CHURCH FINANCE

The Complete Guide to Managing Ministry Resources

Michael E. Batts, CPA
Richard R. Hammar J.D., LL.M., CPA

CHRISTIANITY TODAY
a global media ministry

For any other use, including tuition-based classroom use, advance permission must be obtained from the copyright holder. For information, contact:

Church Finance Permissions
Christianity Today International
465 Gundersen Drive
Carol Stream, IL 60188
Phone: (877) 247-4787
E-mail: clttodaycustserv@christianitytoday.com

This publication is designed to provide accurate and authoritative information in regard to the subject matter covered. It is sold with the understanding that the publisher is not engaged in rendering legal, accounting, or other specific service. If legal advice or other expert assistance is required, the services of a competent professional person should be sought. From a *Declaration of Principles jointly adopted by a Committee of the American Bar Association and a Committee of Publishers and Associates.*

Visit our website, ChurchLawAndTax.com.

Unless otherwise noted, Scripture quotations are taken from HOLY BIBLE: NEW INTERNATIONAL VERSION®. © 1973, 1978, 1984, 2011 by International Bible Society. All rights reserved. Used with permission.

Credits
    Authors: Michael E. Batts, CPA
              Richard R. Hammar, J.D., LL.M, CPA
      Editor: James H. Bolton
Art Director: Phil Marcelo
Editor/Designer: Claudia Volkman
Cover image: © blackred/iStockphoto

1614079145
978-1-61407-914-9

19 18 17 16 15   1 2 3 4
Printed in the United States of America.

Acknowledgement

I would like to express deepest appreciation to my wife, Karen, without whose steadfast love, patience, and encouragement of my work would merely be as sounding brass or a tinkling cymbal.

Mike Batts

Table of Contents

7. Maintaining Sound Internal Control

8. Audits and Other Financial Accountability Activities

9. Tax Law Compliance: A Priority for Financial Management

10. Insurance and Risk Financing

Table of Contents

Introduction

INTRODUCTION

Financial administration of a church is a critically important and foundational element of a sound and healthy church. Done well, financial administration helps the church establish its solid foundation. When financial administration is done poorly, every day can bring a new emergency or crisis, which can impair the credibility of the church's message or otherwise impede the church's ability to carry out its mission effectively. And, while sound financial administration is critical to a church's health, we must remember that financial administration is a supporting role to the church's true ministry purpose. Financial administration is not the "main thing" and should never become the "tail that wags the dog."

In some ways, financial administration is like the marker lines, guard rails, and signs on an interstate highway—with messages like "Caution," "Rough Shoulder," "Steep Grade Ahead," and "Speed Limit." The driver on the highway has a mission—to get to his destination. The signs, markings, and guard rails on the highway let him know what to watch out for along the way…and help him get to his destination safely. The signs and markings are not obstacles or impediments to the journey—they are aids. Those of us who serve in the arena of financial administration must keep that in mind. Our role is to aid the church's leaders in the journey and help them arrive safely at their destination. Of course, a fundamental premise in this metaphor is that the church leaders themselves (the drivers) are safety-minded… that they share the desire to arrive at the destination safely. When those dynamics exist together, the church can be incredibly effective.

An important aspect of financial administration is the principle of financial integrity. If there were ever an organization that should be the model for financial integrity, it should be the church. If a church cannot and will not stand for integrity in its finances—at least two very serious questions arise:

- How can any other aspect of its operations be trusted?
- What kind of message does that convey about the faith of its leaders in the teachings of Scripture?

We start from the premise in this book that the church's leaders desire to operate with financial integrity—indeed, to be "above reproach."

The topic of church finance can seem daunting—even overwhelming at times. With so many laws, rules, best practices, and other considerations that can apply to the financial administration of a church, even the best financial and administrative leaders need help from time to time in addressing particular issues. It is my privilege to work with Rich Hammar on this project in a diligent effort to provide helpful, practical, straightforward, and concise information on the key topics faced by church leaders in the realm of financial administration. I know Rich joins me in a sincere hope that this book will serve as a helpful resource to those who are serving the church. Your work has an eternal impact. May God bless you in it.

Mike Batts

Chapter 1

Mission, Purpose, and Budgeting

IT ALL STARTS WITH MISSION AND PURPOSE

Addressing church budgets starts with understanding the broader context of a church's mission and purpose. If a budget represents the financial blueprint for carrying out a church's ministry plan for a particular period of time, then logic would dictate that such a blueprint and its related ministry plan should be a function—a derivative—of the church's mission and purpose. Many times, however, churches engage in elaborate budget development processes without first evaluating whether their activities are in alignment with their mission and purpose. In some cases, churches operate without a well-defined expression of their mission and purpose. Ensuring that the church's budget is a function of its mission and purpose will help church leaders avoid putting the cart before the horse, or for that matter, having the cart *detached from* the horse.

Not all churches have the same mission and purpose

It may be tempting to assume that all churches have a similar mission and purpose and, accordingly, that there is little value for a church to take the time to clearly express its mission and purpose. Church leaders may assume churches are places of worship with a religious purpose, at least ostensibly, at their core. Such an assumption would be misguided, however, since each church is as unique as the individuals who comprise it.

For example, some churches place a high priority on activities that support foreign missions, while others may focus more on serving their local communities. Some churches heavily use volunteers to conduct many of their activities while other churches hire paid staff to conduct many activities. Some churches heavily emphasize Christian education in the form of grade schools or Sunday school classes, while other churches conduct relatively few educational activities outside the scope of their regular worship services. Some churches emphasize small groups to facilitate fellowship and engagement while other churches rely on other activities to accomplish such purposes. Some churches place a high priority on recreational and social activities while other churches focus on endeavors that are more overtly religious.

In addressing and expressing its own mission and purpose, a church must evaluate its own identity—its own calling.

For what *specific* purposes does our church exist?

What are the *specific* objectives our church is called to accomplish or carry out?

Are we on mission?

Once a church has identified and clearly articulated its mission and purpose, it must identify the *specific* programs, activities, and initiatives that it intends to employ in order to accomplish its mission and purpose. In performing this step, the church should evaluate all of its existing programs, activities, and initiatives to determine whether they *significantly* assist the church in effectively accomplishing its mission and purpose. This step of the introspection process presents a great opportunity for churches to critically evaluate the effectiveness of each of their programs, activities, and initiatives. The church is also able to make wise stewardship decisions by eliminating programs, activities, and initiatives that are not on mission or do not significantly carry out the church's mission and purpose.

Examples of programs, activities, and initiatives commonly conducted by many churches include, but are not limited to:

- Worship services
- Adult education classes
- Small group ministries
- Children's education classes
- Day care and similar ministries
- Preschools
- K-12 schools
- Children and youth ministries
- Senior ministries
- Benevolence ministries
- Short-term mission trips
- Funding for foreign missions agencies
- Adult recreation ministries
- Community service events
- New church planting
- Spiritual counseling

- Bookstores and media distribution
- Food service ministries
- Broadcasting ministries
- Fine arts ministries
- Special events (concerts, etc.)
- Cemeteries and columbaria

ZERO-BASED BUDGETING

The concept of critically evaluating the church's programs, activities, and initiatives is highly compatible with the practice of "zero-based budgeting." Zero-based budgeting is the practice of deciding what specific activities should be conducted in order to carry out the church's mission and what those activities will cost.

Zero-based budgeting does not involve increasing or decreasing the prior year budget, a practice commonly referred to as "incremental budgeting." Rather, it starts with a blank sheet and asks the youth minister, for example, to list each activity or program he or she believes should be conducted and to apply a cost to each activity or program. Accordingly, when adjustments are made, they are not in the form of "10 percent across the board." Rather, they are in the form of "let's not take the kids on that whitewater rafting trip this year." Applied across the entire church to every department, a genuine use of zero-based budgeting has an amazing knack for ferreting out waste and nonessential activity. It also allows church leaders to make specific priority decisions on an activity-by-activity or program-by-program basis, rather than in simple percentages or dollar amounts. It facilitates surgery with a scalpel as opposed to an axe.

ATTRIBUTES OF EXCELLENCE: WHAT CONSTITUTES EXCELLENCE IN A PROGRAM, ACTIVITY, OR INITIATIVE?

Once the church has identified the programs, activities, and initiatives that it believes will help the church effectively carry out its particular mission and purpose, church leaders should take the appropriate next step, which is to identify the attributes of each program, activity, and initiative that represent God-honoring excellence. In other words, church leaders should ask the following question with respect to each program, activity, or initiative in which it plans to engage:

What attributes of this program, activity, or initiative would constitute excellence?

Or, stated another way:

How will we need to conduct this program, activity, or initiative in order for it to be carried out in a God-honoring, excellent manner?

Once a church's leaders have determined the answers to this question, the church will have a much clearer ability to identify the costs associated with a particular program, activity, or initiative.

EXAMPLE. FOOD SERVICE MINISTRY— ATTRIBUTES OF EXCELLENCE

Assume that ABC Church plans to operate a food service ministry to serve meals in connection with its Wednesday evening services and certain other special events. The leaders of ABC Church would identify the "attributes of excellence" for such a food service ministry. They might include:

- Offering high quality, nutritious, and acceptable food to those who are health-conscious.
- Providing gluten-free, vegetarian, and vegan options.
- Polling church members periodically about food allergies, with staff adapting accordingly as potential risks are identified.
- Serving food and beverages cafeteria style, with a very high quality presentation.
- Training servers to be very positive, friendly, and professional.
- Upholding the highest standards for sanitation practices.
- Using quality reusable dinnerware and flatware (not disposable), and ensuring it is thoroughly cleaned and dried.
- Creating an attractive environment, including the purchase of tables and chairs that are of high quality in function and appearance.
- Limiting costs to $10 per person per meal or less.

SPENDING PHILOSOPHY

Every church has a spending philosophy, whether it realizes it or not. In fact, many churches rarely articulate their particular spending philosophy. But a visitor can walk into a church's facilities and quickly observe the church's spending philosophy. A church sanctuary with ornate architecture, travertine floors, dramatic lighting, an expansive pipe organ, a grand piano, and manicured grounds clearly communicates a specific spending philosophy. On the other hand, a humble church building

1

Mission, Purpose, and Budgeting

3

with worn carpet, exposed wiring, a patchwork of architecture, faded paint, and basic musical instruments clearly communicates a different spending philosophy.

In the budgeting process, it is helpful for a church to define its spending philosophy. Such an expression provides useful parameters for spending prioritization decisions, which is immensely helpful when a church is considering construction or renovation of its facilities. While there are no specific standards for an objective assessment of a church's spending philosophy, the following three categories are possibilities:

- Polished and refined;
- Nice and adequate; or
- Modest and thrifty.

COMPENSATION PHILOSOPHY

Compensation typically represents the largest single category of expense for any church, and often comprises 40 percent to 50 percent of a church's operating budget. Accordingly, staff compensation is arguably the most important element of the church's budget.

Before a church can begin making appropriate decisions about the compensation of its staff, the church must determine its compensation philosophy. Specifically, the church should decide how the compensation of its staff should compare with the compensation of other comparable churches. In determining how a church's compensation of its employees compares with that of similar churches, the church should look to church salary survey information. Christianity Today conducts a biannual national church compensation survey, which becomes the basis of its *Compensation Handbook for Church Staff (http://ChurchLawAndTaxStore.com)*. Other sources include Leadership Network's biannual large church salary survey and The Church Network (formerly NACBA)'s Ministry Pay.

Determining how a church's staff compensation compares to that of its peers is only part of the process. A church's compensation philosophy dictates *how* that particular church intends for its staff compensation to compare to its peer group. Some churches express their compensation philosophy in terms of a *percentile* of their peer group. For example, a church may decide that

it generally intends for its staff compensation to be in about the 75th percentile of its peer group. Alternatively, a church may express its compensation philosophy in terms of a relationship to the *average* (e.g., above average, average, and so on). Whichever way the church chooses to express its compensation philosophy, it is important and helpful for the church to do so, and for the church to express the basis for its particular philosophy.

In doing so, the church should also take into consideration the demographics and expectations of its own congregation.

A church's staff compensation philosophy generally may be described by one of the following classifications:

- Well above average
- Above average
- Average
- Modest
- Vow of poverty

Consider individuality

While a compensation philosophy will guide the church broadly in its compensation planning, the church must take into consideration the individual skills, performance, abilities, and contribution of each employee in setting compensation for specific individuals. As a result, the compensation of individual employees may vary somewhat (within reason) from the norm established by the church's compensation philosophy. Of course, the church should document its basis for deciding to compensate an individual at a level that exceeds that supported by comparable data and the church's general compensation philosophy.

The need to document the church's basis for an individual compensation decision is particularly important when establishing compensation for the church's top leaders. As is described in more detail in Chapter 5, federal tax laws provide parameters for determining the reasonableness of the compensation of the top leaders of a church or other 501(c)(3) nonprofit organization. Failure to comply with federal tax law in this area can subject the church's leaders to potential personal financial penalties and can, in extreme cases, jeopardize the church's federal tax-exempt status.

Don't forget benefits

When establishing compensation for the church's staff, church leaders not only must consider the regular salary or wages paid to each person, but also the benefits provided. The benefits package provided to a church's employees are just as relevant as salary or wages when it comes to performing any analysis of comparability. Accordingly, when a church compares the compensation of its staff to that of various peer groups by using salary survey data or other similar information, the church must be careful to ensure that benefits are not neglected in the analysis.

Additionally, under federal tax law, when determining whether a church leader's compensation is reasonable, all forms of compensation (including benefits) are taken into consideration—both taxable and nontaxable.

BUDGETING AS A STRATEGY TO IMPROVE LIQUIDITY AND FINANCIAL POSITION

A church's budgeting process should be much more strategic than simply estimating revenues and expenses. The budgeting process for a church is a pivotal moment in time in which the church has a unique opportunity to implement and follow a strategic financial plan for the church.

This chapter on the topic of "Mission, Purpose, and Budgeting" should be read jointly with Chapter 6 on the topic of "Managing Liquidity and Financial Position," as these two topics go hand-in-glove. As described in more detail in Chapter 6, a church should set specific, targeted objectives for achieving a desired financial position as well as a timeframe for doing so. The combination of a specific, targeted financial position and a timeframe provides a roadmap for the church's leaders in their planning and budgeting.

How does the budget fit into the church's overall financial plan and how does it help the church achieve its financial objectives?

Before a church can answer that question, it must assess whether it has a financial plan and financial objec-tives. A financial plan and financial objectives include such elements as:

- Establishing cash operating reserves or debt service reserves of $ (amount) within a stated period of time.
- Reducing debt by $ (amount) within a stated period of time.
- Building a maintenance and replacement fund of $ (amount) within a stated period of time.

The false comfort of a "balanced budget"

In order to ensure that the church has adequate financial capacity to carry out its programs, activities, and initiatives, its leaders must ensure that the church's financial plan is sound. Sound financial management includes development and approval of a responsible operating budget. Many churches operate under the belief that there is something improper about generating a positive bottom line—that is, a surplus of revenues over expenses. In fact, in many churches, a desirable budget is a "balanced budget." While operating a balanced budget may seem like an admirable goal, it simply means that the church expects to incur expenses equal to its revenues. The term "balanced budget" sounds attractive because the term has a positive connotation (what's the alternative—an "*imbalanced* budget?"). But, if the church's budget is prepared on a cash basis and the church has a "balanced budget," the church is essentially saying that it plans to spend every nickel of revenue that it brings in, with little or no room for error. An unexpected dip in revenues can cause immediate financial stress for such a church and its leaders. That is no way to improve a church's financial position.

A better approach to budgeting involves determining the church's desired or targeted financial position (liquidity, reserves, debt levels, and so on) and the desired timetable for achieving it. With a long-term plan for improving financial position, the church can develop operating budgets that not only provide for carrying out its mission and purpose, but also can contemplate using reasonable surpluses to contribute toward the targeted financial position.

Improving a church's liquidity and financial position requires intentional effort as an essential part of the planning and budgeting process. That effort must include planning to spend less than what the church receives in cash revenues. For a church that has been following the habit of spending all of its cash receipts annually, the transition can be challenging. If the church's revenues are growing, the church may be able to make progress in this area by slowing or stopping spending increases as revenues rise. For churches whose revenues are not growing significantly, the transition will require the church to pursue additional revenue (through additional giving or from alternative revenue sources—see Chapters 3 and 4 for more information on these topics), employ expense reductions, or apply a combination of the two.

ACCOUNTING METHODS APPLIED IN BUDGETING

Churches often prepare their operating budgets using the cash basis of accounting. Budgets prepared in this manner are, essentially, cash flow budgets. A primary weakness of cash basis budgets is the fact that they exclude depreciation expense. As is more fully described in Chapter 2, depreciation is a non-cash expense that represents the "using up" or deterioration of a long-lived asset. Property and equipment other than land generally deteriorate over time and typically must be either repaired, refurbished, or replaced in the future. Churches often overlook this very real economic expense that occurs continuously as assets deteriorate or are used up. Failure to recognize depreciation expense in the budgeting process creates an inadequate representation of the church's total expenses and can make it difficult for a church to achieve its targets for liquidity and financial position.

EXAMPLE. A church prepares its operating budgets using the cash basis of accounting. Depreciation expense is not recognized. The operating budget reflects estimated revenues for the year of $2.5 million and estimated cash operating expenses of an equal amount. The church considers this a "balanced budget," and follows this practice every year. If it were recognized, depreciation expense related to the deterioration of the church's property and equipment would amount to $400,000 annually. In reality, this church's operating budget is planning for a $400,000 deficit for the year because the very real economic expense of depreciation is not being recognized in its cash flow budget.

At some point in the future, the church will be required to deal with the deterioration of its assets. The fact that the church has operated with no cash flow surpluses in prior years will not help the church build reserves to address its future property and equipment needs.

Funding depreciation

The practice of including depreciation expense in a church's operating budget, while still maintaining a bottom line that is either breakeven ("balanced") or better, is sometimes referred to as "funding depreciation."

The practice of funding depreciation in an operating budget can be a big and challenging step for a church that has never done it, as implementing such a change could significantly affect other areas of the operating budget. As a result, church leaders may be reluctant to implement such a change. In such cases, the church should implement the practice of funding depreciation over a period of time, rather than all at once. Churches should recognize depreciation expense in their operating budgets regardless of whether the depreciation is fully funded. This practice will result in an operating budget that reflects a deficit, but the more accurate the budget picture, the better the chances the church's leaders and those responsible for the church's financial oversight will realize the effects of depreciation on the church's overall economics. This picture may serve as an impetus to make funding depreciation a regular practice for the church's budget, even if it takes a period of time for the church to fully do so.

The accounting method used for budgeting should align with the accounting method used for internal financial reporting

Chapter 2 describes, in detail, the accounting methods used by churches for internal financial reporting purposes. Whatever the method of accounting used by a church's leaders to monitor the church's ongoing financial activities, the same method of accounting should be used in developing the church's operating budget.

Use of the same accounting method for budgeting and internal financial reporting purposes makes it possible to effectively monitor and evaluate the church's actual operating results compared to its budget. Such a comparison is difficult, if not impossible, when the accounting methods used for budgeting and internal financial reporting are different. That fact notwithstanding, many churches employ accounting methods for budgeting that differ from those used for the church's internal financial reporting—an unsound and even dangerous practice.

TYPES OF BUDGETS

A church operating budget should reflect the church's estimated revenues and expenses. Two significant elements of a church's cash disbursements do not constitute expenses—capital expenditures and debt principal reduction. Rather, a capital expenditure represents the purchase of, or improvement to, one or more assets. A debt principal reduction expenditure results in a decrease of one or more of the church's liabilities.

EXAMPLE. ABC Church developed the following capital expenditures and debt principal reduction budgets for the year 20XX:

CAPITAL EXPENDITURES BUDGET

Roof replacement—sanctuary	$100,000
New carpet—education building	$ 40,000
New computers—pastoral staff	$ 12,000
New bus for seniors	$ 60,000
Total capital expenditures	**$212,000**

Sources of Funds

Building fund	$140,000
Operating surplus	$ 72,000
Total source of funds	**$212,000**

DEBT PRINCIPAL REDUCTION BUDGET

Required principal reduction per terms of note	$ 64,300
Additional planned principal reduction	$ 35,700
Total debt principal reduction	**$100,000**

Sources of Funds

Operating surplus	$100,000
Total sources of funds	**$100,000**

Accordingly, a church should prepare both an *operating budget* and a *capital expenditures budget* for the applicable period. If the church has outstanding debt, it should also prepare a *debt principal reduction budget*.

For a capital expenditures budget or a debt principal reduction budget, it is essential for the church to identify the sources of funds that will be used to make the capital or debt principal reduction expenditures. The sources of funds may be a surplus from the operating budget, cash reserves, special gifts expected to be raised for the particular purpose, or other sources.

BUDGETING FOR AUXILIARY ACTIVITIES

Some churches do not include in their operating budgets the revenues and expenses related to auxiliary activities—particularly those that are self-supporting or that generate revenues from fees or other charges. For auxiliary ministries that are partially self-supporting, churches sometimes include in their operating budget an estimate for the "subsidy" that the church intends to provide from general funds to support the auxiliary activity. Examples of auxiliary activities for which churches sometimes fail to fully budget include, but are not limited to, food service operations, Mom's Day Out and similar programs, sports and recreational programs, and educational programs for which fees are charged. For a variety of reasons, it is a best practice for a church to budget the entire amount of revenues and expenses for its auxiliary activities. One significant reason to follow such a practice is that the operating budget serves as an internal control mechanism; comparing actual results to budgeted results can help identify aberrations or anomalies in revenues or expenses that require further attention. Additionally, failure to budget for the details of auxiliary activities often goes hand-in-hand with a failure to monitor financial reports for such activities—which is definitely a dangerous practice.

Is it ethical to use donor-restricted funds to replace regularly budgeted expenses?

A frequent question among churches is whether it is ethical for a church to use donor-restricted funds to replace regularly budgeted ministry operating expenses. For example, assume that a church regularly budgets and spends 5 percent of its operating budget on contributions to its denominational missions agency. A member of the church's congregation makes a large gift to the church with a restriction stipulating that the gift must be used to support missions. Would it be ethical for the church to use these restricted funds to replace the funds that the church would normally spend from its operating budget on contributions to its denominational missions agency—thereby freeing such funds for general use?

Using donor-restricted funds to replace regularly budgeted expenses is viewed by some as an unethical practice. Such a practice can be perceived as "sleight-of-hand" in the arena of financial administration. Additionally, such a practice has the potential to offend donors or, in the case of donors who are deceased, their families. If a donor makes a gift to a church that is restricted for a particular purpose, the donor should have a reasonable basis for believing that the restricted gift will be used to fund programs, activities, or initiatives that would not otherwise be funded by the church's regular operating budget. Given our scriptural mandate to operate above reproach and to do what is right in the sight of God and people, it is a best practice to avoid using donor-restricted gifts to replace regularly budgeted operating expenses. Churches that adhere to such a philosophy may wish to adopt policy language to that effect.

BUDGETING FOR USE OF DONOR-RESTRICTED FUNDS

Interestingly, churches rarely have a formal policy that addresses who among the church leadership has the authority to release donor-restricted funds and to make specific decisions as to how such funds are to be spent. Additionally, churches rarely budget for the specific use of donor-restricted funds other than building funds. For example, many churches maintain donor-restricted funds to support missions.[1] As money accumulates in the church's missions fund, decisions are made regarding expenditures made from the missions fund. But who makes those decisions? And by what authority do they make those decisions? Does the church's governing board make the decisions? Is the church's staff leadership authorized to make such decisions? Are the

expenditures budgeted? This area is often a "twilight zone" for churches. Frequently, churches simply follow a pattern of practices that they have developed over the years—and no one questions those practices—at least not until a misunderstanding or disagreement erupts.

Lack of a clear policy and board-approved practices for the expenditure of donor-restricted funds has been a source of numerous conflicts—some of them very serious—in churches across America. Such conflicts have, in some cases, resulted in allegations of misappropriation, terminations of top church leaders, and/or splits in the congregation.

EXAMPLE. Gertrude Johnson left a bequest in her will for ABC Church in the amount of $500,000 with a stipulation that the gift is to be used by the church to support its youth ministry. The church received the bequest in 20X1. The church's business administrator decided to apply $100,000 from Gertrude's bequest toward regular youth ministry activities in each of the years 20X1 through 20X5, thereby reducing the amount that the church would ordinarily budget and spend from its general fund on its youth ministry expenses. The business administrator's decision to apply Gertrude's bequest in this manner was not well communicated to the church's governing board. Additionally, the church had no policy addressing who among the church's leaders has the authority to make spending decisions with respect to donor-restricted gifts, and the church's budgets do not address the use of donor-restricted gifts. In the year 20X6, the church began to explore constructing a new building to be dedicated to serving the church's youth. Members of the church's board and congregation thought that it would be a wise and appropriate use of Gertrude's bequest to use it for the construction of the new youth building. Members of the church board and congregation were shocked to learn that Gertrude's bequest had already been fully expended on the regular operations of the church's youth ministry under the direction of the business administrator. Allegations of misappropriation and impropriety began to swirl, and members of the congregation began to accuse the church's board of failure to adequately oversee the church's finances. Allegations were also made that using Gertrude's restricted gift funds to replace regularly budgeted youth ministry expenses was unethical and was inconsistent with Gertrude's expectations. Church board members were livid over the business administrator's decision to expend the funds. The business administrator, however, argued that historically the business administrator has always made decisions regarding the expenditure of donor-restricted funds, and that the use of Gertrude's funds aligned with the stipulation in her bequest. A significant portion of the church's congregation left the church over concerns about the church's fiscal management. Three of the church's

---

1   The term "missions" does not have a precise meaning in the church arena—the term may refer to funding foreign missions agencies, direct engagement in foreign evangelistic activities, engagement in local or domestic evangelistic activities, humanitarian or disaster relief activities, church planting, or any number of other activities. Accordingly, the scope and intent of such a term should be clearly defined by each church so that donors to such a fund have an appropriate understanding of how funds are to be used.

board members resigned. The business administrator was terminated. And, the new youth building was never built.

This tragic example is an all-too-real scenario in the church arena.

Budgeting for use of donor-restricted funds as a control mechanism

A church can avoid tragic occurrences like the one described in the example above by having a clear policy governing the expenditure of donor-restricted funds. As a best practice, the policy needs to have clearly delineated lines of authority for approving the release of donor-restricted funds and for making individual expenditures of such funds. The policy should also require planned expenditures of donor-restricted funds to be incorporated into specific budgets (e.g., the operating budget, capital expenditures budget, or debt principal reduction budget) as appropriate. To incorporate the expenditure of donor-restricted funds into the operating budget, a line item adjacent to the estimated revenues can be included that represents "release of donor-imposed restrictions" or "resources provided from donor-restricted gifts." Including such a line item would reflect the authorization to use donor-restricted gifts. The expenditures related to use of the

EXAMPLE. Following is an example of a capital expenditures budget incorporating the use of donor-restricted gifts as an element of the budget:

CAPITAL EXPENDITURES BUDGET

New youth building	**$500,000**
New computers—pastoral staff	**$ 12,000**
New bus for seniors	**$ 60,000**
Total capital expenditures	**$ 572,000**

Sources of Funds	
Release of restricted gift— Gertrude Johnson bequest for youth ministry	**$500,000**
Operating surplus	**$ 72,000**
Total sources of funds	**$572,000**

funds would be included in the appropriate section of the budget for expenditures. Requiring that the release of donor-restricted funds and related expenditures be incorporated into the budgeting process adds an element of healthy control to the use of such funds.

BUDGETING AS AN EXPENSE CONTROL MECHANISM

Church leaders have widely varying views on the purpose and function of the church's operating budget. For some, the operating budget is merely an estimate or a rough guideline of expectations for financial activities during the applicable period. For church leaders who espouse this view of the operating budget, the budget is not an authoritative document, nor is it an expense control mechanism. For others, an operating budget—once approved—is an official expression of limitation on the amount of expenses that may be incurred by the church. For churches that espouse this view, any expenditure in excess of what is authorized in the operating budget may not be incurred without specific approval.

A church's view on whether the budget acts as an expense control mechanism or is simply a helpful guide depends in large part on the church's governance model and church polity. Traditionally, it has been common for churches to view the annual operating budget as an official limitation on the church's spending that cannot be exceeded without specific authorization. In many traditional churches, the church's membership or congregation votes to approve the official annual budget. In hierarchical churches, an overseer or bishop may establish or approve the operating budget for a particular church or congregation. Many churches formed in recent years—especially independent and nondenominational churches—follow different models. Some newer churches are governed entirely by members of the church's staff. Such churches often have nontraditional views of the budgeting process.

Regardless of a church's view of the role and authority of the budget with respect to expense control, every church should still actively engage in a meaningful and thorough budgeting process as a best practice for financial planning purposes, good stewardship, and as an element of sound internal control.

So we're going over-budget ... now what?

For churches that view the operating budget as an expense control mechanism, the matter of how to deal with expenditures in excess of budgeted amounts is an important element of policy that is poorly developed in many churches. For example, a church operating budget will typically include line items for each of the church's main areas of ministry operations. Line items will exist for worship activities, educational activities, children and youth ministries, missions, and so on.

Suppose a church develops and approves an operating budget for the year 20X1 reflecting total expenses of $1.5 million, of which $200,000 relates to educational activities. Also suppose that, due to unexpected developments, it appears the church's expenses for its educational activities will exceed the amount budgeted by $50,000 for the year.

Is it acceptable for the church's staff leadership to make the additional expenditures for the educational ministries, so long as total expenses do not exceed the total amount of expenses budgeted for the church of $1.5 million? Even if church staff leaders are permitted to reallocate budget line items so long as the total amount spent remains within the amount of total expenses authorized by the budget, who on the church staff leadership has the authority to make such a reallocation decision? Or, should church staff leaders be required to obtain specific authorization to incur expenses that exceed the amount budgeted for the educational ministries? If authorization is required in order to exceed expenses for an individual line item or for the budget as a whole, who must provide that authorization? If the congregation approved the annual budget, must the congregation be involved in an authorization for such a variance? Or, may such approval be granted by the governing body of the church or by some other group? Would the answer to these questions change, depending on the amount by which actual expenditures are expected to exceed budgeted amounts?

Many churches do not have good answers to these questions. For churches that view the operating budget as an expense control mechanism, it is essential to have an appropriate budget policy that clearly addresses such matters and leaves little room for misunderstanding.

Following is a sample budget policy statement that may be helpful for churches wishing to adopt a policy of their own:

Sample Church Budget Policy *(For churches in which budgeting serves as an expense control mechanism)*

1. Budget methods and approvals—operating

Annually, the Administrator shall, in cooperation with department heads, develop a detailed proposed operating budget for each department, reflecting income and expenses using the same method of accounting used by the Church in preparing its regular financial statements for Finance Committee and Board consideration. The detailed proposed operating budget shall be presented to the Finance Committee for approval no later than _____. Upon approval by the Finance Committee, the approved budget (with any modifications) shall be summarized by department and submitted to the Board for approval no later than _____. Upon approval by the Board of the summarized budget (with any modifications), the budget shall be officially adopted for the respective year. Notwithstanding the official adoption of any budget, management of Church is not permitted to authorize expenses in excess of income for any year-to-date period without specific approval of the Finance Committee. The Finance Committee is not permitted to authorize expenses in excess of income of more than $____ for any year-to-date period without specific approval of the Board.

Subject to the limitations described in the preceding paragraph, the Administrator is permitted to reallocate budgeted amounts from one department to another, so long as the total budget remains unchanged. Subject to the limitations described in the preceding paragraph, department heads are permitted to incur expenses for their respective departments which vary from the amounts budgeted for individual line items, so long as the total expenses for each such department remain within the total amount budgeted for the department.

Variances (expenses in excess of budgeted amounts) by individual departments must be approved by the Administrator. Variances in the total operating budget of up to $____ annually must be approved by the Finance Committee. Variances in the total operating budget in excess of $____ annually must be approved by the Board.

All approvals of budgets and variances should be duly recorded in the minutes of the body exercising such authority.

2. Budget methods and approvals—capital expenditures and debt principal reduction

Annually, the Administrator shall develop a detailed proposed capital expenditures budget and a proposed debt principal reduction budget reflecting expected sources of funds and proposed expenditures for capital items and principal reduction. The detailed budgets shall be presented to the Finance Committee for approval no later than _____ (date). Upon approval by the Finance Committee, the approved capital expenditures and debt principal reduction budgets (with any modifications) shall be summarized and submitted to the Board no later than _____ (date) for approval. Upon approval by the Board of the summarized capital expenditures and debt principal reduction budgets (with any modifications), the budgets shall be officially adopted for the respective year. Capital expenditures and debt principal reduction may only be made from fund sources identified in and approved as part of the respective budgets. Notwithstanding the official adoption of any budget, Management of Church is not permitted to authorize expenditures in excess of actual authorized fund sources received or available for any year-to-date period without specific approval of the Finance Committee. The Finance Committee is not permitted to authorize expenditures in excess of authorized fund sources received or available of more than $____ for any year-to-date period without specific approval of the Board. Funds from new borrowings of debt are considered authorized fund sources only if the proceeds of the specific debt are included in the authorized capital expenditures or debt principal reduction budget and the specific debt is approved in advance by

the Board pursuant to applicable provisions of the Articles of Incorporation and Bylaws.

All approvals of budgets and variances should be duly recorded in the minutes of the body exercising such authority.

3. Budget methods and approvals—auxiliary activities

Annually, the Administrator shall, in cooperation with department heads, develop a detailed proposed auxiliary activities budget for ABC Church, reflecting income and expenses using the same method of accounting used by ABC Church in preparing its regular financial statements for Finance Committee and Board consideration. The detailed proposed auxiliary activities budget shall be presented to the Finance Committee for approval no later than _____ (date). Upon approval by the Finance Committee, the approved budget (with any modifications) shall be officially adopted for the respective year. Notwithstanding the official adoption of any budget, Management of ABC Church is not permitted to authorize expenses in excess of income for any year-to-date period without specific approval of the Finance Committee. The Finance Committee is not permitted to authorize expenses in excess of income of more than $____ for any year-to-date period without specific approval of the Board.

As an alternative to providing a separate budget for auxiliary activities as described in the preceding paragraph, budgeted revenues and expenses for auxiliary activities may be incorporated into the church's annual operating budget.

All approvals of budgets and variances should be duly recorded in the minutes of the body exercising such authority.

4. Disbursement and use of restricted funds

All disbursements of donor-restricted funds, to the extent not covered in specifically approved budgets (for example, capital expenditures budgeted from building fund contributions included in the capital expenditures budget) must be approved in advance by the Finance Committee.

Management of ABC Church must establish proper accounting and tracking of donor-restricted contributions so as to ensure that donor-restricted funds are held until spent for authorized purposes, and that expenditures of such funds are in accordance with applicable donor restrictions. The church shall not utilize donor-restricted funds to replace funds for regular, recurring operating activities that are ordinarily and customarily budgeted and funded by the church's general revenues.

ALTERNATIVES TO THE ANNUAL BUDGET

American churches tend to operate with the mindset that budgeting is a formal, annual process that must be performed in a manner and timeframe that aligns with the church's fiscal year. In reality, there is no legal requirement for such a formal or annual process.[2] With improved technologies and availability of more timely financial information on a regular basis, churches are able to monitor and forecast activities and costs on a more dynamic basis than has been the case in the past. As a result, some churches have adopted alternatives to (either as a supplement or in lieu of) the formal, annual budgeting process that are more fluid and dynamic. Such an approach allows church leaders to adapt on an ongoing basis to changing expectations regarding revenues and other dynamic developments. A more dynamic budgeting or forecasting process is likely essential for a church undergoing rapid change—particularly a church experiencing rapid growth or a church that has experienced a sudden and unexpected challenge or crisis. Whether a church chooses to abandon formal, annual budgeting, or not, is a decision to be made by its governing body and possibly (depending on the church's governance model) its membership.

A commonly used alternative to the formal, annual budgeting process is some form of rolling forecast or rolling budget. For example, a church may adopt a rolling forecast looking forward to the next 12 months and update the forecast each quarter. For obvious reasons, utilizing a rolling forecast or rolling budget in which forecasted or budgeted amounts change frequently

presents challenges for a church that wishes to use its budget as an expense control mechanism. Accordingly, it may be wise for a church that utilizes a rolling forecast or rolling budget model to officially adopt policies or constraints on spending. For example, a church may adopt a resolution providing that the financial management of the church shall result in a minimum cash flow surplus for each calendar quarter or for a calendar year. Such a resolution may also adopt targeted benchmarks for the church to reach each quarter, or year, as progress toward its longer-term targets for improved liquidity and financial position.

If a rolling forecast or rolling budget model is used, it is still important for the church to utilize its forecast or budget as a tool for effective stewardship and internal control. Comparing actual results with budgeted or forecasted amounts for the applicable periods of time is a particularly effective financial oversight exercise and an important element of sound internal control. The fact that the church may not utilize a formal, annual budgeting process is not a basis for abandoning the process of comparing actual results with forecasted or budgeted amounts.

IDENTIFYING EXPENSE REDUCTIONS

No discussion of budgeting would be complete without addressing the topic of reducing expenses. As a normal part of the budgeting process, churches find themselves wishing to conduct more programs, activities, and initiatives than available funds will allow. Additionally, churches that wish to improve their liquidity and financial position may need to reduce expenses in an effort to generate reasonable and appropriate cash flow surpluses to reach their targets.

The "no noticeable impact" phenomenon
An interesting phenomenon developed in some churches during the Great Recession of 2008. Faced with sudden revenue decreases of as much as 20 percent, 30 percent, or more, some churches were forced to quickly make dramatic expense reductions. These churches reduced or eliminated multiple programs, ministries, and staff positions in short order to avoid catastrophic cash flow deficits. In some cases, when the churches informed their congregations of the massive expense reductions, congregation members remarked that the expense cuts had "no noticeable impact" on their ex-

---

2   Consideration must be made, however, of an individual church's governing documents (articles of incorporation, constitution, bylaws, etc.) and polity, including denominational books of order or other similar authoritative sources that may impose specific, formal, annual budgeting requirements.

periences in worship or similar activities. Such perceptions on the part of congregations raised some interesting questions. For example, how is it that a church was able to reduce its operating expenses by 30 percent with no noticeable effects on the key elements of the church's worship and educational activities? Was the church previously wasting that money? Why can't the church ordinarily operate with such a lower level of expenses?

These are reasonable questions, and church leaders should contemplate the answers to such questions as part of their overall evaluation of the effectiveness of the church's spending. Church leaders should carefully evaluate whether a particular program, activity, or initiative contributes significantly and effectively to the accomplishment of the church's overall mission and purpose before committing funds to it.

The obvious places to look

Churches looking to reduce their expenses will typically look first at the rather obvious areas of potential opportunity for cost savings, such as:

- Reducing or eliminating specific programs, activities, and initiatives;
- Eliminating staff positions;
- Reducing staff work hours and compensation;
- Reducing employer-paid staff benefits;
- Renegotiating costs with vendors;
- Renegotiating debt terms; and,
- Deferring maintenance on property and equipment.

A note about eliminating staff positions or terminating employees

Church leaders who are considering terminating employees for expense reduction purposes should remember churches are exempt from both the federal and state unemployment compensation tax and benefit systems. Accordingly, terminated employees will not be eligible for unemployment benefits attributable to their services in the employ of a church. Church leaders who terminate staff members may wish to consider offering a severance package to terminated employees. Of course, the cost of any severance benefits must be taken into consideration when evaluating the cost savings associated with terminations.

Some not-so-obvious places to look

Following are some not-so-obvious suggested ways that churches may be able to reduce expenses:

Mission and purpose exercise

This chapter begins with the observation that "it all starts with mission and purpose." The exercise of clearly identifying a church's specific mission and purpose, followed by critically evaluating its programs, activities, and initiatives, can be an extraordinarily effective process for ferreting out waste or marginally beneficial expenses. The evaluation should help church leaders determine whether each program, activity, or initiative significantly and effectively contributes to the accomplishment of the church's mission and purpose. Coupled with a zero-based budgeting approach (described earlier in this chapter), such an exercise can efficiently help church leaders identify those aspects of the church's operations that are prime candidates for expense reductions. It can also assist church leaders in reallocating expense priorities toward those activities that are more effective in accomplishing the church's mission and purpose.

Streamlining processes and systems

- *How much does it cost for your church to pay a bill with a check? (Not the bill itself ... the **process** of paying the bill.)*
- *Does your staff use computerized bank account reconciliation applications? How much time does the account reconciliation process take?*
- *Are your expense reports submitted on paper with paper receipts attached? How much collective staff time (all staff) is spent preparing and addressing paper expense reports for reimbursement?*
- *How much collective staff time does your church spend completing, approving, and otherwise addressing purchase orders and similar authorizations?*
- *Have you made an active effort to encourage your congregation to give electronically? Is giving to your church as easy as buying a book on*

Amazon.com? How much time does your staff spend processing check-based offerings?

- *When people make a purchase in your church cafeteria with a credit card, must they sign a receipt, and must you then store that receipt? Have you considered that many vendors now do not require signatures for such purchases and offer a receipt only if requested?*
- *How much time does your staff spend filing documents and retrieving (or searching for) documents in paper files? If your church operates with a paperless filing system, how many steps are involved when your staff members scan documents for electronic storage? Does the scanning process involve them leaving their desks to scan the documents at a central scanner? Do they then return to their desks to find the document they just scanned on the network server?*
- *Do you still have a person answering your telephones? If yes, is that belief based on the premise that callers prefer that? Have you reconsidered that premise?*

Addressing these questions and many others like them can help a church streamline its processes and systems and, as a result, operate more efficiently and at a lower cost. As mentioned in Chapter 5, a *Wall Street Journal* article stated that a business check costs between $4 and $20 to fully prepare and process, and that the cost of writing a check can be as much as five times the cost of an e-payment. Or, consider the fact that a staff member who must leave her desk and go to a centralized scanner (as opposed to using a scanner at her desk) every time a document requires scanning may spend three to five extra minutes on that process. Multiply that three to five extra minutes by 10 times a day, and the result is an extra 30 to 50 minutes per staff member per day. Churches typically have many processes and systems that have not been seriously evaluated for efficiency. A church that wishes to reduce its expenses should consider whether there is a significant opportunity to do so by streamlining its processes and systems.

Church leaders may decide to undertake an effort to streamline the church's processes and systems themselves. Larger churches may seek out a consultant to assist. A professional discipline exists around the practice of streamlining processes and systems. Much of the professional work conducted in this area utilizes principles of "Lean Six Sigma"—a term attributed to authors Michael George and Robert Lawrence, Jr. Various levels and types of certification exist in this arena. A church considering engaging a consultant to assist with streamlining its activities should perform appropriate due diligence and check references for comparable clients of the consultant.

Energy studies and adaptations

Many churches throughout the United States have found it helpful to engage experts to perform energy usage analyses. Such an expert will typically recommend adaptations to equipment, fixtures, insulation, lighting, software, and usage management systems in order to help the church operate with greater energy efficiency. The changes necessary to generate significant energy savings may require a substantial initial investment. Of course, a church must evaluate its expected return on that investment to determine whether making it is a wise decision. Analyses performed for larger churches by reputable energy consulting companies (and, in some cases, utility companies themselves) have generally brought cost savings and satisfaction to the churches that performed them. A church interested in pursuing the possibility of an energy study should reach out to other churches for referrals to a reputable service provider in this area. The church may also wish to consult its own electrical utility company to identify energy analysis options that may be available.

Outsourcing

Many churches outsource certain aspects of their operations—some for decades. For example, churches commonly outsource the administration of their employee retirement plans, cafeteria (Section 125) plans, and other employee benefit plans. Many churches with investment portfolios outsource the asset management function for those portfolios. Churches commonly outsource the processing and disbursement of their payrolls. Other services commonly outsourced include grounds maintenance, information technology (IT) services, vehicle maintenance, and security.

Why are such functions and activities commonly outsourced? In many cases, the church believes the function or activity can be performed more effectively, more efficiently, and less costly by persons or companies that concentrate their work and expertise in the particular field.

Churches that do not outsource some of the functions and activities described above may wish to consider doing so. Other functions and activities that the church may wish to consider outsourcing include, but are not limited to:

- Regular accounting and financial reporting activities
- Bill-paying activities
- Human resources (or some aspects of it, such as employee screening; the service provider must be fully aware of the unique legal attributes that apply to churches in the HR arena)
- Document printing, preparation, and graphic design
- Document editing and proofing
- Website and social media management
- Public relations

Collaboration

In order to more effectively and efficiently carry out their mission and purpose, churches sometimes collaborate with each other or with other Christian ministries. While such collaboration is very common in connection with international missions and humanitarian relief activities, collaboration with domestic ministry activities is also an area of growing interest among churches. Collaboration can take forms that are similar to outsourcing (described above) and can offer many of the same advantages. The primary differences between collaboration and outsourcing are that:

1. In collaboration arrangements, the church often participates directly in conducting the respective activities along with the other churches or ministries with which it is collaborating.
2. Outsourcing is most commonly a purely contractual arrangement with a vendor or service provider, whereas some aspects of collaboration may not involve formal contractual agreements.

Following are some examples in which a church may collaborate with other churches or ministries to carry out particular programs, activities, or initiatives:

- Elm Church has a desire to meet the needs of some of the homeless people in its area. Rather than starting its own direct ministry to the homeless, Elm Church collaborates with a Christian homeless ministry in the same community. One of Elm Church's staff members works directly with the staff of the local Christian homeless ministry as part of his duties for Elm Church. Elm Church also provides volunteers from its congregation to serve at the homeless ministry center, and Elm Church makes grants to the homeless ministry to help fund its operations.
- Elm Church has a desire to provide spiritual counseling for its members and their families. Rather than starting its own direct Christian counseling ministry, Elm Church collaborates with Lighted Way Counseling, a reputable local Christian ministry dedicated to providing spiritual counseling. Elm Church encourages its members and their families to utilize the services of Lighted Way Counseling. Elm Church enters into a cooperation agreement with Lighted Way Counseling that stipulates

certain spiritual principles and practices that will be followed whenever Lighted Way counselors work with members of Elm Church and their families. Elm Church provides financial support to Lighted Way Counseling on a regular basis.

- Elm Church and Oak Church both desire to plant new churches that will do work similar to theirs in the state of Oklahoma. Rather than engaging directly in church planting activity individually, Elm Church and Oak Church decide to jointly form a new ministry, Elm and Oak Seeds Ministry. Elm and Oak Seeds Ministry will engage in church-planting activities that carry out the objectives of both Elm Church and Oak Church. The governing documents (articles of incorporation and bylaws) of Elm and Oak Seeds Ministry provide for board members to be appointed by both Elm Church and Oak Church and also stipulate the terms of cooperation by the two churches. Both churches provide the financial funding necessary to operate Elm and Oak Seeds Ministry.

A church that considers collaborating with other churches or ministries should take care to ensure that the expectations of all parties involved are clearly spelled out. Depending on the nature and extent of the collaboration, a legal agreement may be appropriate and necessary. Collaboration agreements can take various forms. However, it is wise for a church considering such an arrangement to consult with its legal counsel in order to ensure that a proposed collaboration arrangement and its related agreements are appropriate for the church and do not subject the church to unintended risks or other unanticipated consequences.

12 Steps for Sound Church Budgeting

1	Identify and/or evaluate the church's mission and purpose.
2	Identify, evaluate, and critically screen the programs, activities, and initiatives that significantly assist the church in carrying out its mission and purpose.
3	For each program, activity, and initiative the church plans or wishes to conduct, determine and define the attributes of excellence.
4	Identify or define the church's spending philosophy • Polished and refined • Nice and adequate • Modest and thrifty.
5	Identify or define the church's compensation philosophy • Well above average • Above average • Average • Modest • Vow of poverty.
6	Identify the church's targets for sound liquidity and financial position and the timeframe for reaching them, with annual milestones/interim targets.
7	Determine capital expenditure and principal reduction requirements for the relevant period.
8	Identify and determine the costs for carrying out the programs, activities, and initiatives in an excellent manner as identified in Step 3, applying the church's spending philosophy and compensation philosophy. Aggregate costs with capital expenditure and principal reduction requirements identified in Step 7.
9	Estimate the resources/funds (revenues) expected to be available for the applicable period.
10	Assess the estimated revenues as compared with the total costs determined in Step 8 and the desired progress toward liquidity and financial position targets identified in Step 6.
11	Make prioritization decisions as necessary to reduce specifically-identified costs so that resulting estimated excess of revenues over costs is satisfactory.
12	Pursue approval of operating, capital expenditures, and debt reduction budgets in accordance with church policy. Identify specific specific sources of funds for capital expenditures and debt reduction budgets.

Chapter 2

Accounting and Financial Reporting

INTRODUCTION

Church officials responsible for the church's accounting and financial reporting should view the church's decision-making leaders like drivers of an automobile. When a person gets behind the wheel of a car, he or she continuously uses information from numerous sources. A driver keeps within the lines of the highway; follows road signs; watches other vehicles; checks dashboard gauges; and, listens to GPS directions. A good and healthy system of accounting and financial reporting is much like the sources of information for a driver on the highway. The accounting and financial reporting system provides church leaders with critical information necessary for good decision-making and safe navigation toward the goal of carrying out the church's mission and purpose. As such, the accounting and financial reporting system must provide *accurate*, *timely*, and *relevant* information.

GENERAL DEFINITIONS

Accounting is the process by which the church's financial operations and transactions are observed, measured, processed, recorded, organized, stored, and formatted. The primary purpose and result is to facilitate **financial reporting**.

Financial reporting may be either **internal** or **external**.

Internal financial reporting provides church leaders with financial information to assess the financial condition of the church and to make informed decisions about the operations and activities of the church.

External financial reporting provides financial statements, which cover a specific period of time, to users who are external to the leadership of the church. These financial statements facilitate an understanding of the church's financial position and financial activities. External users of the financial statements may include, but are not limited to, church members, lending institutions, denominational organizations, and accrediting organizations, such as the Evangelical Council for Financial Accountability (ECFA).

INTERNAL FINANCIAL REPORTING

Given the analogy above about the information a driver uses on the highway, a few key points about the role of internal financial reporting in a church setting are worthy of consideration:

The internal financial reporting function is a means, not an end. Just as a driver uses a variety of sources of information to make decisions while driving toward a destination, church leaders use financial reporting for wise decision-making regarding the church's operations and activities. The accounting and financial reporting function serves a supporting and informational role with respect to the leadership of the church. The accounting function and its people are not, and never should be, viewed as the "driver" or the "destination" with respect to a church's activities or operations.

Information provided by the financial reporting process must be timely, accurate, and relevant. Drivers need to know that their automobile is low on fuel before it is empty. Similarly, church leaders need t*imely, accurate,* and *relevant* financial information; this information keeps them apprised of current conditions so that they can make the best possible decisions.

Financial reports must be clear and understandable. Financial reports presented in a highly detailed or technical format often are of limited value to church leaders. Those who prepare financial reports must take into consideration the fact that the internal users of the reports are not generally accountants. Financial reports must be provided to decision-makers in a form and language that they understand.

Who says internal financial reports must look like financial statements?

The most helpful financial reporting information for church leaders is likely to include a combination of financial and nonfinancial information. Financial information alone often presents an incomplete picture. For example, if a church leader learned contribution revenues increased for the first half of the year by 20 percent, that statement alone may sound excellent.

However, if the 20 percent increase in contributions were annotated with information that a single donor made a large gift accounting for more than the 20 percent increase, and that church attendance actually declined during the first half of the year, then the church's leadership would receive a more complete picture—and likely reach different conclusions.

With respect to internal financial reporting, there are no rules or laws that dictate the nature, scope, or format of the reports.[1] Accordingly, financial reports should be presented in the manner most helpful to those who use them. Graphs, charts, dashboard-like "gauges," and plain-language narratives are likely to provide the most helpful information in most circumstances.

Examples of financial reports:

1. Sample Narrative Report on Liquidity and Financial Position

The church's overall financial position improved during the month of October as compared with September. Weekly giving averaged approximately $28,000 for the month of October, compared to approximately $24,000 for September. The

church's operating cash balance increased from approximately $230,000 at the end of September to approximately $270,000 at the end of October. Average weekly church attendance for October also increased to approximately 1,050 people compared to about 950 for September. The age of accounts payable invoices remains consistent at approximately 17 days. The church continues to pay its bills in a timely manner. Debt payments as a percentage of overall church revenue year-to-date is at approximately 20.2 percent, which is within the range the church has deemed acceptable. Given the upward trend in attendance and giving, the overall outlook is good at this time.

We have not yet made meaningful progress toward achieving our goal of maintaining a debt service reserve equal to six months of debt service costs. We plan to begin to address that goal as part of the upcoming year's budgeting process.

2. Gauges

Below is a more visually driven approach to providing the same information described in the sample narrative above.

---

1   Of course, there are laws prohibiting fraud, misappropriation, and other similar activities.

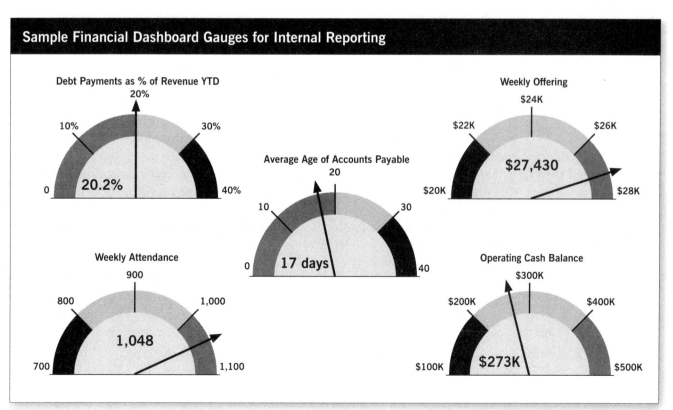

Sample Financial Dashboard Gauges for Internal Reporting

Who are the users?

The users of internal financial reports typically include members of the church's leadership team, financial oversight committee, and governing body. In designing a system of internal financial reporting, those who are responsible for preparing financial reports must consider the specific people who will read and use them. They must also consider the nature and scope of information that each user or group of users needs in order to effectively carry out their roles. For example, the business administrator of a church will likely need financial information that is more detailed in nature and scope than the information needed by the church's governing board. Additionally, the business administrator will likely need specific information regarding the financial activities of all areas of the church's operations, whereas department heads may only need information regarding the financial activities of their respective departments.

What information should be covered by the internal financial reporting process?

Church leaders should determine the nature and scope of information they need in order to carry out their respective responsibilities. An effective way to make such a determination is to identify the "key questions" they need answered. Once the key questions are identified, church leaders can evaluate and modify the financial reporting content and format to ensure that the financial reports adequately address the key questions. Following are examples (not intended to be exhaustive) of questions that church leaders might incorporate into their list:

(1) Is the church's current liquidity sound or strong? How do we know?

(2) Is the trending in the church's liquidity improving or declining? Elaborate.

(3) What is the church's current balance for cash and other liquid assets? What is the balance net of donor-restricted and designated amounts? Provide details.

(4) If current accounts payable and other similar liabilities were paid, how many months of cash operating expenses would the current cash and liquid assets balance (net of donor-restricted and designated amounts) cover?

(a) How does the answer to this question compare to the church's objectives for this matter?

(b) Is there a plan in place to improve the operating cash reserves balance? What is the plan? How are we doing with respect to implementing the plan?

(5) Is the church paying all of its bills on time? How do we know?

(6) Has the church had any trouble in recent weeks or months meeting its cash flow demands? If yes, elaborate.

(7) Does the church expect to have any trouble in the foreseeable future with respect to meeting its cash flow demands? How do we know? If yes, elaborate.

(8) Has the church borrowed any money to fund regular operations or noncapital outlays? If yes, elaborate.

(9) Has the church dipped into donor-restricted or designated cash or investment balances in order to fund operations at any point during the last year? How do we know? If yes, elaborate.

(10) What is the current balance of the church's mortgage debt?

(11) Are debt payments being made in a timely manner, without any difficulty?

(12) Are there any specific financial covenants contained in the church's loan agreements that stipulate specific financial requirements the church must meet as a condition of complying with the terms of the loan? If yes, provide details with respect to the nature of each covenant as well as the church's compliance with the terms of the covenant.

(13) What percentage of the church's total revenues is being spent on servicing the church's mortgage debt?

(a) How does the answer to this question compare to the church's objectives with respect to servicing debt?

(14) What is the ratio of the church's total liabilities to the church's unrestricted net assets?

(a) How does the answer to this question compare to the church's objectives with respect to this matter?

(15) What is the balance of the church's debt service reserves?

(a) How many months of debt service for the church's existing mortgage debt will this balance cover?

(b) How does the answer to this question compare with church's objectives with respect to this matter?

(c) Is there a plan in place to improve the debt service reserves balance? What is the plan? How are we doing with respect to implementing the plan?

(16) Is there any other information regarding the church's overall liquidity or financial position that the church's leadership should know that the questions above do not address? If yes, provide details.

(17) Is the trending with respect to overall revenue for tithes and offerings favorable or declining?

(a) If declining, what are the causes and what is the church's leadership doing to address the matter?

(b) Does the trending in the church's overall giving levels align with the trending in the church's overall attendance? Elaborate and provide details.

(18) Is per capita giving trending favorably or unfavorably? Provide details.

(19) What other information about the church's revenues (especially revenues not related to tithes and offerings) is relevant to church leadership?

(20) With respect to expenditures, is the church's staff leadership adhering to budget parameters? How do we know?

(21) Are expenditures increasing or decreasing?

(22) Are appropriate approval processes in place for all expenditures? Elaborate and succinctly describe the approval process for all areas of expenditure.

(23) Is there any additional information about the church's expenditures not covered by the questions above that would be relevant to the church's leaders?

(24) Is the church generating a cash flow surplus from its operating activities? Why or why not?

(25) How do the church's financial operating results compare with expectations as set forth in the approved budget?

(26) Are there any current vulnerabilities, specific risks, threats, or other similar matters that could adversely affect the church's financial condition? If yes, elaborate.

(27) On a scale of 1 to 10, with 1 very weak and 10 extraordinarily strong, how would the church's staff leadership rate the church's current financial condition? Explain the basis for the rating.

NOTE: Responses to key questions should be provided in plain language. A perfectly acceptable format for a portion of the church's internal financial reporting very well may be a Q&A format, with questions like those in the examples above provided, along with appropriate responses by members of the accounting and financial management team. Such a format can cover a particular period of time. Once responses are formulated to the questions, the responses can be updated each time new reports are required. If changes to the responses are highlighted, users of the reports can quickly and easily identify new information. Of course, the church's accounting and finance team should have appropriate schedules and details available to support the responses.

Church leaders shouldn't be intimidated

If a church leader does not completely understand the internal financial reports, or feels that additional information is needed, that leader should work with the church's accounting team to revise and improve the financial reporting process. A church leader should never be intimidated if he or she does not understand information in the financial reports. If the leader has significant overall management responsibilities for the church and does not adequately comprehend the financial reporting information, the leader cannot carry out his or her responsibilities adequately. While a church leader responsible for overseeing the business activities of a church should have business experience, if the financial reports do not provide information in a manner that facilitates understanding, the problem is not likely with the key church leader. More likely, the problem is with the internal financial reporting process.

Effective internal financial reporting is always based on the idea that meaningful, usable, relevant, and timely information is provided to decision-makers in a format that they can easily understand. When that is not happening, the solution is not to attempt to convert a decision-making church leader into an accountant. Rather, the church's accounting team must adapt to the needs, language, and experience of the church's decision-makers. If the church's accounting team is unable to do so, the church leadership may need to evaluate the makeup of the accounting team.

Reporting to the Body Charged with Financial Oversight

Church leaders do not need to be accountants in order to carry out and manage the day-to-day business activities of a church. But those charged with overseeing the church's financial activities—be it the members of the governing body, such as a board, or a committee—should have financial expertise. Most often, the board assigns a finance committee or its equivalent to oversee the church's financial operations. The members of this committee must diligently and consistently perform their tasks and responsibilities. Otherwise, the board can't effectively govern in the manner it is required. And even worse, it will fall short of fulfilling its legal duties.

Because so much is at stake, at least some of the people responsible for performing governance-level financial oversight should be financial professionals—accountants, corporate finance executives, bankers, and so on.

Since at least a portion of those serving on the body responsible for the church's financial oversight will—or should be—composed of financial professionals, the nature and format of reporting to the financial oversight body may vary from the reporting provided to other church leaders. For example, financial professionals may be accustomed to reading and evaluating formal *financial statements*. An effective church financial reporting system will include the ability to produce accurate and timely financial statements in a proper format for the financial oversight body. The church's accounting team should also produce whatever other reports the oversight body requires and should do so in the format prescribed by the oversight body.

As further described in Chapter 8, appropriate financial oversight may involve the use of audits or other accountability measures designed to evaluate the veracity and propriety of financial reports and other information the church's leadership uses.

CHURCH ACCOUNTING DEFINITIONS

Certain key terms are central to church accounting. Here are the ones most commonly used:

Assets

Assets represent items of value that the church owns or to which the church has certain rights that relate to future benefits. The most common assets recognized in the financial reports of churches include cash, investment securities, and property and equipment (frequently referred to as "PP&E"--the second "p" is for "plant"). Property and equipment is also sometimes referred to as "fixed assets." Other types of assets include accounts receivable (such as amounts due from families for school tuition for churches that operate schools), inventories (such as bookstore or food service inventory items), loans receivable, and prepaid expenses (payments made in advance of receiving goods or services).

Liabilities

Liabilities represent obligations of the church to pay money or to provide goods or services to another party. The most common liabilities recognized in church financial reports include accounts payable (amounts due to vendors), accrued expenses (expenses that have been incurred but not invoiced by a vendor, such as payroll earned by employees but not yet paid, interest that has accumulated with respect to outstanding debt but is not yet due, and so on), and debt payable (frequently referred to as "note payable," "mortgage payable," or "loan payable"). Another type of liability sometimes seen in church financial statements is unearned revenue (for example, tuition money that has been received from parents for education services to be provided by the church's school in future months).

Net Assets

In the purest and simplest sense, net assets comprise the difference between a church's assets and its liabilities. However, in accounting for nonprofit organizations, net assets are classified into as many as three categories, depending on whether the church has received contributions subject to donor-imposed restrictions and the nature of any such restrictions.

The three categories of net assets that a church may have are as follows:

- **Permanently restricted net assets.** Permanently restricted net assets arise when a donor makes a gift to the church and stipulates that the gift amount (or some portion of it) is to be invested permanently and not expended by the church. Donors who make permanently restricted gifts frequently stipulate how the distributions or earnings from the invested gift are to be utilized. An example of a contribution that results in permanently restricted net assets is an endowment gift; the donor stipulates that the gift amount is to be invested permanently and that distributions from the endowment fund are to be used to fund scholarships.

- **Temporarily restricted net assets.** Temporarily restricted net assets arise when a donor makes a gift to the church and stipulates that the gift is to be used for a specific purpose or at a specific future time. A common example of a gift that results in temporarily restricted net assets is a gift by a donor to the church's missions fund, where the church tells its congregation that all contributions to its missions fund will carry out the church's various missions programs. Another common example of a temporarily restricted gift is a contribution to a church's building fund, where donors have been advised that such contributions will be used to fund a particular building project.

NOTE: Permanently and temporarily restricted net assets represent the church's "equity" in the related assets. A church's net assets balance is distinct from the church's "actual" assets (cash, investments, and so on). For example, if a donor makes a cash gift of $1 million to a church to fund a permanent scholarship endowment, the accounting entry is to recognize an asset (cash) of $1 million and permanently restricted contribution revenue of $1 million. The permanently restricted contribution revenue results in an increase in permanently restricted net assets of $1 million. The ultimate effect on the church's financial position is that the church has additional assets of $1 million (cash) and permanently restricted net assets of $1 million.

While net assets and actual assets are distinct, a church should always ensure that it has actual assets (typically in liquid form) sufficient to cover its restricted net assets (whether permanent or temporary). Failure to do so typically constitutes a violation of one or more donor-imposed restrictions, which can be a significant legal matter.

- **Unrestricted net assets.** Unrestricted net assets comprise the balance of net assets that are not subject to either permanent or temporary donor restrictions. A church's governing body may "designate" a portion of the church's net assets for a particular purpose. Designations made by the church itself (as contrasted with a donor-imposed restriction) do not constitute temporarily or permanently restricted net assets, but rather, are a component of unrestricted net assets. The fundamental reason for such treatment is that internal designations made by church officials may be undone or reversed, whereas a donor-imposed restriction is a more significant legal matter.

Income, revenue, and gains

Income, revenue, and gains generally result from the church receiving one or more assets, experiencing an increase in the recognizable value of one or more assets, or experiencing a decrease in the recognizable value of one or more liabilities. In plain words, income, revenue, and gains generally result when positive (good) things happen to the church's assets or liabilities. Common examples of income and revenue are contributions, interest and dividend income from investments, and fees received for program activities conducted by the church. Gains commonly occur from appreciation of a church's investment assets.

Expenses or losses

Expenses or losses generally result when the church transfers assets (e.g., cash) to other parties to cover operating costs, experiences a decrease in the recognizable value of one or more assets, or experiences an increase in the recognizable value of one or more liabilities. The most common expenses incurred by a church are the cash operating costs associated with regular activities (e.g., salaries, utilities, repairs, maintenance, transportation, and so on). The most common example of a non-cash expense incurred by churches is depreciation—defined and described below. A common way a church may experience losses is a decline in the value of a church's investment assets.

Depreciation – Depreciation is a non-cash expense that represents the "using up" or deterioration of a long-lived asset. Property and equipment other than land generally deteriorates over time and ultimately must be either repaired, refurbished, replaced, or simply discarded. Accountants estimate the useful life of a particular asset and then recognize its deterioration over the estimated useful life. For example, assume that a church acquires an item of electronic equipment for $50,000. The estimated useful life of the equipment is 5 years. The church may recognize depreciation expense of $10,000 per year over the 5-year estimated useful life of the asset. As another example, assume that the church constructs a new building for a cost of $4 million and estimates that the building has a useful life of 40 years. The church may recognize depreciation expense of $100,000 per year over the 40-year estimated life of the building. (While churches commonly recognize depreciation expense evenly over the life of an asset, other methods of recognizing depreciation (typically, accelerated) may be permissible. In reality, churches rarely use depreciation methods other than recognizing the expense evenly over the estimated life of an asset—a method that is referred to as "straight-line" depreciation.)

The accounting entry necessary to recognize depreciation expense involves increasing an expense account (depreciation expense) and increasing an account commonly referred to as "accumulated depreciation." Accumulated depreciation is a "contra-asset" account, which simply means that it is a negative account in the church's assets. For example, using the information described in the preceding paragraph for the electronic equipment, the equipment is originally recognized as an asset on the books of the church for $50,000. After the first year of depreciation expense is recognized, accumulated depreciation in the amount of $10,000 will be recognized as a contra-asset, thereby reducing the net amount of the equipment asset on the church's books from $50,000 to $40,000.

Even though depreciation expense is a non-cash expense in the year in which it is recognized, it is a very real expense in the sense that it represents the genuine deterioration of an asset that is being used up over time. As further described in Chapter 1, churches often overlook or ignore the reality of depreciation expense, which can adversely affect a church's ability to reach its targeted financial objectives.

Resources for detailed accounting guidance

Some resources provide specific, detailed guidance with respect to accounting for various aspects of a church's transactions and activities, including numerous resources from ECFA (http://ecfa.org), as well as *PPC's Guide to Religious Organizations*, available from Thomson Reuters.

CHURCH ACCOUNTING METHODS

Churches apply a variety of accounting methods in their financial statements and reports. Current professional accounting literature refers to a comprehensive method of accounting as a *"financial reporting framework."* The three financial reporting frameworks most commonly used by churches in the United States are:

(1) Generally Accepted Accounting Principles (GAAP),
(2) The Cash Basis, and
(3) The Modified Cash Basis.

Generally Accepted Accounting Principles (GAAP)

Accounting principles that are formally and officially recognized by the accounting profession in the United States are commonly referred to as "generally accepted accounting principles," a term that is frequently abbreviated using the acronym "GAAP." The official accounting literature comprising GAAP is promulgated by the Financial Accounting Standards Board—an independent nonprofit organization. GAAP is used by many regulated businesses (e.g., banks) and companies whose stock is publicly traded on U.S. stock exchanges. GAAP is also used by many privately held businesses, as well as many nonprofit organizations. The GAAP framework is used most frequently for external financial reporting (described further below). Outside the context of regulated and publicly traded companies, its use for *internal* financial reporting is much less common.

The primary distinction between GAAP and the other frameworks described below is that GAAP generally attempts to recognize revenues and expenses as they are *incurred*, rather than when an organization receives or pays the cash (or other assets) related to the revenues and expenses.

For example, when a church has a company repair the church's air-conditioning equipment, the repair expense is *incurred* at the time the repair is performed. Under GAAP, the church would recognize the repair expense at the time the repair is performed and would recognize a payable to the vendor for the amount due.

As another example, assume that a church operates a school and families are required to pay tuition for the school year in advance. When the church receives the tuition money from the families, it has not yet provided the services for the tuition paid. Under GAAP, the church would recognize the cash it receives as an asset and it would also recognize a liability associated with the church's obligation to provide services in the future. Such a liability is frequently referred to as "unearned revenue." The church would then recognize the revenue over the period during which the services are provided.

As a final example, assume that a church's fiscal year ends on June 30, which happens to fall in the middle of the church's payroll period. As of that date, the church's employees have worked several days for which they have not yet been paid, since the payroll date has not yet arrived. Under GAAP, the church will recognize "accrued payroll expense"—a liability for the services that have been provided to the church but for which the church has not yet paid.

Due to the fact that the GAAP framework typically involves recognizing "accruals" such as those described in the preceding paragraph, GAAP is sometimes referred to as the "full accrual" method of accounting.

Even though the GAAP framework is formally and officially recognized by the accounting profession, use of the GAAP framework for external financial reporting is not generally a requirement of the law outside the context of regulated and publicly traded companies. However, the use of GAAP for external financial reporting purposes may be required as a contractual or legal condition for churches and other nonprofit organizations in certain circumstances. For example, a bank or other lender may require a church to apply the GAAP framework to financial statements submitted to the lender on an annual basis. Similarly, a government agency or other grant-funding organization may require a church to submit GAAP-basis financial state-

ments as a condition of receiving a grant. Regardless of whether such a contractual or legal condition applies, a church may still voluntarily choose to use the GAAP framework for its external financial reporting. Regardless of whether a contractual or legal condition applies to the use of GAAP in external financial reporting, and regardless of whether a church voluntarily uses GAAP in its external financial reporting, the church is free to use whatever financial reporting framework it considers most helpful for its internal accounting and financial reporting purposes.

The primary advantage of the GAAP framework is that it is almost universally accepted by all parties for external financial reporting. Lending institutions, regulatory bodies, taxing authorities, grant-making organizations, prospective donors, accrediting organizations, and virtually all other external users of the church's financial statements will accept financial statements prepared using GAAP. GAAP is the "highest common denominator" of the financial reporting frameworks. There is no higher or better method of financial reporting.

Accordingly, a church that applies the GAAP reporting framework to its external financial statements will be in a position to provide acceptable financial statements to virtually any party who may require them in virtually any scenario. That is not the case with respect to the other reporting frameworks described below. For example, if a church were to apply for a new mortgage loan, it is possible that the lender would require the use of the GAAP reporting framework in the church's financial statements. If the church's external financial statements are not ordinarily prepared using the GAAP framework, the church may be required to rework its accounting and financial reporting in order to satisfy the lender.

The cash basis

The cash basis financial reporting framework is really quite simple. Sometimes colloquially referred to as the "pure cash basis" of accounting (to distinguish it from the "modified cash basis" described below), the premise of the cash basis framework is to recognize only cash transactions in the church's financial statements. For this purpose, organizations frequently define the term "cash" to include balances in bank deposit accounts as well as highly liquid investment securities. Accordingly, under the cash basis framework, the only assets recognized in the church's financial statements are cash and highly liquid investment securities. No other assets are recognized, and no liabilities are recognized.

Income and revenues are recognized when cash is received, and expenses are recognized when cash is paid. With GAAP, cash spent to purchase a long-lived asset would result in the recognition of the long-lived asset in the church's financial statements (and not an immediate expense), but the cash basis framework dictates that any such expenditure is simply a cash disbursement that reduces the church's cash balance. Similarly, while GAAP would dictate that a principal payment made by a church to reduce its outstanding debt would reduce the liability on the financial statements of the church, the cash basis framework does not recognize liabilities, meaning a payment to reduce the outstanding principal of debt is simply another type of cash expenditure that reduces the church's cash balance.

Accordingly, a financial statement prepared using the cash basis framework for a particular period of time will generally report only the following items:

- Beginning cash balance,
- Cash receipts,
- Cash disbursements, and
- Ending cash balance.

(The financial statement may provide descriptions or categories of cash receipts and cash disbursements.)

Given the fact that the cash basis financial reporting framework is so simple and limited, it is typically used only by very small organizations with very simple financial operations. For a very small church, the cash basis framework may be adequate to meet the needs of the church's leaders for both *internal* and *external* financial reporting. This is especially true for churches that do not have significant property and equipment or significant outstanding debt. The primary virtue of the cash basis framework is its simplicity. Very little, if any, accounting experience is required to maintain an accounting system using the cash basis financial reporting framework.

While the simplicity of the cash basis financial reporting framework may be a virtue for very small

churches, its limitations make it an inadequate framework for most larger churches—especially churches with significant property and equipment or significant outstanding debt. Due to the fact that the cash basis framework does not recognize assets other than cash or any liabilities, applying the cash basis framework to a church with significant property and equipment or debt will produce financial statements that do not reflect the church's significant assets or obligations. The absence of such information would make it difficult—if not impossible—for church leaders to accurately and adequately assess the church's financial condition.

The modified cash basis

The modified cash basis reporting framework takes the cash basis framework (as described above) and adds to it the recognition of limited types of assets in addition to cash and limited types of liabilities. As is the case with the cash basis framework, the term "cash" in the modified cash basis framework is typically defined to include highly liquid investment securities. Generally, in the modified cash basis framework, property and equipment is recognized as an asset (along with its contra-asset, accumulated depreciation) in addition to cash. Additionally, outstanding debt and other "hard" liabilities (not regular accounts payable or accruals) are recognized as liabilities.

Other types of assets and liabilities are generally not recognized under the modified cash basis reporting framework. For example, accounts receivable, inventories, and prepaid expenses are not generally recognized as assets under the modified cash basis. Similarly, regular accounts payable, accrued expenses, and unearned revenue are not generally recognized as liabilities. Some professional judgment may be required in determining whether it is appropriate to recognize a particular asset or liability under the modified cash basis framework. The basic concept of the modified cash basis framework is to recognize "hard" assets and liabilities, and not to recognize accrual-type assets and liabilities.

Many churches use the modified cash basis framework for financial reporting. The primary advantage that the modified cash basis offers over the GAAP basis is its relative simplicity. Since accrual-type assets and liabilities are not recognized, the accounting is simpler.

For many churches, including some larger churches, the modified cash basis reporting framework may be used for both *internal* and *external* financial reporting (if acceptable to external users). Churches that use the modified cash basis often favor it because, while it is relatively simple (as compared to the GAAP basis), it does provide information about the church's most significant assets and liabilities—its cash and investments, its property and equipment, and its outstanding debt. For many church leaders, the omission of accrual-type assets and liabilities is not a significant factor in their evaluation of the church's financial condition. Further, if church leaders want to assess information about the church's accrual-type assets and liabilities, such as accounts receivable, inventories, and accounts payable, that information can be measured and reported to church leaders as of any given date separately from the church's financial statements.

NOTE: *While some variations of the modified cash basis framework exist that differ slightly from that described above, the methodology and principles described above represent the most commonly used version of the modified cash basis framework.*

EXTERNAL FINANCIAL REPORTING

External financial reporting typically involves the church issuing formal *financial statements* to users who are external to the church's leadership. The nature, content, and format of the external-use financial statements will vary based on the reporting framework used by the church. Following is a summary description of the financial statements typically included for churches with respect to each of the three financial reporting frameworks described above.

Generally Accepted Accounting Principles (GAAP)

- **Statement of financial position.** Sometimes informally referred to as the "balance sheet," the statement of financial position reports the assets, liabilities, and net assets of the church. The balance of each of the three components of net assets is also reported—unrestricted, temporarily restricted (if applicable), and permanently restricted (if applicable).
- **Statement of activities.** Sometimes informally referred to as the "income statement" or the "P & L" (which stands for "profit and loss"—a term commonly used in the business sector), the statement of activities reports the income, revenues, gains, expenses, and losses of the church. The net amount of these items is reported as the "change in net assets." The statement of activities reports the change in each of the three components of net assets—unrestricted, temporarily restricted (if applicable), and permanently restricted (if applicable).
- **Statement of cash flows.** The statement of cash flows reports the church's sources and uses of unrestricted cash. Inflows and outflows of cash are grouped into three categories—operating cash flows, investing cash flows, and financing cash flows.
- **Notes to the financial statements.** Specific disclosures regarding various aspects of the church's financial position and activities are required by GAAP.

See the sample GAAP-basis church financial statements on page 49.

The cash basis

- **Statement of cash receipts and disbursements.** The statement of cash receipts and disbursements is a very simple report that includes the following components:

  - Beginning cash and investment balances;
  - Cash receipts;
  - Cash disbursements; and
  - Ending cash and investment balances.

Appropriate detail should be provided for each of the components.

- **Notes to the financial statements.** A statement of cash receipts and disbursements prepared under the cash basis reporting framework may or may not be accompanied by notes to the financial statements providing additional disclosures about the church and the information in the statement. *It is a best practice to provide notes to the financial statement under the cash basis framework. Appropriate notes are required if the financial statement is to be audited and the church wishes to receive an unqualified ("clean") audit opinion.*

The modified cash basis

- **Statement of financial position – modified cash basis.** The statement of financial position – modified cash basis reports the cash (including highly liquid investment securities), property and equipment (net of accumulated depreciation), and outstanding debt of the church, along with the resulting net assets balance. It is a generally accepted practice for the statement of financial position – modified cash basis to include the balance of each of the three components of net assets—unrestricted, temporarily restricted (if applicable), and permanently restricted (if applicable).

- **Statement of activities – modified cash basis.** The statement of activities – modified cash basis reports the income, revenues, gains, expenses, and losses of the church in a manner consistent with the modified cash basis financial reporting framework as described above. The net amount of these items is reported as the "change in net assets – modified cash basis." It is a generally accepted practice for the statement of activities – modified cash basis to report the change in each of the three components of net assets—unrestricted, temporarily restricted (if applicable), and permanently restricted (if applicable).

- **Notes to the financial statements.** Financial statements prepared under the modified cash basis reporting framework may or may not be accompanied by notes to the financial statements providing additional disclosures about the church and information in the statements. *It is a best practice to provide notes to the financial statements under the modified cash basis framework. Appropriate notes are required if the financial statements are to be audited and the church wishes to receive an unqualified ("clean") audit opinion.*

CHURCH ACCOUNTING SOFTWARE

Virtually all churches use some type of accounting software to create and maintain appropriate accounting records and financial reporting. Some smaller churches use software with functionality that is limited to the accounting and financial activities arena (e.g., QuickBooks). Larger churches generally use "church management" applications with both accounting and other capabilities—including tools that assist with various operational areas of the church (e.g., membership records, facilities usage, inventory management, school administration, and so on). Some accounting and church management applications can run on the church's own computer network, while others are offered as "cloud-based" applications accessible by users through the Internet.

Each of the church management applications offers distinct features. Nick Nicholaou of Ministry Business Services publishes an annually updated comparison of the features of some of the more well-known church management applications. Mr. Nicholaou's analysis is available at *mbsinc.com/church-donor-management-software-chms/. See pages 58-63.*

In determining whether a specific church management application is appropriate for a particular church, church leaders should take into consideration not only the operating functionality of the application, but also the strength and reputation of the application with respect to internal control. (See Chapter 7 for more information about maintaining sound internal control.) Additionally, church leaders should evaluate the financial strength and viability of the company providing the application to address the possible risk of the provider going out of business. Cessation of business by a church's accounting and operations application provider could have adverse implications with respect to the church's accounting and other important records—especially if the application is cloud-based and becomes inaccessible. Lastly, the church will want to fully understand the security controls put into place by the provider to keep sensitive private data protected.

Cloud-based paperless accounts payable applications

Certain cloud-based applications for accounts payable management exist which are independent of accounting and general ledger software applications. Independent cloud-based accounts payable applications typically integrate or interface with a variety of general ledger and accounting software packages. A church considering using such an application should evaluate whether it will integrate or interface with the church's accounting software package. Even if the cloud-based accounts payable application does not directly interface or integrate with the church's accounting software

NonProfit Accounting Essentials

Not all computerized accounting systems are created equal! What are the essentials a church or ministry should look for when selecting a new accounting system? Here are some of the features many in ministry consider highest priority.

Secure Audit Trail

The audit trail is the record of every transaction that is posted in the accounting system. The best accounting systems have audit trails that cannot be altered in any way or at any time. If a mistake is posted, the correction must be done in a separate entry rather than just erasing and re-entering.

The benefit of a secure audit trail is that nothing can be hidden from scrutiny. The danger with unsecured audit trails—those that can be modified or erased—is they can more easily hide fraud and embezzlement. That is, inappropriate entries are less obvious and may thus go on longer than in a secure audit trail system.

Fund Accounting

Churches and ministries track multiple fund balances, and this is sometimes referred to as fund accounting. What we're referring to here is different than having multiple designated contributions or support opportunities, but rather the ability to have various income and expense accounts close to different balance sheet fund accounts. You might think of them similarly to equity accounts on a corporate balance sheet.

Cash vs Accrual Flexibility

GAAP (Generally Accepted Accounting Principals) refers to the rules and concepts that govern the field of accounting. GAAP requires that reports be presented based on accrual accounting. Accrual accounting means posting income or expense transactions at the time they are incurred. However, many churches and ministries prefer to manage themselves based on the cash basis of accounting, or a mixture of both that is referred to as modified cash.

An easy example of the difference between the accrual basis and the cash basis is asking when you want to post the expense of an invoice received from a vendor to your general ledger: at the time the expense was incurred (accrual, based on the invoice date) or when it is paid (cash, based on the check date).

Most in the nonprofit sector want the flexibility to satisfy GAAP (accrual basis), but also want to manage by the cash basis— all from the same set of books. To do this they sometimes keep everything in accrual except AP (modified cash basis). Some of the better systems allow this flexibility.

Module Integration

Accounting systems usually have many modules (GL, AP, AR, Payroll, Bank Reconciliation, etc). When all of these modules are integrated— which means they are all interconnected, there is less chance of accidental entry mistakes. A well-integrated system allows people with differing system security rights to process the data for which they are responsible (contributions or accounts payable, for example) and no other data, and yet all the entries flow into the general ledger where a person with a higher level of security rights can review the work that was done in those other modules.

This supports the concept of separating duties to improve internal controls (for instance, the person handling contributions usually should not also have check writing authority).

Government Forms

There are a number of government forms that need to be printed by all organizations each year. 1099s, W-2s, and other state and federal forms can be printed directly from some modern accounting systems, saving your team a lot of time while also improving accuracy.

CPA Approval

When looking for a new accounting system, be sure to ask your CPA firm if they're comfortable with the system you are considering. This is especially important if you have your books audited by your CPA firm; having their blessing in advance will save you time, money, and headaches!

package, other advantages of the cloud-based application may still outweigh that disadvantage.

Cloud-based accounts payable applications offer significant advantages over applications that are built into a church's regular accounting software. For example, with a cloud-based application, church leaders may use their computer, smart phone, iPad, or similar device to review, approve, and pay bills from literally anywhere in the world at any time, so long as they have an Internet connection. Additionally, the better cloud-based applications incorporate user rights and user profiles with built-in internal controls as a standard feature. Accordingly, church leaders can receive reminder emails at selected intervals (daily, weekly, and so on) of bills requiring review, approval, and payment. When the leader who is vested with the authority to approve actual payments (bills that have been properly approved by others) selects specific bills for payment and executes the "pay" command, the bills are actually paid.

Disbursements are either made electronically or the cloud-based application service provider actually prints checks at its location and mails them to the respective vendors. The cost of such applications is typically insignificant in light of the dramatic streamlining and improvement in efficiency that typically result from their use.

Two popular examples of cloud-based accounts payable management applications are *Bill.com* and AnyBill (*anybill.com*).

In addition to providing significant efficiencies, electronic accounts payable management systems generally facilitate improved internal control by requiring multiple individuals to provide approvals in connection with disbursements (assuming the application has been properly set up with segregated user rights). For example, such an application offers "roles," such as the accountant role, with duties that align with the principle of segregation of duties. An accountant, for example, would not be permitted to execute a "pay" command. Another feature that enhances internal control is that such systems do not produce physical checks to be signed by the church's employees and mailed or delivered from the church's office. Instead, disbursements are either made electronically through the ACH system

or checks are actually cut and mailed by the service provider directly to the vendors. Cloud-based paperless accounts payable management systems offer significant advantages over traditional paper-check-based systems. The applications integrate with a number of accounting software applications.

OUTSOURCING ACCOUNTING AND FINANCIAL REPORTING

As the complexity of the accounting, tax, and regulatory compliance environment for churches continues to increase, more churches are outsourcing their accounting and financial reporting functions to others. As was the case with payroll processing beginning in the 1980s and 1990s, churches are beginning to find that outsourcing their accounting and financial reporting can, in some cases, result in better information with less risk and at a cost that is lower than performing the functions internally. Church accounting, financial reporting, and tax compliance are very different from the accounting, financial report, and tax compliance conducted in the business sector. Accordingly, when a church hires an accountant or bookkeeper from the general business sector, there is typically a steep learning curve with respect to the unique attributes of the church sector. The availability of accountants and bookkeepers with significant and high-quality church experience is limited.

True outsourcing of a church's accounting and financial reporting function is very different from traditional bookkeeping services. Traditional bookkeeping services are typically "after the fact" and involve preparing financial statements and reports for the church after the end of each month (or quarter). Under the traditional bookkeeping service model, church employees typically prepare checks and pay the church's bills on a day-to-day basis. The bookkeeper takes the information from the church after the end of each month (or quarter) and uses it to prepare financial reports.

True outsourcing of a church's accounting and financial reporting function, however, involves having the outsourcing firm actually coordinate the day-to-day bill paying process, payroll, and similar functions as they occur. In some outsourced accounting and financial reporting arrangements, the outsourcing firm maintains real-time financial reports and dashboards that are accessible to the church's leaders on a continuous basis. Additionally, in some outsourced accounting arrangements, the church's bills are paid through an electronic bill-paying process, thereby eliminating the need for anyone to print, sign, and mail checks. When outsourcing of a church's accounting and financial reporting function is performed by a firm with significant experience in the church arena, the quality of the accounting and information available to the church's leaders may exceed anything available to the church if the church were to hire an accountant or bookkeeper internally from the general business sector. Also, since outsourcing by definition involves having people external to the church performing the accounting and financial reporting function, outsourcing typically facilitates an improvement in internal controls by enhancing the segregation of incompatible duties.

Outsourcing the accounting and financial reporting function is most commonly done by moderate to large-sized churches (e.g., those with annual revenues between $500,000 and $4,000,000). "Mega-churches" do not commonly (currently) outsource their accounting and financial reporting functions. Outsourcing can be an affordable option – often costing less than performing services of comparable quality internally. The cost of outsourcing will vary based on a variety of factors, including the nature of the specific services to be provided and the experience of the people performing the outsourced services. A church that employs its accounting team internally understandably may be reluctant to consider switching to outsourcing if doing so would mean that one or more of the church's employees would be terminated. If the church's internal accounting person or people are performing well, the church may wish to wait until a change in their employment occurs naturally (e.g., when the key accounting person resigns or retires).

RETENTION OF CHURCH RECORDS

State nonprofit corporation laws generally require incorporated churches to maintain the following records:

- Correct and complete books and records of account;
- Minutes of the proceedings of its members;

- Minutes of the proceedings of its board of directors;
- Resolutions of its board of directors;
- Minutes of the proceedings of committees; and
- A current list of voting members.

These documents, in addition to the corporate charter, constitution, bylaws, certificate of incorporation, correspondence, insurance policies, employment files, contracts, and tax forms and documentation constitute the records of a church corporation. **The Model Nonprofit Corporation Act**, under which many churches are incorporated, states:

> Each corporation shall keep correct and complete books and records of account and shall keep minutes of the proceedings of its members, board of directors and committees having any of the authority of the board of directors; and shall keep at its registered office or principal office in this State a record giving the names and addresses of its members entitled to vote. All books and records of a corporation may be inspected by any member, or his agent or attorney, for any proper purpose at any reasonable time.[2]

The Revised Model Nonprofit Corporation Act, which has been adopted in some states, specifies:

> (a) A corporation shall keep as permanent records minutes of all meetings of its members and board of directors, a record of all actions taken by the members or directors without a meeting, and a record of all actions taken by committees of the board of directors . . . .
>
> (b) A corporation shall maintain appropriate accounting records.
>
> (c) A corporation or its agent shall maintain a record of its members in a form that permits preparation of a list of the name and address of all members, in alphabetical order by class, showing the number of votes each member is entitled to cast.
>
> (d) A corporation shall maintain its records in written form or in another form capable of conversion into written form within a reasonable time.

---

2   MODEL NONPROFIT CORPORATION ACT § 25.

(e) A corporation shall keep a copy of the following records at its principal office:

(1) its articles or restated articles of incorporation and all amendments to them currently in effect;

(2) its bylaws or restated bylaws and all amendments to them currently in effect;

(3) resolutions adopted by its board of directors relating to the characteristics, qualifications, rights, limitations and obligations of members or any class or category of members;

(4) the minutes of all meetings of members and records of all actions approved by the members for the past three years;

(5) all written communications to members generally furnished within the past three years, including the financial statements furnished for the past three years under section 16.20;

(6) a list of the names and business or home addresses of its current directors and officers; and

(7) its most recent annual report delivered to the secretary of state . . . .[3]

All records should be as complete as possible, which means that each record should be dated and indicate the action taken, the persons present, and the voting results if any. It is often helpful to include a brief statement of the purpose for each action if it would not otherwise be clear. The secretary of the board of directors usually is the custodian of the corporate records, while accounting records customarily are maintained by the treasurer.

The income tax regulations state that "any person subject to tax . . . shall keep such permanent books of account or records, including inventories, as are sufficient to establish the amount of gross income, deductions, credits, or other matters required to be shown by such person in any return of such tax . . . ."[4]

Inspection of Church Records

Can church members inspect church records? If so, which records can be inspected and under what circumstances? What about nonmembers? Generally, there is no inherent right to inspect church records. Such a right must be granted in some legal document

---

3   REVISED MODEL NONPROFIT CORPORATION ACT § 16.01.
4   Treas. Reg. § 1.6001-1(a).

such as a church's bylaws or state nonprofit corporation law. Some of the possible justifications for a right of inspection are reviewed in this section.

Nonprofit corporation law

Section 25 of the Model Nonprofit Corporation Act, previously quoted, gives members of an incorporated church the right to inspect corporate records for any proper purpose at any reasonable time. The Revised Model Nonprofit Corporation Act gives members broad authority to inspect corporate records, but specifies that "the articles or bylaws of a religious corporation may limit or abolish the right of a member . . . to inspect and copy any corporate records."[5]

Can a church incorporated under the Model Nonprofit Corporation Act refuse a member's request to inspect church records on the ground that such a right conflicts with the church's constitutional guaranty of religious freedom? The courts have reached conflicting answers to this question.

> **CASE STUDY.** The Arkansas Supreme Court ruled that members of a church incorporated under the Model Nonprofit Corporation Act do not have a right to inspect church records if doing so would "impinge upon the doctrine of the church." When church elders rejected members' requests to inspect church records, the members incorporated the church under a state nonprofit corporation law making the "books and records" of a corporation subject to inspection "by any member for any proper purpose at any reasonable time." When church elders continued to reject the members' request for inspection, the members asked a state court to recognize their legal right to inspection under state law. The elders countered by arguing that application of state corporation law would impermissibly interfere with the religious

---

5   REVISED MODEL BUSINESS CORPORATIONS ACT § 16.02. Some of the special provisions under the revised Act include: (1) ordinarily, a member must give the corporation written notice at least five business days before the date of inspection; (2) the right to inspect includes the right to make copies; (3) the corporation may charge a reasonable fee for the duplicating expenses; (4) for certain types of records, a member's request for inspection must be "in good faith and for a proper purpose," and the member must describe with "reasonable particularity the purpose of the records the member desires to inspect," and the records must be directly related to such purpose; and (5) a member's agent or attorney has the same inspection and copying rights as the member. In addition, the revised Act empowers the civil courts to order a corporation to grant a member's request for inspection.

doctrine and practice of the church, contrary to the constitutional guaranty of religious freedom. Specifically, the elders argued that according to the church's "established doctrine," the New Testament "places within the hands of a select group of elders the sole responsibility for overseeing the affairs of the church," and that this authority is "evidenced by biblical admonitions to the flock to obey and submit to them that have rule over the flock." The state supreme court agreed that "application of our state corporation law would almost certainly impinge upon the doctrine of the church" as described by the elders, and accordingly would violate the constitutional guaranty of religious freedom. The court concluded that if the application of a state law would conflict with the "doctrine, polity, or practice" of a church, then the law cannot be applied to the church without a showing of a "compelling state interest." No such showing was made in this case, the court concluded, and therefore the state law giving members of nonprofit corporations the legal right to inspect corporate records could not be applied to the church.[6]

Other courts have rejected the claim that the First Amendment insulates church records from inspection by members. To illustrate, members of one church sought a court order authorizing them to examine the church's financial records. The church was incorporated under the state's general nonprofit corporation law, which gave members the right to inspect corporate records at any reasonable time. The church and its pastor objected to the inspection on the ground that the First Amendment prohibits the courts from involving themselves in church affairs. The court disagreed with this contention, concluding that "First Amendment values are plainly not jeopardized by a civil court's enforcement of a voting member's right to examine these records."[7]

It is doubtful that most courts would permit churches incorporated under the Model Act to refuse members' requests to inspect church records on the basis of the

First Amendment guaranty of religious freedom. The statutory right of inspection is a "neutral law of general applicability" that is presumably constitutional without the need for demonstrating a compelling state interest.[8] As a result, church leaders should not assume that the First Amendment permits them to deny inspection rights given to members under state corporation law.

A right of inspection, however, generally applies only to *members*. Persons who are not members of a church generally have no right to demand inspection of church records under nonprofit corporation law.

> **CASE STUDY.** The Alabama Supreme Court ruled that a dismissed church member no longer had a legal right to inspect church records.[9]

> **CASE STUDY.** A Georgia court ruled that a member of a nonprofit corporation failed to prove that he had a proper purpose for his request to inspect several categories of corporate records, and therefore he had no legal right under the state nonprofit corporation law to inspect the records.

> **CASE STUDY.** Some of the members of a charitable organization incorporated under the state nonprofit corporation law demanded to see various corporate records. Their request was denied by corporate officers, and the members sued. An Illinois state appeals court ruled that the members had a broad right to inspect the corporation's records. The court noted that the state nonprofit corporation law specified that "all books and records of a corporation may be inspected by any member . . . for any proper purpose at any reasonable time." The court continued, "The [member] has the burden to establish he has a proper purpose to inspect the corporation's records. A proper purpose is shown when a shareholder has an honest motive, is acting in good faith, and is not proceeding for vexatious or speculative reasons; however, the purpose must be lawful in character and not contrary to the interests of the corporation. A proper purpose is one that seeks to protect the interests of the corporation and the [member] seeking the information.

---

6   *Gipson v. Brown*, 749 S.W.2d 297 (Ark. 1988). A "compelling state interest" no longer is required with respect to "neutral laws of general applicability," according to the United States Supreme Court's decision in *Employment Division v. Smith*, 494 U.S. 872 (1990).

7   *Bourgeois v. Landrum*, 396 So.2d 1275, 1277 78 (La. 1981).

8   *Employment Division v. Smith*, 110 S. Ct. 1595 (1990).

9   *Lott v. Eastern Shore Christian Center*, 908 So.2d 922 (Ala. 2005). Accord *Ex parte Board of Trustees*, 2007 WL 1519867 (Ala. 2007).

. . . [A member's] right to inspect a corporation's books and records must be balanced against the needs of the corporation depending on the facts of the case. Proof of actual mismanagement is not required; a good faith fear of mismanagement is sufficient to show proper purpose. The [member] is not required to establish a proper purpose for each record he requests. Once that purpose has been established, the [member's] right to inspect extends to all books and records necessary to make an intelligent and searching investigation and from which he can derive any information that will enable him to better protect his interests."[10]

CASE STUDY. A Louisiana court ruled that an incorporated church had to allow members to inspect church records. Four members asked for permission to inspect the following records of their church: (1) bank statements; (2) the check register and cancelled checks for all the church's bank accounts; (3) the cash receipts journal; and (4) monthly financial reports. The pastor denied the members' request. The members then sought a court order compelling the church to permit them to inspect the records. The pastor insisted that such an order would interfere with "internal church governance" in violation of the First Amendment. A state appeals court ruled that allowing the members to inspect records, pursuant to state nonprofit corporation law, would not violate the First Amendment. The court quoted from an earlier Louisiana Supreme Court ruling: "A voting member of a nonprofit corporation has a right to examine the records of the corporation without stating reasons for his inspection. Since the judicial enforcement of this right does not entangle civil courts in questions of religious doctrine, polity, or practice, the First Amendment does not bar a suit to implement the statutory right. First Amendment values are plainly not jeopardized by a civil court's enforcement of a voting member's right to examine these records. No dispute arising in the course of this litigation requires the court to resolve an underlying controversy over religious doctrine."[11]

CASE STUDY. A New York court ruled that a church member had the legal authority to inspect church records despite the pastor's refusal to allow him to do so. A church member (and former church officer) suspected that the senior pastor and several current church trustees diverted or misappropriated church funds. When his request to inspect church financial records was denied, he sued the church, citing a provision in the state nonprofit corporation law authorizing members of nonprofit corporations to inspect specified corporate records. A state appeals court ruled that the member had a legal right to inspect the church's financial records as a result of the nonprofit corporation law. It observed: "Not-For-Profit Corporation Law § 621 authorizes any person who is a member of a not-for-profit corporation for at least six months immediately preceding an unsuccessful demand to inspect the corporation's books and records to commence a special proceeding to compel the production of those books and records. . . . The issue of whether the plaintiff, who seeks to enforce a statutory right, is entitled to the production of the church's books and records, can be determined by resort to neutral principles of law" involving no inquiry into church doctrine.[12]

CASE STUDY. A Tennessee court ruled that church members were not legally entitled to inspect certain records of their church on the basis of a provision in the state nonprofit corporation law giving members a right of inspection, since they lacked a "proper purpose" for their request. The Tennessee nonprofit corporation law specifies that members have a legal right to inspect "accounting records" only if "a demand is made in good faith and for a proper purpose, the member describes with reasonable particularity the purpose and the records the member desires to inspect; and the records are directly connected with the purpose for which the demand is made." Several members of a church sought to inspect the church's financial records as part of their investigation into financial mismanagement by the pastor and other church leaders. The church resisted this request, arguing that the members' request failed to satisfy all of the conditions required for inspection, and turning over the records would violate the church's consti-

---

10 *Meyer v. Board of Managers, 583 N.E.2d 14 (Ill. App. 1 Dist. 1991).*
11 *Jefferson v. Franklin, 692 So.2d 602 (La. App. 1997).* The court quoted from the Louisiana Supreme Court's decision in *Burgeois v. Landrum, 396 So.2d 1275 (La. 1981),* referred to in the text.

12 *Tae Hwa Yoon v. New York Hahn Wolee Church, Inc. 870 N.Y.S.2d 42 (N.Y.A.D. 2008).*

tutional right to freely exercise its religion. The trial court ruled that the members had a proper purpose since they were investigating suspected financial mismanagement, and therefore had a "property interest in the church assets." A state appeals court reversed the trial court's decision, and ruled that the members failed to satisfy the requirements of the nonprofit corporation law for inspection of the church's financial records: "The members relied upon their property rights in the church building and its funds as the proper purpose. The purpose presented by the members . . . was to determine their property rights. However . . . unless there is an agreement to the contrary in some bylaw or associational agreement, any decision about control of church property is to be decided by a majority vote of the church. It has likewise been found that church members have no property rights in their contributions to a church. Consequently, the members have no property rights in the church building or its assets. This is in accord with the generally accepted law on the subject. Generally, a non-profit corporation, and not its members, owns the property of the nonprofit. Absent a departure by the majority from doctrine accepted by the articles of incorporation, the minority has no right to claim church property from a majority at the church membership."[13]

CASE STUDY. The Texas Supreme Court ruled that a state nonprofit corporation law that granted a limited right to inspect corporate records did not mandate the disclosure of donor records.[14] The Texas Nonprofit Corporation Act specifies that nonprofit corporation "shall maintain current true and accurate financial records with full and correct entries made with respect to all financial transactions of the corporation." It further specifies that "all records, books, and annual reports of the financial activity of the corporation shall be kept at the registered office or principal office of the corporation . . . and shall be available to the public for inspection and copying there during normal business hours." Based on these provisions, a group of persons demanded that a charity turn over documents revealing the identities of all donors

and the amounts of donors' annual contributions. The charity resisted this request, claiming that the inspection right provided under the nonprofit corporation law did not refer to inspection or disclosure of donor lists, and that even if it did, such a provision would violate the First Amendment freedom of association. The state supreme court ruled that the right of inspection did not extend to donor lists. It noted that "the statute does not expressly require that contributors' identities be made available to the public." And, it found that the intent of the legislature in enacting the inspection right "was not to force nonprofit corporations to identify the exact sources of their income; rather, it was to expose the nature of the expenditures of that money once received from the public and to make nonprofit organizations accountable to their contributors for those expenditures." As a result, the statute "can be upheld as constitutional when interpreted as not requiring disclosure of contributors' names."

➤ TIP. The Privacy Act and Freedom of Information Act have no application to religious organizations. They do not provide church members with any legal basis for inspecting church records.

Church charter or bylaws
A right of inspection may be given by the bylaws or charter of a church corporation or association.

State securities law
Churches that raise funds by issuing securities (such as bonds or promissory notes) may be required by state securities laws to allow investors—whether members or not—to inspect the financial statements of the church.

Subpoena
Members and nonmembers alike may compel the production (i.e., disclosure) or inspection of church records as part of a lawsuit against a church, if the materials to be produced or inspected are relevant and not privileged. For example, Rule 34 of the Federal Rules of Civil Procedure, adopted by several states and used in all federal courts, specifies that any party to a lawsuit:

> May serve on any other party a request (1) to produce and permit the party making the request, or someone acting on his behalf, to inspect and copy,

---

13 *Two Rivers Baptist Church v. Sutton, 2010 WL 2025444 (Tenn. App. 2010).*
14 *In re Bacala, 982 S.W.2d 371 (Tex. 1998).*

2

Accounting and Financial Reporting

any designated documents . . . which are in the possession, custody or control of the party upon whom the request is served; or (2) to permit entry upon designated land or other property in the possession or control of the party upon whom the request is served for the purpose of inspection. . . .

Similarly, Rule 45(b) of the Federal Rules of Civil Procedure states that a subpoena may command the person to whom it is directed "to produce the books, papers, documents, or tangible things designated therein . . . ." Rule 45 also stipulates that a subpoena may be quashed or modified if it is "unreasonable and oppressive." Federal, state, and local government

agencies are also invested with extensive investigative powers, including the right to subpoena and inspect documents. However, this authority generally may not extend to privileged or irrelevant matters.

Since church records are not inherently privileged, they are not immune from production or inspection. Although most states consider confidential communications to be privileged when they are made to clergy acting in their professional capacity as spiritual advisers, several courts have held that the privilege does not apply to church records.

> **CASE STUDY.** In upholding an IRS subpoena of the records of a religious corporation over its objection that its records were privileged, a federal court observed that the "contention of violation of a penitent clergyman privilege is without merit. A clergyman must be a natural person."[15]

> **CASE STUDY.** The Ohio Supreme Court, in upholding the admissibility of a church membership registration card over an objection that it was privileged, noted that "this information by any flight of the judicial imagination cannot conceivably be considered as a confession made to [a clergyman] in his professional character in the course of discipline . . . and, of course, is not privileged."[16]

> **CASE STUDY.** A New York court ruled that a church's books and records were subject to government inspection as part of an investigation into alleged wrongdoing in soliciting contributions.[17] The state attorney general received reports that the church forced residents of its homeless shelter to "panhandle" contributions on the streets in exchange for room, board, and 25 percent of the monies collected. There also were allegations that most of the contributions were appropriated for the personal benefit of the church's founder. Accordingly, the attorney general issued a subpoena to the church, directing it to make

---

Inspection of Church Records

Do church members have a legal right to inspect church records as a result of state nonprofit corporation law? Consider the following:

- Most state nonprofit corporation laws give members a limited right to inspect corporate records.
- The right of inspection is not absolute. It only exists if a church is incorporated under a state nonprofit corporation law that gives members such a right.
- The right of inspection only extends to members.
- The right of inspection only extends to those records specified in the statute creating the right.
- Most such laws provide that the member may inspect documents only "for a proper purpose" at a "reasonable time."
- Some courts have ruled that the right of inspection is limited by considerations of privacy, privilege, and confidentiality.[1] That is, some documents may be protected from disclosure by legitimate considerations of privacy (such as an employee's health records); privilege (such as communications protected by the clergy-penitent privilege); or confidentiality (such as reference letters submitted by persons who were given an assurance of confidentiality).
- Any decision to withhold documents from a member should be made with the advice of an attorney.

---

1   See, e.g., *Lewis v. Pennsylvania Bar Association*, 701 A.2d 551 (Pa. 1997).

15   *United States v. Luther*, 481 F.2d 429, 432 (9th Cir. 1973) (the court did state that its holding would not prevent "a later determination at a time when the issue is properly raised and supported by a proper showing"). See also *Abrams v. Temple of the Lost Sheep, Inc.*, 562 N.Y.S.2d 322 (Sup. Ct. 1990); *Abrams v. New York Foundation for the Homeless, Inc.*, 562 N.Y.S.2d 325 (Sup. Ct. 1990).

16   *In re Estate of Soeder*, 220 N.E.2d 547, 572 (Ohio 1966).

17   *Abrams v. New York Foundation for the Homeless, Inc.*, 562 N.Y.S.2d 325 (Sup. Ct. 1990); *Abrams v. Temple of the Lost Sheep, Inc.*, 562 N.Y.S.2d 322 (Sup. Ct. 1990).

available for inspection its (1) books and records, (2) leases and deeds, (3) minutes of its governing body and the names and addresses of all directors, officers, and trustees, and (4) copies of all materials used to solicit contributions. The church refused to respond to this subpoena on the ground that it violated its "religious rights." In rejecting the church's claim, the court observed: "There is no doubt that the attorney general has a right to conduct investigations to determine if charitable solicitations are free from fraud and whether charitable assets are being properly used for the benefit of intended beneficiaries." It makes no difference whether or not the organization soliciting the donations is a church or other religious organization, since "religious corporations . . . are still within the attorney general's subpoena power, and investigations by the attorney general of alleged fraudulent behavior may proceed based upon law and the public interest against fraudulent solicitations by so-called religious groups." The court emphasized that the attorney general's investigation did not prevent the church or its members "from practicing their religious activity, nor is it disruptive to such activity."[18]

CASE STUDY. The Pennsylvania Supreme Court ruled that the clergy-penitent privilege did not excuse a Roman Catholic diocese from turning over internal documents pertaining to a priest in response to a subpoena. An individual (the "defendant") was charged with the murder of a Roman Catholic priest. The defendant admitted that he shot the priest, but he insisted that he did so in self-defense. In attempting to prove that he acted in self-defense, the defendant subpoenaed documents from the local Catholic Diocese. Specifically, the defendant requested the priest's personnel records and the Diocese's records concerning the priest's alleged alcohol and drug abuse and sexual misconduct. The defendant insisted that these documents could help prove that he acted in self-defense because of the priest's past violent conduct. The Diocese turned over some documents but refused to turn over any records kept in its "secret archives." It insisted that documents in its secret archives were protected from disclo-

sure by the clergy-penitent privilege since they had been obtained in confidence by the bishop or other clergy in the course of their duties. The court disagreed, noting that there was no proof that the secret records reflected communications between members of the clergy in confidence and for confessional or spiritual purposes.[19]

⊙ KEY POINT. Most courts have viewed requests by church members for an "accounting" of church funds to be an internal church matter over which the civil courts have no jurisdiction.

Do church members, or a government agency or officer have the right to demand an accounting of church funds? The courts have reached conflicting answers to this question.

CASE STUDY. A group of church members who had contributed funds to their church demanded that the church give an "accounting" of the use of the contributed funds. When the church refused, the members turned to the courts for relief. A trial judge ordered an immediate accounting, as well as annual audits "forever," and required the church to disclose the contents of a church safety deposit box to the complaining members. The church appealed, arguing that the civil courts had no jurisdiction over a church, and even if they did, they had no authority to order accountings or annual audits. A Florida court, in upholding the trial judge's ruling regarding an accounting and inspection of the church's safety deposit box, observed that "we are of the opinion that this is not an improper interference by the government into a church, or ecclesiastical, matter. When the members of the church decided to incorporate their body under the laws of the state of Florida, they submitted themselves to the jurisdiction of the state courts in all matters of a corporate nature, such as accounting for funds." However, the court reversed the trial judge's order requiring annual audits forever, since "we cannot agree it is proper to order annual, ad infinitum, audits of the books" of a church.[20]

18 *Id. at 328.*

19 *Commonwealth v. Stewart, 690 A.2d 195 (Pa. 1997).*

20 *Matthews v. Adams, 520 So.2d 334 (Fl. App. 1988).*

2

Accounting and Financial Reporting

CASE STUDY. The Supreme Judicial Court of Maine ruled that a state has the authority to demand an accounting of church trust funds. In 1939, a wealthy individual made a gift of a substantial amount of stock to a church, subject to the following two conditions: (1) the church was to use the trust fund for "charitable uses and purposes," and (2) the church was not to sell or transfer the stock for a period of 50 years. In 1983, after faithfully observing the terms of the trust for 44 years, the church sought court permission to sell the stock. It noted that the value of the stock had fallen sharply and the rate of return was substantially less than could be achieved with other investments. The court permitted the church to sell the stock (then valued at $733,000) in order to protect the trust fund. In 1987, the state attorney general received information suggesting that the church was not carrying out the terms of the trust. The attorney general asked the church for an accounting of the trust fund. When the church refused to comply, the attorney general sought a court order compelling the church to provide an accounting. The church argued that the First Amendment guaranty of religious freedom protected the church from complying with the demand for an accounting. The court rejected the church's position. It noted that the attorney general had the legal authority to ensure that the church was complying with the trust purpose, and this authority included the right to demand an accounting of trust funds. In rejecting the church's First Amendment argument, the court observed: "The attorney general is not attempting to inquire into the financial affairs of the church, or impose a regulatory scheme, but only to obtain the information necessary for him to fulfill his statutory obligation to the public. Because we find that the trust is a public trust, separate and distinct from the church, the court ordered accounting can be accomplished by application of neutral principles of law and therefore, does not impinge upon the church's First Amendment freedoms."[21]

CASE STUDY. An Illinois court ruled that it lacked jurisdiction to resolve a lawsuit brought by church members who demanded an accounting of church funds. Six members of a church filed a lawsuit asking the court to order an accounting of church funds as a result of what they perceived to be financial irregularities involving their minister. A state appeals court declined the members' request. It observed, "It is eminently clear that the basis of this lawsuit is to have the courts examine the way the church is managing its financial affairs; to substitute the prudence of a court's judgment for that of the [minister] who is entrusted by church doctrine to exercise such judgment; to impose court supervision over all financial matters of an entire religious faith; and to have a court interfere with the proper succession in the hierarchy of a religious faith. These matters, however, are beyond the realm of judicial jurisdiction."[22]

Public inspection of tax-exemption applications

Any organization that is exempt from federal income taxation (including churches and religious denominations) must make available a copy of the following materials in response to a request from a member of the public:

- The exemption application form (Form 1023) submitted to the IRS;
- any supporting documents submitted with the exemption application, including legal briefs or a response to questions from the IRS; and
- any letter or document issued by the IRS with respect to the exemption application (such as a favorable determination letter or a list of questions from the IRS about the application).[23]

The exemption application must be made available for inspection, without charge, at the organization's principal office during regular business hours. The organization may have an employee present during inspection, but must allow the individual to take notes freely and to photocopy at no charge if the individual provides the photocopying equipment.

An exempt organization also must provide a copy of its exemption application to anyone who requests a copy, either in person or in writing at its principal office dur-

---

21 *Attorney General v. First United Baptist Church, 601 A.2d 96 (Me. 1992).*

22 *Rizzuto v. Rematt, 653 N.E.2d 34 (Ill. App. 1995).*
23 *IRS Notice 88-120, 1988-2 C.B. 4541.*

ing regular business hours. If the individual made the request in person, the copy must be provided on the same business day the request is made unless there are unusual circumstances. The organization must honor a written request for a copy of documents or specific parts or schedules of documents that are required to be disclosed. However, this rule only applies if the request (1) is addressed to the exempt organization's principal office; (2) is sent to that address by mail, electronic mail (e-mail), facsimile (fax), or a private delivery service approved by the IRS; and (3) gives the address to where the copy of the document should be sent. The organization must mail the copy within 30 days from the date it receives the request. The organization may request payment in advance and must then provide the copies within 30 days from the date it receives payment.

The organization may charge a reasonable fee for providing copies. It can charge no more for the copies than the per-page rate the IRS charges for providing copies. The IRS may not charge more for copies than the fees listed in the Freedom of Information Act (FOIA) fee schedule (*foia.gov/faq.html#cost*). Although the IRS charges no fee for the first 100 pages, the organization can charge a fee for all copies. The organization can also charge the actual postage costs it pays to provide the copies.

Many churches never filed an exemption application with the IRS because they are covered by a "group exemption" obtained by their denomination. If such a church receives a request for inspection of its exemption application, it must make available for public inspection, or provide copies of: (1) The application submitted to the IRS by the central or parent organization to obtain the group exemption letter, and (2) those documents which were submitted by the central or parent organization to include the local or subordinate organization in the group exemption letter. However, if the central or parent organization submits to the IRS a list or directory of local or subordinate organizations covered by the group exemption letter, the local or subordinate organization is required to provide only the application for the group exemption ruling and the pages of the list or directory that specifically refer to it.

In lieu of allowing an inspection, the local or subordinate organization may mail a copy of the applicable documents to the person requesting inspection within

the same time period. In this case, the organization can charge the requester for copying and actual postage costs only if the requester consents to the charge. If the local or subordinate organization receives a written request for a copy of its annual information return, it must fulfill the request by providing a copy of the group return in the time and manner specified earlier. The requester has the option of requesting from the central or parent organization, at its principal office, inspection or copies of group returns filed by the central or parent organization. The central or parent organization must fulfill such requests in the time and manner specified earlier.

If an exempt organization maintains one or more "regional or district offices," the exemption application (and related materials) "shall be made available at each such district or regional office as well as at the principal office." This rule will be relevant to many religious denominations. Churches and religious denominations should be aware of these requirements, since some undoubtedly will receive requests for inspection.

The penalty for failure to allow public inspection of exemption applications is $20 for each day the failure continues. The penalty for willful failure to allow public inspection of an exemption application is $5,000 for each return or application. The penalty also applies to a willful failure to provide copies.

Government inspection of donor and membership lists

Whether the government has the right to compel religious organizations to release the *names of members and contributors* is a hotly contested issue.

In 1958, the United States Supreme Court ruled that the freedom to associate with others for the advancement of beliefs and ideas is a right protected by the First Amendment against governmental infringement, whether the beliefs sought to be advanced are political, economic, religious, or cultural.[24] The Court acknowledged that the right of association is nowhere mentioned in the First Amendment, but it reasoned that such a right must be inferred in order to make the express First Amendment rights of speech and assem-

---

24 *National Association for the Advancement of Colored People v. Alabama, 357 U.S. 449 (1958).*

bly more secure. The court concluded that an order by the State of Alabama seeking to compel disclosure of the name of every member of the National Association for the Advancement of Colored People in Alabama constituted an impermissible restraint upon members' freedom of association, since on past occasions "revelation of the identity of its rank and file members has exposed these members to economic reprisal, loss of employment, threat of physical coercion, and other manifestations of public hostility. Under these circumstances, we think it apparent that compelled disclosure of [the NAACP's] Alabama membership is likely to affect adversely the ability of [the NAACP] and its members to pursue their collective effort to foster beliefs which they admittedly have the right to advocate, in that it may induce members to withdraw from the Association and dissuade others from joining it. . . ."

It is clear that governmental actions with the possible effect of curtailing the freedom of association are subject to the closest scrutiny. Yet the courts have made it clear that the right to associate is not absolute; a "significant interference" with the right may be tolerated if the government (1) avoids unnecessary interference, (2) demonstrates a sufficiently important interest, and (3) employs the least intrusive means of achieving its interests.

> The Supreme Court has observed that "decisions . . . must finally turn, therefore, on whether [the government] has demonstrated so cogent an interest in obtaining and making public the membership lists . . . as to justify the substantial abridgement of associational freedom which such disclosures will effect. Where there is a significant encroachment upon personal liberty, the state may prevail only upon showing a subordinating interest which is compelling."

Government demands for the production and inspection of membership and contributor lists frequently are approved on the ground that a compelling governmental interest exists.

CASE STUDY. A federal appeals court upheld the enforcement of an IRS summons seeking the name of every individual who had contributed property other than securities to Brigham Young

University (BYU) during a three-year period. Before issuing the summons, the IRS had audited the returns of 162 taxpayers who had contributed property to the university during the years in question. In each instance the amount of the contribution claimed by the taxpayer was overvalued, and in many cases grossly overvalued. As a result, the IRS surmised that many other contributors had overvalued their contributions as well. The university challenged the summons on the ground that the IRS was without a reasonable basis for believing that the remaining contributors had overvalued their contributions. The university further asserted that the information sought was readily available to the IRS through its own files, and that enforcement of the summons would infringe upon the contributors' freedom of association under the First Amendment. The court, in upholding the summons, observed that "having previously examined the returns of some 162 donors of gifts in kind to BYU and having found that all were overvalued, the IRS has established a reasonable basis for believing that some of the remaining donors of in kind gifts may have also overvalued their gifts."

CASE STUDY. The Federal Communications Commission (FCC) received complaints that a religious broadcaster was not expending contributed funds as indicated in over the air solicitations. As part of its investigation, the FCC ordered the broadcaster to divulge the names of all contributors and the amount of each contribution. The broadcaster refused to comply on the ground that such information was protected by the First Amendment freedoms of religion and association. An FCC administrative tribunal ruled that, under the circumstances, the agency had a compelling interest in obtaining disclosure of the names of contributors and the amounts of contributions, and that this interest outweighed the freedoms of religion and association. A federal appeals court affirmed this determination on the grounds that (1) the government has a compelling interest in preventing the diversion of funds contributed for specific, identified purposes, especially when such funds are obtained through the use of the public airwaves, which, by congressional mandate, must be operated in the public interest; (2) the allegations of diversion of funds were made by a former employee and therefore they were entitled to a greater inference of reliability; (3) the government's investigation was narrow and avoided unnecessary interference with the free exercise of religion; and (4) the government's request for records was necessary to serve its compelling interest in investigating the alleged diversion of funds.

CASE STUDY. A federal court in the District of Columbia ruled that a church could not be forced to disclose the names of its members in a lawsuit. The court observed: "There is . . . implicit in the First Amendment's guarantee of religious freedom, the right to choose whether or not to disclose one's religious affiliation lest forced disclosure inhibit the free exercise of one's faith. I have to believe that, when a person provides her name and address to a church that has asked her to become a member, she reasonably expects that her name and address will be disclosed to other church members, used by the church to invite her to other church functions, and used to solicit her contribution to the church's financial welfare. There is nothing I know of in the American experience that suggests to me that by giving one's name and address to a church one thereby agrees to the publication of one's religious affiliation to the whole world."

CASE STUDY. A California court ruled that the right to associational privacy extends to private lawsuits as well as governmental investigations, and thus a litigant has no right to compel disclosure of the membership list of a church unless he can establish a compelling state interest justifying disclosure.

It is not clear whether the government needs to prove a "compelling interest" to inspect church membership or donor records following the Supreme Court's 1990 decision in the Smith case. In Smith, the Court ruled that "neutral laws of general applicability" are presumably valid without the need for demonstrating a "compelling state interest." Statutes that give government agencies a broad authority to collect information (including

church membership or donor information) may well be deemed "neutral laws of general applicability" by the courts. But this does not necessarily mean that such agencies can inspect church records without proof of a compelling state interest.

In the *Smith* case, the Supreme Court observed that the compelling government interest test applies if a neutral and generally applicable law burdens not only the exercise of religion, but also some other First Amendment right (such as the right of association, described above). The Court observed: "The only decisions in which we have held that the First Amendment bars application of a neutral, generally applicable law to religiously motivated action have involved not the free exercise clause alone, but the free exercise clause in conjunction with other constitutional protections, such as freedom of speech and of the press. . . ." In other words, if a neutral and generally applicable law or governmental practice burdens the exercise of religion, then the compelling governmental interest standard can be triggered if the religious institution or adherent can point to some other First Amendment interest that is being violated. In many cases, this will not be hard to do.

If the identities of all members or contributors are not reasonably relevant to a particular governmental investigation, the government's interest in disclosure will not be sufficiently compelling to outweigh the constitutionally protected interests of members and contributors.

➤ TIP. Neither the Privacy Act of 1974 nor the Freedom of Information Act applies to church records.

Who owns a church's accounting records?
Who owns a church's accounting records, and who has the right to maintain possession of them? Consider the following points:

1. The nonprofit corporation laws under which most churches are incorporated require that corporations maintain various kinds of records, including financial books of account. To illustrate, the Model Nonprofit Corporation Act, which has been adopted by most states, provides that "a

corporation shall maintain appropriate accounting records." While this language does not directly address ownership, an important question arises: *How can a church maintain appropriate accounting records if they are possessed and "owned" by the treasurer?* As a result, it should be assumed that the church is the owner of its financial records, and not a volunteer treasurer who takes them home. The takeaway point is that location, and even possession, does not determine ownership.

2. Allowing a volunteer treasurer to take the church's accounting records home is not recom-

mended for several reasons, including the following: (1) Such a procedure violates two of the core principles of internal control—segregation of duties and oversight over operations. Imagine the financial improprieties that could go undetected under such an arrangement. (2) Irreplaceable financial records may be lost, stolen, or destroyed while in the home of the church treasurer, and confidential information may be accessed by family members. (3) Church staff will be frustrated in the performance of their duties because of the inaccessibility of the church's financial records. (4) Such an arrangement can provide a treasurer with "leverage" that can be

Corporate Records

The following chart summarizes the most common record retention guidelines for corporate records.

Document	Description	How long to keep (minimum)	Comments
charter (articles of incorporation)	a legal document usually issued by the Secretary of State confirming corporate status	permanently	• the "charter" is the articles of incorporation that have been approved by the Secretary of State • contains basic information such as name, address, the initial board members, duration, and purpose • be sure to append all amendments to the charter
constitutions or bylaws	rules of internal church governance	permanently	be sure the current version is distinguishable from obsolete versions (i.e., affix an effective date and version identifier to all copies)
certificate of incorporation	a legal document issued by the Secretary of State confirming incorporation	permanently	a corporation's "birth certificate"
certificate of good standing	a legal document issued by the Secretary of State confirming current corporate status	permanently	it is a good practice to obtain one annually to validate corporate status
minutes of membership meetings	summaries of actions taken at regular and special membership meetings	permanently	minutes contain important information on many issues of church governance
minutes of board meetings	summaries of actions taken at regular and special board meetings	permanently	minutes contain important information on many issues of church governance
annual corporate reports	an annual report that in many states must be filed annually with the Secretary of State by any corporation incorporated under the general nonprofit corporation law	permanently	• failure to file this report can result in a "lapse" of corporation status • obtaining an annual certificate of good standing ensures that the corporate status has not lapsed

exerted to achieve ulterior objectives. (5) Such an arrangement may result in the permanent inaccessibility of church records in the event of a dispute with the treasurer or at such time as the treasurer leaves office voluntarily or involuntarily.

3. Church leaders should check the church's bylaws or other governing document to determine what, if any, authority the treasurer may have over the church's financial records. Some church bylaws state that the treasurer shall have "custody" of the church's financial records, or "be responsible" for them. But custody and responsibility are not the same as ownership, although such terminology suggests that the treasurer is authorized to remove the church's financial records to his or her home. For the reasons stated, this generally is not advisable, and so church leaders should review their governing document in order to identify and amend such a provision should one exist.

4. The same logic applies to paid employees. A church's bookkeeper, business administrator, or other paid employee should not keep financial records at home. An additional consideration applies to employees—the federal Fair Labor Standards Act. The FLSA guarantees overtime pay for hours worked in excess of 40 during the same week. States have their own requirements. The point is that churches have no way to monitor hours worked by an employee in his or her residence, and so compliance with the FLSA is virtually impossible. Some churches allow employees to take church records home to work on them as unpaid "volunteers." But this is not permissible, according to Department of Labor interpretations of the FLSA. The bottom line is that allowing church employees to take church records home in order to work with them may expose a church to significant liability under the FLSA or a state counterpart.

5. Some church leaders allow financial records to be kept in the private residence of a treasurer or other church officer or employee to preserve them from theft or a natural disaster affecting the church office. This risk can be managed by storing the records in a locked and immovable fireproof cabinet. After data on financial records is integrat-

ed into the church's computer software, backup copies can be stored off-site.

6. U.S. auditing standards require CPAs to maintain specified kinds of documentation when performing an audit. Most states have enacted laws specifying that CPAs own the working papers and other documentation they prepare in performing their duties. As a result, a church ordinarily cannot assert ownership in the working papers of CPAs who are retained to perform an audit of the church.

Establishing a records retention policy

Most church leaders struggle with the question of how long to retain church records. After all, church offices can become overwhelmed with old records and forms.

What is needed is a *records retention policy*. Such a policy should be based on applicable legal considerations and your church's needs. This will make records retention and disposal decisions systematic and rational. The table reproduced in this chapter will assist you in developing such a policy with regard to corporate records.

In establishing a records retention policy, you should consider a number of factors in addition to how long to keep records. These include: (1) when to make copies of records; (2) how to maintain the security of records (especially records you plan to keep permanently), including backups of computer records; and (3) how to follow a record retention schedule (a document that summarizes records, lists how long you plan to keep them, and indicates where they are kept).

Here are some additional factors to consider in developing a records retention policy for your church:

- Make an inventory of existing records.
- The church board should develop and approve your records retention policy.
- Your records retention policy should be reviewed by a local attorney (who can check local and state requirements), a CPA, and your insurance agent.
- There are many reasons to keep church records. These include legal requirements, potential relevance in future litigation, the needs of the organization, and historical importance. The table reproduced here suggests minimum periods of

time for retaining various church records. Some of the suggested retention periods are based on legal requirements, while others are based on practical considerations. You may want to keep some records longer than the table suggests.

- Some organizations maintain a "destruction of records journal." When the period of time for keeping a record has expired, the record is described in the journal before being destroyed.
- Do not destroy records, even when the period for keeping them has expired, if they may be relevant in pending or threatened litigation or in pending or threatened government (including IRS) investigations.

This section will summarize the recordkeeping rules for corporate, employment, and tax-related forms.

Tax records

IRS Publication 1828 contains the following information on the retention of church records: "The law does not specify a length of time that records must be retained; however, the following guidelines should be applied in the event that the records may be material to the administration of any federal tax law." *Publication 1828* lists the following guidelines:

This information is little help to church leaders in deciding how long to retain tax records. The following Chart provides guidance for deciding how long to retain tax records:

Insurance policies

It is imperative that all insurance policies, and especially liability and umbrella policies, be retained permanently. Here's why. The molestation of minors is one of the most virulent and frequent sources of church litigation. The statute of limitations for such claims does not begin to run until the victim is 18 years old. In most states, the statute of limitations is extended even further by the so-called "discovery" rule. Under this rule, the statute of limitations does not begin to run until the victim "discovers" the connection between the abuse and his or her emotional or other injuries. This can expose churches to liability for several decades.

When a church is sued for a case of child abuse that allegedly occurred decades in the past, it will need to locate its liability insurance policies for the year or years that the molestation occurred in order to trigger coverage pursuant to the terms of the policy, which generally includes a legal defense and the payment of any judgment or settlement (indemnification) up to the policy limits. If a church has disposed of its insurance policies for the years in question, it may have a difficult time establishing coverage.

Tax Records

Type of record	Length of time to retain
records of revenue and expenses, including payroll records	retain for at least four years after filing the return to which they relate
records relating to acquisition and disposition of property (real and personal, including investments)	retain for at least four years after the filing of the return for the year in which disposition occurs

2

Accounting and Financial Reporting

Record Retention Guidelines for Tax Records

Document	Description	How Long To Keep (minimum)	Comments
Form W-2 (wage and tax statement)	reports wages paid and taxes withheld	at least 4 years after filing the return	• retain the employer's copy of W-2 forms issued to employees
Form W-4 (withholding allowance certificate)	employees report withholding allowances on this form to enable their employer to withhold the correct amount of income taxes	at least 4 years after filing the return	• all lay employees should complete and submit this form to the church treasurer • ministers' wages are not subject to tax withholding, but ministers who report their income taxes as employees can elect voluntary withholding of taxes by completing and submitting this form to the church treasurer
Form 941 (employer's quarterly tax return)	used by employers to report wages paid and taxes withheld for each calendar quarter	at least 4 years after filing the return	• churches must file this form if they have at least one lay employee (or one minister who has elected voluntary withholding) • amounts reported on W-2 forms issued by the church should reconcile with the 941 forms for the year
Form 990-T (unrelated business income tax return)	tax return that tax-exempt organizations (including churches) file to report taxable income from an unrelated trade or business	at least 3 years after filing the return	• some exceptions apply (such as activities conducted by volunteers, sale of donated goods, and activities not regularly carried on) • rent from debt-financed property may be taxable (some exceptions apply)
Form 1023 (application for recognition of exemption)	used to apply for IRS recognition of exemption from federal income taxes	permanently	• churches are not required to file this form, since they are automatically assumed to be exempt • it often is desirable to have IRS recognition of exemption (though not required), mostly to assist members in substantiating charitable contributions • many churches are recognized by the IRS to be exempt because they are included in denominational group exemptions • churches not covered by group exemptions can file this form to obtain IRS recognition of exemption
Form 1099-MISC (miscellaneous income)	used to report compensation paid to nonemployees of $600 or more during the year	at least 4 years after filing the return	• churches use this form to report compensation of $600 or more paid to self-employed clergy or any other self-employed worker, including itinerant evangelists and guest speakers • not issued to corporations • $600 amount is net of accountable expense reimbursements and housing allowance
Form 5578 (annual certification of racial nondiscrimination)	filed annually by private schools (preschool through graduate school)	at least 4 years after filing the return	• used by private schools even if church-affiliated to certify compliance with federal nondiscrimination requirements (due by the 15th day of the 5th month following the close of each fiscal year)
Form 8274 (certification by churches requesting exemption from FICA taxes)	used to exempt a church from the employer's share of FICA taxes	permanently	• Churches with nonminister employees in July 1984 could exempt themselves from the employer's share of FICA taxes by filing this form with the IRS by October 30, 1984. • An exemption makes nonminister church employees self-employed for Social Security (they pay the full 15.3% self-employment tax like ministers). They are not exempt. • Churches hiring their first nonminister employee after 1984 have until the day before the due date for their first quarterly 941 form to file the exemption application.

Record Retention Guidelines for Tax Records (cont'd.)

Document	Description	How Long To Keep (minimum)	Comments
accountable reimbursement policy	church policy that reimburses employees' substantiated business expenses	permanently	• the policy usually is reflected in a board resolution or employee handbook • be sure all amendments are dated
accountable reimbursement policy receipts	employees must substantiate reimbursements with adequate documentation	at least 4 years from the filing deadline of the employee's tax return (but see "comments" for an exception)	• the regulations require employers to maintain receipts and other records used by employees to substantiate their reimbursed business expenses • the IRS has indicated that it may relax this requirement, but it has not done so • if an employer does not maintain these records, its employees will have to substantiate expenses if audited
all records associated with non-accountable expense reimbursements	reimbursement of personal expenses, or unsubstantiated business expenses	at least 4 years from the filing deadline of the employee's tax return	• churches must report non-accountable reimbursements as taxable income to the employee • failure to do so can expose the employee to substantial penalties (intermediate sanctions)
housing allowance	board or church resolution or budget item designating a portion of a pastor's compensation as a housing allowance	at least 4 years from the filing deadline of the pastor's tax return	• housing allowances are nontaxable (for income taxes) only to the extent they are used for housing expenses, and, for ministers who own their home, do not exceed the home's fair rental value
estimated housing expense form	churches often base housing allowances on a list of estimated housing expenses provided by a pastor	at least 4 years from the filing deadline of the pastor's tax return	• if estimated expenses are significantly above the fair rental value of a pastor's home, the allowance should be reduced (otherwise the pastor's W-2 wages will be too low, which can create tax liabilities for a pastor who assumes that the W-2 reflects true compensation)
safety net housing allowance	continuing resolution designating a specified percent of the salary of any staff pastor as a housing allowance if no allowance has otherwise been declared	permanently	• such resolutions avoid loss of the housing allowance if a church neglects to designate an allowance for the year, or is late in doing so • also useful when a church hires a pastor in mid-year (when designation of a housing allowance is often neglected)
job descriptions of staff pastors	describe the duties for which the pastor is employed	at least 4 years from the filing deadline of the pastor's tax return	• a housing allowance must represent compensation paid to a pastor for the exercise of ministry • job descriptions will indicate whether a pastor's duties constitute the exercise of ministry
property tax exemption applications and certificates	application form used to apply for exemption of church property from taxation, and the certificate issued by the taxing authority recognizing the exemption	consult local law	• churches generally must apply for property tax exemption under local law • in some states the exemption must be renewed periodically • an exemption application must be filed by the "tax day" specified by local law
sales tax exemption applications and certificates	application form used to apply for exemption of state sales taxes, and the certificate issued by the taxing authority recognizing the exemption	consult local law	• churches are exempt from sales tax in 41 states • exemption generally requires an application • exemption generally must be renewed periodically • the exemption varies from state to state

2

Accounting and Financial Reporting

Record Retention Guidelines for Tax Records (cont'd.)

Document	Description	How Long To Keep (minimum)	Comments
tax-sheltered annuity salary reduction agreements	designations by employees of the amount of their salary to be reduced and placed in their retirement account	at least 4 years from the filing deadline of the employee's tax return	• tax-sheltered "403(b)" annuities are the most common retirement program for church staff
cafeteria plan	popular fringe benefit plan allowing employees to use pre-tax salary reductions to pay for a menu of fringe benefits	permanently	• be sure all plan amendments (with dates) are recorded
retirement gifts	generally a resolution of the board or membership authorizing a gift to a retiring staff member	at least 4 years from the filing deadline of the employee's tax return	• retirement "gifts" paid by a church to a retiring employee are taxable (even if labeled "love gifts") • exception for some gifts of insignificant value • exception for some "employee achievement awards" (property valued at less than $400)
special occasion gifts	generally a resolution of the board or membership authorizing a holiday, birthday, or anniversary gift to a staff member	at least 4 years from the filing deadline of the employee's tax return	• special occasion "gifts" paid by a church to an employee are taxable (even if labeled "love gifts") • exception for some gifts made directly to an employee by a church member
health plans	plans adopted by an employer for the payment of some medical expenses of employees	permanently	• amounts received by employees from an employer as reimbursement for medical expenses may be nontaxable if made pursuant to a "plan" • be sure all plan amendments (with dates) are recorded
documents defining compensation	generally in minutes of church board or membership meetings	at least 4 years from the filing deadline of the employee's tax return	• compensation includes salary, expense reimbursements, fringe benefits, housing allowance, retirement plan contributions, insurance coverage, etc. • documentation may be needed in the event an employee's tax return is audited
correspondence received from the IRS or state and local tax agencies	may pertain to questions about a tax return (W-2, 941, etc.), a donor's contributions, eligibility for property tax exemption, etc.	permanently	• correspondence from taxing authorities may be relevant in future years

Sample GAAP-Basis Financial Statements for External Reporting with Sample Report of Independent Auditors

[Audit Firm Letterhead]

REPORT OF INDEPENDENT AUDITORS

The Governing Body
ABC Church
City, State

We have audited the accompanying financial statements of **ABC Church** ("the Church"), which comprise the statement of financial position as of June 30, 20XX, and the related statements of activities and cash flows for the year then ended, and the related notes to the financial statements.

Management's Responsibility for the Financial Statements
Management is responsible for the preparation and fair presentation of these financial statements in accordance with accounting principles generally accepted in the United States of America; this includes the design, implementation, and maintenance of internal control relevant to the preparation and fair presentation of financial statements that are free from material misstatement, whether due to fraud or error.

Auditor's Responsibility
Our responsibility is to express an opinion on these financial statements based on our audit. We conducted our audit in accordance with auditing standards generally accepted in the United States of America. Those standards require that we plan and perform the audit to obtain reasonable assurance about whether the financial statements are free from material misstatement.

An audit involves performing procedures to obtain audit evidence about the amounts and disclosures in the financial statements. The procedures selected depend on the auditor's judgment, including the assessment of the risks of material misstatement of the financial statements, whether due to fraud or error. In making those risk assessments, the auditor considers internal control relevant to the Church's preparation and fair presentation of the financial statements in order to design audit procedures that are appropriate in the circumstances, but not for the purpose of expressing an opinion on the effectiveness of the Church's internal control. Accordingly, we express no such opinion. An audit also includes evaluating the appropriateness of accounting policies used and the reasonableness of significant accounting estimates made by management, as well as evaluating the overall presentation of the financial statements.

We believe that the audit evidence we have obtained is sufficient and appropriate to provide a basis for our audit opinion.

Opinion
In our opinion, the financial statements referred to above present fairly, in all material respects, the financial position of ABC Church as of June 30, 20XX, the changes in its net assets, and its cash flows for the year then ended in accordance with accounting principles generally accepted in the United States of America.

[Audit Firm Signature]

City, State
(Date of Report)

2

Accounting and Financial Reporting

ABC CHURCH

Statement of Financial Position

June 30, 20XX

Assets	
Cash and cash equivalents	$ 3,210,000
Certificate of deposit	450,000
Cash and investments restricted for long-term purposes	1,480,000
Property and equipment, net	26,400,000
Other assets	50,000
Total assets	**$ 31,590,000**
Liabilities	
Accounts payable and accrued expenses	$ 400,000
Unearned revenue	360,000
Note payable	4,420,000
Total liabilities	**5,180,000**
Net assets	
Unrestricted	
Undesignated	24,010,000
Board designated	700,000
Total unrestricted	24,710,000
Temporarily restricted	900,000
Permanently restricted	800,000
Total net assets	**26,410,000**
Total liabilities and net assets	**$ 31,590,000**

1

ABC CHURCH

Statement of Activities

For The Year Ended June 30, 20XX

	Unrestricted	Temporarily Restricted	Permanently Restricted	Total
Public support and revenue and net assets released from restrictions				
Contributions	$ 6,000,000	$ 1,890,000	$ 200,000	$ 8,090,000
Tuition and fees, net	4,000,000	—	—	4,000,000
Auxiliary activities and other revenue	1,300,000	—	—	1,300,000
Gains on investments	—	110,000	—	110,000
Net assets released from restrictions	1,500,000	(1,500,000)	—	—
Total public support and revenue and net assets released from restrictions	12,800,000	500,000	200,000	13,500,000
Expenses				
Program activities				
Church activities	6,650,000	—	—	6,650,000
School activities	3,700,000	—	—	3,700,000
Total program activities	10,350,000	—	—	10,350,000
Supporting activities				
General and administrative	1,650,000	—	—	1,650,000
Fundraising	150,000	—	—	150,000
Total supporting activities	1,800,000	—	—	1,800,000
Total expenses	12,150,000	—	—	12,150,000
Change in net assets	650,000	500,000	200,000	1,350,000
Net assets - Beginning of year	24,060,000	400,000	600,000	25,060,000
Net assets - End of year	$ 24,710,000	$ 900,000	$ 800,000	$ 26,410,000

2

Accounting and Financial Reporting

2

ABC CHURCH

Statement of Cash Flows

For The Year Ended June 30, 20XX

Operating cash flows	
Cash received from contributors	$ 7,470,000
Cash received from tuition and fees	4,040,000
Other revenue received	1,300,000
Cash paid for operating activities and costs	(11,189,000)
Interest paid	(121,000)
Net operating cash flows	1,500,000
Investing cash flows	
Redemption of certificate of deposit	170,000
Net investment in assets restricted for long-term purposes	(290,000)
Purchases of and improvements to property and equipment	(1,470,000)
Net investing cash flows	(1,590,000)
Financing cash flows	
Proceeds from contributions restricted for investment in property and equipment and endowments	620,000
Principal payments on debt	(230,000)
Net financing cash flows	390,000
Net change in cash and cash equivalents	300,000
Cash and cash equivalents - Beginning of year	2,910,000
Cash and cash equivalents - End of year	$ 3,210,000
Reconciliation of change in net assets to net operating cash flows	
Change in net assets	$ 1,350,000
Adjustments to reconcile change in net assets to net operating cash flows	
Depreciation	800,000
Contributions restricted for investment in property and equipment and endowments	(620,000)
Gains on investments	(110,000)
Change in other assets	10,000
Change in accounts payable and accrued expenses	30,000
Change in unearned revenue	40,000
Net operating cash flows	$ 1,500,000

3

ABC CHURCH
NOTES TO FINANCIAL STATEMENTS
June 30, 20XX

NOTE 1
NATURE OF ACTIVITIES

ABC Church ("the Church") is a not-for-profit corporation, incorporated in the state of XXXXX. The purpose of the Church is to worship God and share the Gospel of Jesus Christ with others. The Church conducts various activities in accomplishing its purposes, including worship services, operation of a kindergarten through twelfth-grade school ("the School"), educational training, support of missionary endeavors, and other similar activities. The Church is located in City, State.

NOTE 2
SUMMARY OF SIGNIFICANT ACCOUNTING POLICIES

RESTRICTED AND UNRESTRICTED REVENUE AND SUPPORT
Contributions received are recorded as unrestricted, temporarily restricted, or permanently restricted support, depending on the existence and/or nature of donor restrictions. Donor-restricted support is reported as an increase in temporarily or permanently restricted net assets, depending on the nature of the restriction. When a restriction expires (that is, when a stipulated time restriction ends or purpose restriction is accomplished), temporarily restricted net assets are reclassified to unrestricted net assets and reported in the statement of activities as "net assets released from restrictions."

REVENUE RECOGNITION
The School's tuition and fees are reported net of discounts for families who are members of the Church and families who are provided financial assistance in the form of reduced tuition at the School. Tuition is recognized ratably throughout the School's academic year. All other revenue is recognized in the period earned. Accounts receivable as of the Church's fiscal year-end are insignificant.

CASH AND CASH EQUIVALENTS
Investment instruments which are purchased or donated with original maturities of three months or less are considered to be cash equivalents.

CASH AND INVESTMENTS RESTRICTED FOR LONG-TERM PURPOSES
Certain cash and investments have been restricted pursuant to agreements with donors which stipulate that the funds be held in perpetuity or are donor-restricted for the acquisition of long-lived assets such as property and equipment.

PROPERTY AND EQUIPMENT
Property and equipment are stated at cost, if purchased, or estimated fair value on the date of donation, if donated. Depreciation is provided using the straight-line method over the estimated useful lives of the assets.

UNEARNED REVENUE
Unearned revenue consists of tuition payments and other fees received in advance of their recognition as revenue.

BOARD DESIGNATED NET ASSETS
Net assets were designated by the Board as a contingency fund for building repairs and maintenance.

4

ABC CHURCH
NOTES TO FINANCIAL STATEMENTS
June 30, 20XX

NOTE 2 (CONTINUED)

INCOME TAXES

The Church is exempt from federal income tax as an organization described in Section 501(c)(3) of the Internal Revenue Code and from state income tax pursuant to applicable state law. The Church is further classified as a public charity and not a private foundation for federal income tax purposes. The Church has not incurred unrelated business income taxes. As a result, no income tax provision or liability has been provided for in the accompanying financial statements. The Church has not taken any material uncertain tax positions for which the associated tax benefits may not be recognized under accounting principles generally accepted in the United States of America. Federal and state tax authorities may generally examine the Church's income tax positions or (if applicable) returns for periods of approximately three to six years.

USE OF ESTIMATES

Management uses estimates and assumptions in preparing the financial statements. Those estimates and assumptions affect the reported amounts of assets and liabilities, the disclosure of contingent assets and liabilities, and reported revenues and expenses. Significant estimates used in preparing these financial statements include those related to the useful lives of property and equipment. Actual results could differ from the estimates.

SUBSEQUENT EVENTS

The Church has evaluated for possible financial reporting and disclosure subsequent events through (Date of Audit Report), the date as of which the financial statements were available to be issued.

NOTE 3
CONCENTRATIONS

The Church maintains its cash, cash equivalents, and certificate of deposit in deposit accounts which may not be federally insured, may exceed federally insured limits, or may be insured by an entity other than an agency of the federal government. The Church has not experienced any losses in such accounts, and believes it is not exposed to any significant credit risk related to cash, cash equivalents, and the certificate of deposit.

The Church's debt is held by a single financial institution.

NOTE 4
CASH AND INVESTMENTS RESTRICTED FOR LONG-TERM PURPOSES

Cash and investments restricted for long-term purposes consisted of the following as of June 30, 20XX:

Marketable securities	$ 880,000
Cash and cash equivalents	600,000
Total cash and investments restricted for long-term purposes	**$ 1,480,000**

5

ABC CHURCH
NOTES TO FINANCIAL STATEMENTS
June 30, 20XX

NOTE 5
FAIR VALUE MEASUREMENTS

Accounting principles generally accepted in the United States ("GAAP") define fair value for an investment generally as the price an organization would receive upon selling the investment in an orderly transaction to an independent buyer in the principal or most advantageous market for the investment. The information available to measure fair value varies depending on the nature of each investment and its market or markets. Accordingly, GAAP recognizes a hierarchy of "inputs" an organization may use in determining or estimating fair value. The inputs are categorized into "levels" that relate to the extent to which an input is objectively observable and the extent to which markets exist for identical or comparable investments. In determining or estimating fair value, an organization is required to maximize the use of observable market data (to the extent available) and minimize the use of unobservable inputs. The hierarchy assigns the highest priority to unadjusted quoted prices in active markets for identical items (Level 1 inputs) and the lowest priority to unobservable inputs (Level 3 inputs).

A financial instrument's level within the fair value hierarchy is based on the lowest level of any input that is significant to the fair value measurement.

Following is a description of each of the three levels of input within the fair value hierarchy:

Level 1 – unadjusted quoted market prices in active markets for identical items

Level 2 – other significant observable inputs (such as quoted prices for similar items)

Level 3 – significant unobservable inputs

Estimated fair values of assets measured on a recurring basis as of June 30, 20XX, are as follows:

	Total	Level 1	Level 2	Level 3
Equity securities:				
Common and preferred stocks	$ 480,000	$ 480,000	$ —	$ —
Mutual funds	400,000	400,000	—	—
Total equity securities	$ 880,000	$ 880,000	$ —	$ —

NOTE 6
PROPERTY AND EQUIPMENT

Property and equipment consisted of the following as of June 30, 20XX:

Land and land improvements	$ 5,400,000
Buildings and building improvements	24,000,000
Furniture and equipment	3,800,000
Vehicles	200,000
Total	33,400,000
Less: Accumulated depreciation	(7,000,000)
Net property and equipment	$ 26,400,000

Depreciation expense for the year ended June 30, 20XX amounted to $800,000.

6

ABC CHURCH
NOTES TO FINANCIAL STATEMENTS
June 30, 20XX

NOTE 7
NOTE PAYABLE

Note payable as of June 30, 20XX consisted of a note payable to a bank which is payable in monthly installments including interest at the one-month LIBOR plus 2.50% per annum and which is collateralized by a mortgage on certain real property. The note matures during May 20XX.

Approximate future maturities of the note payable are as follows:

For The Year Ended June 30,	
20X1	$ 275,000
20X2	300,000
20X3	315,000
20X4	340,000
20X5	360,000
Thereafter	2,830,000
Total	**$ 4,420,000**

Interest expense for the year ended June 30, 20XX amounted to $121,000.

NOTE 8
TEMPORARILY RESTRICTED NET ASSETS

Net assets were temporarily restricted for the following purposes:

	Beginning Balance July 1	Contributions and income	Releases	Ending Balance June 30
Building fund	$ 400,000	$ 420,000	$ (220,000)	$ 600,000
Benevolence and other activities	—	180,000	(50,000)	130,000
Missions	—	1,290,000	(1,200,000)	90,000
Net appreciation on endowments	—	110,000	(30,000)	80,000
Total	**$ 400,000**	**$ 2,000,000**	**$ (1,500,000)**	**$ 900,000**

NOTE 9
PERMANENTLY RESTRICTED NET ASSETS

Net assets were permanently restricted for the following purposes as of June 30, 20XX:

Endowments with distributions restricted for scholarships	$ 500,000
Endowments with distributions restricted for general ministry purposes	300,000
Total permanently restricted net assets	**$ 800,000**

The Church preserves the estimated fair value of the endowment gift as of the gift date, which management deems is in compliance with state law. Accordingly, the Church classifies as "permanently restricted net assets" (a) the original value of gifts donated to the permanent endowment and (b) the original value of subsequent gifts to the permanent endowment. The Church has adopted an investment policy for endowment assets that attempts to provide a predictable stream of funding to supported programs while seeking to maintain the purchasing power of the endowment assets and to preserve the invested capital. The Church seeks the advice of investment counsel, as well as management and the governing body, when determining amounts to be spent on supported programs. The Church has adopted a current annual spending rate of 5% of the estimated fair value of the endowment funds.

ABC CHURCH
NOTES TO FINANCIAL STATEMENTS
June 30, 20XX

NOTE 10
TUITION AND FEES

Tuition and fees are reported net of discounts of approximately $300,000 for church members, need-based financial aid, multiple children, and other discounts. Employee tuition reductions amounted to approximately $175,000 for the year ended June 30, 20XX and are reflected in "School activities" expense in the accompanying statement of activities.

NOTE 11
RETIREMENT PLAN

Certain employees of the Church are enrolled in a retirement plan administered by XYZ ("the Plan"). The Church contributes 8% of each eligible employee's gross wages to the Plan each pay period. Participating employees may make elective deferral contributions by entering into a salary reduction arrangement. Employer contributions to the Plan amounted to approximately $300,000 during the year ended June 30, 20XX.

8

Church & Donor Management Systems (ChMS) 2015

Legend: ■ = full support, ◪ = partial support

Category	Feature	ACS Technologies	Active Network Fellowship One	Aplos Software	Breeze Church Management	BVCMS	By The Book	CahabaCreek Software	CCIS Church Software	CDM+
Focus	Church Management	■	■		■	■	■	■	■	■
	Parachurch / Donor Management	■	■	■	■				■	■
	Denomination "Editions" Available	■								■
	Multilingual Versions Available (Spanish, French, etc)	■					■			
Database	Can Separately Track Multiple Congregations Within One Database	■	■	■	■	■	■	■	■	■
	Stores Individual and Family Photos	■	■	■	■	■	■	■	■	■
	Prints Directories-- with or without Photos	■	■		■	■	■	■	■	■
	Prints U.S. Postal Bar Codes	■				◪				■
	Certified Postal CASS & PAVE	■	◪			◪				■
	National Change of Address (NCOA) Updates	■				◪	■			■
Contributions	Tracks Contribution of Gifts in Kind	■	■	■	■	■	■	■	■	■
	Checks Can Be Input via Check21-Compliant Scanner	■	■			◪				■
	Gifts in Kind (GIK) Can Satisfy Pledge without Setting GIK Value	■	■			■				■
	Can Post Gifts Received via Website without Manual Entry	■	■	■	■	■	■	◪		■
	Can Store Check & Envelope Images		■							■
	Congregants / Donors Can View Check Images Online		■							■
	Statements Can Be Automatically Sent via Email	■				■	■	■	■	■
Assimilation	Tracks Attendance	■	■		■	■	■	■	■	■
	Can Post Attendance Using Geo-Fencing									■
	Security / Check-In Capability	■	■		■	■	■	■		■
	Check-In Tracks Allergies, Allowable Check-Out Persons, etc	■	■		■	■	■	■		■
	Tracks Volunteer Involvements, Interests, etc	■	■		■	■	■		■	■
	Has Background Check Interface	■	■			■	■			■
	Approved Volunteers Can Schedule Themselves for Service	■				■				■
	Manages Small Groups	■	■		■	■	■	■	■	■
Facilities & Events	Facility / Equipment Calendar Scheduler	■	■							■
	Calendar Scheduler Can Feed Public Events to Ministry's Website	■	■							■
	Retreat / Event Registrations with A/R Tracking	■	■			■				■
	Can Post Registrations Received via Website without Manual Entry	■	■		■	■				■
	Library Module	◪								■
	Fixed Assets Tracking (Inventory, Depreciation, Maintenance)	■								■

(Row grouping: all features above are under **Non-Accounting Features**.)

"Church & Donor Management Systems (ChMS)," by Nick Nicholaou, © 2015. To view updated versions of this chart, and to learn more about church management software providers, visit *mbsinc.com/church-donor-management-software-chms/*

Column headers (left to right):

- Church Community Builder
- Church Windows
- ChurchStack
- ChurchTeams
- ChurchTrac
- Concordia Technology Solutions
- Diakonia
- DonorPerfect
- Elexio
- Excellerate
- FlockBase
- Fresh Vine
- Helpmate Technology Solutions
- Iglesia HOY
- Intacct
- Nuverb Systems
- ParishSOFT / LOGOS
- PowerChurch Software
- ProclaimCRM
- Servant Keeper
- Shelby Systems
- SimpleChurchCRM
- Software4Nonprofits
- Specialty Software
- White Mountain Software

**The " ■ " symbol indicates features ChMS companies provide directly, and
The " ◢ " symbol indicates needs they meet through an outside (third party) source.**

"Church & Donor Management Systems (ChMS)," by Nick Nicholaou, © 2015. To view updated versions of this chart, and to learn more about church management software providers, visit *mbsinc.com/church-donor-management-software-chms/*

Church & Donor Management Systems (ChMS) 2015

			ACS Technologies	Active Network Fellowship One	Aplos Software	Breeze Church Management	BVCMS	By The Book	CahabaCreek Software	CCIS Church Software	CDM+
Accounting Features	**General Ledger**	General Ledger	■		■				■	■	■
		Automatically Tracks Multiple Fund Balances	■		■		■		■	■	■
		Automatically Balances Funds on Interfund Transactions	■		■				■	■	■
		Audit Trail is Secure / Unalterable (not just password protected)	■		■				■	■	■
		Can Select Straight Line or Seasonal Budgeting by Account	■		■				■	■	■
		Has Method for Budgeting Capital Expense Items	■						■		■
		Graphic Analysis	■							■	◪
	Accounts Payable	Accounts Payable / Bill Pay	■		■				■	■	■
		Can Set Up as Accrual or Cash Basis	■		■					■	■
		Invoices Can Be Automatically Distributed to Multiple GL Accounts	■		■						■
		Checks / Check Runs Can Post Against Multiple Funds	■		■				■	■	■
		Can Partial Pay Invoices; Balance Payable with Same Invoice #	■		■					■	■
		Can Automate Recurring Entries	■						■	■	■
		Can Void Checks with Option of Reopening the Invoice	■		■				■	■	■
		Annual 1096 & 1099s	■		■				■	■	■
		Purchase Order Tracking (Authorization, Budget, & GL Interface)	■								■
	Payroll / Human Resources	Payroll with Minister's Salary Capabilities (Housing, SECA)	■						■	■	■
		Can Split Payroll & Benefit Costs across Multiple Departments	■		■				■	■	■
		Time Clock Interface	■							■	■
		Payroll ACH Direct Deposit	■							■	■
		Accrues Vacation & Sick Time by Hours Worked or Pay Period	■							■	■
		Hiring / Termination Process & Documentation w Self-Audit								■	■
		Vacation Scheduler with Schedule View by Department	■								■
		Tracks & Stores Images of HR Forms	■								■
		Tracks Employee Discipline Records	■								■
		State & Federal Tax Tables are Maintained by Software Provider	■						■	■	■
		All Federal & State Payroll Tax Forms	■						■	■	◪
		Workers' Compensation Audit	■							■	■

The " ■ " symbol indicates features ChMS companies provide directly, and The " ▪ " symbol indicates needs they meet through an outside (third party) source.

"Church & Donor Management Systems (ChMS)," by Nick Nicholaou, © 2015. To view updated versions of this chart, and to learn more about church management software providers, visit *mbsinc.com/church-donor-management-software-chms/*

2

Accounting and Financial Reporting

Church & Donor Management Systems (ChMS) 2015

Infrastructure Features		Feature	ACS Technologies	Active Network Fellowship One	Aplos Software	Breeze Church Management	BVCMS	By The Book	CahabaCreek Software	CCIS Church Software	CDM+
	Communication	Tracks & Uses People's Preferences for Text Messages, Mail, Email	■	■			■	■		■	■
		Can Send Individual Text Messages	■	◪		■	■	■			■
		Can Send Individually-Addressed Mail-Merged Bulk Email	■	■		■	■	■	■		■
		Email Can Have Multiple Attachments	■	◪		■	■				■
		System Integrates w/Outlook Contacts & Tasks for Staff Follow-Up	■								■
		Connects with Social Media Accounts like Facebook	■	◪						■	■
		Constant Contact and/or MailChimp HTML Interface	■					■			■
	Mobile & Web	Data is Accessible in Realtime via iOS & Android Mobile Devices	■	■	■	■	■	■		■	■
		Tablet App (iPhone, Android, etc)	■	■			■			■	■
		Congregants / Donors Can Update Personal Data Online	■	■		■	■	■			
		Congregants Can Set Which of Their Online Data is Private	■	■							■
	Requirements & Capabilities	Can be Network-Based w/Multiple Concurrent User Access	■		■	■	■	■	■	■	■
		Web Browser Interface	■	■	■	■	■	■		■	■
		Administration-Level Users Can Add / Modify Fields in Database	■	■		■	■	■	■		■
		Includes a User-Accessible Customizable Report System	■	■	■		■	■		■	■
		Data is Accessible & Fully Exportable in Multiple Formats	■	■	■		■	■		■	■
		Excel Pivot Table Interface	■	■							■
		Graphics-Capable Dashboard with Drill-Down Capabilities	■	■							■
		Field-Level Access / Entry Security	■	■			■	■	■	■	■
		Maintains Transactional Database of Who Made Changes	■	■	■		■			■	■
	How Hosted	Can Run on Ministry's Server	■				■	■	■	■	■
		Can Run Hosted on ChMS Provider's Server	■			■	■	■			■
		If Hosted by ChMS Provider, Datacenter is Certified Tier 3 or Higher	■	■			■			■	■
		Solution has a Completely Open API	■	■			■				

Column headers (left to right):

- Church Community Builder
- Church Windows
- ChurchStack
- ChurchTeams
- ChurchTrac
- Concordia Technology Solutions
- Diakonia
- DonorPerfect
- Elexio
- Excellerate
- FlockBase
- Fresh Vine
- Helpmate Technology Solutions
- Iglesia HOY
- Intacct
- Nuverb Systems
- ParishSOFT / LOGOS
- PowerChurch Software
- ProclaimCRM
- Servant Keeper
- Shelby Systems
- SimpleChurchCRM
- Software4Nonprofits
- Specialty Software
- White Mountain Software

The " ■ " symbol indicates features ChMS companies provide directly, and
The " ◢ " symbol indicates needs they meet through an outside (third party) source.

"Church & Donor Management Systems (ChMS)," by Nick Nicholaou, © 2015. To view updated versions of this chart, and to learn more about church management software providers, visit *mbsinc.com/church-donor-management-software-chms/*

Chapter 3

Charitable Contributions

INTRODUCTION

For church leaders to fully understand finances, they need to master the subject of charitable contributions. Charitable contributions represent much—if not all—of a church's annual income, and as such, they demand a great deal of attention every week. By mastering the many aspects of charitable contributions, leaders will free themselves of time-consuming efforts to research the questions that inevitably arise whenever money or resources are given to the church.

This chapter explores the definitions of various types of charitable contributions, giving special attention to the many nuances that each often present. In addition, it explores the intricacies of designated contributions, and provides specific guidance on how to best substantiate contributions.

CHARITABLE CONTRIBUTIONS DEFINITION

It's important to start with the basic definition of a charitable contribution. Section 170 of the tax code states that "there shall be allowed as a deduction any charitable contribution. . . payment of which is made within the taxable year." To be deductible, a contribution must meet six conditions. A charitable contribution must be

(1) a gift of cash or property;
(2) claimed as a deduction in the year in which the contribution is made;
(3) unconditional and without personal benefit to the donor;
(4) made "to or for the use of" a qualified charity;
(5) within the allowable legal limits; and
(6) properly substantiated.

Let's look more closely at these six conditions.

(1) Gift of cash or property
Charitable contributions are limited to gifts of cash or property, but almost any kind of property will qualify, including cash, charges to a bank credit card, real estate, promissory notes, stocks and bonds, automobiles, art objects, books, building materials, collections, jewelry, easements, insurance policies, and inventory.

Here are several important things to note about gifts of cash or property:

Donated services
No deduction is allowed for a contribution of services. Church members who donate labor to their church may not deduct the value of their labor.

While the value of labor or services can never be deducted as a charitable contribution, any unreimbursed expenses incurred while performing donated labor for a church may constitute a deductible contribution. The income tax regulations specify:

> Unreimbursed expenditures made incident to the rendition of services to an organization contributions to which are deductible may constitute a deductible contribution. For example, the cost of a uniform without general utility which is required to be worn in performing donated services is deductible. Similarly, out-of-pocket transportation expenses necessarily incurred in performing donated services are deductible. Reasonable expenditures for meals and lodging necessarily incurred while away from home in the course of performing donated services are also deductible. *Treas. Reg. 1.170A-1(g).*

IRS Publication 526 (Charitable Contributions) states:

> You may be able to deduct some amounts you pay in giving services to a qualified organization. The amounts must be:

> - Unreimbursed,
> - Directly connected with the services
> - Expenses you had only because of the services you gave, and
> - Not personal, living, or family expenses.

Contributions of less than a donor's entire interest in property
Contributions of less than a donor's entire interest in property ordinarily are not deductible unless they qualify for one of the following exceptions:

- A contribution (not in trust) of an irrevocable remainder interest in a personal residence or farm. To illustrate, a donor who wants to give his home or farm to his church, but who wants to retain possession during his life, can retain a "life estate" in the property and donate a "remainder interest" to the church. The donor may deduct the value of the remainder interest that he has conveyed to the church, though this interest represents less than the donor's entire interest in the property. The valuation of a remainder interest is determined according to income tax regulation *1.170A-12.*

- A contribution (not in trust) of an undivided interest in property. Such an interest must consist of a part of every substantial interest or right the donor owns in the property and must last as long as the donor's interest in the property lasts. To illustrate, assume that a church member owns a 100-acre tract of land and that she donates half of this property to her church. While this represents a gift of only a portion of the donor's interest in the property, it is nevertheless deductible. *Treas. Reg. 1.170A-7.*

- A contribution of an irrevocable remainder interest in property to a charitable remainder trust. A charitable remainder trust is a trust that provides for a specified distribution, at least annually, to one or more noncharitable income beneficiaries for life or for a term of years (ordinarily not more than 20), with an irrevocable remainder interest to a charity.

A contribution of a partial interest in property that does not fit within one of the three categories described above ordinarily is not deductible as a charitable contribution. To illustrate, an individual who owns an office building and donates the rent-free use of a portion of the building to a charitable organization is not entitled to a charitable contribution deduction, since the contribution consists of a partial interest in property that does not fit within one of the exceptions described above.

This principle is illustrated in the income tax regulations with the following example: "T, an individual owning a 10-story office building, donates the rent-free use of the top floor of the building. . . to a charitable organization. Since T's contribution consists of a partial interest to which section 170(f)(3) applies, he is not entitled to a charitable contribution deduction for the contribution of such partial interest."

The same principle would apply to rent-free use of equipment. *IRC 170(f)(3)(A).*

Pledges

Pledges and subscriptions are commitments to contribute a fixed sum of money or designated property to a church or other charity in the future. Many churches base their annual budget, or the construction of a new facility, on the results of pledge campaigns. Pledges raise two questions of interest to church leaders: (1) can pledges be deducted as charitable contributions, and if so, when; and (2) are pledges legally enforceable?

The income tax regulations specify that "any charitable contribution . . . actually paid during the taxable year is allowable as a deduction in computing taxable income irrespective of the method of accounting employed or of the date on which the contribution is pledged." *Treas. Reg. 1.170A-1.* The IRS ruled that "the satisfaction of a pledge" is a tax-deductible charitable contribution. *Revenue Ruling 78-129.*

CASE STUDY. A federal appeals court ruled that pledges not paid during the year are not allowed as charitable contribution deductions for that year. *Mann v. Commissioner, 35 F.2d 873 (D.C. Cir. 1932).*

Are such commitments enforceable by a church? Traditionally, the courts have refused to enforce pledges on the basis of contract law. Since donors who make a pledge normally receive nothing in exchange for the pledge, their commitment was considered "illusory" and unenforceable. In recent years, however, several courts have enforced pledge commitments. In most cases, enforcement is based on the principle of detrimental reliance. That is, a church that relies to its detriment on a pledge in assuming debt or other legal obligation should be able to enforce the pledge. One court has noted:

> The consideration for a pledge to an eleemosynary [i.e., charitable] institution or organization is the accomplishment of the purposes for which such institution or organization was organized and created and in whose aid the pledge is made, and such consideration is sufficient. We therefore conclude that pledges made in writing to eleemosynary institutions and organizations are enforceable debts supported by consideration, unless the writing itself otherwise indicates or it is otherwise proved. *Hirsch v. Hirsch, 289 N.E.2d 386 (Ohio 1972)*. See also *Estate of Timko v. Oral Roberts Evangelistic Association, 215 N.W.2d 750 (Mich. 1974)*.

Another court observed that "the real basis for enforcing a charitable [pledge] is one of public policy—enforcement of a charitable pledge is a desirable social goal." The court continued: "Lightly to withhold judicial sanction from such obligations would be to destroy millions of assets of the most beneficent institutions in our land, and to render such institutions helpless to carry out the purposes of their organization." *Jewish Federation v. Barondess, 560 A.2d 1353 (N.J. Super. 1989)*.

Gifts of blank checks

A blank check is a check that is complete in all respects except for the designation of a payee. The person issuing the check specifies the date and an amount and signs the check but does not identify a payee. Occasionally a church will receive a blank check in the offering or in the mail. This can occur for a number of reasons. Some elderly church members may forget to complete the check. Others may assume that the church will insert (or stamp) its name as payee.

Can church members claim a charitable contribution deduction for a blank check? Possibly not, according to a Tax Court case summarized in the following example.

EXAMPLE. A husband and wife claimed a charitable contribution of $34,000 to their church. The couple attempted to substantiate their deductions with canceled checks and carbon copies of checks from their two personal checking accounts on which they left the payee lines blank. The Tax Court ruled that "because these canceled blank checks fail to list [the church] as the donee, these checks do not establish" that the couple made tax-deductible charitable contributions to the church. *Dorris v. Commissioner; T. C. Memo. 1998-324.*

(2) Claimed as a deduction in the year in which the contribution is made

Ordinarily, a contribution is made at the time of delivery. For example, a check that is mailed to a church (or other charity) is considered delivered on the date it is mailed. A contribution of real estate generally is deductible in the year that a deed to the property is delivered to the charity. A contribution of stock is deductible in the year that a properly endorsed stock certificate is mailed or otherwise delivered to the charity. A promissory note issued in favor of a charity (and delivered to the charity) does not constitute a contribution until note payments are made. Contributions charged to a bank credit card are deductible in the year the charge was made. Pledges are not deductible until actually paid.

Predated checks

Section 1.170A-1(b) of the income tax regulations states: "Ordinarily, a contribution is made at the time delivery is affected. The unconditional delivery or mailing of a check which subsequently clears in due course will constitute an effective contribution on the date of delivery or mailing."

According to this language, a check made payable to a church and dated December 31, but not physically delivered to the church until January of the following year, is deductible only on the donor's federal tax return for the following year. This is so, whether a donor predated a check to read "December 31" during the first church service in the new year or in fact completed and dated the check on December 31 of the prior year but deposited it in a church offering the following January.

The only exception to this rule is a check that is dated, mailed, *and postmarked* in one year but received in the next year. The fact that the church does not receive the check until January does not prevent the donor from deducting it on his or her federal tax return for the prior year.

Postdated checks

Churches occasionally receive a postdated check (a check that bears a future date). For example, Frank writes a check for $100 on March 1 of the current year that he dates April 15. Such checks often are received at the end of the year, when some donors decide they will be better off for tax purposes if they delay their contribution until the following year. Other donors make gifts of postdated checks before leaving on an extended vacation or business trip.

One court defined a postdated check as follows: "A postdated check is not a check immediately payable but is a promise to pay on the date shown. It is not a promise to pay presently and it does not mature until the day of its date, after which it is payable on demand the same as if it had not been issued until that date."

In other words, a postdated check is treated like a promissory note. It is nothing more than a promise to pay a stated sum on or after a future date. It is not an enforceable obligation prior to the date specified.

Since a postdated check is no different than a promissory note, it should be treated the same way for tax purposes. If someone issues a note to a church, promising to pay $1,000 in one year, no charitable contribution is made when the note is signed (assuming the donor is a "cash basis" taxpayer). Rather, a contribution is made when the note is paid. Until then, there is only a promise to pay. Like a promissory note, a church ordinarily should simply retain a postdated check until the date on the check occurs. There is no need to return it. A bank may be willing to accept such a check for deposit before the date on the check has occurred, with the understanding that the funds will not be available for withdrawal.

Promissory notes

Churches occasionally receive gifts of promissory notes. For example, during a church building campaign, Bob gives his church a promissory note in which he promises to pay the church $10,000 over a three-year term. How much does the church treasurer report as a charitable contribution for the current year? The full amount of the note? Some other amount?

The Tax Court has addressed this question. An attorney gave his church a promissory note for a substantial amount and then claimed a charitable contribution deduction for the entire face amount of the note, even though very little had been paid that year. The court ruled that the attorney could claim a charitable contribution deduction only for amounts he actually paid on the note in the year in question, not for the entire amount of the note. *Investment Research Associates v. Commissioner, T.C. Memo. 1999-407 (1999).*

(3) Unconditional and without personal benefit

The word "contribution" is synonymous with the word "gift," and so a contribution is not deductible unless it is a valid gift. Since no gift occurs unless a donor absolutely and irrevocably transfers title, dominion, and control over the gift, it follows that no charitable contribution deduction is available unless the contribution is unconditional. Similarly, no charitable contribution deduction is permitted if the donor receives a direct and material benefit for the contribution, since a gift by definition is a gratuitous transfer of property without consideration or benefit to the donor other than the feeling of satisfaction it evokes.

If a donor does receive a return benefit in exchange for a contribution, then a charitable contribution exists only to the extent that the cash or property transferred by the donor exceeds the fair market value of the benefit received in return. These two requirements of a charitable contribution—unconditional transfer without personal benefit to the donor—are illustrated by the examples below:

The income tax regulations specify that if a contribution to a charity is dependent on the performance of some act or the happening of some event in order for it to be effective, then no deduction is allowable unless the possibility that the gift will not become effective is so remote as to be negligible. Further, if the contribution specifies that it will be voided if a specified future event occurs, then no deduction is allowable unless the possibility of the future event occurring is so remote as to be negligible. *Treas. Reg. 1.170A-1(e)*.

To illustrate, if a donor transfers land to a church on the condition that the land will be used for church purposes and will revert to the donor if the land ever ceases to be so used, the donor is entitled to a charitable contribution deduction if on the date of the transfer the church plans to use the property for church purposes and the possibility that it will cease to do so is so remote as to be negligible. *IRS Letter Ruling 9443004.*

The United States Supreme Court has summarized these rules as follows:

> The [essence] of a charitable contribution is a transfer of money or property without adequate consideration. The taxpayer, therefore, must at a minimum demonstrate that he purposely contributed money or property in excess of any benefit he received in return. [A contribution is deductible] only if and to the extent it exceeds the market value of the benefit received . . . [and] only if the excess payment [was] made with the intention of making a gift. *United States v. American Bar Endowment, 106 S. Ct. 2426 (1986).*

Returning contributions to a donor
Should churches ever return a contribution to a donor? This is a question that nearly every church leader faces eventually. Such requests can arise in a variety of ways. Consider the following:

EXAMPLE. A church member donates $1,000 to the church building fund. Three years later the church abandons its plans to construct a new building. The member asks the church treasurer to return her $1,000 contribution.

EXAMPLE. A church member donates $2,500 to his church during the current year. Later in the year, due to a financial crisis, he asks for a refund of his contributions.

EXAMPLE. A church member donates $2,000 to her church during the first six months of the current year. In July she becomes upset with the pastor and begins attending another church. She later asks the treasurer of her former church for a refund of her contributions.

A charitable contribution is a gift of money or property to a charitable organization. Like any gift, a charitable contribution is an irrevocable transfer of a donor's entire interest in the donated cash or property. Since the donor's entire interest in the donated property is transferred, it generally is impossible for the donor to recover the donated property.

(4) Contributions made to or for the use of a qualified organization
Only those contributions made to qualified organizations are deductible. Section 170(c) of the tax code defines "qualified organizations" to include, among others, any organization that satisfies all of the following requirements:

(1) created or organized in the United States (or a United States possession);
(2) organized and operated exclusively for religious, educational, or other charitable purposes;
(3) no part of the net earnings of which inures to the benefit of any private individual; and,
(4) not disqualified for tax exempt status under section 501(c)(3) by reason of attempting to influence legislation, and which does not participate or intervene in any political campaign on behalf of any candidate for public office.

The IRS website lists those organizations that have been recognized by the IRS to be qualified organizations. This listing is not exhaustive, however, since many organizations, including churches, are automatically exempt from federal income taxes without filing an exemption application, and therefore their names ordinarily do not appear on the official IRS list. Some organizations are covered by a "group exemption ruling."

To be deductible, a contribution must be made to or for the use of a qualified organization. Contributions and gifts made directly to individuals are not deductible. To illustrate, the courts have ruled that payments made directly to individual ministers or to needy individuals are not deductible. However, contributions to individuals will, in some cases, be deductible on the ground that they were for the use of a qualified organization. Contributions to foreign missionaries under the control and supervision of a religious organization often are considered to be deductible on this basis. The contribution is not made to the organization, but it is made *for the use of* the organization. Similarly, contributions often are made payable to a church, but with a stipulation that the funds be distributed to a specified individual. Common examples include Christmas gifts to a minister, scholarship gifts to a church school, and contributions to a church benevolence fund.

Church members sometimes make contributions directly to religious organizations or ministries overseas. Or they make contributions to a United States religious organization for distribution to a foreign organization. Are these contributions tax-deductible? Federal law specifies that a charitable contribution, to be tax-deductible, must go to an organization "created or organized in the United States or in any possession thereof." In addition, the organization must be organized and operated exclusively for religious or other charitable purposes. This means that contributions made directly by church members to a foreign church or ministry are not tax-deductible in this country.

A related question addressed by the IRS in a 1963 ruling is whether a donor can make a tax-deductible contribution to an American charity with the stipulation that it be transferred directly to a foreign charity. The IRS ruled that such a contribution is not deductible, since in effect it is made directly to the foreign charity. *Revenue Ruling 63-252.* In its 1963 ruling the IRS did concede that contributions to a U.S. charity are deductible even though they are earmarked for distribution to a foreign charity, so long as the foreign charity "was formed for purposes of administrative convenience and the [U.S. charity] controls every facet of its operations." The IRS concluded: "Since the foreign organization is merely an administrative arm of the [U.S.] organization, the fact that contributions are ultimately paid over to the foreign organization does not require a conclusion that the [U.S.] organization is not the real recipient of those contributions."

Note some additional details about contributions made to organizations in Canada, Mexico, and Israel:

- You may be able to deduct contributions to certain Canadian charitable organizations covered under an income tax treaty with Canada. To deduct your contribution to a Canadian charity, you generally must have income from sources in Canada. See *IRS Publication 597 (Information on the United States–Canada Income Tax Treaty)* for information on how to figure your deduction.
- You may be able to deduct contributions to certain Mexican charitable organizations under an income tax treaty with Mexico. The organization must meet tests that are essentially the same as the tests that qualify U.S. organizations to receive deductible contributions. The organization may be able to tell you if it meets these tests. To deduct your contribution to a Mexican charity, you must have income from sources in Mexico.
- You may be able to deduct contributions to certain Israeli charitable organizations under an income tax treaty with Israel. To qualify for the deduction, your contribution must be made to an organization created and recognized as a charitable organization under the laws of Israel. The deduction will be allowed in the amount that would be allowed if the organization was created under the laws of the United States but is limited to 25 percent of your adjusted gross income from Israeli sources.

(5) Within the allowable legal limits

In general, donors can deduct contributions they make to most charitable organizations up to 50 percent of their adjusted gross income (AGI). The 50 percent limit applies to contributions to all public charities, including churches and most religious organizations. Donors who contribute noncash property generally can claim a deduction in the amount of the fair market value of the donated property. The amount of a charitable contribution deduction may be limited to 20 percent, 30 percent, or 50 percent of a donor's adjusted gross

3

Charitable Contributions

income, depending on the type of property given and the nature of the charity.

Contributions in excess of the 50 percent or 30 percent ceilings can be carried over and deducted in each of the five succeeding years until they are used up. Your total charitable deduction for the year to which you carry your contributions cannot exceed 50 percent of your adjusted gross income for the year.

Charitable contributions are available only as an itemized deduction on Schedule A (Form 1040). This means that taxpayers who do not itemize deductions cannot claim a deduction for charitable contributions. No charitable contribution deduction is available to taxpayers who use Form 1040A or 1040-EZ. As a result, most taxpayers are prevented from deducting any portion of their charitable contributions, since it is estimated that about 70 percent of all taxpayers have insufficient deductions to use Schedule A.

The deduction for charitable contributions is reduced for some higher-income taxpayers.

(6) Properly substantiated

Section 170 of the tax code, which authorizes deductions for charitable contributions, states that a charitable contribution shall be allowable as a deduction only if verified. Because of the importance of this issue, it is addressed in a separate section of this chapter.

DESIGNATED CONTRIBUTIONS

Designated contributions are contributions made to a church for a specified purpose. In most cases a donor either designates a specific project (such as the church building fund) or a specific individual (such as a missionary, student, minister, or needy person). In this section, both kinds of designated contributions are addressed. More emphasis is given to contributions designating individuals, since this is the type of designated contribution that has caused the most confusion.

Contributions designating a project or program

If the purpose is an approved project or program of the church, the designation ordinarily will not affect con-

tribution deductibility. An example is a contribution to a church building fund.

IRS Letter Ruling 200530016 (2005) addressed charitable contributions that designate specific projects. A charity began construction of a cultural center and solicited contributions for this project. It asked the IRS for a ruling affirming that contributions toward the project would be deductible even if donors requested that their donations be applied to the project and the charity "provides no more than assurances to such donors that it will attempt in good faith to honor such preferences."

The IRS provided an exhaustive analysis of the deductibility of designated contributions and made the following helpful clarifications and observations:

- In *Revenue Ruling 60-367* the issue was gifts to a university for the purpose of constructing housing for a designated fraternity. The college accepted gifts designated for improving or building a house for a designated fraternity and honored such designation so long as it was consistent with the policy, needs, and activities of the college. The college retained and exercised discretion and control, with respect to the amount spent on the fraternity house, consistent with the standards and pattern of the college for other student housing and consistent with the expressed housing policy of the college. The ruling thus held that the contributions made to the college under such circumstances were allowable deductions.
- Where funds are earmarked, it is important that the charity has full control of the donated funds and discretion as to their use, to ensure that the funds will be used to carry out the organization's functions and purposes. If the charity has such control and discretion and the gift is applied in accordance with the organization's exempt purposes, the donation ordinarily will be deductible, despite the donor's expressed hope that the gift will be applied for a designated purpose.
- The charity must maintain discretion and control over all contributions. Accordingly, the charity may endeavor to honor donors' wishes that designate use of donated funds. However, the charity must maintain control over the ultimate

determination of how all donated funds are allocated. Donors should be made aware that although the charity will make every effort to honor their contribution designation, contributions become the property of the charity, and the charity has the discretion to determine how best to use all contributions to carry out its functions and purposes.

The IRS concluded, based on this precedent, that charitable contributions to the charity would be deductible even if the donors requested that their donations be used to cover costs and expenses relating to the cultural center and the charity provided no more than assurances to such donors that it would attempt in good faith to honor such preferences.

> **EXAMPLE.** A church establishes a "new building" fund. Bob donates $500 to his church with the stipulation that the money be placed in the "new building" fund. This is a valid charitable contribution and may be treated as such by the church treasurer.

> **EXAMPLE.** Barb would like to help her church's music director buy a new home. She contributes $10,000 to her church with the stipulation that it be used "for a new home for our music director." Neither the church board nor the congregation has ever agreed to assist the music director in obtaining a home. Barb's gift is not a charitable contribution. As a result, the church treasurer should not accept it. Barb should be advised to make her gift directly to the music director. Of course, such a gift will not be tax-deductible by Barb. On the other hand, the music director may be able to treat it as a tax-free gift.

Contributions designating a specific individual

If a donor stipulates that a contribution be spent on a designated individual, no deduction ordinarily is allowed unless the church exercises full administrative control over the donated funds to ensure that they are being spent in furtherance of the church's exempt purposes. To illustrate, contributions to a church or missions agency for the benefit of a particular missionary may be tax deductible if the church or missions agency exercises full administrative and accounting control over the contributions and ensures that they are spent in furtherance of the church's mission.

As noted above, a charitable contribution must be made to or for the use of a qualified organization. Con-tributions and gifts made directly to individuals are not deductible. However, contributions to individuals will, in some cases, be deductible on the ground that they were for the use of a qualified organization. Contributions to foreign missionaries under the control and supervision of a religious organization often are deductible on this basis. The contribution is not made to the organization, but it is made for the use of the organization. Similarly, contributions often are made payable to a church, but with a stipulation that the funds be distributed to a specified individual. Common examples include Christmas gifts to a minister, scholarship gifts to a church school, and contributions to a church benevolence fund.

Of course, donors can designate the specific charitable activity to which they would like their contribution applied. For example, a donor can contribute $500 to a church and specify that the entire proceeds be applied to foreign missions or to a benevolence or scholarship fund. Designating a charitable activity, as opposed to an individual, presents no legal difficulties.

> **CASE STUDY.** A taxpayer made payments to a boys' school on behalf of a ward of the Illinois Children's Home and Aid Society. The court held that the payments were not contributions to or for the use of the charitable organization but were gifts for the benefit of a particular individual. *S.E. Thomason v. Commissioner, 2 T.C. 441 (1943).*

> **CASE STUDY.** An individual gave money to a university, requiring that it use the money to fund the research project of a particular professor. The university had no discretion over the use of the funds. The IRS ruled that the university was a "conduit" only and that the real donee was the professor. As a payment to an individual, the gift was not deductible. IRS Revenue Ruling 61-66 (1961).

IRS Letter Ruling 200530016 (2005) addresses charitable contributions that designate specific projects and individuals. The IRS provided an exhaustive analysis of the deductibility of designated contributions and made these clarifications and observations:

3

Charitable Contributions

- An important element for a taxpayer donor of a qualified charitable contribution is the charity's control over the donated funds. The donor must show that the charity retained control over the funds. To have control over donated funds is to have discretion as to their use. In instances where a donor designates a gift to benefit a particular individual and the individual does benefit from the gift, the determination of whether the gift is deductible depends upon whether the charity has full control of the donated funds and discretion as to their use. Such control and discretion ensures that the funds will be used to carry out the organization's functions and purposes.

- If contributions to a fund are earmarked by the donor for a particular individual and the charity exercises no control or discretion over their use, they are treated as gifts to the designated individual and are not deductible as charitable contributions.

- In *Tripp v. Commissioner, 337 F.2d 432 (7th Cir. 1964)*, a taxpayer's illusory gifts to a scholarship fund subject to the college's discretionary use were, in fact, designated by the donor and used for the sole benefit of a named individual and did not qualify as deductions for charitable contributions.

- When contributions are restricted by the donor to a class of beneficiaries, the class of potential beneficiaries may still be too narrow to qualify as a deductible charitable contribution. Thus, in *Charleston Chair Co. v. United States, 203 F. Supp. 126 (E.D.S.C. 1962)*, a corporation was denied a deduction for amounts given to a foundation established to provide educational opportunities for employees and their children. The court noted that the narrow class of persons who might benefit, the more restricted group that did benefit, and the preference given to the son of the director, stockholder, and trustee disclose that the Foundation was not operated exclusively for charitable purposes.

- However, a deduction is allowable where it is established that a gift is intended by the donor for the use of the organization rather than a gift to an individual. *Revenue Ruling 62-113*. This revenue ruling concerned contributions to a church fund by the parent of one of the church's missionaries. The ruling noted that if contributions to the fund are earmarked by the donor for a particular indi-

vidual, they are treated, in effect, as being gifts to the designated individual and are not deductible. However, a deduction will be allowable where it is established that a gift is intended by a donor for the use of the organization and not as a gift to an individual. The test in each case is whether the organization has full control of the donated funds and discretion as to their use, so as to insure that they will be used to carry out its functions and purposes. The ruling held that unless the taxpayer's contributions to the fund are distinctly marked by him so that they may be used only for his son or are received by the fund pursuant to a commitment or understanding that they will be so used, they may be deducted by the taxpayer.

- A charitable contribution may be permitted where preferences expressed at the time of contribution are precatory rather than mandatory, or where preference is given to relatives who otherwise qualify as charitable beneficiaries. . . . In addition, retention by the donor, or his family members, of the right to determine which individuals actually receive benefits does not preclude a charitable deduction.

- Where funds are earmarked, it is important that the charity has full control of the donated funds and discretion as to their use, so as to ensure that the funds will be used to carry out the organization's functions and purposes. If the charity has such control and discretion and the gift is applied in accordance with the organization's exempt purposes, the charitable gift ordinarily will be deductible, despite the donor's expressed hope that the gift will be applied for a designated purpose. Thus, in *Peace v. Commissioner, 43 T.C. 1 (1964)*, the court permitted a deduction for funds donated to a church mission society with the stipulation that specific amounts should go to each of four designated missionaries because an examination of the totality of the facts and evidence demonstrated that the contribution went into a common pool and the church retained control of the actual distribution of the funds.

- In *Winn v. Commissioner, 595 F.2d 1060 (5th Cir. 1979)*, at issue was a contribution in response to an appeal by a church to assist a certain person in her church missionary work. Central to the court's finding was that even though the contribution was made payable to a fund named for the individual, an officer of the church took the funds donated and dealt with them as the church wished. That is, possession of the contribution by a church official was held to be one of the elements establishing control by the church. The court concluded, "We also note that a donor can earmark a contribution given to a qualified organization for specific purposes without losing the right to claim a charitable deduction. Such a contribution still would be to or for the use of a charitable entity despite the fact that the donor controlled which of the qualified entity's charitable purposes would receive the exclusive benefit of the gift. . . . Proof that the church sponsored the appeal for the express purposes of collecting funds for this part of its work, that an officer of that church took the funds donated and dealt with them as the church wished, and that the funds went to the support of the work the church intended is sufficient to establish that the funds were donated for the use of the church."

In summary, funds donated to a charitable organization restricted for the benefit of a private individual are not deductible. This is in contrast to funds contributed for a particular purpose, but the charity maintains control and discretion over actual use of the funds.

The charity must maintain discretion and control over all contributions. Accordingly, the charity may endeavor to honor donors' wishes that designate the use of donated funds. However, the charity must maintain control over the ultimate determination of how all donated funds are allocated. Donors should be made aware that although the charity will make every effort to honor their contribution designation, contributions become the property of the charity, and the charity has the discretion to determine how best to use contributions to carry out its functions and purposes.

● **KEY POINT.** In *Revenue Ruling 62-113* the IRS affirmed the deductibility of a donor's contribution to a church fund out of which missionaries, including his son, were compensated. The IRS concluded:

> If contributions to the fund are earmarked by the donor for a particular individual, they

are treated, in effect, as being gifts to the designated individual and are not deductible. However, a deduction will be allowable where it is established that a gift is intended by a donor for the use of the organization and not as a gift to an individual. The test in each case is whether the organization has full control of the donated funds, and discretion as to their use, so as to insure that they will be used to carry out its functions and purposes. In the instant case, the son's receipt of reimbursements from the fund is alone insufficient to require holding that this test is not met. Accordingly, unless the taxpayer's contributions to the fund are distinctly marked by him so that they may be used only for his son or are received by the fund pursuant to a commitment or understanding that they will be so used, they may be deducted by the taxpayer in computing his taxable income.

This principle has been consistently applied by the courts in determining the deductibility of designated contributions to charitable organizations. The IRS noted that this test is to be used in evaluating the tax-deductibility of contributions that designate a student as well as contributions that designate other individuals "such as a fund to help pay for an organ transplant or to help a particular family rebuild a home destroyed by a tornado . . . [and] religiously motivated programs to support designated missionaries." *IRS Exempt Organizations Continuing Professional Education Technical Instruction Program for 1996.*

Returning donated funds to donors

Donors whose designated gifts to their church are not honored may seek to enforce their designations in two ways. First, they may ask a civil court to order the church to honor the designation; or, second, they may ask a court to order a return of their contribution. Either option involves a judicial recognition of the legally enforceable nature of the donor's designation.

The Uniform Prudent Management of Institutional Funds Act (UPMIFA)

This Act specifies that "if the donor consents . . . an institution may release or modify, in whole or in part, a restriction contained in a gift instrument on the management, investment, or purpose of an institutional fund. A release or modification may not allow a fund to be used for a purpose other than a charitable purpose of the institution." Further, if written consent of the donor cannot be obtained, a court, "upon application of an institution, may modify a restriction contained in a gift instrument regarding the management or investment of an institutional fund if the restriction has become impracticable or wasteful, if it impairs the management or investment of the fund, or if, because of circumstances not anticipated by the donor, a modification of a restriction will further the purposes of the fund."

Conclusions

In deciding whether to disregard donors' designations, church leaders should consider several factors, including the following:

(1) In some states donors have the legal authority to enforce their designated gifts in the civil courts.

(2) In many states donors have the legal authority to enforce their designated gifts if they have a "special interest."

(3) In most states the attorney general is empowered to enforce the terms of charitable gifts.

(4) Ethical and practical considerations (mentioned above) are associated with any decision to disregard donors' designations.

(5) The Uniform Prudent Management of Institutional Funds Act (UPMIFA) only applies to perpetual "institutional funds." But if it applies, it will provide a church with a possible way to avoid a restriction on a designated gift.

(6) Church leaders should never disregard donors' designations without first consulting with legal counsel.

Substantiation of Charitable Contributions

Charitable contributions to churches and other tax-exempt organizations are deductible only if they satisfy certain conditions. One important condition is that the donor must be able to substantiate the contribution. The substantiation requirements vary depending on the kind of contribution. They are summarized below.

The many substantiation rules are presented in this section in the form of ten rules. Simply find the rules that apply to a particular contribution and follow the substantiation requirements.

CONTRIBUTIONS OF CASH

Rule 1—requirements for all cash contributions

Donors cannot deduct a cash contribution to a church or charity, regardless of the amount, unless they keep one of the following:

- a bank record (a statement from a financial institution, an electronic fund transfer receipt, a canceled check, a scanned image of both sides of a canceled check obtained from a bank website, or a credit card statement) showing the charity's name, date of the contribution, and the amount of the contribution, or
- a written communication (including "electronic mail correspondence") from the charity showing the charity's name, date of the contribution, and the amount of the contribution.

The substantiation requirements *may not be satisfied by maintaining other reliable written records.* In the past, donors could substantiate cash contributions of less than $250 with "other reliable written records showing the name of the donee, the date of the contribution, and the amount of the contribution" if no canceled check or receipt was available. This is no longer allowed.

▲ **CAUTION.** *As noted below, additional substantiation requirements apply to individual contributions of $250 or more, and these must be satisfied as well.*

CASE STUDY. A church member makes cash contributions to his church of between $20 and $50 each week. He uses offering envelopes provided by the church, but the church provides no other receipt or statement substantiating the contributions. The member will not be able to claim a charitable contribution deduction for any of these payments. All cash contributions, regardless of amount, must be substantiated by either a bank record (such as a canceled check) or a written communication from the donee showing the name of the donee organization, the date of the contribution, and the amount of the contribution. The recordkeeping requirements cannot be satisfied by other written records, including offering envelopes.

CASE STUDY. The IRS audits a taxpayer's federal income tax return and questions an alleged contribution of $100 to a church for which the taxpayer has no canceled check or church receipt. The taxpayer does maintain a daily diary. A diary entry on the alleged date of the contribution shows that a contribution of $100 was made to the church. This is inadequate substantiation. Cash contributions can only be substantiated with bank records (including canceled checks) or a written communication from the donee charity showing the name of the donee, the date of the contribution, and the amount of the contribution. They cannot be substantiated with other written records, including diary entries.

Offering envelopes

Many churches use offering envelopes. They have a number of advantages, including the following:

- they help the church connect cash contributions to individual donors;
- they promote privacy in the collecting of contributions;
- they give members the opportunity to designate specific programs or projects;
- they provide members with a weekly reminder of the need to make contributions and honor pledges; and,
- they reduce the risk of offering counters pocketing loose bills.

In the past, another reason for using offering envelopes was to assist donors in substantiating cash contributions of less than $250. Offering envelopes no longer can be used for this purpose. The tax code now states that all cash contributions, regardless of amount, must be substantiated with (1) a bank record (such as a canceled check) or a written communication from the charity (2) showing the charity's name, date of the contribution, and the amount of the contribution. Offering envelopes will not satisfy these requirements and cannot be used to substantiate a donor's cash contributions.

Church leaders often ask how long they must keep offering envelopes. If your church uses offering envelopes, one option is to issue donors a periodic (quarterly, semiannual, or annual) summary of contributions and include in this summary a statement similar to the following: "Any documentation, including offering envelopes, that the church relied upon in preparing this summary will be disposed of within six months. Therefore, please review this summary carefully and inform the church treasurer of any apparent discrepancies within six months of the date of this summary."

Such a statement provides the church with a reasonable basis for destroying envelopes and other written records after the specified period of time. The burden is on members to promptly call attention to discrepancies. Of course, you can change the six-month period to any other length of time you desire. This statement will relieve the church of the responsibility of warehousing offering envelopes and other supporting documentation for long periods of time.

CASE STUDY. A church member ordinarily contributes cash (in church envelopes and in individual amounts of less than $250) rather than checks. Since the member will have no canceled checks to substantiate her contributions, she must rely upon the periodic receipts provided by her church. If the church does not issue the member a receipt, the member will not be able to deduct any of her cash contributions. The offering envelopes will not suffice.

Rule 2—individual cash contributions of $250 or more

Written acknowledgment

Donors must substantiate individual cash contributions of $250 or more "by a contemporaneous written acknowledgment of the contribution by the donee organization." *Donors cannot substantiate individual cash contributions of $250 or more with canceled checks.* They must receive a written acknowledgment from the church or other charity.

The IRS has clarified that "as long as it is in writing and contains the information required by law, a contemporaneous written acknowledgment may be in any format." The law specifies that a written acknowledgment must include the following information:

- name of organization;
- amount of cash contribution;
- description (but not the value) of noncash contribution;
- statement that no goods or services were provided by the organization in return for the contribution, if that was the case;
- description and good faith estimate of the value of goods or services, if any, that an organization provided in return for the contribution; and,
- statement that goods or services, if any, that an organization provided in return for the contribution consisted entirely of intangible religious benefits (described later) if that was the case.

It is not necessary to include the donor's Social Security number on the acknowledgment.

⊙ **KEY POINT.** Although it is a donor's responsibility to obtain a written acknowledgment, a church can assist a donor by providing a timely, written acknowledgment that meets the requirements summarized above.

The IRS has provided the following clarification regarding acceptable written acknowledgments:

A separate acknowledgment may be provided for each single contribution of $250 or more, or one acknowledgment, such as an annual summary, may be used to substantiate several single contributions of $250 or more. There are no IRS forms for the acknowledgment. Letters, postcards, or computer-generated forms with the above information are acceptable. An organization can provide either a paper copy of the acknowledgment to the donor, or an organization can provide the acknowledgment electronically, such as via an e-mail addressed to the donor. A donor should not attach the acknowledgment to his or her individual income tax return, but must retain it to substantiate the contribution. Separate contributions of less than $250 will not be aggregated. An example of this could be weekly offerings to a donor's church of less than $250, even though

the donor's annual total contributions are $250 or more. *IRS Publication 1771.*

Contemporaneous

The tax code requires that written acknowledgments must be contemporaneous. The IRS explains this requirement as follows: "For the written acknowledgment to be considered contemporaneous with the contribution, a donor must receive the acknowledgment by the earlier of the date on which the donor actually files his or her individual federal income tax return for the year of the contribution, or the due date (including extensions) of the return."

Goods or services

The acknowledgment must describe goods or services a charity provides in exchange for a contribution of $250 or more. It must also provide a good faith estimate of the value of such goods or services, because a donor must generally reduce the amount of the contribution deduction by the fair market value of the goods and services provided by the charity. Goods or services include cash, property, services, benefits, or privileges. However, two important exceptions are described below:

1. Token exception. Insubstantial goods or services a charitable organization provides in exchange for contributions do not have to be described in the acknowledgment. The IRS announces each year the maximum value for "token" goods and services.

2. Intangible religious benefits exception. If a religious organization provides only intangible religious benefits to a contributor, the acknowledgment does not need to describe or value those benefits. It should simply state that the organization provided intangible religious benefits to the contributor. What are intangible religious benefits? The IRS defines them as follows:

Generally, they are benefits provided by a tax-exempt organization operated exclusively for religious purposes, and are not usually sold in commercial transactions outside a donative (gift) context. Examples include admission to a religious ceremony and a de minimis tangible benefit, such as wine used in a religious ceremony. Benefits that are not intangible religious benefits include education leading to a recognized degree, travel services, and consumer goods. *IRS Publication 1771.*

To substantiate an individual charitable contribution of $250 or more, a donor must obtain a receipt from the charity that states whether the charity provided any goods or services in exchange for a contribution of $250 or more (other than intangible religious benefits), and if so, a description and good faith estimate of the value of those goods and services.

IRS regulations define a "good faith estimate" as an estimate of the fair market value of the goods or services provided by a charity in return for a donor's contribution. The fair market value of goods or services may differ from their cost to the charity. The charity may use any reasonable method it applies in good faith in making the good faith estimate.

However, a taxpayer is not required to determine how the charity made the estimate. IRS regulations specify that a taxpayer generally may treat an estimate of the value of goods or services as the fair market value for purposes of computing a charitable contribution deduction if the estimate is in a receipt issued by the charity. For example, if a charity provides a book in exchange for a $100 payment and the book is sold at retail prices ranging from $18 to $25, the taxpayer may rely on any estimate of the charity that is within the $18 to $25 range (the charitable contribution deduction is limited to the amount by which the $100 donation exceeds the fair market value of the book that is provided to the donor). However, a taxpayer may not treat an estimate as the fair market value of the goods or services if the taxpayer knows, or has reason to know, that such treatment is unreasonable. For example, if the taxpayer is a dealer in the type of goods or services it receives from a charity, or if the goods or services are readily valued, it is unreasonable for the taxpayer to treat the charity's estimate as the fair market value of the goods or services if that estimate is in error and the taxpayer knows, or has reason to know, the fair market value of the goods or services.

Unreimbursed expenses
If a donor makes a single contribution of $250 or more in the form of unreimbursed expenses (such as out-of-pocket transportation expenses) incurred in order to

perform donated services for a church, the donor must obtain a written acknowledgment from the church containing the following information: (1) a description of the services provided by the donor; (2) a statement of whether the organization provided goods or services in return for the contribution; (3) a description and good faith estimate of the value of goods or services, if any, that an organization provided in return for the contribution; and (4) a statement that goods or services, if any, that an organization provided in return for the contribution consisted entirely of intangible religious benefits (described above) if that was the case. In addition, a donor must maintain adequate records of the unreimbursed expenses. The church's acknowledgment must meet the contemporaneous requirement (see above).

> **CASE STUDY.** A chosen representative to an annual church convention purchases an airline ticket to travel to the convention. The church does not reimburse the delegate for the $500 ticket. The representative should keep a record of the expenditure, such as a copy of the ticket. The representative should obtain from the church a description of the services the representative provided and a statement that the representative received no goods or services from the organization.

> **CASE STUDY.** Greg participates in a short-term mission project sponsored by his church and incurs $700 of unreimbursed out-of-pocket travel expenses. Here is an example of an abbreviated written acknowledgment that complies with the regulations: "Greg Jones participated in a mission trip sponsored by [name of church] in the nation of Panama. His services included [working in a medical clinic]. The church provided no goods or services in return for these services." The church should be sure that Greg receives this receipt before the earlier of (1) the date he files a tax return claiming the contribution deduction, or (2) the due date (including extensions) for the tax return for that year.

Examples of written acknowledgments
Here are examples of acceptable written acknowledgments:

- "Thank you for your cash contribution of $300 that First Church received on December 12,

20XX. No goods or services were provided in exchange for your contribution."

- "Thank you for your cash contribution of $350 that First Church received on May 6, 20XX. In exchange for your contribution, we gave you a cookbook with an estimated fair market value of $30." Federal tax law permits you to deduct as a charitable contribution only the excess (if any) of your gift over the value of items you received in exchange.
- "Thank you for your contribution of a used oak baby crib and matching dresser that First Church received on March 15, 20XX. No goods or services were provided in exchange for your contribution other than intangible religious benefits." Federal tax law permits you to deduct as a charitable contribution only the excess (if any) of your gift over the value of items you received in exchange.

Below are a few additional points to note concerning the substantiation rules.

No reporting to the IRS

A church's written acknowledgments are issued to donors. They are not sent to the IRS. Exceptions exist for some contributions of noncash property and vehicles, as noted later in this chapter.

Why church contribution receipts often are inadequate

Most churches provide some form of periodic written statement to donors, acknowledging their contributions. However, any statements currently being used must be carefully reviewed to ensure compliance with the requirements summarized above. In some cases, they will need to be changed. Here are a few common examples of receipts that do not comply with the law:

- A church's receipts do not specify whether the church provided any goods or services in exchange for each individual contribution of $250 or more.
- A church occasionally provides goods or services to donors in exchange for their contributions of $250 or more, but the receipts it issues to these donors do not include a good-faith estimate of the value of the goods or services the church provided. Note that if such goods or services consist solely of intangible religious benefits, the church's

receipt must include a statement to that effect. Such receipts should also include a statement such as the following: Federal tax law permits you to deduct as a charitable contribution only the excess (if any) of your gift over the value of items you received in exchange.

- Some churches issue receipts in February or March of the following year. Such a practice will jeopardize the deductibility of every individual contribution of $250 or more to the extent a receipt is received by a donor after a tax return is filed.

The $250 threshold

If a donor makes a $50 cash contribution each week to a church, the substantiation requirements addressed in Rule 2 do not apply, even though the donor will have made $2,600 in contributions for the year, because no individual contribution was $250 or more. The donor can rely on canceled checks to substantiate the contributions or on an acknowledgment provided by the church that satisfies the requirements of Rule 1.

Combining separate contributions of $250

If a donor makes 10 separate contributions of $250 or more to her church in the same year, must the church issue a receipt listing each contribution separately, or can the 10 contributions be combined as one amount? The IRS has provided the following clarification: "A separate acknowledgment may be provided for each single contribution of $250 or more, or one acknowledgment, such as an annual summary, may be used to substantiate several single contributions of $250 or more." *IRS Publication 1771*. This may mean that a single acknowledgment may be issued by a church that combines all individual contributions into a lump sum. Or, it may mean that in lieu of providing donors with separate receipts for each contribution of $250 or more it may provide a single receipt that itemizes all such contributions. Since this issue has not been clarified by the tax code, regulations, or the courts, it would prudent to take the more conservative approach and separately itemize individual contributions of $250 or more on one receipt.

Effect of noncompliance

No penalty is imposed on a church that does not issue written acknowledgments to donors who comply with Rule 2. However, a donor will not be able to substantiate individual charitable contributions of $250 or more if audited, and a deduction for such contributions may be denied. Thus it is essential for church leaders to be familiar with these rules and issue acceptable written acknowledgments to donors who have made one or more individual contributions to the church of $250 or more during the year. Note that a penalty ($10) may be imposed on churches that fail to provide donors with an appropriate written acknowledgment for quid pro contributions of more than $75, as noted below.

CASE STUDY. A donor made a cash contribution of $25,000 to a religious organization. The IRS audited the donor's tax return and denied the charitable contribution deduction on the ground that it was not properly substantiated. The donor appealed to the United States Tax Court. The Tax Court agreed with the IRS that the charitable contribution was not tax-deductible:

> Because the amount of the alleged contribution exceeds $250, it must be evidenced by a contemporary written acknowledgment in order to be deductible. As evidence of his alleged contribution [the donor] provided a self-generated letter signed by himself. The letter states that the amount of cash contributed was $25,000, but it does not include any of the other required information. In particular, the letter is silent as to whether the donor received any goods or services in exchange for the cash. Both the Code and the regulations provide that such information is a necessary element of the contemporary written acknowledgment. Because he failed to provide a contemporary written acknowledgment of his contribution, we find that he is not entitled to deduct any amount for contribution.

This case illustrates the consequences that can result from a church's failure to comply with the substantiation requirements for charitable contributions. Those requirements are stricter for contributions of $250 or more, and, as this case demonstrates, require the written acknowledgment (receipt) provided by a charity to donors to be contemporaneous and include a statement indicating whether the charity provided goods or services to the donor in consideration of the contribution.

If goods or services were provided, the church's written acknowledgment must provide a description and good faith estimate of the value of those goods or services, or, if only intangible religious benefits were provided, a statement to that effect. The Tax Court stressed that whether or not the donor actually made the donation was irrelevant. Even assuming that he did make the $25,000 contribution, he was not entitled to a charitable contribution deduction because he was unable to meet the strict substantiation requirements that apply to contributions of $250 or more. *Longino v. C.I.R., T.C. Memo. 2013-80 (2013).*

Rule 3—individual quid pro quo cash contributions of $75 or less

While the special quid pro quo substantiation rules (discussed below) do not apply to contributions of $75 or less, these contributions are still only deductible to the extent they exceed the value of the goods or services provided in exchange. To illustrate, a donor who contributes $50 to a charity and receives a "free" book with a market value of $10 is entitled to a deduction of only $40, since donors may only deduct the amount by which a contribution exceeds the value of any goods or services received in return.

Raffle tickets

Some churches use raffles to raise funds for a project or activity. Numbered tickets are sold to church members, and a ticket is randomly selected as the winner of a prize. Does the possibility of winning a prize make all of the raffle tickets nondeductible? The IRS addressed raffle tickets offered by charities in a 1967 ruling and made the following observation:

> A taxpayer paid $5 for a ticket which entitled him to a chance to win a new automobile. The raffle was conducted to raise funds for the X Charity. Although the payment for the ticket was solicited as a "contribution" to the X Charity and designated as such on the face of the ticket, no part of the payment is deductible as a charitable contribution. Amounts paid for chances to participate in raffles, lotteries, or similar drawings or to participate in puzzles or other contests for valuable prizes are not gifts in such circumstances, and therefore, do not qualify as deductible charitable contributions. *Revenue Ruling 67-246.* [Emphasis added.]

3

Charitable Contributions

The key language here is "for valuable prizes." To the extent that a raffle ticket entitles a purchaser to valuable prizes, it is nondeductible according to this ruling. The vast majority of religious congregations that use raffles as a means of raising funds do not offer "valuable prizes." Rather, they offer prizes of token value. Everyone is aware that the purpose of the raffle is to raise funds, and the value of the prize is incidental. However, if a congregation offers valuable prizes to raffle ticket purchasers, then the treatment of raffle tickets as charitable contributions is in doubt.

The IRS issued a similar ruling in 1983. *Revenue Ruling 83-130.* It quoted its previous 1967 ruling and noted that "amounts paid for chances to participate in raffles, lotteries, or similar drawings or to participate in puzzles or other contests *for valuable prizes* conducted by a charity are not gifts and therefore do not qualify as charitable contributions" (emphasis added). Again, note that the emphasis is on "valuable prizes."

The Tax Court addressed raffle tickets in a 1966 ruling. *Goldman v. Commissioner, 46 T.C. 136 (1966), aff'd 388 F.2d 476 (6th Cir. 1967).* A taxpayer purchased raffle tickets in the following amounts from the following organizations: Good Samaritan Hospital ($50), Jewish Community Center ($10), Chofetz Chaim (Hebrew School) Bazaar ($10), and Cancer Aid ($10). The taxpayer received tickets for these payments and these tickets were placed in a "blind draw" from which he conceivably might have won something. The taxpayer acknowledged that he would have won something if his ticket number had been drawn in the lottery but contended that in purchasing the tickets he did not intend to gamble on a risk but intended to make a gift, characterizing his payments as "a regular donation that is made year after year, to these institutions." The taxpayer insisted that "the odds of winning were infinitesimal" and that "the amount of the payment far exceeded the actuarial value of the 'chance.'"

The taxpayer treated all of these purchases as charitable contributions on his tax return. The IRS challenged these deductions, and the case was appealed to the Tax Court. The court acknowledged that "it is possible to hypothesize a raffle ticket situation where the charitable nature of the gift would scarcely be debated, as where the purchase for $10 is one of one thousand chances and the

prize a nosegay of violets." In other words, the purchase of a raffle ticket may be treated as a charitable contribution if either or both of the following conditions is met: (1) the chance of winning a prize is low because of the number of tickets sold; or (2) the value of the prize is low. On the other hand, the court noted that there are other situations in which the purchase of a raffle ticket cannot be treated as a charitable contribution because neither of these two conditions is satisfied.

The court concluded that the raffle tickets could not be treated as charitable contributions, since the prizes offered by the various charities were of "substantial" value, and the taxpayer had failed to establish that his chances of winning were sufficiently low to entitle him to a charitable contribution deduction.

Conclusion
In conclusion, note the following two considerations:

First, the precedent summarized above allows raffle tickets to be treated as a charitable contribution so long as the chance of winning is remote because of the number of tickets sold or the value of the prize is insubstantial. Many congregational raffles satisfy either or both of these conditions, so there is a reasonable basis for treating the tickets as charitable contributions.

Second, these rulings never raised any concerns about the legality of conducting raffles. The IRS addressed various "games of chance" conducted by charities in *Announcement 89-138, I.R.B. 1988-45.* The IRS did not express any concerns about the legality of such activities but did note that they may generate unrelated business taxable income if they are "regularly carried on" as opposed to an intermittent activity.

Rule 4—individual quid pro quo contributions of more than $75
In addition to providing a written acknowledgment for contributions of $250 or more (as discussed under Rule 2 above), a church must issue a written disclosure statement to persons who make *quid pro quo contributions* of more than $75. A quid pro quo contribution is a payment "made partly as a contribution and partly in consideration for goods or services provided to the donor by the donee organization." For example, a

donor contributes $100 to her church, but in return she receives a dinner worth $30.

The written disclosure statement a church or charity provides to a donor of a quid pro quo contribution of more than $75 must

- inform the donor that the amount of the contribution that is tax-deductible is limited to the excess of the amount of any money (or the value of any property other than money) contributed by the donor over the value of any goods or services provided by the church or other charity in return; and
- provide the donor with a good faith estimate of the value of the goods or services furnished to the donor. *IRC 6115.*

CASE STUDY. A donor gives a charitable organization $100 in exchange for a concert ticket with a fair market value of $30. In this example the donor's tax deduction may not exceed $70. Because the donor's payment (quid pro quo contribution) exceeds $75, the charitable organization must furnish a disclosure statement to the donor even though the deductible amount does not exceed $75.

Exceptions to the quid pro quo reporting rule
A written statement need not be issued to a donor of a quid pro contribution in any of the following situations:

Token goods or services are given to the donor by the charity. Token goods or services are defined annually by the IRS.

The donor receives an intangible religious benefit. The term "intangible religious benefit" is defined by the tax code as "any intangible religious benefit which is provided by an organization organized exclusively for religious purposes and which generally is not sold in a commercial transaction outside the donative context." A congressional committee report states that the term "intangible religious benefit" includes "admission to a religious ceremony" or other insignificant "tangible benefits furnished to contributors that are incidental to a religious ceremony (such as wine)." However, the committee report clarifies that "this exception does

apply, for example, to tuition for education leading to a recognized degree, travel services, or consumer goods."

Penalties
The tax code imposes a penalty of $10 per contribution (up to a maximum of $5,000 per fund-raising event or mailing) on charities that fail to make the required quid pro quo disclosures, unless a failure was due to reasonable cause. The penalties will apply if a charity either fails to make the required disclosure in connection with a quid pro quo contribution (as explained above) or makes a disclosure that is incomplete or inaccurate.

CONTRIBUTIONS OF NONCASH PROPERTIES

The substantiation requirements for contributions of noncash property (e.g., land, equipment, stock, books, art, vehicles) are more stringent than for contributions of cash or checks. It is important to note that more than one rule may apply to a particular contribution. For example, any contribution of property valued by the donor at less than $250 will trigger only Rule 5. But contributions of property valued at $250 or more will trigger Rule 6 and possibly Rule 7 or Rule 10 (depending on the value of the donated property).

Rule 5—individual contributions of noncash property valued by the donor at less than $250
The church's written acknowledgment
The income tax regulations specify that any taxpayer who makes a charitable contribution of property other than money . . . shall maintain for each contribution a receipt from the donee showing the following information:

(1) The name of the donee.
(2) The date and location of the contribution.
(3) A description of the property in detail reasonably sufficient under the circumstances. Although the fair market value of the property is one of the circumstances to be taken into account in determining the amount of detail to be included on the receipt, such value need not be stated on the receipt. *Treas. Reg. 1.170A-13.*

A letter or other written communication from the church acknowledging receipt of the contribution and containing the information in (1), (2), and (3) above will serve as a receipt. You are not required to have a receipt where it is impractical to get one (for example, if you leave property at a charity's unattended drop site).

Records maintained by donors

In addition to the receipt provided by the church, donors themselves must keep reliable written records for each item of donated property. Records must include the following information:

- The name and address of the organization to which you contributed.
- The date and location of the contribution.
- A description of the property in detail reasonable under the circumstances. For a security, keep the name of the issuer, the type of security, and whether it is regularly traded on a stock exchange or in an over-the-counter market.
- The fair market value of the property at the time of the contribution and how you figured the fair market value. If it was determined by appraisal, you should also keep a signed copy of the appraisal.
- The cost or other basis of the property if you must reduce its fair market value by appreciation. Your records should also include the amount of the reduction and how you figured it. If you choose the 50 percent limit instead of the special 30 percent limit on certain capital gain property (discussed earlier), you must keep a record showing the years for which you made the choice, contributions for the current year to which the choice applies, and carryovers from preceding years to which the choice applies.
- The amount you claim as a deduction for the tax year as a result of the contribution, if you contribute less than your entire interest in the property during the tax year. Your records must include the amount you claimed as a deduction in any earlier years for contributions of other interests in this property. They must also include the name and address of each organization to which you contributed the other interests, the place where any such tangible property is located or kept, and the name of any person in possession of the property, other than the organization to which you contributed.

- The terms of any agreement or understanding entered into by the donor which relates to the use, sale, or other disposition of the donated property, including, for example, the terms of any agreement or understanding which (1) restricts the church's right to use or dispose of the donated property, (2) confers upon anyone other than the church any right to the income from the donated property or to the possession of the property, or (3) earmarks donated property for a particular use. *Treas. Reg. 1.170A-13(b)(2)(ii).*

Rule 6—individual contributions of noncash property valued by the donor at $250 to $500

The church's written acknowledgment

Donors who claim a deduction of at least $250 but not more than $500 for a noncash charitable contribution must get and keep an acknowledgment of their contribution from the church. Donors who make more than one contribution of $250 or more must have either a separate acknowledgment for each contribution or one acknowledgment that shows the total contributions. The church's written acknowledgment must contain the same information as under Rule 5 (above). It also must meet these tests:

- It must be written.
- It must include (1) a description (but not necessarily the value) of the donated property, (2) a statement of whether the church provided any goods or services as a result of the contribution (other than certain token items and membership benefits), and (3) a description and good faith estimate of the value of any goods or services described in (2). If the only benefit provided by the church was an intangible religious benefit (such as admission to a religious ceremony) that generally is not sold in a commercial transaction outside the donative context, the acknowledgment must say so and does not need to describe or estimate the value of the benefit.
- The donor must receive the church's written acknowledgment on or before the earlier of (1) the date the donor files his or her tax return claiming the contribution; or (2) the due date, including extensions, for filing the return.

Records maintained by donors

IRS regulations specify that donors who make contributions of $250 or more, but not more than $500, are required to obtain a contemporaneous written acknowledgment from the donee charity and, in addition, maintain all of the donor records described under Rule 5 above.

Rule 7—individual contributions of noncash property valued by the donor at more than $500 but not more than $5,000

Donors who claim a deduction of more than $500 but not more than $5,000 for a noncash charitable contribution must have the acknowledgment and written records described under Rule 6, and their records must also include:

- a description of how the donor acquired the donated property, for example, by purchase, gift, bequest, inheritance, or exchange;
- the approximate date the donor acquired the property;
- the cost or other basis, and any adjustments to the basis, of property held less than 12 months and, if available, the cost or other basis of property held 12 months or more. This requirement, however, does not apply to publicly traded securities.

◉ **KEY POINT.** Donors whose total deduction for all noncash contributions for the year is more than $500 must complete Section A of Form 8283 and attach it to Form 1040. However, donors should not complete Section A for items reported on Section B (see Rule 9). The IRS can disallow a deduction for a noncash charitable contribution of more than $500 if a donor does not submit Form 8283 with his or her tax return.

Rule 8—quid pro quo contributions of noncash property

The quid pro quo rules are explained fully in the previous section dealing with cash contributions (see Rules 3 and 4). Those rules apply to contributions of property as well and should be reviewed at this time.

Rule 9—individual contributions of noncash property valued by the donor at more than $5,000

Many donors and church leaders are not familiar with the substantiation rules required for a contribution of property valued by the donor at more than $5,000. This can lead to unfortunate consequences, since IRS regulations warn that no deduction for any contribution of property valued by the donor at more than $5,000 will be allowed unless these requirements are satisfied.

The requirements discussed below ordinarily are triggered by a contribution of a single item of property valued by the donor at more than $5,000, but they also can be triggered by contributions of *similar items* within a calendar or fiscal year if the combined value claimed by the donor exceeds $5,000.

Publicly traded stock listed on a stock exchange is not subject to these requirements, since its value is readily ascertainable. Note, however, that gifts of publicly traded stock must be substantiated by completing Part A of Form 8283, even if the stock is valued at more than $5,000. Part A does not require a qualified appraisal.

Contributions of nonpublicly traded stock (i.e., stock held by most small, family-owned corporations) are subject to the qualified appraisal requirement, but only if the value claimed by the donor exceeds $10,000.

Contributions of cars, boats, and planes are subject to special rules, as explained in Rule 10.

The substantiation requirements that apply to contributions of $250 or more were enacted to make it more difficult for donors to improperly reduce taxable income by intentionally overvaluing contributed property and then claiming inflated charitable contribution deductions on their income tax returns.

The donor's obligations

Donors who contribute property valued at more than $5,000 to a church or other charity must satisfy each of the following three requirements in order to claim a charitable contribution deduction:

(1) Obtain a qualified appraisal. A donor's first obligation is to obtain a qualified appraisal. The income tax regulations define a qualified appraisal as an appraisal that (a) is "made, signed, and dated" by a "qualified appraiser"; (b) is made no earlier than 60 days prior to the date the appraised property was donated; (c) does not involve a prohibited appraisal fee (i.e., based on a percentage of the appraised value or on the amount allowed as a deduction); and (d) includes the following information:

- an adequate description of the donated property;
- the physical condition of the property;
- the date (or expected date) of the contribution;
- the terms of any agreement or understanding entered into by, or on behalf of, the donor pertaining to the use or disposition of the donated property;
- the name, address, and identifying number of the qualified appraiser;
- the qualifications of the qualified appraiser who prepared and signed the qualified appraisal;
- a statement that the appraisal was prepared for income tax purposes;
- the date on which the property was valued;
- the appraised fair market value of the property on the date (or expected date) of the contribution;
- the method of valuation used to determine the fair market value;
- the specific basis for the valuation; and,
- a description of the fee arrangement between the donor and appraiser.

In addition, a qualified appraisal must be prepared in accordance with generally accepted appraisal standards and any regulations or other guidance prescribed by the IRS. The income tax regulations define a qualified appraisal as an appraisal prepared by a qualified appraiser in accordance with generally accepted appraisal standards. Generally accepted appraisal standards are defined in the proposed regulations as "the substance and principles of the Uniform Standards of Professional Appraisal Practice (USPAP), as developed by the Appraisal Standards Board of the Appraisal Foundation."

Qualified appraiser. A qualified appraisal, as noted above, is one prepared by a *qualified appraiser.* The regulations define the term "qualified appraiser" as an individual who:

- has earned an appraisal designation from a recognized professional appraiser organization or has otherwise met minimum education and experience requirements to be determined by the IRS in regulations;

- has met certain minimum education and experience requirements. For real property, the appraiser must be licensed or certified for the type of property being appraised in the state in which the property is located. For property other than real property, the appraiser must have successfully completed college or professional-level coursework relevant to the property being valued; must have at least two years of experience in the trade or business of buying, selling, or valuing the type of property being valued; and must fully describe in the appraisal his or her qualifying education and experience;
- regularly prepares appraisals for which he or she is paid;
- demonstrates verifiable education and experience in valuing the type of property being appraised. To do this, the appraiser can make a declaration in the appraisal that, because of his or her background, experience, education, and membership in professional associations, he or she is qualified to make appraisals of the type of property being valued;
- has not been prohibited from practicing before the IRS at any time during the three-year period ending on the date of the appraisal;
- is not an "excluded individual." This term includes the donor or donee of the property, or a party to the transaction in which the donor acquired the property being appraised, unless the property is donated within two months of the date of acquisition and its appraised value is not more than its acquisition price. See *IRS Publication 561* for additional information.

The qualified appraisal must be received by the donor before the due date (including extensions) of the federal income tax return on which the deduction is claimed. Finally, note that a qualified appraisal must be obtained for each item of contributed property valued by the donor in excess of $5,000.

Exceptions. You do not need an appraisal if the property is

- nonpublicly traded stock of $10,000 or less;
- a vehicle (including a car, boat, or airplane) for which your deduction is limited to the gross proceeds from its sale (see Rule 10, below);

- publicly traded securities listed on a stock exchange for which quotations are published on a daily basis, or regularly traded in a national or regional over-the-counter market for which published quotations are available; or
- inventory.

⊙ **KEY POINT.** The requirement that a donor obtain a qualified appraisal of property donated to charity if the amount of the deduction exceeds $5,000 applies to both individuals and C corporations.

Donors and appraisers may be subject to penalties, as follows:

Penalties against the appraiser. An appraiser who prepares an incorrect appraisal may be subject to a penalty if: (1) the appraiser knows, or should have known, the appraisal would be used in connection with a return or claim for refund and (2) the appraisal results in the 20 percent or 40 percent penalty for a valuation misstatement described below. The penalty imposed on the appraiser is the smaller of

- the greater of (i) 10 percent of the underpayment due to the misstatement or (ii) $1,000, or
- 125 percent of the gross income received for the appraisal.

In addition, any appraiser who falsely or fraudulently overstates the value of property described in a qualified appraisal of a Form 8283 that the appraiser has signed may be subject to a civil penalty for aiding and abetting as understatement of tax liability and may have his or her appraisal disregarded.

Penalties against the donor. You may be liable for a penalty if you overstate the value or adjusted basis of donated property. The penalty is 20 percent of the underpayment of tax related to the overstatement if

- the value or adjusted basis claimed on the return is 150 percent or more of the correct amount and
- you underpaid your tax by more than $5,000 because of the overstatement.

The penalty is 40 percent, rather than 20 percent, if

- the value or adjusted basis claimed on the return is 200 percent or more of the correct amount and
- you underpaid your tax by more than $5,000 because of the overstatement.

(2) Prepare a qualified appraisal summary. A donor must also complete an appraisal summary and enclose it with the tax return on which the charitable contribution deduction is claimed. The appraisal summary is a summary of the qualified appraisal and is made on Section B (side 2) of IRS Form 8283. You can obtain copies of Form 8283 by contacting your nearest IRS office, by calling the toll-free IRS forms hotline at 1-800-829-3676, or by downloading them from the IRS website (*irs.gov*).

Section A (side 1) of Form 8283 is completed by donors who contribute property valued between $500 and $5,000, as noted under Rule 7.

Section B of Form 8283 contains four parts. Part I is completed by the donor or appraiser and sets forth information from the qualified appraisal regarding the donated property, including its appraised value. Part II is completed by the donor and identifies individual items in groups of similar items having an appraised value of not more than $500. Part II contains the appraiser's certification that he or she satisfies the definition of a qualified appraiser. Part IV is a donee acknowledgment, which must be *completed by the church.* The church simply indicates the date on which it received the contribution and agrees to file an information return (Form 8282) with the IRS if it disposes of the donated property within three years. The regulations specify that the church's acknowledgment "does not represent concurrence in the appraised value of the contributed property. Rather, it represents acknowledgment of receipt of the property described in the appraisal summary on the date specified in the appraisal summary."

The instructions for Form 8283 permit a church to complete Part IV before the qualified appraisal is completed. They instruct the donor to "complete at least your name, identification number, and description of the donated property," along with Part II if applicable, before submitting the Form 8283 to the church (or other donee). In other words, the donor should fill in his or her name and Social Security number on the

3

Charitable Contributions

lines provided at the top of page 1 of the form, and also complete line 5(a) of Section B, Part I (on the back page of the form) before submitting the form to the church. After completing Section B, Part IV, the church returns the form to the donor, who then completes the remaining information required in Part I. The donor should also arrange to have the qualified appraiser complete Part II at this time.

If the amount of a contribution of property other than cash, inventory, or publicly traded securities exceeds $500,000 (if art, $20,000), the qualified appraisal must be attached to the donor's tax return. For purposes of the dollar thresholds, property and all similar items of property donated to one or more charities are treated as one property.

(3) Maintain records. The donor's third obligation is to have the acknowledgment and written records described under Rule 7. Many of these items will be contained in the qualified appraisal, which should be retained by the donor.

> **EXAMPLE.** A member contributes equipment valued at $15,000 to his church. The member asks an appraiser who attends the church to appraise the property. Such an appraiser may not satisfy the definition of a qualified appraiser, since his relationship to the church might cause a reasonable person to question his independence.

> **EXAMPLE.** A member contributes property to a church that is worth well in excess of $5,000. To assist the member in complying with the substantiation requirements, the church should (1) acknowledge receipt of the contribution in a signed document; (2) inform the member of the necessity of obtaining a qualified appraisal; and (3) inform the member of the obligation to complete an appraisal summary (Form 8283) prior to the due date for the income tax return (and, as a convenience, give the member a copy of the current form). The church is required to sign Section B, Part IV, of the donor's Form 8283 and to complete and file with the IRS an information return (Form 8282) within 125 days of the date it disposes of the property (if it does so within 3 years of the date of the contribution).

> **CASE STUDY.** The Tax Court ruled that a married couple (the "donors") was not eligible for a charitable contribution deduction for a donation of property because their appraisal failed to comply with the qualified appraisal requirements. The donors argued that their appraisal should be accepted

because it was in substantial compliance with the law. The court rejected this argument for two reasons. First, the tax code contains no provision suggesting that substantial compliance is sufficient to meet the substantiation requirements enumerated in the code and regulations. Second, even if such an exception existed, it would not benefit the donors, since their compliance was far from substantial:

> Assuming *arguendo* that the [substantial compliance] doctrine indeed could apply in such taxpayer actions, the court finds that the appraisal at issue wholly lacks even a modicum of content in critical areas to say that it substantially complies with numerous statutory and regulation mandates. The substantial compliance doctrine is not a substitute for missing entire categories of content; rather, it is at most a means of accepting a nearly complete effort that has simply fallen short in regard to minor procedural errors or relatively unimportant clerical oversights. The required content the donors neglected does not constitute such instances of technicalities. Much of the content provides necessary context permitting the Internal Revenue Service to evaluate a claimed deduction. Without, for example, the appraiser's education and background information, it would be difficult if not impossible to gauge the reliability of an appraisal that forms the foundation of a deduction. The simple inclusion of an appraiser's license number does not suffice given that there are distinctions between appraisers that the required information targets. . . .

Nowhere is it more apparent that donors' actions negate the equitable safe haven they pursue than in recognizing that the purpose of the qualified appraisal is to present an understandable rationale for the claimed deduction, and the deduction of $287,400.00 claimed here hardly matches the $520,000.00 appraisal offered. *Hendrix v. Commissioner, 2010 WL 2900391 (S.D. Ohio 2010).*

The church's obligations

Churches receiving contributions of property valued by the donor at more than $5,000 have the following two obligations (assuming that the donor plans to claim a deduction for the contribution):

Written acknowledgment. The church should provide the donor with a written acknowledgment described under Rule 7, above.

Form 8283. The church must complete and sign Part IV of Section B of the donor's Form 8283 appraisal summary.

Form 8282. Churches are required to file a Form 8282 (Donee Information Return) with the IRS if three conditions are met: (1) a donor makes a contribution of noncash property to the church that is valued at more than $5,000 (other than publicly traded securities); (2) the donor presented the church with a qualified appraisal summary (Form 8283, Section B, Part IV) for signature; and (3) the church sells, exchanges, consumes, or otherwise disposes of the donated property within three years of the date of contribution. The purpose of this reporting requirement is to ensure that donors do not claim inflated values for donated property.

Note the following specific rules that apply to the Form 8282 reporting requirement:

(1) When to file. If your church is required to file a Form 8282 (no exception applies), it should file Form 8282 within 125 days of the date it disposed of the property. An exception applies if the church did not file a Form 8282 because there was no reason to believe that the qualified appraisal requirement applied to a donor, but you later learned that it did apply. Then you must file Form 8282 within 60 days of learning of your obligation to file.

(2) Missing information. The instructions for Form 8282 specify that you must complete at least "column a" of Part II. If you do not have enough information to complete the other columns, you may leave them blank. This may occur if you did not keep a copy of the donor's appraisal summary (Form 8283, Section B).

◗ **KEY POINT.** The IRS has addressed the question of the penalty that should be assessed against a church or other charity that does not list the donor's Social Security

number on Form 8282. It concluded that section 6721 of the tax code imposes a penalty in such a case of $50 for each return that does not contain a donor's Social Security number. The IRS pointed out, however, that this penalty can be reduced to $30 per return if a return is filed with the correct information within 30 days following the due date of the return. Further, the instructions for Form 8282 state that the form does not have to be filled out completely if, for example, the information is not available to the church because it does not have the donor's appraisal summary (Form 8283). *IRS Letter Ruling 200101031.*

(3) Where to file. Send the completed Form 8282 to the address listed on the form.

(4) Informing the donor. You must provide the donor with a copy of the Form 8282 you filed with the IRS.

(5) Exceptions. A Form 8282 does not need to be filed if either or both of the following exceptions apply: (a) The church consumes the donated property or distributes it without charge to another organization or individual. The consumption or distribution must be in furtherance of the church's tax-exempt purposes. (b) At the time the church signed the donor's appraisal summary, the donor had signed a statement on the appraisal summary (Form 8283, Section B, Part II) that the appraised value of the donated property was not more than $500. This exception will apply if a donor contributes several similar items of property (having a combined value in excess of $5,000) to a church during a calendar year, and the church disposes of, or consumes, one item that is separately valued by the donor at $500 or less.

(6) Certification. The charitable contribution deduction available to donors who contribute tangible personal property to a charity is not reduced (from market value to cost basis) if the donee charity makes a certification to the IRS by written statement, signed under penalties of perjury by an officer of the charity, that either (a) certifies that the use of the property by the charity was related to the purpose or function constituting the basis for its exemption and describes how the property was used and how such use furthered such purpose or function, or (b) states the intended use of the property by the charity at the time of the contribution and certifies that such use became impossible or infeasible to implement. This certification is made in Part IV of Form 8282.

Rule 10—special rules for donations of (a) cars, boats, and planes; (b) stock; and (c) clothing and household items

Donations of cars, boats, and planes

Special rules apply to donations of cars, boats, and planes. It is important for church leaders to be familiar with these rules for two reasons. First, churches have reporting requirements that must be followed; and second, church leaders need to be ready to explain the rules to members who indicate an interest in donating a car (or a boat or plane) to the church.

The substantiation and reporting requirements that apply to donations of cars, boats, and planes are summarized in the chart below. Note the following:

- Mere application of the proceeds from the sale of a qualified vehicle to a needy individual to any charitable purpose does not directly further a donee organization's charitable purpose within the meaning of this rule.
- To constitute a significant intervening use, a charity must actually use the donated car to substantially further its regularly conducted activities, and the use must be significant. Incidental use is not a significant intervening use. Whether a use is a significant intervening use depends on its nature, extent, frequency, and duration.
- Material improvement includes a major repair or improvement that improves the condition of a car in a manner that significantly increases the value. To be a material improvement, the improvement

Donations Of Vehicles To Charity (for vehicles valued at more than $500)

Rule	Form of donation	Amount of charitable contribution deduction	Charity's obligations
1	A taxpayer donates a vehicle to a charity, and the charity sells it without any significant use or material improvement.	• Gross proceeds received by the charity from the sale of the vehicle • No deduction allowed unless a donor itemizes expenses on Schedule A and attaches either of the following to the tax return claiming the deduction: (1) IRS Form 8283, Section A and (2) either a "written acknowledgment" (described in next column) or a completed Form 1098-C • Appraisal not required if donor's deduction is limited to the gross proceeds of the sale	• Provide the donor with a written acknowledgment, within 30 days of the sale, containing donor's name and Social Security number; vehicle identification number; date of contribution; date of sale; amount of gross proceeds from the sale; certification that the vehicle was sold in an "arm's length transaction" to an unrelated party; statement that the deductible amount may not exceed the amount of the gross proceeds from the sale; and whether the charity provided any goods or services in consideration of the donation (and a description and good faith estimate of the value of any such goods or services, or, if the goods or services consist solely of intangible religious benefits, a statement to that effect). • IRS Form 1098-C may be used as a written acknowledgment (if provided to the donor within 30 days of the sale). • Submit Form 1098-C to the IRS by February 28 of the following year (April 1 if filed electronically).
2	A taxpayer donates a vehicle to a charity, and the charity "significantly uses" the vehicle (e.g., regular use over an extended period of time in performing the charity's exempt purposes).	• Fair market value of the donated vehicle • No deduction allowed unless a donor itemizes expenses on Schedule A and attaches the following to the tax return claiming the deduction: (1) IRS Form 8283, Section A and (2) either a "written acknowledgment" (described in next column) or a completed Form 1098-C • Qualified appraisal and appraisal summary (Form 8283) required for a deduction in excess of $5,000 if the deduction is not limited to gross proceeds from the sale of the vehicle (a written acknowledgment or Form 1098-C is still required, but not Form 8283, Section A)	• Provide the donor with a written acknowledgment, within 30 days of the contribution, containing donor's name and Social Security number; vehicle identification number; date of contribution; whether the charity provided any goods or services in consideration of the donation (and a description and good faith estimate of the value of any such goods or services, or, if the goods or services consist solely of intangible religious benefits, a statement to that effect); a certification and description of the intended significant intervening use by the charity and the intended duration of the use; and a certification that the vehicle will not be sold before completion of the use. • IRS Form 1098-C may be used as a written acknowledgment (if provided to the donor within 30 days of the contribution). • Submit Form 1098-C to the IRS by February 28 of the following year (April 1 if filed electronically).

may not be funded by an additional payment to the donee organization from the donor of the qualified vehicle. Services that are not considered material improvements include application of paint or other types of finishes (such as rust proofing or wax), removal of dents and scratches, cleaning or repair of upholstery, and installation of theft deterrent devices.

- A donor claiming a deduction for the fair market value of a car must be able to substantiate the fair market value. A reasonable method of determining fair market value is by reference to an established used-vehicle pricing guide. A used-vehicle pricing guide establishes the fair market value of

a particular vehicle only if the guide lists a sales price for a vehicle that is the same make, model, and year, sold in the same area, in the same condition, with the same or substantially similar options or accessories and with the same or substantially similar warranties or guarantees as the vehicle in question.

Deductions of $500 or less. A donation of a car with a claimed value of at least $250 must be substantiated by a contemporaneous written acknowledgment of the contribution by the charity. For a donation of a car with a claimed value of at least $250 but not more than $500, the acknowledgment must contain the follow-

	Donations Of Vehicles To Charity (for vehicles valued at more than $500)		
Rule	**Form of donation**	**Amount of charitable contribution deduction**	**Charity's obligations**
3	A taxpayer donates a vehicle to a charity, and the charity "materially improves" the vehicle (e.g., major repairs that significantly increase the vehicle's value).	Same as Rule 2	• Provide the donor with a written acknowledgment, within 30 days of the contribution, containing donor's name and Social Security number; vehicle identification number; date of contribution; whether the charity provided any goods or services in consideration of the donation (and a description and good faith estimate of the value of any such goods or services, or, if the goods or services consist solely of intangible religious benefits, a statement to that effect); a certification and description of the intended material improvement by the charity; and a certification that the vehicle will not be sold before completion of the improvement. • IRS Form 1098-C may be used as a written acknowledgment (if provided to the donor within 30 days of the contribution). • Submit Form 1098-C to the IRS by February 28 of the following year (April 1 if filed electronically).
4	A taxpayer donates a vehicle to a charity, and the charity transfers it to a needy person for significantly below market value in furtherance of its charitable purposes.	Same as Rule 2	• Provide the donor with a written acknowledgment, within 30 days of the contribution, containing donor's name and Social Security number; vehicle identification number; date of contribution; whether the charity provided any goods or services in consideration of the donation (and a description and good faith estimate of the value of any such goods or services, or, if the goods or services consist solely of intangible religious benefits, a statement to that effect); and a certification that the charity will sell the vehicle to a needy individual at a price significantly below fair market value (or, if applicable, that it will gratuitously transfer the vehicle to a needy individual) and that the sale (or transfer) will be in direct furtherance of the charity's exempt purpose of relieving the poor and distressed or the underprivileged who are in need of a means of transportation. • IRS Form 1098-C may be used as a written acknowledgment (if provided to the donor within 30 days of the contribution). • Submit Form 1098-C to the IRS by February 28 of the following year (April 1 if filed electronically).

ing information (as noted above): the amount of cash and a description (but not value) of any property other than cash contributed; whether the donee organization provided any goods or services in consideration, in whole or in part, for the cash or property contributed; and a description and good faith estimate of the value of any goods or services provided by the donee organization in consideration for the contribution, or, if such goods or services consist solely of intangible religious benefits, a statement to that effect.

If a donor contributes a car that is sold by the charity without any significant intervening use or material improvement, and if the sale yields gross proceeds of $500 or less, the donor may be allowed a deduction equal to the lesser of the fair market value of the qualified vehicle on the date of the contribution or $500. Under these circumstances the donor must substantiate the fair market value and, if the fair market value is $250 or more, must substantiate the contribution with an appropriate acknowledgment.

Penalties. The tax code imposes penalties on any charity required to furnish an acknowledgment to a donor that knowingly furnishes a false or fraudulent acknowledgment or knowingly fails to furnish an acknowledgment in the manner, at the time, and showing the information required under the rules summarized above. For example, the penalty applicable to an acknowledgment relating to the sale of a donated car is the greater of (1) the product of the highest individual income tax rate (currently 39.6 percent) and the sales price stated on the acknowledgment, or (2) the gross proceeds from the sale of the qualified vehicle.

The penalty applicable to an acknowledgment relating to a vehicle that was materially improved or used significantly by the church for its religious purposes is the greater of (1) the claimed value of the vehicle multiplied times the highest individual income tax rate or (2) $5,000.

> **EXAMPLE.** A church receives a contribution of a used car. It sells the car without any significant intervening use or material improvement. Gross proceeds from the sale are $300. The church provides an acknowledgment to the donor in which it knowingly includes a false or fraudulent statement that the gross proceeds from the sale of the vehicle were $1,000. The church is subject to a penalty for knowingly furnishing a false or fraudulent acknowledgment to the donor. The amount of the penalty is $396, the product of the sales price stated in the acknowledgment ($1,000) and 39.6 percent, because that amount is greater than the gross proceeds from the sale of the vehicle ($300).

Donations of stock

With more than half of all Americans now owning stock, it is not surprising that many of them are donating shares of stock to their church. As a result, it is important for church leaders and donors to be familiar with the tax rules that apply to stock donations. Unfamiliarity with these rules can result in additional taxes. This section will review what donors and church leaders need to know.

Why should donors consider donating stock to their church? Gifts of stock can provide donors with a double tax benefit. First, they may be able to claim a charitable contribution deduction in the amount of the current market value of the donated stock. That is, they can deduct not only the original cost they paid for the donated shares but also the value of any increase in the value of those shares. Second, donors avoid paying taxes on the appreciated value of the donated stock.

> **EXAMPLE.** Bob purchased 100 shares of ABC stock 10 years ago at a cost of $1,000, and he donates these shares to his church this year when their value is $3,000. Subject to the limitations discussed later in this section, Bob would be able to deduct the full $3,000 market value, and he would not have to pay capital gains tax on the $2,000 gain in the value of the stock.

Many church members own stock that has appreciated in value. The greater the amount of appreciation, the more capital gains tax the shareholder will face if the stock is sold. But this tax can be avoided if the member donates the stock to his or her church. And remember, the church pays no capital gains tax when it sells the donated stock, so the entire amount of the gift furthers the church's mission.

What about gifts of privately held stock? Most stock is either publicly traded or privately held by the owners of a business that has not offered its shares for sale to the public. When donors make gifts of privately held stock, three special rules must be understood by both donors and church leaders:

Qualified appraisals. If privately held stock valued at more than $10,000 is donated, a donor must obtain a qualified appraisal of the donated shares no earlier than 60 days prior to the date of the contribution. The cost of obtaining a qualified appraisal of privately held shares can be high and has caused some donors to reconsider making such a gift.

Qualified appraisal summaries (Form 8283). The donor must complete a qualified appraisal summary (IRS Form 8283) and enclose it with the Form 1040 on which the contribution deduction is claimed. Note that the church must sign this appraisal summary. Unfortunately, some donors have sent this form to their church for signature only to have it discarded or misplaced. The failure of a donor to submit a properly executed appraisal summary will jeopardize the deductibility of the contribution.

If the donor buys back the donated shares. It is common for donors who donate privately held stock to a church to buy back those shares after the gift. After all, there usually is little, if any, market for shares in privately held companies, so the church cannot easily sell the shares to anyone else. However, if an agreement exists at the time the shares are donated for the donor to buy back the shares or for the church to sell them to the donor, the charitable contribution may be disallowed by the IRS, and any gain in the value of the shares may be taxed to the donor. Such transactions should never be consummated without legal advice.

What limitations apply to gifts of stock? Three limitations apply to a gift of stock that has appreciated in value:

(1) The one-year rule. When contributing capital gain property, such as stock, to a church or other public charity, a donor generally is entitled to claim a deduction in the amount of the fair market value of the donated property on the date of the gift. Property is capital gain property if its sale at fair market value on the date of the contribution would have resulted in long-term capital gain. Capital gain property includes capital assets held more than one year.

Donated stock that was held by the donor for less than one year is not capital gain property. The IRS classifies it as "ordinary income property," since a sale of

the stock would result in ordinary taxable income rather than capital gain on any appreciation in value. The amount a donor can deduct for a contribution of ordinary income property is its fair market value less the amount that would have been ordinary income or short-term capital gain if the donor had sold the property for its fair market value on the date of the gift. Generally, this rule limits the deduction to the donor's basis (cost) in the property.

> **EXAMPLE.** Barb donates stock that she held for five months to her church. The fair market value of the stock on the date of the donation was $1,000, but Barb paid only $800 (her "basis") for the stock. Because the $200 of appreciation would be short-term capital gain if she had sold the stock on the date of the contribution, her deduction is limited to $800 (fair market value less the appreciation).

(2) The 30 percent limit. Donors generally can deduct contributions to their church only up to 50 percent of their adjusted gross income (AGI), with any excess being carried over to the next year (up to five years in all, with the 50 percent limit applying to each year). However, gifts of capital gain property (including stock) to a church are deductible only up to 30 percent of a donor's AGI. The 30 percent limit does not apply to donors who elect to reduce the fair market value of donated property by the amount that would have been long-term capital gain had the property been sold on the date of the gift. In such cases, the 50 percent limit applies.

◉ KEY POINT. Donors may elect a 50 percent limit for gifts of capital gain property instead of the 30 percent limit. Donors who make this election must reduce the fair market value of the donated property by the appreciation in value that would have been long-term capital gain if the property had been sold on the date of the gift. This choice applies to all capital gain property contributed to churches and other public charities during a tax year. Donors make the election on their tax return or on an amended return filed by the due date for filing the original return.

Donors can carry over contributions that they could not deduct in the current year because they exceed the 30 percent of AGI limit. Donors can deduct the excess in each of the next five years until it is used up, but not beyond that time. Contributions that are carried over are subject to the same percentage limits in the year to which they are carried. For example, contributions subject to the 30 percent limit in the year in which they are made are subject to the same limit in the year to which they are carried. Donors deduct carryover contributions only after deducting all allowable contributions in that category for the current year.

(3) Itemized deductions. Donors claim charitable contribution deductions as itemized expenses on Schedule A of Form 1040. Donors who do not itemize their expenses cannot claim a charitable contribution deduction for a gift of stock.

What about stock that has declined in value? Some donors give their church stock that has declined in value. In general, donors who contribute stock with a fair market value that is less than their basis (cost) are entitled to a deduction in the amount of the stock's fair market value. They cannot claim a deduction for the difference between the stock's basis and its fair market value (the decrease in value). Persons who have stock that has declined in value generally will pay less taxes if they sell the stock, give the proceeds to charity, and then claim a loss on their income tax return.

What about selling the stock and donating the proceeds? Some donors consider selling their stock and then donating the cash proceeds to their church. Is this a good idea? Not if the stock has increased in value. Let's illustrate this with an example. Assume that Bill buys shares of stock 5 years ago for $6,000 that is worth $10,000 today. Bill sells the stock for $10,000 and donates the proceeds to his church. By selling the stock, Bill realized capital gains on the appreciation and he will have to pay taxes on this amount. However, if Bill had donated the stock to his church without selling it, he would have avoided capital gains tax on the appreciation and still could have claimed a charitable contribution.

By giving the stock directly to the church, Bill avoids paying tax on the $4,000 gain on his stock investment, and he gets a charitable contribution deduction for the full value of his shares (unless one of the limitations previously mentioned applies).

▲ **CAUTION.** *Stock that has been held more than a year and that has declined in value ordinarily should not be given directly to a church or charity. It often is more desirable, from a tax perspective, for the owner to sell the stock and give the proceeds to charity,* *because this will create a "realized loss" that the donor may be able to deduct in computing his or her taxes.*

How does a donor value donated stock? Donors who contribute publicly traded stock to a church or charity can claim a charitable contribution deduction in the amount of the fair market value of the donated shares, subject to the limitations previously discussed. The fair market value of donated stock is determined by (1) determining the "mean price" of the donated shares by adding the high and low quoted prices of the stock on the day of the gift, and dividing by two; then (2) multiplying the mean price by the number of donated shares.

◉ **KEY POINT.** The date of a gift of stock is addressed in the income tax regulations as follows: "Ordinarily, a contribution is made at the time delivery is effected. The unconditional delivery or mailing of a check which subsequently clears in due course will constitute an effective contribution on the date of delivery or mailing. If a taxpayer unconditionally delivers or mails a properly endorsed stock certificate to a charitable donee or the donee's agent, the gift is completed on the date of delivery or, if such certificate is received in the ordinary course of the mails, on the date of mailing. If the donor delivers the stock certificate to his bank or broker as the donor's agent, or to the issuing corporation or its agent, for transfer into the name of the donee, the gift is completed on the date the stock is transferred on the books of the corporation." *Treas. Reg. 1.170A-1(b).*

▲ **CAUTION.** *Donors often make gifts of stock at the end of the year by calling their stockbroker and asking that the shares be transferred. Donors who expect a year-end charitable contribution deduction should make their desire clear when communicating with their broker. In some cases, brokers do not transfer donated shares until the beginning of the new year, resulting in the loss of any deduction for the previous year.*

What are the mechanics of donating stock? Donors can donate stock in a number of ways:

- by electronic transfer (if available);
- by physical transfer (personally or through the mail). For security purposes, donors usually transfer unsigned stock certificates and separately execute a "stock power" form with a signature guaranteed by the donor's bank or broker. The

stock power form should be sent on the same day as the stock certificate, but in a separate envelope. If donated stock is held in the names of more than one person, all owners must sign the stock power form. If using the mail, donors should send all documents by registered mail;

- through a stockbroker.

▲ **CAUTION.** *Donors who contribute stock to their church through a broker should be sure that the broker understands that they are donating the stock, not selling it. If the broker sells stock held by the donor for more than one year and transfers the proceeds to the donor's church rather than giving the shares directly to the church, the donor will have to pay capital gains tax on any gain in the value of the stock.*

What about gifts of mutual fund shares? Donors generally determine the fair market value of donated mutual fund shares by multiplying the net asset value on the date of the gift by the number of donated shares.

How do donors substantiate gifts of stock? Gifts of stock are subject to special substantiation rules. Note the following:

- A church is not an appraiser and should never provide donors with a value for donated stock. Instead, provide a receipt that acknowledges the date of gift, the donor's name, the number of shares given, and the name of the company.
- A donor who gives publicly traded stock valued at more than $5,000 is not required to obtain a qualified appraisal or complete a qualified appraisal summary (Section B of Form 8283).
- A donor who gives publicly traded stock valued at more than $500 must complete Section A, Part I, of Form 8283. This requirement applies even if the stock is valued at more than $5,000 (in which case the stock is exempt from the qualified appraisal requirement).
- A donor who gives nonpublicly traded stock valued at $10,000 or less is not required to obtain a qualified appraisal and complete a qualified appraisal summary (Form 8283). However, donors who give nonpublicly traded stock valued at more than $10,000 must obtain a qualified appraisal of the stock no earlier than 60 days prior to the date of the gift, and they must also complete a

qualified appraisal summary (IRS Form 8283) that summarizes the qualified appraisal and is enclosed with the tax return on which the deduction is claimed. Failure to comply with these requirements can lead to a loss of any charitable contribution deduction.

CASE STUDY. A donor contributed nonpublicly traded stock worth more than $10,000 to a church, but obtained no qualified appraisal and attached no qualified appraisal summary to the tax return on which the charitable contribution deduction was claimed. The Tax Court ruled that the donor was not entitled to a charitable contribution deduction, even though there was no dispute as to the value of the donated stock. *Hewitt v. Commissioner, 109 T.C.12 (1997).*

◉ **KEY POINT.** Do not assume that donors are familiar with the substantiation rules that apply to gifts of stock. Church treasurers should obtain several copies of Form 8283 each January to give to persons who donate stock to the church during the year. You can order multiple copies of Form 8283 by calling the IRS forms hotline or by downloading them from the IRS website (irs.gov).

Donations of clothing and household items

Americans love to donate used clothing and household items to charity. The IRS reports that the amount claimed as deductions in a recent year for clothing and household items was more than $9 billion. These items are notoriously difficult to value, and the attempt to do so wastes valuable time and resources.

The tax code responds to this dilemma by denying a charitable contribution deduction for a contribution of clothing or household items unless the clothing or household items are in "good used condition or better." The Treasury Department is authorized to deny (by regulation) a deduction for any contribution of clothing or a household item that has minimal monetary value, such as used socks and used undergarments.

A deduction may be allowed for a charitable contribution of an item of clothing or a household item not in good used condition or better only if the amount claimed for the item is more than $500 and the taxpayer obtains a qualified appraisal of the property and attaches a qualified appraisal summary (Form 8283) to the tax return claiming the deduction.

Household items include furniture, furnishings, electronics, appliances, linens, and other similar items. Food, paintings, antiques, and other objects of art, jewelry and gems, and collections are excluded from the definition.

If the donated item is in good used condition or better and a deduction in excess of $500 is claimed, the taxpayer must file a completed Form 8283 (Section A or B, depending on the type of contribution and claimed amount), but a qualified appraisal is required only if the claimed contribution amount exceeds $5,000.

If the donor claims a deduction of less than $250, the donor must obtain a receipt from the church or charity or maintain reliable written records of the contribution. A reliable written record for a contribution of clothing or a household item must include a description of the condition of the item. If the donor claims a deduction of $250 or more, the donor must obtain from the church or charity a receipt that meets the requirements of a contemporaneous written acknowledgment (see Rule 6, above).

PLANNED AND DEFERRED GIVING

The terms "planned giving" and "deferred giving" are often used interchangeably to refer to any method of giving by a donor to the donor's church or other charitable organization at some point in the future, after the donor's execution of an agreement or other gift instrument gives effect to the gift. This book will use the terms "planned giving" and "planned gift" to refer to such methods of giving.

The most common examples of planned giving by church donors in the United States are:

- Charitable bequests pursuant to a will or similar document;
- Gifts of life insurance;
- Charitable gift annuities; and
- Charitable remainder trusts.

Other, less common forms of planned giving by church donors do exist and are outside the scope of this book. A few examples are charitable lead trusts, pooled income funds, and gifts of remainder interests in property. A church that is approached by a donor interested in making a planned gift should consider the donor's proposal together with knowledgeable legal and tax counsel. The mere fact that a proposed planned gift may seem complex is not a reason for a church to reject such a proposal out of hand. To do so could represent poor stewardship. With proper legal and tax advice, a church may determine that accepting a seemingly complex proposed planned gift is in its best interests.

CHARITABLE BEQUESTS

One of the simplest ways donors may make a planned gift is to leave assets to their church as part of a will or other similar estate document (such as a revocable living trust). Since the provisions of the will or revocable living trust may be changed from time to time, a donor is not entitled to an income tax deduction during his or her lifetime for simply naming a church or charity as a beneficiary in a will or similar document.

Requests by donors for estate planning assistance

At times, donors may seek advice or referrals from their church leaders regarding their estate planning. Sometimes, donors seek such advice from the church because they wish to include the church as a beneficiary in their estate plans. Churches should obtain advice from experienced legal counsel in determining whether or to what extent they should assist a donor with estate planning matters. On the one hand, a church wants to encourage and (to the extent appropriate) facilitate a donor's desire to make a testamentary gift to the church. On the other hand, a church is not a law firm and if the church provides advice to a donor regarding legal matters, the church would likely be in violation of state law. Additionally, if the church facilitates a donor's decision to include the church in his/her will or other estate planning documents as a beneficiary, the church could be open to allegations of undue influence over the donor's decisions. If family members of the donor or others protest the validity of the designation of the church as a beneficiary, the result could be that a court may rule that the designation by the donor of the church as a beneficiary was invalid. Churches and their legal counsel should consider these issues carefully in determining how to properly address a request by a donor for estate planning assistance.

GIFTS OF LIFE INSURANCE

As has long been the case, there are perfectly acceptable ways for donors to make gifts of life insurance to a church or other charitable organization. Unfortunately, due to negative publicity in recent years surrounding questionable practices involving donors, charities, and life insurance providers, much confusion exists in the area of tax law associated with gifts of life insurance.

Inappropriate Life Insurance Transactions

The negative publicity in recent years in the area of charitable gifts of life insurance relates primarily to practices involving "charitable split-dollar life insurance." Charitable split-dollar life insurance arrangements typically involve a donor or a member of the donor's family being entitled to certain benefits in connection with the contribution of all or part of a life insurance policy to a church or charity along with payments by the donor to cover the premiums of such a policy.

In *Notice 99-36,* the Internal Revenue Service addressed charitable split-dollar life insurance arrangements by stating:

> In general, a charitable split-dollar insurance transaction involves a transfer of funds by a taxpayer to a charity, with the understanding that the charity will use the transferred funds to pay premiums on a cash value life insurance policy that benefits **both the charity and the taxpayer's family**. [Emphasis added.] Typically, as part of this transaction, the charity or an irrevocable life insurance trust formed by the taxpayer (or a related person) purchases the cash value life insurance policy. The designated beneficiaries of the insurance policy include both the charity and the trust. **Members of the taxpayer's family (and, perhaps, the taxpayer) are beneficiaries of the trust.** [Emphasis added.]

> In a related transaction, the charity enters into a split-dollar agreement with the trust. The split-

dollar agreement specifies what portion of the insurance policy premiums is to be paid by the trust and what portion is to be paid by the charity. The agreement specifies the extent to which each party can exercise standard policyholder rights, such as the right to borrow against the cash value of the policy, to partially or completely surrender the policy for cash, and to designate beneficiaries for specified portions of the death benefit. The agreement also specifies the manner in which it may be terminated and the consequences of such termination. Although the terms of these split-dollar agreements vary, the common feature is that, over the life of the split-dollar agreement, the trust has access to a disproportionately high percentage of the cash-surrender value and death benefit under the policy, compared to the percentage of premiums paid by the trust.

Charitable Split-Dollar Insurance Transactions

As part of the charitable split-dollar insurance transaction, the taxpayer (or a related person) transfers funds to the charity. Although there may be no legally binding obligation expressly requiring the taxpayer to transfer funds to the charity to assist in making premium payments, or expressly requiring the charity to use the funds transferred by the taxpayer for premium payments in accordance with the split-dollar agreement, both parties understand that this will occur.

The structure of charitable split-dollar insurance transactions varies. In some cases, a member of the taxpayer's family, a family limited partnership, or another type of intermediary related to the taxpayer is used as an intermediary rather than an irrevocable life insurance trust. This notice applies to any charitable split-dollar insurance transaction, regardless of whether a trust or some other type of related intermediary is used in the transaction.

Generally, to be deductible as a charitable contribution…, a payment to charity must be a gift. A gift to charity is a payment of money or transfer of property without receipt of adequate consideration and with donative intent…However, regardless of whether a taxpayer receives a benefit in return for a transfer to charity or has the requisite donative intent, sections 170(f)(3) and 2522(c)(2) provide that generally no charitable deduction is allowed for a transfer to charity of less than the taxpayer's entire interest (i.e., a partial interest) in any property. Thus, **no charitable contribution deduction is permitted when a taxpayer assigns a partial interest in an insurance policy to a charity**. [Emphasis added.]

The IRS considers charitable split-dollar life insurance arrangements to be abusive transactions, as is made clear by the following excerpts from *Notice 99-36*:

> Depending on the facts and circumstances, **the Service may challenge, on the basis of private inurement or impermissible private benefit, the tax-exempt status of a charity that participates in charitable split-dollar insurance transactions** … [Emphasis added.]

> In addition, the Service may impose penalties on participants in charitable split-dollar insurance transactions, including the accuracy-related penalty under section 6662, the return-preparer penalty under section 6694, the promoter penalty under section 6700, and the penalty under section 6701 for aiding and abetting the understatement of tax liability.

Clearly, the IRS is not a fan of charitable split-dollar life insurance arrangements. **Churches should avoid participation in such arrangements.**

Permissible Life Insurance Gifts

Donors may make life insurance-related gifts to churches in a variety of acceptable ways.

Simply naming the church as a beneficiary of a life insurance policy. A donor may simply name his or her church as a beneficiary of a life insurance policy. In doing so, the donor may make the church either the sole beneficiary or one of multiple beneficiaries. In such an arrangement, the donor retains ownership of the insurance policy and makes the related premium payments. There is no transfer of ownership of the insurance policy to the church, nor does the church have any responsibility with respect to making premium payments. Additionally, the owner of the insurance policy is typically permitted to change

the beneficiaries of his or her life insurance policy while the insured person is living.

Since no ownership transfer is made to the church in connection with naming the church as a beneficiary, and since a donor may change a beneficiary designation, a donor is not entitled to a charitable contribution deduction for federal income tax purposes in connection with naming his or her church as a beneficiary of a life insurance policy. As is the case with many other types of planned gifts, a church may not be aware of the fact that it has been named by a donor as a beneficiary of a life insurance policy. The church may simply receive a death benefit payment upon the death of the insured person. Such arrangements are both common and permissible.

Transferring ownership of an insurance policy to the church. A donor may transfer ownership of an insurance policy to the church. Of course, in so doing, the beneficiary designation should be changed as well so that the church is the sole beneficiary. It is important to note here that a transfer of the entire ownership interest of an insurance policy to the church is an acceptable charitable practice, unlike the scenario described above for charitable split-dollar life insurance arrangements.

Life insurance policies typically exist in one of two broad types: term insurance (which does not accumulate cash value and typically only pays a death benefit) and insurance that can accumulate cash value as well as provide a death benefit (often referred to as "whole life," "universal life," or "variable life" insurance.) The provisions of life insurance policies, including premium payment obligations, vary widely and no attempt to provide simple descriptions or categorizations of all such policy variations would be adequate here.

When a donor transfers his or her entire interest in a life insurance policy to the church, the donor may be entitled to a charitable contribution deduction for federal income tax purposes. A contribution of a life insurance policy to a church is considered a non-cash contribution and is subject to the ordinary rules that apply to non-cash charitable contributions. A term life insurance policy may have little or no economic value, especially if premiums must continue to be paid in order to keep the policy in force. On the other hand, a term life insurance policy may have significant value if the person whose life is insured has a short life expectancy. A cash-value type life insurance policy may have economic value if the owner may surrender the policy in exchange for cash. A donor making a gift of a life insurance policy must determine the value of the policy contributed to the church. If the donor wishes to claim the value of the policy as a charitable contribution deduction, the donor should follow guidance for non-cash contributions such as that found in *IRS Publication 561* and *IRS Publication 526*, as well as IRS Form 8283 and its related instructions. If the donor claims a value for a contributed life insurance policy in excess of $5,000, the donor likely will request the church to sign Form 8283 acknowledging receipt of the life insurance policy.

Determining whether to accept a gift of a life insurance policy. When a donor offers to contribute ownership of a life insurance policy to a church, the church should evaluate the form and economics of the proposed gift. For policies that do not require future premium payments, the decision likely will be quite simple. For policies that require future premium payments, the church should evaluate whether the donor intends to make future contributions to the church that are sufficient to cover the premiums. (Such plans are permissible under federal tax law, provided that the church is the sole owner and beneficiary of the policy. In such arrangements, assuming that the church is the sole owner of the life insurance policy as well as the sole beneficiary, the donor is not receiving anything in exchange for contributions that are intended to help the church make future premium payments. Accordingly, such contributions would ordinarily be deductible just like other charitable contributions.)

With most insurance policies, the only adverse consequence of failing to pay premiums is that the policy lapses. If the church accepts a gift of a policy that requires future premium payments and the donor fails to make contributions to fund the payments, the church must decide whether to make the premium payments without a subsidy from the donor, or to stop making the payments and allow the policy to lapse. Cash-value type life insurance policies may have accumulated value that will permit deferral of premium payments for a period of time. The church may also wish to consider the life expectancy of the donor in making a decision about whether to accept a proposed gift of a

life insurance policy or to continue making premium payments for a policy it owns. The church should consider all relevant economic factors in making the decision. It would be wise for the church to consult with a knowledgeable life insurance broker or agent and legal counsel in evaluating proposed gifts of life insurance.

CHARITABLE GIFT ANNUITIES

Charitable gift annuities represent a method of accommodating an **irrevocable** planned gift. A charitable gift annuity is an agreement between a donor and a church (or other charity) pursuant to which the donor transfers something of value to the church (typically money) in exchange for the church's promise to make regular payments to the donor for a stated period of time. The stated period of time may be a fixed number of years or the remainder of the donor's life. Payments may begin immediately or they may be deferred for an agreed-upon period of time.

When payments are to be made only to one beneficiary, such arrangements are commonly referred to as "single-life" gift annuities. A donor may stipulate that payments are to be made as long as one of two beneficiaries is still living. Such arrangements are commonly referred to as "joint and survivor" gift annuities. Other variations of gift annuities exist as well.

Gift annuity payments are typically described in terms of a percentage of the value of property or money that the donor transfers to the church at the time the annuity is established.

> **EXAMPLE.** Ted and Mildred Wilson entered into a gift annuity agreement with First Pine Church pursuant to which Mr. and Mrs. Wilson transferred $100,000 to the church. Ted is 70 years old and Mildred is 68 years old. The agreement calls for the church to make 6-percent annuity payments in monthly installments to the couple so long as either of them is living beginning on the first month after the annuity agreement is executed. Accordingly, the church will make payments of $6,000 per year (6 percent multiplied by $100,000) to the couple in monthly installments of $500 so long as either of them is living. This is an example of a typical joint and survivor *immediate* charitable gift annuity arrangement.

If the facts stated above were the same, except that the annuity payments did not begin until five years after

3

Charitable Contributions

the annuity agreement was executed, such an agreement would represent a joint and survivor *deferred* charitable gift annuity arrangement.

Legal and Regulatory Considerations for Gift Annuities

A church must consider legal and regulatory implications prior to offering gift annuities to its donors. The offering of gift annuities and the related administration of gift annuities is an activity that is regulated by many states in the U.S. For states that regulate gift annuities, statutory requirements are typically part of the state's insurance laws and the regulatory agency that oversees gift annuities is typically the same agency that oversees insurance regulation in the state. States that regulate gift annuities typically have specific requirements for the content of annuity agreements, the annuity rates that churches or charities may pay, the manner in which charitable gift annuity funds must be invested, and the amount of "reserves and surplus" that an issuing organization must maintain in connection with its outstanding gift annuities.

Churches must have experienced legal counsel advising them with respect to the issuance and administration of charitable gift annuities under applicable state law.

Tax aspects of charitable gift annuities

A donor is typically entitled to a charitable contribution deduction for federal income tax purposes in connection with establishing a charitable gift annuity. A calculation must be made of the present value of estimated future annuity payments to be made under the agreement. The present value of the future annuity payments is subtracted from the value of money or property transferred by the donor to the church at the inception of the agreement. The net result, which is the present value of the church's estimated remainder interest in the annuity, is typically the amount deductible by the donor. Additionally, annuity payments made to the beneficiaries (or "annuitants") are typically only partially taxable, as a portion of the annuity payment is considered a return of the donor's original investment in the agreement.

Churches offering gift annuities should do so only under the advice of knowledgeable tax and legal counsel, who can assist in compliance matters as well as in making the present value calculations described above.

Alternatives to Administering Charitable Gift Annuities Directly

Some organizations offer to accept and/or administer charitable gift annuities for the benefit of churches or other charitable organizations that do not wish to engage in such activities themselves. A church's legal counsel can assist the church in evaluating the advisability of such arrangements.

The American Council on Gift Annuities

Significant additional information about gift annuities and related topics is available from the American Council on Gift Annuities (ACGA) at *acga-web.org*. The ACGA publishes recommended charitable gift annuity rates which are updated periodically and are typically utilized by churches and charities that issue gift annuities.

CHARITABLE REMAINDER TRUSTS

A charitable remainder trust has features that are similar to a charitable gift annuity, but unlike a charitable gift annuity (which is an agreement directly between the donor and the issuing church or other charitable organization), a charitable remainder trust is actually a separate legal entity created by a donor for the purpose of accommodating a planned gift. A trust is typically created pursuant to a trust document and must generally have one or more trustees and one or more beneficiaries. A charitable remainder trust will have one or more **income beneficiaries**, who receive payments initially, and one or more **remainder beneficiaries**, such as the donor's church or other charitable organization.

Church as trustee?

It is possible that a donor may ask the church to serve as trustee of a charitable remainder trust. Since the church will be a remainder beneficiary of the trust, and because there are significant legal considerations, churches should not accept the role of trustee of a charitable remainder trust unless they have evaluated the matter carefully under the advice of legal counsel and determined that serving as trustee would be appropriate in the circumstances. The risks can be greater for a trust in which the church is not the sole remainder beneficiary (due to the fact that the church is responsible for managing the trust's assets for the ultimate benefit of another church or charitable organization, in addition to itself.) Some churches and charitable organizations will not, as a matter of internal policy, accept the role of trustee for charitable remainder trusts.

Types of charitable remainder trusts

There are *many* variations of charitable remainder trusts. The two broadest categories of charitable remainder trusts (of which there are many subtypes) are:

1. Charitable remainder annuity trusts; and
2. Charitable remainder unitrusts.

A common form of **charitable remainder annuity trust** (often referred to as a "CRAT") is a trust wherein a donor transfers money or property to the trust in exchange for **equal annual payments** to be made over an agreed-upon period of time, with the remainder interest going to a designated charity such as the donor's church.

A CRAT operates in a manner very similar to a charitable gift annuity. However, since a trust is a separate legal entity and the church is not the "issuer," such arrangements are not subject to the same regulatory requirements that apply to charitable gift annuities under the laws of many states. State law may, however, govern the manner in which the trustee of such a trust must administer it. Note that as a remainder beneficiary, a church may not be aware that a donor has formed such a trust until it is notified of its right to receive the remainder proceeds. Such occurrences are rather common.

> **EXAMPLE.** Ted and Mildred Smith formed a charitable remainder annuity trust and named their bank as trustee and First Pine Church as the remainder beneficiary. Mr. and Mrs. Smith contributed $100,000 to the trust. The trust document stipulates that Mr. and Mrs. Smith will receive 6 percent of the original trust principal annually for as long as either one of them is living. Accordingly, Mr. and Mrs. Smith will receive $6,000 per year from the trust as long as either one of them is living. At the second death, First Pine Church will receive the remaining assets of the trust.

Ted and Mildred Smith are entitled to an income tax deduction at the time they fund the trust. The deduction is determined in a manner similar to that for gift annuities as described above.

A common form of **charitable remainder unitrust** (often referred to as a "CRUT") is a trust wherein a donor transfers money or property to the trust in exchange for payments equal to **a fixed percentage of the value** of the trust's assets each year for a stated period of time. A remainder interest goes to a designated charity such as the donor's church. Since the value of the trust's assets may change from year to year, the amount of the payments to the beneficiaries may vary from year to year, while the percentage remains fixed.

As is the case with CRATs, CRUTs are not regulated in the same manner as charitable gift annuities under the laws of many states. State law may, however, govern the manner in which the trustee of such a trust must administer it. Note that as a remainder beneficiary, a church may not be aware that a donor has formed such a trust until it is notified of its right to receive the remainder proceeds. Such occurrences are rather common.

> **EXAMPLE.** Ted and Mildred Smith formed a charitable remainder unitrust and named their bank as trustee and First Pine Church as the remainder beneficiary. Mr. and Mrs. Smith contributed $100,000 to the trust. The trust document stipulates that Mr. and Mrs. Smith will receive 6 percent of the value of the trust's assets as of the beginning of each year annually for as long as either one of them is living. Accordingly, Mr. and Mrs. Smith will receive $6,000 in the first year from the trust. Assume that at the beginning of Year 2, the value of the trust's assets is $110,000. In Year 2, Mr. and Mrs. Smith will receive 6 percent of $110,000, or $6,600. This annual process will continue as long as either one of them is living. At the second death, First Pine Church will receive the remaining assets of the trust.

Ted and Mildred Smith are entitled to an income tax deduction at the time they fund the trust. The deduction is determined by calculating the estimated present value of the church's remainder interest pursuant to guidelines prescribed by the IRS.

CLAWBACKS OF CHARITABLE CONTRIBUTIONS – A CONTINUING CHALLENGE

One of the more insidious risks churches face with respect to charitable contributions is the risk that contributions received from a particular donor may later be ruled "fraudulent transfers" or "fraudulent conveyances" under federal bankruptcy law or applicable state law. The church that receives the contributions may have no idea that a donor is facing bankruptcy or that a donor may have obtained the donated funds in an ill-gotten manner (such as a Ponzi scheme). If such conditions

3

Charitable Contributions

are present, a bankruptcy trustee, creditors of a donor, or law enforcement authorities may assert that contributions made to the church were "fraudulent transfers" and, as a result, must be returned by the church to a receiver, trustee, or other party to pay the creditors or to be used for other purposes. The laws that require such refunds are often referred to as "clawback" laws.

Clawbacks of charitable contributions can be particularly damaging to a church – especially in cases where the contributions are large and the church has spent the money on operations or assets before learning of the clawback claim. Accordingly, **church leaders would be well-advised to carefully evaluate large or unusual gifts...and if there is any concern about the possibility of a clawback claim, consult with legal counsel and consider holding the assets for a period until it is deemed safe by the church's legal counsel to spend them – possibly three years or more.**

Numerous instances of clawbacks of charitable contributions occurred during the Great Recession and they still occur today.

The federal government and many states have laws that provide churches and other nonprofits *very limited protection* from clawbacks. For example, Florida law (which is comparable to the laws of a number of states) provides that **a natural person's charitable contributions are fraudulent transfers if they were received within 2 years before the commencement of a Florida Uniform Fraudulent Transfer Act, bankruptcy, or insolvency proceeding, unless:**

> (a) **The transfer was made consistent with the debtor's practices in making charitable contributions, or**
> (b) **The transfer was received in good faith and did not exceed 15% of the debtor's gross annual income for the year in which the transfer was made.**

(These provisions are also comparable to those found in the federal Bankruptcy Code's protection for charitable contributions against a bankruptcy trustee's clawback action.)

Chapter 4

Other Revenue Sources

INTRODUCTION

While the primary source of revenue for churches is contributions, churches often generate revenue from other sources. For purposes of this chapter, we will refer to revenue from sources other than contributions as *alternative source revenue*. Alternative source revenue may be generated by church activities and programs (such as foodservice programs in which patrons are charged for meals or preschool ministries in which patrons are charged tuition) or by more passive activities (such as investing funds to produce income). In this chapter we will explore the variety of alternative sources of revenue, plus discuss the legal and tax implications that churches must consider in this area.

ALTERNATIVE SOURCE REVENUE

Here are some of the more common forms of alternative source revenue:

Investment Income (From Investment of Liquid Funds)

Investment income (interest, dividends, and capital gains) is one of the most common sources of alternative source revenue for churches, as they invest cash reserves in various income-producing vehicles, such as interest-bearing bank accounts, certificates of deposit, stocks, bonds, mutual funds, and so on. Important considerations related to investment management practices and related topics are addressed in detail in Chapter 6.

Rental Income

Rental income is a form of investment income, typically generated by churches that allow other parties to use all or a portion of their real estate in exchange for rent. (Rental income also may be generated by allowing other parties to use *tangible personal property*, such as furniture and equipment, although such arrangements are rare among churches.) Churches may generate rental income from real estate in a variety of scenarios. For example, churches may rent unused classroom space to groups during the week for educational activities. They may rent the church sanctuary to outside groups for special events. They may rent their "fellowship hall" or equivalent space to

groups for meetings, banquets, or other gatherings. In some cases, churches may own real estate as investment property (either residential or commercial) and generate rental income. For example, some churches own commercial office buildings and rent space in them to commercial tenants. Some churches own retail shopping centers and rent space in the property to retail merchants.

Income from Parking Lots or Garages

Churches typically have significant parking capacity at their facilities due to the nature of their activities. While a church may use its parking capacity heavily during worship services and during other significant church activities, most churches do not continuously utilize their full parking capacity. Some churches are located in areas where parking is scarce and needed by people in the area during times when the church's use is minimal. For example, a church located in an urban commercial area, such as the "downtown" area of a city, may have significant parking capacity that is not used by the church during typical business work hours on Monday through Friday. In many such situations, a church will allow others to use its parking facilities for a fee. Such arrangements may be made in bulk, where the church rents its entire parking lot to another party, or the church may directly operate the parking facility, charging individual patrons for using it. As another example, some church campuses are located near venues that attract large crowds, such as sports stadiums and arenas. Churches in such locations often generate income from their parking areas in connection with events at those venues. As described in the section below related to tax considerations of alternative source revenue, the manner in which a church generates revenue from its excess parking capacity will dictate whether the income is considered rental income for federal income tax purposes, which will affect the federal income tax treatment of the income generated.

Activity Revenues

Many churches conduct a variety of activities that generate revenue—some with more of a connection to the church's ministry activities and religious purposes than others. Motivations for conducting such activities vary widely. Following are some common examples:

Bookstores

A church may operate a bookstore selling Bibles, prayer books, religious music, Bible study guides, and other religious items. Some church bookstores sell other types of merchandise, including clothing, jewelry, and cosmetics. Some church bookstores are operated in locations deep within the church campus, are open only at limited times, and are intended primarily to serve the people in attendance at the church's activities. Other church bookstores are located in high-traffic street-front retail locations (either on or off the church's campus), and are open during typical retail hours in an effort to attract the general public.

Thrift shops

Some churches operate thrift shops in which they sell used household goods and clothing that have been donated by supporters of the church. Church thrift shops vary in sophistication from small spaces on the church campus to large, appealing retail thrift stores operated in high-traffic commercial areas.

Schools and other educational programs

Many churches operate educational programs or similar ministries, such as schools (kindergarten through 12th grade, or portions thereof), preschools, day care ministries, "Mom's Day Out" programs, and so on. Some churches conduct such activities because they consider them to be an integral part of the church's overall mission and purpose. Some churches have found that certain educational and similar activities can generate positive cash flow for the church and thereby help reduce overall operating costs—which may serve as at least partial motivation for conducting the activities.

Cafés, coffee shops, and restaurants

In recent years, many churches have begun operating cafés, coffee shops, and other similar activities—typically in connection with ministry activities. The nature and sophistication of such activities range from simple kiosks selling coffee and pastries in the church lobby, to food courts comparable to those found in shopping malls, to full-service restaurants at which members of the public can make reservations. The church's primary motivation for conducting such activities is typically to serve the people who attend or participate in the church's ministry activities. For some very large churches that have relatively continuous activities on their campuses, foodservice operations are often more extensive and elaborate. Some churches even offer catering to patrons at offsite locations.

Special events

Many churches conduct special events that generate revenue, such as festivals, carnivals, banquets, concerts, and similar activities. Motivations for conducting such events vary, and may be primarily related to the church's overall religious mission or, alternatively, primarily related to generating income for the church. The sophistication of such events also varies widely. A simple church banquet celebrating Mother's Day, for example, may consist of providing a meal and a simple program in exchange for an admission fee. As a contrast, a church might conduct a multi-day festival featuring carnival rides, games, concessions, and entertainment that may be funded by sales of admissions, concessions revenues, sales of tickets for individual entertainment activities, and corporate sponsorships. Churches may also host music concerts featuring popular religious recording artists or entertainers, or other similar activities, typically in exchange for admission fees.

Event hosting

Churches may also host events for church members and, in some cases, for outside groups. For example, many churches will host weddings, banquets, reunions, and other special meetings, for which the group uses the church facilities and for which the church provides foodservice and other services. For example, at a wedding, the church may provide the minister for the service, the music, the decorations, and more. While seemingly similar to the rental activity described above, event hosting is distinct because it involves the provision of significant services in addition to the use of the church's property. Some churches offer event hosting for events that have no religious purpose, such as business meetings or private parties.

Broadcasting activities

Some churches operate radio and television stations licensed by the Federal Communications Commission (FCC). The FCC license may be an "educational" or "noncommercial" license (restricting the content to noncommercial content) or it may be a regular "commercial" license (which permits advertising and other commercial content). Operators of noncommercial television and radio stations may sell noncommercial programming time on the station and/or accept corporate sponsorships as a way to generate revenue. Commercial license operators may sell programming time on the station, corporate sponsorships, and/or spots for regular commercials.

ISSUES TO CONSIDER: MISSION AND PURPOSE

Surprisingly, many churches embark on the conduct of alternative revenue source activities without much thought for whether the activities are "on mission" for the church or not. In fact, as addressed in Chapter 1, many churches do not have a clearly defined and specific expression of mission and purpose—which can make it impossible to determine whether a given activity is "on mission." Such considerations should be the starting place for any church contemplating an alternative source revenue activity. If the church does not have a clear and specific sense of mission and purpose, developing and expressing that is the first step. (See Chapter 1 for more details on the topic of Mission and Purpose.)

"Watershed" criteria

There really are only two possible valid motivations for a church to engage in a particular revenue-generating activity, and at least one of them should be present to justify further consideration of an activity by the church. The activity should:

(a) significantly help the church advance its mission and purpose,
(b) generate significant net income or positive cash flow for the church, or
(c) do both of the above.

Some churches will not consider an activity that does not meet the first criterion, regardless of whether it meets the second criterion—a position which is understandable.

In addition to the "watershed" criteria described above, churches should evaluate other aspects of a proposed activity before conducting it. Any church considering generating income from an alternative revenue source should do so utilizing a rubric that takes into consideration questions such as the following:

(1) Does conducting the activity help the church carry out its stated mission and purpose? If so, how, and to what extent? Is the activity's positive impact in carrying out the church's mission and purpose truly expected to be significant and worth the effort? What are the metrics for success in this context, and how will they be measured?

(2) Does the church believe that the financial impact of conducting the activity will be significantly positive for the church? If the analysis in #1 is such that the activity is not expected to contribute significantly to the church's overall mission and purpose, is the church's motivation for interest in the activity to generate net income or positive cash flow for the church?

(3) What are the expected financial outcomes of the activity and how well can we predict them? Does conducting the activity present significant financial risk to the church?

(4) Have we adequately evaluated the legal implications of conducting the activity? (See Legal Considerations for Alternative Source Revenue Activities in the section below.)

(5) Have we adequately evaluated the tax implications of conducting the activity? (See Tax

Considerations for Alternative Source Revenue Activities in the section below.)

(6) Can we adequately insure for the risks related to the activity?

(7) Are there public relations risks associated with the activity?

(8) Are there other risks associated with the activity?

(9) Do we have the leadership, management, and staff capacity to adequately conduct, account for, and oversee the activity?

(10) Are the potential risks and disadvantages of conducting the activity outweighed by the expected benefits to the church—either financially or in terms of accomplishing the church's mission and purpose?

LEGAL IMPLICATIONS OF REVENUE-GENERATING ACTIVITIES

There are a number of important legal issues that should be carefully considered before pursuing these or similar activities. These include:

- zoning law
- legal liability
- "public accommodation" nondiscrimination laws
- insurance

Zoning law

Church leaders need to consider the possible application of local zoning laws before pursuing a revenue-generating activity. Most municipalities in the United States have enacted zoning laws. The purpose of a municipal zoning law is:

> to regulate the growth and development of the city in an orderly manner. Among the objectives to be served is to avoid mixing together of industrial, commercial, business and residential uses; the prevention of undue concentrations of people in certain areas under undesirable conditions; making provisions for safe and efficient transportation; for recreational needs; and for the enhancement of aesthetic values, all in order to best serve the purpose of promoting the health, safety, morals and general welfare of the city and its inhabitants.[1]

1 *Naylor v. Salt Lake City Corporation, 410 P.2d 764, 765 (Utah 1966).*

The typical zoning ordinance divides a municipality into zones or districts in which only certain activities or uses are permitted. For example, it is common for a municipal zoning ordinance to divide a municipality into residential, commercial, and industrial districts, with the activities and uses permitted in each district described in the ordinance. Nonconforming uses and activities may be authorized in some cases through variances, special use permits, or by the fact that the nonconforming use preceded the enactment of the zoning ordinance.

Historically, churches presented few problems for municipal planners. Churches were allowed in residential districts so that they would be within walking distance of parishioners' residences. It was unthinkable to locate churches anywhere else. Most municipalities still permit churches in residential zones. With the advent of the automobile, churches became more incompatible with residential districts for two reasons. First, most parishioners drive their automobiles to church, making it less essential for churches to locate within walking distance of their membership. Second, on at least one day each week, the church is the biggest source of traffic congestion, noise, and pollution in many residential neighborhoods. For a growing number of churches, this is becoming true on several days of the week due to additional church services, youth activities, weddings, funerals, child care, rehearsals, civic events, and programs for the poor and elderly. Understandably, many municipalities have reconsidered the traditional view of allowing churches in residential zones without restriction.

This process of reconsidering the proper location of churches within a modern-day community has resulted in a number of views. Most municipalities continue to allow churches in residential zones, but many require churches to obtain a permit prior to obtaining and using property in a residential zone. The permit procedure gives municipal planners greater control over the location of churches within residential zones. Some municipal zoning ordinances prohibit churches in any residential zone, and a few municipalities have attempted to bar churches altogether.

When a church operates a revenue-raising activity on its premises, the issue of zoning law is always implicated. The question is whether the activity is a permissible use under the local zoning law. That is, if a church is located in a residential zone, can it operate what amounts to a "commercial" activity on its premises, or allow a member of a third party to do so?

Many zoning laws permit uses that are "accessory" to a permitted use. As one court has observed:

> *A church is more than merely an edifice affording people the opportunity to worship God. Strictly religious uses and activities are more than prayer and sacrifice and all churches recognize that the area of their responsibility is broader than leading the congregation in prayer. Churches have always developed social groups for adults and youth where the fellowship of the congregation is strengthened with the result that the parent church is strengthened. To limit a church to being merely a house of prayer and sacrifice would, in a large degree, be depriving the church of the opportunity of enlarging, perpetuating, and strengthening itself and the congregation.[2]*

To illustrate, one court upheld a church's right to construct a recreational complex on property adjacent to its sanctuary despite the claim of neighboring landowners that the complex was not a church and thus should not be permitted in a residential district.[3] The court concluded that the term *church* "is broader than the church building itself" and must be interpreted to include "uses customarily incidental or accessory to church uses . . . if reasonably closely related, both in distance and space, to the main church purpose." The court upheld the use of the recreational complex since the activities conducted on the field were an integral part of the church's overall program.

Other courts have found that the following uses were accessory to a permitted church use and therefore were appropriate in a residential district:

- a church activities building and playground;[4]
- a kindergarten play area;[5]
- a parking lot;[6]

- residential use of church buildings by members;[7]
- a home for parochial school teachers;[8]
- a school;[9]
- a commercial day-care center;[10]
- a neon sign constructed on church property to inform the public the time of worship services;[11]
- a center for performing arts;[12]
- a sanctuary or shelter for the homeless.[13]

Not every use of church property, however, will be so approved. The following uses of church property have been disallowed on the ground that they were not accessory to a permitted church use:

- parking of a church bus on church property;[14]
- a ritualarium constructed by a Jewish synagogue;[15]
- a 301-foot radio transmission tower that was more than 10 times higher than neighboring residences;[16]
- a school.[17]

CASE STUDY. The Alabama Supreme Court ruled that a church could not create a parking lot on land located across the street from the church. A church purchased land across the street from the church building in order to expand its parking facilities. Neighboring landowners complained that such a use of the property was not permitted by local zoning law. A local zoning board ruled in favor of the church. It reasoned that churches were permitted uses in the area in question, and that a church parking lot should be permitted as an "accessory use" by a church. The neighbors appealed to a state appeals court, which reversed the decision of the zoning

2   Cash v. Brookshire United Methodist Church, 573 N.E.2d 692 (Ohio App. 1988).
3   Corporation of the Presiding Bishop v. Ashton, 448 P.2d 185 (Ida. 1968).
4   Board of Zoning Appeals v. New Testament Bible Church, Inc., 411 N.E.2d 681 (Ind. 1980).
5   Diocese of Rochester v. Planning Board, 154 N.Y.S.2d 849 (1956).
6   Mahrt v. First Church of Christ, Scientist, 142 N.E.2d 567 (Ohio 1955), aff'd, 142 N.E.2d 678 (Ohio 1955).

7   Havurah v. Zoning Board of Appeals, 418 A.2d 82 (Conn. 1979).
8   Board of Zoning Appeals v. New Testament Bible Church, Inc., 411 N.E.2d 681 (Ind. 1980).
9   City of Concord v. New Testament Baptist Church, 382 A.2d 377 (N.H. 1978); Westbury Hebrew Congregation, Inc. v. Downer, 302 N.Y.S.2d 923 (1969); Diocese of Rochester v. Planning Board, 154 N.Y.S.2d 849 (1956).
10 Noah's Ark Christian Child Care Center v. Zoning Hearing Board, 831 A.2d 756 (Pa. Common. 2003).
11 Parkview Baptist Church v. Pueblo, 336 P.2d 310 (Colo. 1959).
12 North Shore Hebrew Academy v. Wegman, 481 N.Y.S.2d 142 (1984).
13 St. John's Evangelical Lutheran Church v. City of Hoboken, 479 A.2d 935 (N.J. App. 1983); Lubavitch Chabad House of Illinois, Inc. v. City of Evanston, 445 N.E.2d 343 (Ill. App. 1982); Greentree at Murray Hill Condominium v. Good Shepherd Episcopal Church, 550 N.Y.S.2d 981 (1989).
14 East Side Baptist Church v. Klein, 487 P.2d 549 (Colo. 1971).
15 Sexton v. Bates, 85 A.2d 833 (N.J. 1951), aff'd, 91 A.2d 162 (N.J. 1952).
16 Gallagher v. Zoning Board of Adjustment, 32 Pa. D. & C.2d 669 (Pa. 1963).
17 Damascus Community Church v. Clackamas County, 610 P.2d 273 (Ore. 1980), appeal dismissed, 450 U.S. 902 (1981).

board and prohibited the church from establishing the parking lot. The case was then appealed to the state supreme court, which agreed with the appeals court that the parking lot should not be allowed. The court noted that the local zoning ordinance defined an accessory use as a use "on the same lot with" the principal use or structure. The court concluded that "the definition of accessory use in the ordinance is consistent with the general rule that the accessory use must be located on the same lot as the building to which it is accessory." Since the proposed parking lot was across the street from the church, it was not "on the same lot" and accordingly could not be permitted as an accessory use.[18]

CASE STUDY. The Missouri Supreme Court ruled that a church-run child care center is a permissible activity on church property zoned exclusively for church or residential purposes. The court acknowledged that the zoning ordinance did not allow child care facilities in the neighborhood in which the church was located, but it concluded that such an activity was a permissible "accessory" use. The court observed: "The day care program is subordinate to the principal use of the church. It was created by the governing body of the church and funded by the church. The governing body determined the curriculum for the program and hired a director. The record shows that the church operates the day care to attract new members to the church and accomplish its mission of preaching the gospel and serving the community. Similarly, the day care is subordinate in area to the principal building and use of the church. The day care service contributes to the comfort and convenience of the church parishioners by providing child care for them. The day care proper is located on the same lot as the church and it is located in the same zoning district." Accordingly, the child care center was an accessory use of the church under Missouri law and was a permissible use of church property.[19]

---

18 *Ex parte Fairhope Board of Adjustments and Appeals,* 567 So.2d 1353 (Ala. 1990).

19 *City of Richmond Heights v. Richmond Heights Presbyterian Church,* 764 S.W.2d 647 (Mo. 1989). Accord *Shim v. Washington Township Planning Board,* 689 A.2d 804 (N.J. Super. 1997) ("What is clear from this modern trend is that a church's ministry is not confined to prayer or dissemination of its religious beliefs. Religious institutions consider day care centers as part of their spiritual mission, not necessarily in advancing their religious teachings, but by providing a valuable community service. Grounded on this broad-based commitment, we are persuaded that a church-operated day care center is . . . an incidental use of church facilities.")

Communications Towers on Church Property

Many churches have allowed telecommunications companies to construct antennae on church property in exchange for a monthly rental fee. Such arrangements raise a number of legal and tax issues, including those listed below. It is essential for church leaders to discuss these issues with a local attorney before entering into an agreement with a telecommunications company to erect an antenna on church property.

- Terms and conditions. Be sure to have an attorney review the rental agreement before you sign it. Usually, these agreements are very one-sided in favor of the communications company. There should be a definite term, with renegotiation of rental payments on a periodic basis. Also, the church should have the right to terminate the contract at specified intervals for any reason. Many churches have signed rental agreements that they soon regret.

- Zoning law. Is the construction of a telecommunications antenna on church property consistent with the classification of the property under local zoning law? The few courts that have addressed this question have suggested that zoning laws would not be violated by such a use of church property.[1]

- Property tax exemption. It is possible that the use of church property for a telecommunications antenna would jeopardize the exemption of the property from local property taxes. In many states, an exemption from property taxes is conditioned on the fact that the property is not used for the generation of income. Loss of exempt status ordinarily will be limited to the portion of a church's property that is actually being used for the production of income rather than to the entire premises. However, in some states a church may lose an exemption for all of its property though only a small amount is used for an antenna.

- Unrelated business income. Federal law imposes a tax (equal to the corporate income tax) on the net income generated by a tax-exempt organization from any unrelated trade or business that is "regularly carried on." This tax is called the unrelated business income tax (or UBIT for short). There are a number of exemptions, including rental income. However, in order to be exempt from UBIT, the rental income must be from the rental of a debt-free facility. In 1998, the IRS ruled that rental fees received by charities for the erection of telecommunications towers on their property were exempt from UBIT. However, the IRS revoked this ruling in 2001 and concluded that rents received by charities for the use of communications towers or antennae constructed on their property are subject to the unrelated business income tax. The IRS limited its ruling to "receipts attributable solely to the rental of the broadcasting tower." This suggests that the rental of a specified area of church property on which a communications tower is erected may be partially or wholly exempt from the unrelated business income tax. The IRS did not specifically address this issue in its 2001 ruling.[2]

---

1 See, e.g., *AT&T Wireless PCS, Inc. v. City Council,* 979 F. Supp. 416 (E.D. Va. 1997).
2 *IRS Letter Ruling 200104031.*

CASE STUDY. A Pennsylvania state court ruled that a local zoning board acted improperly in refusing to allow a church to use a portion of its property for counseling services. The church sought a permit allowing it to convert a building containing the church offices into a counseling center. The church offered extensive pastoral counseling services to members and non-members alike. A zoning board denied the church's request on the ground that professional counseling was not a permitted use in a residential district (in which the church was located). The board expressed the view that "the counseling sought to be offered was of a secular nature and not directly related to the church's function." The church challenged this ruling in court, and won. The court ruled that the church's properties could lawfully be used for counseling since "counseling is an integral part of the church's activities" and therefore was a permissible "church use."[20]

LEGAL LIABILITY

Many uses of church property as a source of revenue involve persons coming onto the church's premises as workers or customers. Injuries can occur on church premises in a number of ways, including slips and falls, and assaults in a church parking lot.

In most states, the liability of a church for injuries caused on its premises depends upon the status of the victim, since the degree of care which a church must exercise in safeguarding and inspecting its premises depends entirely upon the status of the victim. Most courts hold that a person may be on another's property as an *invitee*, a *licensee*, or a *trespasser*. An *invitee* may be either a public invitee or a business visitor. Section 332 of the *Restatement (Second) of Torts*, which has been adopted in many states, specifies that:

(a) An invitee is either a public invitee or a business visitor.

(b) A public invitee is a person who is invited to enter or remain on land as a member of the public for a purpose for which the land is held open to the public.

(c) A business visitor is a person who is invited to enter or remain on land for a purpose directly or indirectly connected with business dealings with the possessor of the land.

Churches owe the greatest duty of care to *invitees*, since invitees by definition are on a landowner's property because of an express or implied invitation. Most courts hold that property owners owe invitees a duty to use reasonable and ordinary care to keep their premises safe, including the responsibility of correcting those concealed hazards of which they know or reasonably should know, or at least warning invitees of such hazards.

A landowner is not a guarantor of the safety of invitees. So long as a landowner exercises reasonable care in making the premises safe for invitees or if adequate warning is given about concealed perils, a landowner will not be responsible for injuries that occur.

Many courts have refused to hold landowners responsible for an invitee's injuries caused by an obvious hazard or by a concealed hazard of which the invitee was aware.

A few states in recent years have abandoned the prevailing view of assessing a landowner's liability for injuries occurring on his premises by focusing on the status of the victim. These states have substituted a simple standard of reasonable care that a landowner owes to all lawful visitors. In determining a landowner's liability, the status of a victim is still relevant but not controlling. For example, the fact that an injured victim was a trespasser will reduce the landowner's duty of care since a reasonable person would not take the same steps to ensure the safety of trespassers that he would for invitees.

The great majority of cases involving accidents on church property have determined the church's liability on the basis of the status of the victim. Often, an accident victim's recovery of monetary damages against the church depends on his or her characterization as an invitee by a court, since this status creates the highest duty of care on the part of the church. If the victim is deemed to be a mere licensee, then often any monetary recovery is precluded. Many courts have concluded that accident victims are invitees of a church. There is little doubt that persons coming onto church property to patronize a revenue-rais-

---

20 *Church of the Savior v. Zoning Hearing Board*, 568 A.2d 1336 (Pa. Common. 1989). See also *Needham Pastoral Counseling Center, Inc. v. Board of Appeals*, 557 N.E.2d 43 (Mass. App. 1990).

ing venture will be deemed invitees by the courts, imposing upon the church the highest duty of care.

Churches often let outside groups use their premises. Examples include scout troops, preschools, aerobics classes, substance abuse groups, childbirth classes, and music classes. Some courts have found churches liable for injuries occurring on their premises while being used by such groups so long as they maintained "control" over their premises while the outside group was present.

CASE STUDY. An Indiana court ruled that a church was liable for an injury occurring on its premises while being used by an outside group. A church permitted a local community group to use its facilities for an annual one-day celebration. The event was advertised in the church bulletin, and included a religious ceremony. After the ceremony, guests were ushered into another room for a reception where refreshments were served. While refreshments were being served, volunteers disassembled the tables and chairs in the room where the ceremony occurred. Although the guests were asked to proceed to the reception immediately following the ceremony, a few guests remained behind to socialize. As one of these guests proceeded to the reception area a few minutes later, she tripped and fell over some of the disassembled tables. She later sued the church. The church claimed that it was not responsible for the guest's injuries since it had not retained any control over its facilities while they were being used by the community group for its celebration. The church also pointed out that the group was permitted to use the facilities without charge, that it was responsible for cleaning up the facilities following its activities, and that the church did not retain any control over the facilities during the celebration. A state appeals court noted that "the church is correct in observing that control of the premises is the basis of premises liability." However, the court concluded that there was ample evidence of control by the church. It observed: "[The priest] testified . . . that if he chose to do so, he could have decided not to allow the [community group] to hold their function there; that there was a janitor on the premises to make sure the buildings were locked; that the [organization] was

not in charge of securing the premises; that the church placed an announcement in the church bulletin regarding when and where the celebration was to take place; that the church conducted a religious ceremony as a part of the celebration; and that he would not say that the church relinquished control over the property. This testimony was enough to create an issue of fact as to whether the church retained control over the premises."[21]

CASE STUDY. Can a charity be legally responsible for an injury occurring on its premises while being used by an outside group? That was the question addressed by a Louisiana court in a recent decision. A charity permitted an outside group to use its facility for a Christmas party. During the party, a woman suffered serious injuries when she fell on a slippery floor. As a result of her injuries, the woman underwent surgery for a complete hip replacement. She later sued the charity, claiming that it was responsible for her injuries because it had retained control over the premises during the party. She claimed that the floor was unreasonably slippery, and this dangerous condition caused her to fall. One witness testified, "It was obvious that floor was slippery. It was just waxed or something. I mean it wasn't dirty. It was clean. Probably too clean." The charity asked the court to dismiss the case, but its request was denied. On appeal, a state appeals court suggested that there was sufficient evidence that the charity retained control over its premises during the party to send the case to a jury. The court began its opinion by acknowledging that a property owner may be legally responsible for injuries that occur on its premises when they are under its custody or control. The court suggested that the charity had retained control over its premises during the Christmas party on the basis of the following factors: (1) the charity was responsible for setting up tables for the party; (2) the charity provided a custodian during the entire party; and (3) the charity was responsible for opening the premises at the beginning of the party and locking the premises at the conclusion of the party. The charity's custodian admitted that he had cleaned the floor prior to the party and

---

21 *St. Casimer Church v. Frankiewics, 563 N.E.2d 1331 (Ind. App. 1990).*

that he was on duty and responsible for cleaning the floor during the party.[22]

NONDISCRIMINATION BY PLACES OF PUBLIC ACCOMMODATION

The federal government, and several states and municipalities, have enacted laws prohibiting discrimination by "places of public accommodation" on the basis of various factors which often include race, national origin, age, gender, religion, and sexual orientation. These laws generally exempt various nonprofit organizations, including churches that provide goods or services to their members but not to the general public. However, by providing goods or services to the general public, any exemption may be lost.

To illustrate, a church allows its sanctuary to be used for weddings only among members of the congregation. It is highly unlikely that such a church would be deemed a place of public accommodation under federal or state nondiscrimination laws. But if that church decides to rent its sanctuary to the general public for marriage ceremonies, as a means of raising much-needed revenue, it is doubtful that its exemption from a public accommodation nondiscrimination law would apply, and this might mean, for example, that it would have to rent its sanctuary to members of the public for the performance of marriage ceremonies even though they violate the church's religious beliefs.

INSURANCE

Churches often allow outside groups to use or lease their premises. Obviously, the use of church property by an outside group exposes the church to potential liability for injuries that may occur, and this risk escalates if the property is being used for an activity that involves minors. Consider the following examples.

- A church leases a portion of its premises one evening per week to a local scout troop.
- A church leases several rooms to an outside group to operate a preschool.

- A church leases a room one morning each week to an outside group for the operation of an exercise class.

Churches respond to this risk in various ways. Many require the outside group to list the church's name as an "additional insured" in its general liability insurance policy. A recent case in New York suggests that this practice may be unavailing, and may lull church leaders into a false sense of security. A church leased a portion of its premises to an outside group for three days to conduct a dance competition. The lease required the group to name the church as an additional insured in its liability insurance policy.

A woman was injured when she fell on a sidewalk while walking from the parking lot behind the church to the front entrance in order to attend the dance competition. She sued the church, claiming that her fall was caused by the church's negligence. The church contacted the outside group's insurer and requested that it provide a legal defense of the victim's claims and indemnification for any verdict or settlement. When the insurer refused, the church asked a court to compel it to do so.

The court noted that the insurance policy defined an "insured" to include any organization to whom the insurer was obligated, by virtue of a written contract, to provide liability insurance, "but only with respect to liability arising out of [its] operations." In other words, the fact that the church was named as an additional insured on the policy did not mean that it was entitled to a legal defense and indemnification against any loss. The section in the policy limiting coverage to liability "arising out of [the insured's] operations" required that there be "some causal relationship between the injury and the risk for which coverage is provided."

The court concluded that the church failed to demonstrate the existence of such a causal relationship. The outside group's "operations" consisted of conducting a dance competition in the auditorium and three classrooms. Bodily injury occurring on a sidewalk outside the leased premises, in an area which the outside group had no responsibility to maintain or repair, "was not a bargained-for risk." Rather, the group's operations at the school merely furnished the occasion for the accident.

---

22 Aufrichtig v. Progressive Men's Club, 634 So.2d 947 (La. App. 2 Cir. 1994).

Use of Church Property by Outside Groups—Checklist

Many churches allow community groups to use their facilities. Before doing so, there are a number of issues that church leaders should consider, including the following:

☐ Have the outside group sign a "facilities use agreement" that (1) provides the group with a mere license to use the property; (2) contains a hold harmless and indemnification clause; (3) states that the church provides no supervision or control over the property when being used by the group. This document should be prepared by an attorney. The agreement should clearly specify that it is a license agreement and not a lease. The church's potential liability for injuries that occur during the use of its property by an outside group will depend to some extent on the nature of the relationship. A license exposes the church to less liability than a lease.

☐ The church should be named as an additional insured under the group's liability policy.

☐ Review the group's liability policy to ensure that it provides adequate coverage, and does not exclude sexual misconduct.

☐ If the outside group's use of the property will involve any participants who are minors (including minor children of participants), then the outside group should warrant that it has exercised a high degree of care in conducting background investigations on all persons who will have access to one or more minors to determine their suitability for working with, or being present with, minors during the outside group's use of the property. The outside group also should warrant that it will use a high degree of care in supervising all activities involving minors during its use of the property under the terms of the agreement.

☐ Check with the church insurer to determine coverage issues in the event the church is sued as a result of an accident or injury occurring during the group's use of the property.

☐ If you deny use of your property to any group because of its religious affiliation, be sure that you are legally permitted to do so under applicable federal, state, and local laws. Many jurisdictions permit religious organizations to discriminate on the basis of religion when allowing outside groups to use their property. Check with an attorney regarding the application of such laws to your church.

☐ The Americans with Disabilities Act prohibits places of public accommodation from discriminating against persons with a disability. The Act exempts religious organizations from this provision. Be sure to see if state and local law contains a similar exemption.

☐ There are several potential violations of copyright law that may arise when an outside group is using the church, including the following: (1) An outside group that plays copyrighted music or shows copyrighted videos or images may be committing copyright infringement. (2) If the outside group makes audio or video recordings containing copyrighted music, this is another possible example of copyright infringement. (3) If a musical group performs a concert in which copyrighted music is performed, then this may result in copyright infringement. At a minimum, the agreement should include a statement making the outside group solely responsible for compliance with copyright law.

☐ The fees received by the church may be subject to the federal "unrelated business income tax." Generally, this tax will not apply unless the rented facilities are subject to "acquisition indebtedness" (a mortgage loan).

☐ The agreement should clarify that the outside group will be solely responsible for the collection of any sales taxes on the sale of any product during its use of the facilities, and that it will indemnify the church for any taxes it is assessed as a result of the outside group's sales occurring on (or a result of) its use of the premises.

☐ The outside group should agree to indemnify not only the church but also the church's officers, agents, and employees from any and all claims or damages in connection with the use of the property by the outside group.

☐ The agreement should contain a non-assignability clause.

☐ The agreement should state that the church does not warrant or represent that the property is safe or suitable for the purposes for which it is permitted to be used under the terms of this agreement, and that the outside group (for itself and on behalf of all of its members, guests, or participants who will be using the property) acknowledge that the church is providing the property and all appliances on an "as is" basis.

☐ The agreement should clarify that the church will bear no liability if the agreement is canceled due to any legal or regulatory compliance issue, such as a zoning ordinance.

4

Other Revenue Sources

Before allowing outside groups to use or lease church property there are several points to consider, including the following:

- Use of church property by an outside group will expose the church to potential liability, especially for activities involving minors.
- There is no way to create a "firewall" that insulates a church from all risk of liability under these circumstances.
- Churches should consider several risk management options before allowing church property to be used by outside groups.
- All general liability insurance policies have a "named insured," which generally is the entity that procured the insurance. The named insured can add one or more other entities as "additional insureds." Having your church's name added as an "additional insured" to the general liability policy of an outside group that uses or leases church property for a specified purpose or activity is one way that a church can manage the risk of liability in the event of an injury. But, as the New York case illustrates, it is not fool-proof. Conditions apply, and church leaders need to be familiar with the conditions so they can accurately evaluate coverage. The last thing you want to do is assume that having your church named as an "additional insured" will create an effective firewall when in fact this is not the case. So, it is important to discuss this option with your insurance agent, and legal counsel, so that you are fully informed concerning the viability of this option for managing risk.
- The risks associated with the use of church property by outside groups can be mitigated in other ways. Some or all of these should be considered, and implemented, to ensure that the church has adequately responded to the risk of liability. Consider the following:

  ☐ Check with the church's insurance carrier to evaluate coverage in the event of an injury during use of church property by an outside group.
  ☐ You must assess the increased risk of legal liability associated with the use of your property by outside groups. Some risks may be too great to even consider, especially when you consider the relatively modest user's fee, if any, that will be assessed.
  ☐ Any activity involving minors represents the highest risk. The outside group must provide evidence of insurance in an amount that is acceptable to you.
  ☐ Have the outside group sign a "facilities use agreement" that (1) provides the group with a mere license to use the property; (2) contains *hold harmless* and *indemnification* clauses; and, (3) states that the church provides no supervision or control over the property when being used by the group. This document should be prepared by an attorney.
  ☐ Review the outside group's liability policy to ensure that it provides adequate coverage. Be certain that it does not exclude sexual misconduct. Also, pay close attention to the coverage limits. Are they adequate?
  ☐ Add the church as an additional insured under the outside group's liability insurance policy. This may not be effective in all cases, but it may be in some, making it worth doing.
  ☐ If the group's activities will involve minors, have a written acknowledgment from the group that all workers have been adequately screened.
  ☐ Note that release forms are generally unenforceable against minors who are injured since they have no contractual capacity to sign such a release and their parents or guardians lack the legal authority to release a minor's legal rights.
  ☐ There are other issues to be considered when a church allows outside groups to use or lease its facilities that are addressed elsewhere in this text, including the application of the federal unrelated business income tax; the loss of the church's exemption from property tax, either fully or on a prorated basis; and the potential violation of local zoning laws.
  ☐ It is highly recommended that a church seek legal counsel when considering the use of church property by one or more outside groups.

Many churches allow outside groups to use or lease their property. It is common for churches to require that an outside group's insurance policy list the church as an additional insured. But as this case illustrates, such a practice will not necessarily provide coverage for the church in the event of an injury, especially one that bears no direct relationship to the nature of the outside group's activities. This can result in an unexpected and potentially significant liability for the church.

The takeaway point is this—church leaders should not agree to the use of their property by outside groups on the assumption that being listed as an additional insured in the outside group's insurance policy will create an effective firewall against church liability. Before allowing outside groups to use or lease church property, discuss the issue of insurance with your insurance agent as well as legal counsel. Make certain you clearly understand the availability of coverage under the outside group's policy, and, on the basis of this information, make an informed decision about allowing the outside group to have access to church property (and whether any additional precautions may be necessary to allow that access).

TAX CONSIDERATIONS

A primary tax consideration for an alternative source revenue activity is whether the activity constitutes an "unrelated business activity" subject to special rules under federal income tax law.

UNRELATED BUSINESS INCOME – THE GENERAL RULES

U.S. federal law imposes an income tax on a church if the church generates net income from one or more unrelated business activities. Congress adopted the tax on unrelated business income ("UBI") primarily for the purpose of eliminating unfair competition between nonprofit, tax-exempt organizations and for-profit, taxable businesses.

An unrelated business activity is a revenue-generating activity that:

- Constitutes a trade or business;
- Is regularly carried on; and

- Is not substantially related to the church's exempt purposes.

The law also considers the activity of generating income from "debt-financed property" to constitute an unrelated business activity (see **Specific Exclusions from Unrelated Business Income** on page 119 for additional information on this topic).

What constitutes a trade or business?

For purposes of the tax on UBI, a trade or business generally includes any activity carried on for the production of income from the sale of goods or performance of services. Ordinarily, a church must have a motive (but not necessarily its primary motive) of generating profit from an activity in order for the activity to be considered a trade or business. Most fundraising activities would meet the definition of a trade or business, since fundraising activities are generally conducted for the purpose of generating additional funds for the church.

> **EXAMPLE.** A church sells T-shirts in connection with its theme of evangelism for the year. Each shirt costs the church $8 and the church sells them to its congregation for $7 each. The T-shirt selling activity is not carried on for the production of income and is not, therefore, a trade or business.

> **EXAMPLE.** A church sells Christmas trees to the public in a high-traffic area during the period leading up to the Christmas holiday. The church conducts this activity each year for the purpose of raising money for its youth ministry. Christmas trees are generally sold for approximately twice the church's cost. The activity of selling Christmas trees is a trade or business, because one of the church's motives is to generate income from the activity.

When is an activity regularly carried on?

In determining whether an activity conducted by a church is regularly carried on, the frequency and continuity of the activity must be addressed. If the activity is of a type normally conducted by taxable, for-profit businesses, the frequency and continuity of the church's activity is compared to the industry norm. An activity will generally be considered to be regularly carried on if the church conducts the activity with a frequency and continuity that is similar to that of the industry.

EXAMPLE. A church conducts an annual bake sale in connection with a county fair that is held each year. At the bake sale, which is open to the public, a variety of cakes, cookies, pastries, and other similar products are promoted and sold. The sale and fair last two weeks each year. In addressing the frequency and continuity of the activity, the church compares its annual bake sale to the activities of the retail baking industry and with retail stores that sell baked goods. The church's activity is conducted for two weeks each year, while the industry norm for taxable businesses is to conduct their activities year-round. Even though the church's bake sale is conducted every year, it is not conducted with a frequency or continuity that is similar to the business industry norm. Therefore, the church's annual bake sale is not regularly carried on.

EXAMPLE. A church sells Christmas trees to the public in a high-traffic area during the period leading up to the Christmas holiday. The church conducts this activity each year for the purpose of raising money for its youth ministry. In addressing the frequency and continuity of the activity, the church compares its annual Christmas tree sale to the activities of for-profit businesses that sell Christmas trees. The for-profit businesses generally sell Christmas trees at the same time of year and for approximately the same duration of time as does the church. The church's Christmas tree-selling activity is regularly carried on.

How does the church determine whether an activity is substantially related to its exempt purposes?
A revenue-generating activity is not considered to be substantially related to a church's exempt purposes merely because the income generated from the activity is used to fund the church's exempt purpose activities. In order to support the position that an activity is substantially related to a church's exempt purposes, the church must show that the conduct of the activity itself (and not the money from it) contributes importantly to the accomplishment of the church's exempt purposes.

In making this determination, the church must first identify its exempt purposes. This often-overlooked area of the law is extremely important. Most churches (and their tax advisors) assume that their exempt purposes are obvious and that the general concept of having a religious purpose is adequate. However, according to IRS regulations, in determining whether an activity contributes importantly to a church's exempt purposes, the IRS looks to "the purposes for which exemption is granted." Accordingly, a church should be very deliberate when it comes to defining the exempt purposes for which it exists. Some of a church's purposes may be religious, some may be educational, and others may be charitable. The church itself establishes the purposes for which it exists, and such purposes are often stated in the church's governing documents (articles of incorporation or charter and bylaws). A church's stated exempt purposes should be drafted broadly so as to include all of its intended purposes and not merely the most common activities of a local church. A church with a more broadly worded purpose statement will be better able to defend a broader array of revenue-generating activities as contributing importantly to its exempt purposes.

> **EXAMPLE.** An example of a **narrowly worded** church purpose statement is:

> *This corporation shall have as its purpose the gathering of a congregation of believers dedicated to the worship and service of Almighty God.*

> **EXAMPLE.** *An example of a more **broadly worded** church purpose statement is:*

> *This corporation is dedicated exclusively to charitable, religious, educational, scientific, and literary purposes. This corporation's primary purpose is to reach people with the Christian gospel message and to disciple Christian believers by and through as many methods and means as possible (including by conduct of public worship; conduct of missions activities; educational activities; creation, sale, and distribution of Christian media; conduct of Christian events; and other related activities) so as to maximize the number of people who may be reached and discipled for the glory of Almighty God. In addition to its primary purpose, the church has the following additional purposes:*

- *Fostering an appreciation for and participation in the performing arts, recognizing that the arts are a gift from Almighty God;*
- *Serving the needs of the poor, the needy, the outcast, the sick, the widow, and the elderly;*
- *Fostering adequate education among both the young and the old; and,*
- *Conducting other activities in keeping with the Great Commission.*

In addition to establishing a sufficiently broad purpose statement, the church should ensure that the relationship between each of its revenue-producing activities and its purposes is clear. In some cases, such as selling Bibles and other overtly religious literature, the relationship may be obvious. In cases where the relationship is not obvious, the church should maintain documentation to support the relationship.

EXAMPLE. A church sells decorative candles in its bookstore during the Christmas season. The church should create and maintain a document approved by a leader of the church with respect to its candle sales stating that the sale of candles in the Christmas season facilitates the celebration and reverence of Christ's birth and the message of hope and deliverance that he brought to earth. The document supports the church's position that the sale of candles contributes importantly to the church's exempt purposes. The document should make specific reference to the stated exempt purpose(s) supported by the activity.

Activities that include some related and some unrelated elements

A church may engage in some revenue-generating activities that include elements that are substantially related to its exempt purposes and others that are not. For example, the church may operate a bookstore that sells Bibles and religious books along with cosmetics. The fact that an activity (such as operating a bookstore) includes both unrelated and related elements does not cause the entire activity to be considered unrelated to the church's exempt purposes. Federal tax law applies a "fragmentation" rule that requires such activities to be separated into their related and unrelated elements. In this example, the sale of cosmetics would be considered *not* substantially related to the church's exempt pur-

poses, while the sale of Bibles and religious books would be substantially related.

Examples of unrelated business activities

Unrelated business activities in a church may include:

- Operating a public restaurant;
- Operating a revenue-generating parking lot;
- Selling non-religious items in a bookstore (such as computers, cosmetics, secular books);
- Providing administrative services to other unrelated organizations for a fee;
- Conducting travel tours that are not adequately religious or educational in nature; or,
- Selling advertising in the church's newsletter.

A church is permitted to conduct an *insubstantial* amount of unrelated business activity. If a church engages in a *substantial* amount of unrelated business activity, the church could lose its tax-exempt status under Section 501(c)(3) of the Internal Revenue Code.

SPECIFIC EXCLUSIONS FROM UNRELATED BUSINESS INCOME

Federal law provides a number of specific exclusions from the tax on unrelated business income. While there are some exceptions with respect to how certain of the exclusions apply, income from the following sources is generally excluded from UBI:

(1) Dividends, interest, annuities, capital gains, and other investment income;
(2) Gains from the sale of property other than inventory;
(3) Royalties;
(4) Rent from real property;
*(**Note:** For income of the types listed in 1 - 4 above, the exclusion does not apply if the income is "debt-financed income" as described further below. Also, special rules apply if interest, annuities, royalties, or rents are received from an entity that is controlled by the organization receiving the income. Churches should consult highly expe-*

rienced tax counsel to assist in addressing the tax implications of such arrangements.)

(5) A trade or business in which substantially all of the work is performed by persons who are not compensated for their work (the "volunteer exception");

(6) A trade or business conducted primarily for the convenience of the church's members, students, officers, or employees (the "convenience of members exception");

(7) A trade or business that consists of selling merchandise, substantially all of which was received by the church as gifts or contributions (the "donated goods exception");

(8) Qualified sponsorship activities; and,

(9) Bingo games that meet certain criteria (the "bingo games exception").

The volunteer exception

Under the volunteer exception (item five above), a trade or business is not an unrelated business activity if "substantially all" of the work conducting the activity is performed by persons who are not compensated. The law is not specific as to the definition of "substantially all." However, court cases and rulings on the issue indicate that 85 percent or more of the hours of work constitutes "substantially all" of the work for this purpose.

> **EXAMPLE.** A church operates a coffee shop in a retail location that is open to the public. The coffee shop is a trade or business that is regularly carried on and its operation is not substantially related to the church's exempt purposes. The coffee shop is operated entirely by unpaid church volunteers, although a minimal amount of work (less than 10 percent) is performed by the church's accounting staff related to the store's recordkeeping. Even though the operation of the coffee shop would ordinarily be an unrelated business activity, the fact that substantially all of the work conducting the activity is performed by volunteers causes the coffee shop not to be an unrelated business activity.

The convenience of members exception

Under the convenience of members exception (item six above), a trade or business is not an unrelated business activity if it is conducted primarily for the convenience of the church's members, students, officers, or employees. For this purpose,

court cases and rulings have interpreted the term "members" to include people who attend or participate in a church's worship services or other activities, regardless of whether they are actually members of the church.

> **EXAMPLE.** A church operates a coffee and pastry kiosk during worship services and other events held at the church's facilities in order to provide refreshments to those attending or participating in the events. Even if operation of the coffee and pastry kiosk meets the ordinary criteria to be an unrelated business activity, it will be excluded in this case, since it is conducted primarily for the convenience of the church's "members."

The donated goods exception

Under the donated goods exception (item seven above), a trade or business of selling merchandise is not an unrelated business activity if "substantially all" of the merchandise sold is donated to the church. Court cases and rulings indicate that "substantially all" for this purpose means 85 percent or more of the merchandise sold.

> **EXAMPLE.** A church operates a thrift shop in a retail location on Main Street. The store is open six days per week on a schedule comparable to that of other retailers in the area. The store's workers are all paid employees of the church. Virtually all of the items sold in the thrift shop are items received by the church as donations. The shop also sells a few items of new clothing because the church is able to purchase and sell those items at a substantial discount. Sales of purchased inventory comprise approximately five percent of the shop's total sales. The church's operation of the thrift shop is not an unrelated business activity because substantially all of the shop's sales consist of merchandise donated to the church.

Qualified sponsorship activities

Revenue received by a church as payment for a qualified sponsorship activity (item eight above) is not unrelated business income. A qualified sponsorship activity is an activity in which an outside party (typically a business) pays a church to sponsor an event or activity conducted by the church and in exchange receives certain limited types of recognition or acknowledgment. As long as the acknowledgment or recognition made by the church of the sponsor meets certain criteria, and the church does not provide the sponsor with a "substantial return benefit," the transaction constitutes a qualified sponsorship activity.

Permissible recognition

The following information about a business sponsor may be displayed, used, recognized, and acknowledged by the church as part of a qualified sponsorship arrangement:

- Name;
- Logos or slogans that do not contain qualitative or comparative descriptions of the sponsor's products, services, facilities, or company;
- Product lines;
- The fact that the sponsor is an exclusive sponsor of all or part of an event or activity;
- A list of locations, telephone numbers, or Internet addresses;
- Value-neutral descriptions, including displays or visual depictions, of the sponsor's product-line or services; and,
- The sponsor's brand or trade names and product or service listings.

Federal regulations state that logos or slogans that are an established part of a sponsor's identity are not considered to contain qualitative or comparative descriptions. Additionally, the display or distribution of a sponsor's product by the sponsor or the church to the general public at the sponsored activity is permissible.

Advertising is not permissible recognition

Advertising provided by the church in exchange for payment is considered a "substantial return benefit" and is not permissible recognition. For this purpose, the term advertising means any message which is broadcast or otherwise transmitted, published, displayed, or distributed and which promotes or markets any trade or business, or any service, facility, or product. Advertising includes messages containing qualitative or comparative language, price information or other indications of savings or value, an endorsement, or an inducement to purchase, sell, or use any company, service, facility, or product. A single message that contains both advertising and an acknowledgment is advertising.

Acknowledgments provided to a business in a church's newsletter, magazine, or other regularly distributed periodical in exchange for payment are not permissible acknowledgments in a qualified sponsorship arrangement. A program or brochure produced and distributed in connection with a specific event is not a periodical for this purpose, and acknowledgments in such a document may be permissible recognition if they meet the criteria set forth above.

Payments for exclusive provider rights are not qualified sponsorship payments

If a church agrees to permit a business to be the exclusive provider of certain types of products or services in connection with the church's activities or events in exchange for a payment, the payment received by the church for the value of that benefit is not a qualified sponsorship payment.

Payments in excess of the value of substantial return benefits

Payments by a sponsor that exceed the fair value of substantial return benefits constitute qualified sponsorship payments if the applicable criteria are met.

> **EXAMPLE.** A business pays a church $20,000 to sponsor a weekend retreat for married couples. The church provides the business with advertising valued at $12,000 in exchange for the payment. Except for the advertising, all other benefits provided to the business in connection with the arrangement are permissible benefits in a qualified sponsorship arrangement. The $8,000 of the payment by the business is a qualified sponsorship payment.

Special note about arrangements that do not meet criteria for qualified sponsorships

If a church receives a payment in a transaction that does not meet the criteria for a qualified sponsorship payment, the income to the church is not automatically unrelated business income. The transaction would need to be evaluated in light of the definition of unrelated business income in order for that determination to be made. For example, if the church received payment from a business in an arrangement in which the church endorsed the business at one event, one time, the payment may not constitute unrelated business income to the church, since the activity is not regularly carried on.

EXAMPLE. First Church has an annual Family Fun Weekend every October. The event consists of a variety of entertainment, games, and other activities. Big Car Dealer enters into a sponsorship agreement with the church in which Big Car Dealer pays the church $20,000. In exchange for the payment, First Church agrees to prominently display Big Car Dealer's name and logo throughout the event and distribute flyers expressing gratitude to Big Car Dealer for its sponsorship and listing its location, website address, and the types of automobiles sold by the dealership. Additionally, First Church agrees to permit Big Car Dealer to park four of its new vehicles at the entrance to the event. The church provides no other benefits to Big Car Dealer. The income of $20,000 received by First Church in this transaction is a qualified sponsorship payment and is not unrelated business income to First Church.

EXAMPLE. The same facts apply as in the previous example, except that in addition to the benefits provided by the church in that example, the church also agrees to permit Big Car Dealer to be the exclusive sponsor of the event. No other businesses are permitted to sponsor the event. The result is the same. The income received by First Church is not unrelated business income. Exclusive sponsorship is a permissible form of recognition in a qualified sponsorship arrangement.

EXAMPLE. First Church has an annual Family Fun Weekend every October. The event consists of a variety of entertainment, games, and other activities. In connection with the event, Great Cola Company pays First Church $10,000 (the fair market

value) for the right to be the exclusive provider of beverages to the church for the event. The church agrees not to procure beverages from any other vendor for the event. The payment by Great Cola Company is not a qualified sponsorship payment because the exclusive provider benefit provided by the church is not a permissible benefit in a qualified sponsorship arrangement. The determination of whether the payment is unrelated business income to the church would have to be made based on the regular definition of unrelated business income and other possible exceptions.

The need for good tax counsel for significant sponsorship arrangements

If a church wishes to generate significant revenue from qualified sponsorship arrangements, it should engage legal counsel to draft a standard sponsorship agreement and tax counsel to ensure that the standard agreement complies with the requirements for qualified sponsorships. Failure to comply with the requirements of the law can cause all or part of the income from the activity to be taxable as unrelated business income to the church.

The bingo games exception

Bingo games are not considered unrelated business activities if they:

- Meet the legal definition of bingo;
- Are legal where they are played; and,
- Are played in a jurisdiction where bingo games are not regularly carried on by for-profit organizations.

A bingo game, as defined by Treasury Regulations, is:

A game of chance played with cards that are generally printed with five rows of five squares each. Participants place markers over randomly called numbers on the cards in an attempt to form a preselected pattern such as a horizontal, vertical, or diagonal line, or all four corners. The first participant to form the preselected pattern wins the game. As used in this section, the term "bingo game" means any game of bingo of the type described above in which wagers are placed, winners are determined, and prizes or other property is distributed in the presence of all persons placing wagers in that game. The term "bingo game" does not refer to any game of chance (including, but not limited to, keno games, dice games, card games, and lotteries) other than the type of game described in this paragraph.

EXAMPLE. Sycamore Church conducts bingo games each Friday night in Busy City, in which people buy bingo cards and try to be the first contestant to fill a row of spaces on the cards when numbers are called. The winner of each game wins a prize that is distributed at the event. Bingo is legal in Busy City, but only for nonprofit organizations. Income from Sycamore Church's bingo activity is not unrelated business income because it qualifies for the bingo games exception.

EXAMPLE. Sycamore Church also sells scratch-off tickets during its Friday bingo nights in Busy City. Players buy individual "$100 Bingo" scratch-off tickets in the hope that each one is a winner. Most tickets are losers. Selling scratch-off tickets is legal in Busy City, but only for nonprofit organizations and the state government. Income from the sale of the scratch-off tickets does not qualify for the bingo games exception, since the scratch-off game does not meet the legal definition of bingo. It does not matter that the game is labeled "$100 bingo." The determination of whether the income is unrelated business income to the church would have to be made based on the regular definition of unrelated business income and other possible exceptions.

DEBT-FINANCED INCOME

The federal tax laws and regulations related to debt-financed income are quite technical and complex. A church that believes it may have debt-financed income or that wants to proactively prevent or minimize it should consult knowledgeable tax counsel as early in the process as possible. In many cases, good planning may reduce or eliminate a significant tax liability that could otherwise occur.

As stated previously, investment income such as interest, dividends, rents, royalties, and capital gains are ordinarily excluded from unrelated business income.

The ordinary exclusion does not apply, however, if such income is generated from "debt-financed property."

Debt-financed property

According to federal regulations, debt-financed property is property held to produce income (including a gain on sale) for which there is "acquisition indebtedness" at any time during the tax year or during the 12-month period prior to the date the property is sold.

Acquisition indebtedness

Acquisition indebtedness is debt incurred:

- When acquiring or improving the property;
- Before acquiring or improving the property if the debt would not have been incurred were it not for the acquisition or improvement; or,
- After acquiring or improving the property if:

  - The debt would not have been incurred were it not for the acquisition or improvement; and,

  - Incurring the debt was reasonably foreseeable when the property was acquired or improved.

In other words, acquisition indebtedness is debt that is incurred because the church acquired or improved certain property, regardless of whether the debt was incurred before or at the time the church acquired or improved the property. Debt incurred *after* the acquisition or improvement of certain property could also be acquisition indebtedness if it is incurred because of the acquisition or improvement *and* it was "reasonably foreseeable" that the church would incur the debt when the property was acquired or improved.

Collateralization is not relevant

In determining whether debt is acquisition indebtedness, it does not matter whether it is collateralized by the property in question. The relevant question is why the debt was incurred—not what serves as collateral for it.

EXAMPLE. A church has a campus in Town A and owns 20 acres of vacant land in neighboring Town B. The church has no outstanding debt. The church borrows $1 million to buy a new parcel of property near its campus in Town A. In doing so, the church uses the 20 acres it owns in Town B as collateral for the new loan. The new property it acquires in Town A is not mortgaged and does not serve as collateral for the new loan. The new loan represents acquisition indebtedness with respect to the newly acquired parcel, even though the newly acquired parcel is not collateral for the loan, because the debt was incurred to acquire the new parcel. The debt is **not** acquisition indebtedness with respect to the 20 acres in Town B, even though that 20-acre property is collateral for the loan, because the debt was incurred to acquire the new parcel, not the 20-acre parcel the church already owned.

Special rules for identification and tracing of indebtedness

Complex issues may arise in determining whether indebtedness was incurred in connection with the acquisition and improvement of property when debt is refinanced, consolidated with other debt, or when a borrower engages in other similar actions. Federal tax law contains rules governing the manner in which the identity of debt related to a specific property is tracked, or traced, when such transactions occur. The tracing rules and process are extremely complex and should definitely be addressed by knowledgeable tax counsel.

EXAMPLE. First Church buys its first property in Year 1 for $1 million and incurs debt of $800,000 in doing so. In Year 2, First Church acquires a second parcel of land for $500,000. At the time First Church acquires the second parcel, the debt related to the first parcel has been paid down to $700,000. First Church obtains a new loan in the amount of $1.1 million to pay off the original loan and provide financing for the new property. In the new loan, $400,000 (the additional principal borrowed) represents acquisition indebtedness with respect to the second parcel and $700,000 of it relates to the first property acquired. Subsequent principal payments on the combined note must be allocated between the two properties in conformity with federal tax rules for purposes of determining remaining acquisition indebtedness.

Special exception for educational institutions

A special exception (effectively, an exemption) to the ordinary rules for acquisition indebted-

ness exists in the law for organizations that are specifically classified by the Internal Revenue Service as educational institutions and for certain organizations related to such educational institutions. An organization classified by the IRS as an educational institution should have an IRS determination letter indicating that the organization is described in Section 170(b)(1)(A)(ii) of the Internal Revenue Code. This exception would not apply to a church, but it might apply to an entity that is affiliated with a church, such as a school, if that entity is classified by the IRS as an educational institution. The special exception for educational institutions involves several technical criteria which must be met and which should be evaluated by tax counsel.

Exception for property used for exempt purposes

Property used by a church exclusively for exempt purposes is not debt-financed property, regardless of the existence of acquisition indebtedness. Additionally, if "substantially all" (85 percent or more) of the use of the property is substantially related to the church's exempt purposes, the property is excluded from debt-financed property. The measurement of exempt use and total use may be made by time, space, or a combination of the two. If a church uses property with acquisition indebtedness less than 85 percent for exempt purposes, the portion of the property used for exempt purposes is *not* debt-financed property and the remainder is, unless another exception in the law applies.

EXAMPLE. Second Church owns a building that it acquired with debt financing. The building has 10,000 square feet of space. The church uses all of the space for church activities except a 1,000-square-foot space that it rents to a local restaurant. The building is not debt-financed property because the church uses 90 percent of the building for exempt purposes.

EXAMPLE. Second Church owns a building that it acquired with debt financing. The building has 10,000 square feet of space. The church uses all of the space for church activities except a 3,000-square-foot space that it rents to a local restaurant. This means 7,000 square feet, or 70 percent of the building, is **not** debt-financed property. The 3,000 square feet (30 percent) of the building rented to the restaurant is debt-financed property, and the rental income received is debt-financed income unless another exception in the law applies.

Sale of debt-financed property not used for exempt purposes

A church can incur a significant tax liability if it sells debt-financed property that is not used for exempt purposes and generates a gain from the sale. This is an often-overlooked area of the law.

> **EXAMPLE.** Oak Church buys a vacant parcel of land for $1 million in Year 1 and incurs debt in the amount of $800,000 in so doing with the intent of using the property for exempt purposes at some time in the future. The church never uses the property for exempt purposes. In Year 10, Oak Church sells the property for $10 million at a time when the remaining acquisition indebtedness is $500,000. Oak Church will incur a substantial tax liability related to its $9 million gain.

Exception for property used in certain activities

Debt-financed property does not include property that is used to conduct any of the following activities for which the income is exempt from unrelated business income (see the section titled **Specific Exclusions from Unrelated Business Income** above for descriptions of these activities):

- A trade or business in which substantially all of the work is performed by persons who are not compensated for their work (the "volunteer exception");
- A trade or business conducted primarily for the convenience of the church's members, students, officers, or employees (the "convenience of members exception"); or,
- A trade or business that consists of selling merchandise, substantially all of which was received by the church as gifts or contributions (the "donated goods exception").

The neighborhood land rule exception

If a church acquires property with debt financing and intends to use the *land* for exempt purposes within 15 years of the acquisition date, the property will not be considered debt-financed property. This special rule applies only if the plan to use the property for exempt purposes requires demolition of any buildings or structures on the property. A church relying on the neighborhood land rule to exclude rental income from debt-financed income may not abandon its plan to convert the land to exempt use. In the event the church does abandon its plan, the neighborhood land rule exception fails to apply from that point forward.

Additionally, if the church has not converted the land to exempt use within 5 years of the acquisition date, the church must notify the IRS that it is relying on the neighborhood land rule at the end of the fifth year and provide to the IRS information and documents supporting its claimed intent. The IRS will rule as to whether the church may continue to rely on the neighborhood land rule for the remainder of the allowable period (up to a total of 15 years). Even if the IRS does not rule favorably on the request, if the church ultimately does convert the land to exempt use within the allowable period in conformity with the neighborhood land rule, the rule will apply retroactively as if the IRS issued a favorable ruling at the end of the fifth year.

Special note regarding unique treatment for churches

The neighborhood land rule is so-named because in order for it to apply to exempt organizations other than churches, the property acquired must be in the "neighborhood" of the organization's existing exempt-use property. That rule does not apply to churches. Additionally, the maximum allowable period for which the neighborhood land rule can apply for non-church organizations is 10 years, instead of the 15-year period that applies to churches.

As is the case with other aspects of the debt-financed income rules, the neighborhood land rule involves a number of technical requirements and conditions that should be assessed by knowledgeable tax counsel.

> **EXAMPLE.** Pine Church acquires an office building with debt financing at the beginning of Year 1 and rents the office space to commercial tenants. Pine Church intends to demolish the office

4

Other Revenue Sources

building before the end of Year 15 and construct a new education building on the property to be used exclusively for exempt purposes. At the end of Year 5, Pine Church notifies the IRS of its intent and provides the IRS with plans and drawings showing its progress toward using the property for exempt purposes within the allowable 15-year period. The IRS issues a ruling stating that Pine Church may continue to rely on the neighborhood land rule through Year 15. At the beginning of Year 12, the office building is demolished and Pine Church builds an education building on the property which is used exclusively for exempt purposes. The rental income received by Pine Church for the entire 11-year period prior to demolition is not debt-financed income because of the neighborhood land rule.

EXAMPLE. Pine Church acquires an office building with debt financing at the beginning of Year 1 and rents the office space to commercial tenants. Pine Church intends to demolish the office building before the end of Year 15 and construct a new education building on the property to be used exclusively for exempt purposes. At the end of Year 5, Pine Church notifies the IRS of its intent and provides the IRS with plans and drawings showing its progress toward using the property for exempt purposes within the allowable 15-year period. The IRS does **not** issue a favorable ruling stating that Pine Church may continue to rely on the neighborhood land rule through Year 15. Pine Church begins to treat its rental income from the property as debt-financed income beginning in Year 6. At the beginning of Year 12, the office building is demolished and Pine Church builds an education building on the property which is used exclusively for exempt purposes. The rental income received by Pine Church for the entire 11-year period prior to demolition is not debt-financed income because of the neighborhood land rule. Since the church treated the income as debt-financed income for Years 6 through 11, the church may file amended returns and obtain a refund of all taxes paid on the income during that period.

Calculation of debt-financed income subject to tax

In most cases, not all of the net income generated from debt-financed property is actually taxable. The amount that is taxable is based on the amount of applicable debt and the church's basis in the property.

Calculation of unrelated debt-financed income from regular activity (such as rental income)

In determining how much income (such as rental income) is actually unrelated debt-financed income with respect to a specific property, the church needs to know the *average* amount of acquisition indebtedness that was outstanding during the applicable tax year and the *average* tax basis (as defined in the regulations) of the property for the period during the tax year that it held the property. The amount of the rental income that is considered unrelated debt-financed income is determined by multiplying the rental income by the ratio of the average acquisition indebtedness to the average tax basis of the property.

EXAMPLE. Hickory Church owns a building that is debt-financed and rents it to a commercial tenant for $100,000 per year. For the year20XX, Hickory Church had average acquisition indebtedness related to the building of $600,000 and its average tax basis for the building was $1 million. The ratio of the average acquisition indebtedness to the average tax basis is 60 percent. Therefore, 60 percent of the rental income, or $60,000, is considered unrelated gross debt-financed income. The church would also apply the 60 percent ratio to allowable expenses associated with the building's rental activity to determine the expenses that are deductible against the gross revenue of $60,000 in arriving at net unrelated taxable income (or loss) from the activity.

Calculation of unrelated debt-financed income from the sale of property

In determining how much gain from the sale of debt-financed property is actually unrelated debt-financed income with respect to the property, the church needs to know the *highest* amount of acquisition indebtedness that was outstanding during the 12-month period preceding the date of the sale and the *average* tax basis (as defined in the regulations) of the property for the period during the tax year that it held the property. The amount of gain that is considered unrelated debt-financed income is determined by multiplying the gain from the sale by the ratio of the highest acquisition indebtedness to the average tax basis of the property.

> **EXAMPLE.** Oak Church buys a vacant parcel of land for $1 million in Year 1 and incurs $800,000 in debt with the intent of using the property for exempt purposes at some time in the future. The church never uses the property for exempt purposes. At the end of Year 10, Oak Church sells the property for $10 million. The church's acquisition indebtedness related to the property was $600,000 at the beginning of Year 10 and had been paid down to $500,000 by the end of Year 10 when the property was sold. The church's average tax basis for the property was its original purchase price of $1 million. The church has a gain on the sale of the property of $9 million (the difference between the sales price of $10 million and the church's basis for the property of $1 million). The highest acquisition indebtedness related to the property during Year 10 was $600,000. The ratio of the highest acquisition indebtedness to the average tax basis is 60 percent. Therefore, 60 percent of the gain (or $5.4 million) is taxable as unrelated debt-financed income. (At current regular federal corporate tax rates, the federal income tax on the gain would be approximately $1.8 million. It is likely that state corporate income tax would also apply.)

◉ **PLANNING POINTER:** *If Oak Church had paid off the acquisition debt 13 months before it closed on the sale of the property, <u>none</u> of the gain would have been taxable. This is an example of where good tax planning could have resulted in very substantial tax savings!*

FEDERAL AND STATE FILING REQUIREMENTS AND TAX RATES

When a church generates more than $1,000 of gross revenue from unrelated business activities, the church is required to file a federal income tax return (Form 990-T). Form 990-T is due by the 15th day of the 5th month after the church's year-end (May 15 for a church operating on the calendar year) and may be extended for up to six months.

On Form 990-T, the church reports the revenue from its unrelated business activities and the expenses related to generating the revenue are deducted. If the revenue exceeds the deductible expenses, the church has net income from its unrelated business activities, which is subject to federal tax. If the church is incorporated (i.e., it is a corporation, as are most churches in the U.S.) the regular U.S. corporate income tax rates apply.

Most states require a church that files Form 990-T to file a state income tax return as well, and if the church generates net income as calculated under state law, the church will likely also owe state income taxes calculated at applicable state income tax rates.

Implications for state and local taxes other than income taxes

When a church engages in *any* trade or business activity, whether it generates unrelated business income or not, it should consider the possible tax implications in other jurisdictions. For example, selling goods or services may subject the church to state sales tax laws, requiring the church to collect and remit sales tax on transactions subject to the tax. Renting property to tenants may result in similar obligations.

Laws in some states that provide property tax exemptions for churches require that property be used exclusively for exempt purposes in order to qualify for exemption. Where that is the case, a church that engages in a trade or business activity or that rents out its property to others should determine whether the conduct of the activity could adversely affect its exemption. The definition of exempt use of property for property tax exemption purposes is state-specific and is often different from the definition of exempt-purpose activity under federal income tax law.

It is possible, therefore, that engaging in *any* trade or business, including an unrelated business activity, could adversely affect a church's exemptions under various state or local laws and ordinances. Churches should consult with their tax counsel and/or with state and local tax authorities in addressing such matters. Some information may be available on the websites of state departments of revenue or local/county property tax authorities.

4

Other Revenue Sources

Calculating and minimizing net unrelated business income

Once a church determines that it has more than $1,000 of gross revenue from one or more unrelated business activities, it must determine its net taxable unrelated business income (or loss). Many organizations that have significant revenue from unrelated business activities actually generate a net loss from the activities after taking into account deductible expenses.

The manner in which unrelated debt-financed income is calculated is addressed in the previous section on that topic.

To calculate net unrelated business income from other activities, the starting point is gross unrelated business revenue. Allowable expenses attributable to the unrelated business activities are deducted from gross revenue. In addition to expenses incurred by the church, the law allows a standard deduction of up to $1,000 (but the standard deduction cannot create a net loss or make a net loss larger).

In order to be allowable as deductions, expenses must be "directly connected" with carrying on the church's unrelated business activities. Some expenses are attributable solely to an unrelated business activity, and the relationship is straightforward. A church may incur some expenses that are attributable partly to unrelated business activities and partly to exempt activities, in which case a reasonable allocation must be made, and only that portion of the expense attributable to the unrelated business activity is deductible.

A church that engages in unrelated business activities should carefully evaluate all of its expenses to identify every expense that may be properly and reasonably allocated to and deducted from the unrelated business revenue. When all such expenses are identified and deducted, including a reasonably allocable portion of administrative and overhead expenses, the result is often a net loss.

Net losses from unrelated business activities may be carried back or forward to offset net income in other years in the same manner that is allowed under federal tax law for taxable corporations.

Can a Church Have Too Much Unrelated Business Activity?

A church may not devote a substantial amount of its time, resources, or activities to any non-exempt purposes. Accordingly, if a substantial portion of a church's activities are dedicated to the conduct of one or more unrelated business activities, the church can lose its federal tax-exempt status under Section 501(c)(3) of the Internal Revenue Code. Unfortunately, the law is not clear with respect to measuring or determining the limits of unrelated business activity. The conclusions reached in various cases and rulings over the years vary dramatically due to the unique facts and circumstances in each of them. Many tax practitioners suggest that when a tax-exempt organization generates more than about 15 percent of its revenue from unrelated business activities, it should carefully consider (together with knowledgeable tax counsel) whether it may be exposed to risk of loss of exemption. An insubstantial amount of unrelated business activity is not a threat to a church's federal tax-exempt status.

Generating Income from Activities without Generating Unrelated Business Income

Churches may generate income from a variety of sources other than contributions without generating unrelated business income. Using the information described in the previous sections regarding the definition of unrelated business income and the exceptions and exclusions that apply, a church can wisely plan its revenue-generating activities to avoid UBI treatment. Following are examples of income-generating activities in which a church may engage along with descriptions of how to avoid unrelated business income in conducting them.

Bookstores and gift shops
The volunteer exception

Income from a church bookstore or gift shop may be excluded entirely from unrelated business income if the activity is conducted substantially entirely (more than 85 percent) by volunteers (uncompensated workers). If the activity qualifies for the volunteer exception, it doesn't matter whether the items sold in the store or shop are substantially related to the church's exempt purposes or not; nor does it matter whether the store or shop is located on the church's property. When the volunteer exception applies, the activity may be conducted in a regular commercial location without affecting the exemption from unrelated business income.

Selling substantially related items

If all the items sold in the store or shop are of a nature that selling them contributes importantly to one or more of the church's exempt purposes, the activity will not generate unrelated business income. In some cases, the relationship between an item being sold and the church's exempt purposes may be obvious (e.g., Bibles, prayer books, worship music, and so on). As described in the section **Unrelated Business Income-The General Rules** on pages 114, in cases where the relationship is not obvious, the church should maintain adequate documentation to support the relationship between each item or category of similar items sold and the specific exempt purposes of the church.

Selling at off-site locations, through catalogues, and so on

Note that despite popular perception, a church bookstore does not have to be located on the church's property, operated with limited hours, or concealed from the public in order to have its activities qualify for exemption. In fact, a church selling items that are substantially related to its exempt purposes may operate its store or shop in a commercial location, be open during regular commercial hours, promote itself to the public, sell its items in mail-order catalogues or over the Internet, and use other similar methods of promotion without generating unrelated business income. In an authoritative ruling issued in the context of a museum selling substantially related greeting cards, the IRS clearly addressed the issue:

> The organization sells the cards in the shop it operates in the museum. It also publishes a catalogue in which it solic-

its mail orders for the greeting cards. The catalogue is available at a small charge and is advertised in magazines and other publications throughout the year. In addition, the shop sells the cards at quantity discounts to retail stores. As a result, a large volume of cards are sold at a significant profit.

> The museum is exempt as an educational organization on the basis of its ownership, maintenance, and exhibition for public viewing of works of art. The sale of greeting cards displaying printed reproductions of art works contributes importantly to the achievement of the museum's exempt educational purposes by stimulating and enhancing public awareness, interest, and appreciation of art. Moreover, a broader segment of the public may be encouraged to visit the museum itself to share in its educational functions and programs as a result of seeing the cards. *The fact that the cards are promoted and sold in a clearly commercial manner at a profit and in competition with commercial greeting card publishers does not alter the fact of the activity's relatedness to the museum's exempt purpose. (Revenue Ruling 73-104 – emphasis added.)*

The IRS subsequently reaffirmed the conclusion it reached in the Revenue Ruling cited above when it issued a Technical Advice Memorandum (TAM) in a museum context. The question at hand was whether off-site sales by the museum of substantially related items constituted unrelated business activity. In the TAM, in which the museum is referred to as "M," the IRS stated:

> M carries on extensive off-site sales activities. It uses several vehicles to accomplish these sales: retail stores, gift shops, an outlet located in another city, mail-order catalogues, advertisements in various other publications, corpo-

rate/conference program, etc. Clearly, M has developed an off-site outlet network and receives significant revenue from such sales.

It is, therefore, not unreasonable to infer from this that the purpose behind the off-site sales activities is a commercial one. Were this not an exempt organization, such logic would be persuasive. *However, regarding the sale of related items by an exempt organization,* Rev. Rul. 73-104 *holds that neither the proximity of the sale to the museum's location nor the fact that the individual purchaser never sets foot on the property matters.*

In *Rev. Rul. 73-104,* the organization sold large volumes of cards at quantity discounts to retail stores and through its mail order catalogues. The revenue ruling states the following: "The fact that the greeting cards are promoted and sold in a clearly commercial manner at a profit and in competition with commercial greeting card publishers does not alter the fact of the activity's relatedness to the museum's exempt purpose." *Thus, once it is determined that a line of merchandise is related to the purposes of a museum, the broader the market the museum is able to reach, the more it can fulfill its exempt function. … Therefore, exempt product sales occurring outside the Museum Site do not (for that reason alone) constitute unrelated trade or business under section 513 of the Code.* (TAM 9550003—emphasis added. While a TAM is not authoritative, it is helpful in understanding the IRS's position on a particular issue.)

A church that wishes to engage in aggressive, commercial-type sales of items that it believes are substantially related to its exempt purposes should obtain advice from tax counsel to ensure that it is in compliance with the law. Depending on the volume and scope of the activity, it may be wise to obtain a private ruling from the IRS.

Parking lots

The IRS has consistently held that the operation of a revenue-producing parking lot by an exempt organization is not a rental of real estate, but rather, is a trade or business activity. As is the case with other trade or business activities, a church may operate a parking lot in a manner where substantially all (more than 85 percent) of the work is performed by volunteers and the operation will be exempt from the tax on unrelated business income.

As an alternative, the church could rent the property on which the parking lot sits to an unrelated parking company and the parking company could operate the parking lot. In that scenario, the revenue to the church is real estate rental income, which is not unrelated business income (unless the property is debt-financed). Even if the property is debt-financed, the church should consider whether it may qualify for:

- The substantially exempt use exception or
- The neighborhood land rule exclusion, if the church plans to convert the property to exempt use within 15 years of the date it was acquired.

Concerts or other special events

The conduct of revenue-generating concerts or other events by a church will not generate unrelated business income if the event itself contributes importantly to one or more of the church's exempt purposes. The relationship between the event and the church's exempt purposes (e.g., worship, evangelism, and so on) should be well-documented to support the church's position. Again, as with other trade or business activities, conduct of the activity substantially entirely by volunteers will also result in the income being exempt from the tax on unrelated business income.

Thrift shops or other sales of donated merchandise

As described previously, a trade or business of selling merchandise is not an unrelated business activity if "substantially all" of the merchandise sold is donated to the church. Court cases and rulings indicate that "substantially all" for this purpose means 85 percent or more of the merchandise sold. Therefore, the operation of a thrift shop selling donated goods is not an unrelated business activity. Similarly, the sale of donated merchandise using other methods (such as online auctions, including eBay) is not an unrelated business activity. (Note: A portion of eBay's website is dedicated specifically to online sales by nonprofit organizations.)

Corporate sponsorship of events

Also as described extensively above, revenue received by a church as payment for a qualified sponsorship activity is not unrelated business income. A qualified sponsorship activity is an activity in which an outside party (typically a business) pays a church to sponsor an event or activity conducted by the church and receives, in exchange, certain limited types of recognition or acknowledgment. As long as the acknowledgment or recognition made by the church of the sponsor meets certain criteria, and the church does not provide the sponsor with a "substantial return benefit," the transaction constitutes a qualified sponsorship activity.

Scrip programs

Scrip programs are activities in which an organization purchases gift cards (or their equivalent) at a discount and then sells them to supporters, often for face value. For example, a church might purchase $100 gift cards from a grocery chain at a price of $90 each and sell them to church members for $100 each. Since the members are able to use the cards to buy $100 of groceries, the scrip program is an appealing way for many organizations to raise money. Ordinarily, the regular operation of a scrip program by a church would constitute an unrelated business activity. The IRS has ruled, however, that when the volunteer exception applies (i.e., when substantially all of the activity is conducted by volunteers) the activity is not an unrelated business activity.

Coffee shops and cafés

The best way for a church to avoid having a coffee shop or café treated as an unrelated business ac-

tivity is to limit its activity to providing service in connection with events on the church's property. Doing so will help the church take advantage of the "convenience of members" exemption described under **Specific Exclusions from Unrelated Business Income**. If the church wants to have a full-service coffee shop or café open to the public for regular business hours, it should consider having the activity conducted substantially entirely by volunteers to avoid unrelated business income.

Alternatively, the church could rent a portion of its real property to an unrelated company to operate the coffee shop or café on the site. If the property is *not* debt-financed, real estate rental income is not unrelated business income. If the church's real property *is* debt-financed, the church should determine whether an exception may apply to the debt-financed income rules, such as the rule described previously that exempts debt-financed income if substantially all (85 percent or more) of the property is used for exempt purposes.

Churches have a variety of options when it comes to generating revenue from alternative sources. With careful planning and advice from experienced tax and legal counsel where needed, churches can successfully engage in a variety of revenue-generating activities with little or no adverse impact.

4

Other Revenue Sources

129

Chapter 5

Compensation and Benefits

INTRODUCTION

Effective stewardship of a church's finances requires a clear understanding of its most common operating expenses. While it's easy to immediately think of the things that churches spend their money on to do ministry, such as buildings, copier leases, copyright licenses, or curriculum, the reality is that nearly every church nationwide spends the bulk of its budget on people. Time and again, research has shown that 45 to 55 percent of the average church's budget is spent on the salaries and benefits paid to clergy and staff.

This means a firm grasp of compensation will go a long way toward understanding operating expenses. The proper handling of compensation, including the benefits and expense reimbursements paid to clergy and staff, will help keep operating expenses on track and prevent unnecessary costs, such as the stiff penalties that can apply when a compensation-related matter is mishandled. Such mastery allows churches to more effectively address other expenses essential to ministry.

COMPENSATION PLANNING

Compensation constitutes the largest portion of nearly every church budget nationwide. Proper planning and oversight is necessary to effectively lead in this area, including an understanding of several unique tax issues that can result in significant, costly penalties if they are mishandled (for more on setting a compensation philosophy see Chapter 1).

In adopting compensation packages for your ministers and lay staff members, review these possible components of the compensation package.

Salary

The most basic component of church staff compensation is salary. There are two important considerations to keep in mind with respect to staff salaries—the amount of the salary, and the use of "salary reduction agreements." These two issues will be discussed separately.

> *Amount.* Staff salaries ordinarily are set by the church board. Churches generally may pay any amount they wish, with one important excep-

tion—if a church pays unreasonably high compensation to its leaders there are two possible consequences:

(1) Loss of tax-exempt status. In order for a church or any other charity to maintain its tax-exempt status it must meet a number of conditions. One condition is that it cannot pay unreasonably high compensation to its leaders. There are two considerations to note. First, very few charities have lost their exempt status for paying unreasonable compensation. The Internal Revenue Service has been very reluctant to impose this remedy. Second, the law does not define what amount of compensation is unreasonable, and neither the IRS nor the courts have provided much clarification.

> **EXAMPLE.** A federal appeals court concluded that combined annual income of $115,680 paid by a religious organization to its founder and his wife was not excessive.

> **EXAMPLE.** A court ruled that maximum reasonable compensation for a prominent televangelist was $133,100 in 1984, $146,410 in 1985, $161,051 in 1986, and $177,156 in 1987. The court based its conclusions on a comparison of the salaries of other nonprofit officers in the state.

(2) Intermediate sanctions. The IRS can assess substantial excise taxes called "intermediate sanctions" against "disqualified persons" who are paid an "excess benefit" by a church or other charity. A disqualified person is any officer or director, a relative of such a person, and certain entities related to such a person. An excess benefit is compensation and fringe benefits in excess of what the IRS deems "reasonable." Note that the IRS still can revoke the exempt status of a charity that pays excessive compensation to one of its leaders. However, it is more likely that excessive compensation will result in intermediate sanctions rather than loss of exempt status. To illustrate, why should a major private university lose its tax-exempt status because it pays excessive compensation to its head football coach?

The intermediate sanctions the IRS can impose include the following:

- **Tax on disqualified persons.** A disqualified person who benefits from an excess benefit transaction is subject to an excise tax equal to 25 percent of the amount of the "excess benefit" (the amount by which actual compensation exceeds the fair market value of services rendered). This tax is assessed against the disqualified person directly, not his or her employer.

- **Additional tax on disqualified persons.** If a disqualified person fails to "correct" the excess benefit by the time the IRS assesses the 25 percent tax, then the IRS can assess an additional tax of up to 200 percent of the excess benefit. The law specifies that a disqualified person can "correct" the excess benefit transaction by "undoing the excess benefit to the extent possible, and taking any additional measures necessary to place the organization in a financial position not worse than that in which it would be if the disqualified person were dealing under the highest fiduciary standards."

- **Tax on organization managers.** If the IRS assesses the 25 percent tax against a disqualified person, it is permitted to impose an additional 10 percent tax (up to a maximum of $20,000) on any "organization manager" who participates in an excess benefit transaction knowing it is such a transaction, unless the manager's participation "is not willful and is due to reasonable cause." A "manager" is an officer, director, or trustee. IRS regulations clarify that the managers collectively cannot be liable for more than $20,000 for any one transaction.

KEY POINT. The intermediate sanctions law imposes an excise tax on members of a church's governing board who knowingly vote for an excessive compensation package. This makes it essential for board members to carefully review the reasonableness of compensation packages.

Charities, disqualified persons, and governing boards may rely on a "presumption of reasonableness" with respect to a compensation arrangement if it was approved by a board of directors (or committee of the board) that: (1) was composed entirely of individuals unrelated to and not subject to the control of the disqualified person involved in the arrangement; (2) obtained and relied upon objective "comparability" information, such as (a) compensation paid by similar organizations, both taxable and tax-exempt, for comparable positions, (b) independent compensation surveys by nationally recognized independent firms, or (c) actual written offers from similar institutions competing for the services of the disqualified person; and (3) adequately documented the basis for its decision. The documentation should include the terms of the transaction and the date of its approval, the members of the board present during the debate and vote on the transaction, the comparability data obtained and relied upon, the actions of any members of the board having a conflict of interest, and documentation of the basis for the determination. In order to avail itself of this "presumption of reasonableness," church leaders must carefully follow the requirements described in the federal Treasury regulations, and would be well-advised to do so under the advice of experienced tax counsel.

The IRS may refute the presumption of reasonableness only if it develops sufficient contrary evidence to rebut the comparability data relied upon by the board.

KEY POINT. The law creates a presumption that a minister's compensation package is reasonable if approved by a church board that follows the steps outlined in the Treasury regulations, including the requirement to rely upon valid "comparability" information such as independent compensation surveys by nationally recognized independent firms. One of the more comprehensive compensation surveys for church employees is the biannual *Compensation Handbook for Church Staff*, published by Christianity Today. This means that most ministers will be able to use that book to establish the presumption of reasonableness. But it also suggests that the IRS may rely on the data in that book in any attempt to impose intermediate sanctions against ministers.

IRS regulations clarify that "revenue based pay" arrangements in which an employee's compensation is based on a percentage of the employer's total revenues do not automatically result in an excess benefit transaction triggering intermediate sanctions. Rather, "all relevant facts and circumstances" must be considered.

5

Compensation and Benefits

▲ CAUTION. *In a series of rulings published in 2004, the IRS assessed intermediate sanctions against a pastor as a result of excess benefits paid to him and members of his family by his church. The IRS concluded that taxable compensation and benefits a church pays to a "disqualified person" (generally, a church leader, members of his or her family, and certain entities related to him or her) that are not reported as taxable income to the recipient constitute "automatic excess benefits" that trigger intermediate sanctions regardless of the amount involved. The IRS ruled that the following transactions resulted in excess benefits to the pastor because they were not reported as taxable income: (1) personal use of church property (vehicles, cell phones, credit cards, computers, and so on) by the pastor and members of his family; (2) reimbursements of personal expenses; and (3) nonaccountable reimbursements of business expenses (i.e., reimbursements of expenses that were not supported by adequate documentation of the business purpose of each expense). Since these taxable benefits were not reported as taxable income, they amounted to "automatic" excess benefits resulting in intermediate sanctions. This is a stunning interpretation of the tax code and regulations that directly affects the compensation practices of every church, and exposes some ministers and church board members to intermediate sanctions.*

➤ RECOMMENDATION. Churches that pay a minister (or any staff member) significantly more than the highest 25 percent for comparable positions should obtain a legal opinion from an experienced tax attorney confirming that the amount paid is not "unreasonable" and will not expose the employee or the board to intermediate sanctions.

➤ TAX SAVINGS TIP. Ministers and lay employees should carefully review their W-2 or Form 1099 to be sure that it does not report more income than was actually received. If an error was made, the church should issue a corrected tax form (Form W-2c for an employee, or a "corrected" Form 1099 for a self-employed worker).

Salary reduction agreements

Many churches have established "salary reduction agreements" to handle certain staff expenses. The objective is to reduce an employee's taxable income since only the income remaining after the various "reductions" is reported on the employee's W-2 at the end of the year. It is important for church leaders to understand that they cannot reduce an employee's taxable income through salary reductions unless specifically allowed by law.

Here are three ways that taxable income can be reduced through salary reduction agreements:

(1) 403(b) plan contributions. Salary reduction agreements can be used to contribute to a tax-sheltered 403(b) retirement plan if the salary reductions meet certain conditions.

(2) "Cafeteria plans." Salary reduction agreements can be used to fund "cafeteria plans" (including "flexible spending arrangements") if several conditions are met. A cafeteria plan is a written plan established by an employer that allows employees to choose between cash and a "menu" of nontaxable benefits specified by law (including employer-provided medical insurance premiums, group-term life insurance, and dependent care).

(3) Housing allowances. A church can designate a portion of a minister's salary as a housing allowance, and the amount so designated is not subject to income tax if certain conditions are met. Housing allowances are addressed below.

➤ OBSERVATION. *Most other forms of "salary reduction" will not accomplish the goal of reducing a minister's taxable income. The income tax regulations prohibit the widespread practice of funding "accountable" reimbursement arrangements through salary reductions. This topic is addressed later in this chapter.*

There are three additional issues to consider with regard to salary: (1) employees who refuse to accept full salary, (2) employees who return a portion of their salary to the church, and (3) legal challenges involving clergy compensation.

Refusal to accept full salary

Sometimes a minister or lay employee refuses to accept the full amount of his or her church-approved salary, often because the church is experiencing short-term financial problems. Should the church report the amount that is refused as taxable income to the minister or lay employee? The constructive receipt doctrine specifies:

Income although not actually reduced to a taxpayer's possession is constructively received by him in the taxable year during which it is credited to his account, set apart for him, or otherwise made available so that he may draw upon it at any time, or so that he could have drawn upon it during the taxable year if notice of intention to withdraw had been given. Treas. Reg. 1.451-2(a).

A number of courts have ruled that this principle requires employees to include in their taxable income any portion of their stated salary that they refuse to accept. On the other hand, some courts have reached the opposite conclusion. Perhaps the most notable case is *Giannini v. Commissioner, 129 F.2d 638 (9th Cir. 1942)*. This case involved a corporate president whose annual compensation was 5 percent of the company's profits. In the middle of one year, the president informed members of his company's board of directors that he would not accept any further compensation for the year and suggested that the company "do something worthwhile" with the money. The company never credited to the president any further compensation for the year, nor did it set any part of it aside for his use. The amount of salary refused by the president was nearly $1.5 million, and no part of this amount was reported by the president as taxable income in the year in question. The IRS audited the president and insisted that the $1.5 million should have been reported as taxable income. The taxpayer appealed, and a federal appeals court rejected the IRS position:

> The taxpayer did not receive the money, and . . . did not direct its disposition. What he did was unqualifiedly refuse to accept any further compensation for his services with the suggestion that the money be used for some worthwhile purpose. So far as the taxpayer was concerned, the corporation could have kept the money. . . . In these circumstances we cannot say as a matter of law that the money was beneficially received by the taxpayer and therefore subject to the income tax provisions.

The court acknowledged that the United States Supreme Court has observed: "One who is entitled to receive, at a future date, interest or compensation for services and who makes a gift of it by an anticipatory assignment, realizes taxable income quite as much as if he had collected the income and paid it over to the object of his bounty." *Helvering v. Schaffner, 312 U. S. 579 (1941)*. However, the court distinguished this language

by observing that "the dominance over the fund and taxpayer's direction show that he beneficially received the money by exercising his right to divert it to a use." This was not true of the corporate president in the present case, the court concluded.

In summary, a reasonable basis exists for not treating as taxable income the portion of an employee's stated salary that is refused, particularly where the employee does not assign the income to a specified use but is content to leave the unpaid salary with the employer.

Returning excess salary

Some churches have paid an employee more than the salary authorized by the church board. In most cases this is due to an innocent mistake. But what happens if the church later discovers the mistake and attempts to correct it? Can the employee give back the excess to the church? And what if the mistake is discovered in the following year? How does a return of the excess affect the employee's taxable income and the church's payroll reporting obligations? The IRS has listed the following tax consequences when employees return to their employer in "Year 2" excess salary received in "Year 1":

- The employer does not reduce the employee's wages for Social Security and federal income tax withholding purposes for Year 2.
- The employer does not reduce the employee's taxable income for Year 1 or reduce the amount of income taxes withheld in that year.
- The repayment in Year 2 of excess salary received in Year 1 has no effect on the Form W-2 for Year 2. The employer should furnish to the employee a separate receipt acknowledging the repayment for the employee's records.
- To the extent additional Social Security taxes were paid in Year 1 because of the erroneous salary payment, the repayment of the excess salary in Year 2 creates an overpayment of Social Security taxes in Year 1, and credit may be claimed by the employer with respect to its Social Security tax liability for that prior year.
- The employee may claim in Year 2 a miscellaneous itemized deduction on Schedule A in the amount of the excess salary that was repaid.
- To the extent that repayments in Year 2 of erroneous salary paid in Year 1 result in a reduced

amount of Social Security wages for Year 1 and reduced amounts of employee Social Security taxes paid for that year, the employer is required to furnish corrected Forms W-2 for Year 1 showing the employee's corrected "Social Security wages," corrected "Social Security tax withheld," corrected "Medicare wages and tips," and corrected "Medicare tax withheld." No changes should be made in the entries for "Wages, tips, other compensation" (box 1 of Form W-2) or for "Federal income tax withheld" (box 2 of Form W-2). *SCA 1998-026.*

Clergy compensation disputes

In 2012, the United States Supreme Court unanimously affirmed the so-called "ministerial exception" barring civil court review of employment disputes between churches and ministers. The ministerial exception has been applied to a wide range of employment disputes by state and federal courts over the past half century, but has never before been addressed by the Supreme Court. The Court concluded that the exception applied to a claim of disability discrimination brought by an employee of a church school. The Court did not address the application of the ministerial exception to clergy compensation disputes, but some other courts have done so and have concluded that the exception applies. Here are a few examples:

EXAMPLE. A federal appeals court ruled that the ministerial exception prevents clergy from suing their employing church for violating the minimum wage or overtime pay requirements of the federal Fair Labor Standards Act. *Schleicher v. Salvation Army, 518 F.3d 472 (7th Cir. 2008).*

EXAMPLE. A North Carolina court ruled that it was barred by the First Amendment guaranty of religious freedom from resolving a priest's compensation dispute with his diocese. A Catholic priest claimed that his diocese had failed to assign him to a suitable position and failed to properly compensate him for his services. He submitted his grievance to the Vatican's "Congregation for Clergy." The Congregation later instructed the diocese to "provide some priestly ministry for this priest and ensure that he is henceforth to be provided with an adequate means of livelihood."

The priest alleged that the diocese never followed this mandate, and has continued to refuse to give him either an assignment or a salary. As a result, he sued the diocese, claiming that it had violated the

North Carolina Wage and Hour Act. The Act provides that employers must "pay every employee all wages and tips accruing to the employee on the regular payday," and that "employees whose employment is discontinued for any reason shall be paid all wages due on or before the next regular payday either through the regular pay channels." The priest alleged that the diocese had violated these provisions by refusing to comply with the decision and instruction of the Congregation." A trial court dismissed the lawsuit, and the priest appealed.

In affirming the trial court's dismissal of the lawsuit, the appeals court observed:

The First Amendment to the United States Constitution prohibits any law "respecting an establishment of religion, or prohibiting the free exercise thereof." The United States Supreme Court has interpreted this clause to mean that the civil courts cannot decide disputes involving religious organizations where the religious organizations would be deprived of interpreting and determining their own laws and doctrine. Thus, the dispositive question is whether resolution of the legal claim brought against a religious organization requires the court to interpret or weigh church doctrine.

The court concluded that any resolution of the priest's claims would require the court "to determine, under ecclesiastical law, the compensation to which the priest is entitled as an adequate means of livelihood and the appropriate necessities as envisioned in the Code of Canon Law." Such a determination "is beyond the jurisdiction of the North Carolina courts and we must affirm the order of the trial court to dismiss his claim." Tarasi v. Jugis, 692 S.E.2d 194 (N.C. App. 2010).

EXAMPLE. A federal appeals court ruled that it was barred by the ministerial exception from resolving a seminarian's claim for unpaid overtime compensation. The court noted that federal courts "have grappled with determining whether a particular church employee, though not ordained, nevertheless should be considered a 'minister' for purposes of the ministerial exception." It declined to adopt a specific test for deciding who is a ministerial employee, since "under any reasonable construction of the ministerial exception [a seminarian] meets the definition of a minister." It concluded:

We hold that the First Amendment consider-ations relevant to an ordained minister apply equally to a person who, though not yet or-dained, has entered into a church-recognized seminary program to become a minister and who brings suit concerning employment deci-sions arising from work as a seminarian. The principle of allowing the church to choose its representatives using whatever criteria it deems relevant necessarily applies not only to those persons who already are ordained ministers, but also to those persons who are actively in the process of becoming ordained ministers. Similarly, we can no more ask the church for a religious justification for its decisions con-cerning seminarians (ordained ministers in training) than we can ask the church to articu-late a religious justification for its personnel decisions concerning its ordained ministers. . . . [The plaintiff] challenges the sufficiency of his wages for duties performed as part of his seminary training to become an ordained Roman Catholic priest. Because the ministerial exception applies to those claims, we affirm the district court's dismissal of the complaint. Al-cazar v. Corporation of the Catholic Archbishop, 627 F.3d 1288 (9th Cir. 2010).

EXAMPLE. A federal court in Washington ruled that the "ministe-rial exception" prevented it from resolving several claims brought by seminary students against a religious organization, including violation of a state minimum wage law. The court noted that the First Amend-ment guaranty of religious freedom has created a ministerial exception to employment laws, and that this exception prohibits a court from "inquiring into the decisions of a religious organization concerning the hiring, firing, promotion, rate of pay, placement or any other employ-ment related decision concerning ministers and other non-secular church employees." *Alcazar v. Corporation of Catholic Archbishop of Seattle, 2006 WL 3791370 (W.D. Wash. 2006).*

As a concluding thought regarding salary, it's worth noting the revised standard adopted by the Evangelical Council for Financial Accountability (ECFA) regarding salary and benefits packages for clergy and religious leaders. "In recent years, there has been increased scrutiny on churches regarding their processes for set-ting compensation and handling related-party transac-tions," wrote ECFA's Dan Busby and John Van Drunen

in the September/October 2013 issues of *Church Law & Tax Report*. "(G)iven the increasing number of high-profile financial abuses and perceived abuses, the (Commission on Accountability and Policy for Reli-gious Organizations) concluded that churches must set a high bar of excellence in these areas as part of demonstrating their commitment to integrity to their financial supporters and a watching world.

"Consistent with the commission's recommendations, the ECFA board announced a revision to the ECFA standards, providing guidance in the areas of compen-sation-setting and related-party transactions."

That new standard—**ECFA Standard 6 – Compensation-Setting and Related-Party Transactions**—is a worth-while read for all churches, regardless of size. It states:

> *Every organization shall set compensation of its top leader and address related-party transactions in a manner that demonstrates integrity and propriety in conformity with ECFA's Policy for Excellence in Compensation-Setting and Related-Party Transactions.*

While certain ECFA standards require external evi-dence of financial accountability, such as distributing financial statements, Standard 6 deals primarily with internal behavior and decision-making, which are related to intent and integrity.

This standard provides additional assurance to donors and other supporters that the accredited organization sets compensation and handles financial transactions in the best interests of the organization and its min-istry. As with other standards, compliance with this standard does *not guarantee* that all activities are in the best interests of the organization. It does provide for a more objective and accountable environment. Another goal of this standard is to provide to accredited orga-nizations some good financial management principles, helping them to achieve the best long-term results while bringing honor to the Lord.

Anyone who has been involved in the leadership of a church or nonprofit organization has most likely expe-rienced a situation in which a donor, board member, or other influential person has tried to conduct business with the organization in such a way as to gain some personal benefit. This may include offering products or services to a nonprofit organization which could be secured at a lower price from other sources or promising future gifts only if the organization conducts business with a particular individual or company. Compliance with this standard assists leaders in withstanding such efforts by helping them make the right decision for the organization and themselves.

Similarly, one aspect of governance practices that requires special attention is the area of compensation setting. This is a reality that all organizations must firmly handle with utmost accountability and integrity. Ultimately, this responsibility lies with the board, which, in accordance with Standard 2, is comprised of a majority of independent members.

I Samuel 12 provides guidance as we seek to work within the spirit of this standard. In this chapter, Samuel is near the end of his service as high priest of Israel. He is about to admonish Israel for its disobedience, but before he does he reminds them of his integrity in all his dealings with them.

> Samuel said to all Israel, "I have listened to everything you said to me and have set a king over you. Now you have a king as your leader. As for me, I am old and gray, and my sons are here with you. I have been your leader from my youth until this day. Here I stand. Testify against me in the presence of the LORD and his anointed. Whose ox have I taken? Whose donkey have I taken? Whom have I cheated? Whom have I oppressed? From whose hand have I accepted a bribe to make me shut my eyes? If I have done any of these things, I will make it right." "You have not cheated or oppressed us," they replied. "You have not taken anything from anyone's hand." Samuel said to them, "The LORD is witness against you, and also his anointed is witness this day, that you have not found anything in my hand." "He is witness," they said (1 Samuel 12:1–5).

It is on this solid record of faithful, honest service that Samuel has the place of integrity to speak into the lives of his people. To demonstrate this level of integrity, or-

ganizations should avoid inappropriate compensation-setting practices and conflicts of interest.

Compensation-setting practices. Compensation-setting practices should be consistent with generally accepted biblical truths and practices, should not cause a diminished Christian witness, and should comply with ECFA's Policy for Excellence in Compensation-Setting and Related-Party Transactions, as reflected at the end of this commentary.

Every organization should exercise care and diligence in setting compensation and benefits to ensure that total compensation of its top leader and all of its employees is reasonable, taking into consideration the skills, talents, education, experience, performance, and knowledge of the person whose compensation is being set.

For purposes of Standard 6, total compensation includes salary, wages, other payments for services, and benefits of all types, whether taxable or non-taxable, and whether paid directly or indirectly by the organization or one or more of its subsidiaries or affiliates.

Related-party transactions. Related-party transactions are those occurring between two or more parties when one party has a responsibility for promoting one interest (a fiduciary interest) but has a competing interest at the same time. This standard requires that these transactions be conducted in a manner that demonstrates integrity and propriety, while meeting ECFA's Policy for Excellence in Compensation-Setting and Related-Party Transactions.

Certain related-party transactions may clearly be advantageous to, and in the economic benefit of, the organization. However, even if a transaction is economically beneficial to an organization, it may raise a public perception of questionable integrity or create a perception of self-dealing, and thus, should be avoided.

For purposes of Standard 6, payments for the use of property, whether tangible or intangible, including purchases, rentals, licenses, and royalty arrangements are considered payments for property, and to the extent such payments are made to a "disqualified person" (generally those who may exercise substantial influence over an organization, such as leaders or board members), such arrangements constitute related-party transactions.

Seeking professional guidance. Organizations should consult with their tax counsel in establishing compensation for their leaders and in entering into related-party transactions to ensure compliance with federal tax and other applicable law, and consider steps that may be taken by the organizations and their leaders to avail themselves of protections that may be available under the law in connection with compensation-setting and related-party transactions.

Summary. Properly addressing compensation-setting practices and related-party transactions demonstrates integrity in handling some of the most sensitive dealings in the life of an organization. Ensuring that these dealings are always in the best interest of the organization is a fundamental principle.

ECFA Policy for Excellence in Compensation Setting and Related-Party Transactions

Compensation Setting

The board of every organization shall annually approve the top leader's total compensation package, and shall be notified annually of the total compensation package of any member of the top leader's family who is employed by the organization or any of its subsidiaries or affiliates. Such approval and notification shall be documented in the minutes of the organization's board meetings.

The following compensation-setting process is required for organizations with top leaders at annual compensation levels of $150,000 or more and is recommended for the compensated leaders of all organizations:

(1) The board or an authorized committee of the board shall make the decision regarding total compensation, and those participating in the decision-making process may not have any conflict of interest in the decision, whether direct or indirect. That is, no person in the decision-making process may:

(a) be related to the person whose compensation is being addressed,

(b) be subordinate to the person whose compensation is being set,

(c) be a person whose compensation is determined in a manner that involves input or decision-making by the person whose compensation is being set, or

(d) otherwise have a conflict of interest.

(2) The board or committee shall obtain reliable comparability data with respect to the position for which compensation is being set. Such comparability data shall be for functionally comparable positions, and shall be for organizations as similar as possible to the organization and shall be updated at least every five years.

(3) The board or committee shall determine appropriate total compensation, taking into consideration the comparability data referred to above, as well as the skills, talents, education, experience, performance, and knowledge of the person whose compensation is being set.

(4) The board or committee shall document its compliance with the requirements described above.

(5) The board or committee shall contemporaneously document its decision regarding total compensation and, if applicable, its rationale for establishing compensation at a level that exceeds that which is supported by the comparability data.

(6) If the process described in steps 1–5 above is conducted by a committee, the board shall affirm, ratify, or otherwise approve the total compensation package. Board members who have a conflict of interest in determining total compensation (such as employees of the organization) may be recused from this process of approving the top leader's compensation package.

Related-Party Transactions

The board of every organization shall properly address related-party transactions pursuant to a sound conflicts-of-interest policy. An organization may not enter into a business transaction with a person or entity that meets the definition of a "disqualified person" under federal tax law applicable to public charities unless the organization takes affirmative steps in advance to ensure that the following is true with respect to the transaction:

(1) All parties with a conflict of interest (direct or indirect) are excluded from the discussion and vote related to approval of the transaction;

(2) The organization obtains reliable comparability information regarding the terms of the transaction from appropriate independent sources such as competitive bids, independent appraisals, or independent expert opinions;

(3) The organization's board has affirmatively determined that entering into the transaction is in the best interests of the organization; and

(4) The organization contemporaneously documents the elements described above, as well as the board's approval of the transaction.

Tax Counsel

Organizations are encouraged to consult with tax counsel in establishing compensation for their top leaders, including any person who meets the definition of a disqualified person, and in entering into related-party transactions to ensure compliance with federal tax law and other applicable law. Tax counsel may assist an organization and its leaders in taking steps to avail themselves of protections that may be available under the law in connection with compensation-setting and related-party transactions.[1]

BENEFITS

Housing allowances

The most important tax benefit available to ministers who own or rent their homes is the housing allowance. Ministers who own or rent their home do not pay federal income taxes on the amount of their compensation that their employing church designates in advance as a housing allowance to the extent that the allowance represents compensation for ministerial services, is used to pay housing expenses, and does not exceed the annual fair rental value of the home (furnished, plus utilities). Housing-related expenses include mortgage payments, rental payments, utilities, repairs, furnishings, insurance, property taxes, additions, and maintenance.

Unfortunately, many churches fail to designate a portion of a minister's compensation as a housing allow-

ance. This deprives their minister of an important tax benefit that costs the church nothing.

Ministers who live in a church-owned parsonage that is provided "rent-free" as compensation for ministerial services do not include the annual fair rental value of the parsonage as income in computing their federal income taxes. The annual fair rental value is not "deducted" from the minister's income. Rather, it is not reported as additional income anywhere on Form 1040 (as it generally would be by non-clergy workers). Further, ministers who live in a church-provided parsonage do not pay federal income taxes on the amount of their compensation that their employing church designates in advance as a parsonage allowance, to the extent that the allowance represents compensation for ministerial services and is used to pay parsonage-related expenses, such as utilities, repairs, and furnishings.

➤ TAX SAVINGS TIP. Ministers who live in church parsonages, and who incur any out-of-pocket expenses in maintaining the parsonage (such as utilities, property taxes, insurance, furnishings, or lawn care) should ask their employing church to designate a portion of their annual compensation in advance as a "parsonage allowance." Such an allowance is not included on the minister's W-2 or Form 1099 at the end of the year and is nontaxable in computing federal income taxes to the extent the minister incurs housing expenses of at least that amount. This is a very important tax benefit for ministers living in church-provided parsonages. Many ministers and church boards are not aware of this benefit, or are not taking advantage of it.

Note that the parsonage and housing allowance exclusions only apply in computing federal income taxes. Ministers cannot exclude them when computing their self-employment (Social Security) taxes.

➤ RECOMMENDATION. Be sure that the designation of a housing or parsonage allowance for the subsequent year is on the agenda of the church board for one of its final meetings of the current year. The designation should be an official action of the board or congregation, and it should be duly recorded in the minutes of the meeting. The IRS also recognizes designations included in employment contracts and budget line items—assuming in each case that the designation was duly adopted by the church board (or the congregation in a business meeting). Also, if the minister

---

1   Standard 6, ECFA's Seven Standards of Responsible Stewardship™, www.ECFA.org, 2014. Used by permission.

is a new hire, be sure the church designates a housing allowance prior to the date he or she begins working.

How much should a church board or congregation designate as a housing allowance? Many churches base the allowance on their minister's estimate of actual housing expenses for the new year. The church provides the minister with a form on which anticipated housing expenses for the new year are reported. For ministers who own their homes, the form asks for projected expenses in the following categories: down payment, mortgage payments, property taxes, property insurance, utilities, furnishings and appliances, repairs and improvements, maintenance, and miscellaneous. Many churches designate an allowance in excess of the anticipated expenses itemized by the minister. Basing the allowance solely on a minister's actual expenses will penalize the minister if housing expenses turn out to be higher than expected. In other words, the allowance should take into account unexpected housing costs and inaccurate projections of expenses.

➤ RECOMMENDATION. Plan a mid-year review of the housing allowance to make sure that the designated amount is sufficient to cover actual expenses. If a pastor's expenses will exceed the allowance, then the church may amend the allowance. But any amendment will only operate prospectively.

➤ OBSERVATION. Housing allowances are claimed by several associate ministers, administrators, music directors, secretaries, and custodians. However, it is important to note that the housing allowance is available only if two conditions are met: (1) the recipient is a minister, and (2) the allowance is provided as compensation for services performed in the exercise of ministry. In many cases, these conditions will not be satisfied by administrators, music directors, secretaries, or custodians.

Equity allowances

Ministers who live in church-owned parsonages are denied one very important benefit of home ownership—the opportunity to accumulate "equity" in a home over the course of many years. Many ministers who have lived in parsonages during much of their active ministry often face retirement without housing. Their fellow ministers who purchased a home early in their ministry often can look forward to retirement

with a home that is either substantially or completely debt-free. To avoid the potential hardship often suffered by a minister who lives in a parsonage, some churches increase their minister's compensation by an amount that is sometimes referred to as an "equity allowance." The idea is to provide the minister with the equivalent of equity in a home. This is an excellent idea that should be considered by any church having one or more ministers living in church-provided housing. Of course, for the concept to work properly, the equity allowance should not be accessible by the minister until retirement. Therefore, some churches choose to place the allowance directly in a minister's tax-sheltered retirement account.

➤ RECOMMENDATION. Equity allowances should also be considered by a church whose minister rents a home.

Accountable business expense reimbursement policy

An accountable plan is one that meets the following requirements: (1) only business expenses are reimbursed; (2) no reimbursement is allowed without an adequate accounting of expenses within a reasonable period of time (not more than 60 days after an expense is incurred); (3) any excess reimbursement or allowance must be returned to the employer within a reasonable period of time (not more than 120 days after an excess reimbursement is paid); and (4) an employer's reimbursements must come out of the employer's funds and not by reducing the employee's salary. Under an accountable plan, a church's reimbursements of an employee's business expenses are not reported as income to the employee, and the employee does not claim any deductions. This is the best way for churches to handle reimbursements of business expenses, for the following reasons:

- Church staff report their business expenses to the church rather than to the IRS.
- Church staff who report their income taxes as employees, or who report as self-employed and who are reclassified as employees by the IRS in an audit, avoid the limitations on the deductibility of employee business expenses. These limitations include (1) the elimination of any deduction if the employee cannot itemize deductions on Schedule A (most taxpayers cannot), and (2) the deductibility of business expenses on Schedule

5

Compensation and Benefits

A as an itemized expense only to the extent that these expenses exceed two percent of the employee's adjusted gross income.

- The so-called *Deason* allocation rule is avoided. Under this rule, ministers must reduce their business expense deduction by the percentage of their total compensation that consists of a tax-exempt housing allowance.
- The "50 percent limitation" that applies to the deductibility of business meals and entertainment expenses is avoided. Unless these expenses are reimbursed by an employer under an accountable plan, only 50 percent of them are deductible by either employees or self-employed workers.
- Church staff who report their income taxes as self-employed avoid the risk of being reclassified as an employee by the IRS in an audit and assessed additional taxes.

➤ OBSERVATION. Many churches provide automobile allowances to their ministers and lay staff. In many cases, a church will simply provide a fixed dollar amount every month to an employee (for example, $300), and require no substantiation of business miles or a return of any "excess reimbursements" (in excess of substantiated business miles). This is referred to as a "nonaccountable" reimbursement arrangement. What are the tax consequences of such an arrangement? The allowances must be added to the employee's W-2 at the end of the year, and the employee can claim a business deduction on Schedule A. If a worker is an employee with insufficient itemized deductions to use Schedule A, there is no deduction available for business expenses, even though the full amount of the monthly allowances are added to taxable income. This is a very unfortunate tax result that can be avoided completely through an accountable reimbursement arrangement.

EXAMPLE. A church pays its senior pastor an annual salary. In addition, it provides the pastor with a monthly car allowance of $400. This is an example of a nonaccountable reimbursement arrangement. Assume that the church treasurer reports none of these reimbursements as taxable income on the pastor's Form W-2 since she assumes that the pastor had "at least" $4,800 in expenses associated with the business use of his car and so there was no need to report the nonaccountable reimbursements as taxable income. This assumption not only is incorrect, but

it also converts the nonaccountable reimbursements into an "automatic" excess benefit exposing the pastor to intermediate sanctions, as noted previously in this chapter. This assumes that the senior pastor is a "disqualified person" (i.e., an officer or director, or a relative of an officer or director).

The income tax regulations prohibit the funding of accountable reimbursement arrangements through salary reductions.

EXAMPLE. Assume that a church pays Pastor Gary $700 each week, and also agrees to reimburse his substantiated business expenses for each month out of the first weekly payroll check for the following month. Assume further that Pastor Gary substantiated $300 of business expenses for January. The church issued Pastor Gary his customary check of $700 for the first week of February, but only accumulated $400 of this amount to his W-2 form at the end of the year. This arrangement was once common, and still is practiced by some churches. The income tax regulations do not prohibit the funding of business expense reimbursements out of salary reductions. Rather, a church's reimbursements under such arrangements cannot be accountable. This means that a church cannot reduce W-2 income by reducing an employee's salary to pay for business expense reimbursements. In this example, the full $700 paycheck must be accumulated to Pastor Gary's W-2. If it is not, the arrangement may constitute an automatic excess benefit transaction exposing Pastor Gary to intermediate sanctions, as explained previously in this chapter.

Travel expenses of a spouse

There is much confusion regarding the correct reporting of a church's reimbursement of the travel expenses of a spouse accompanying a minister or other staff member on a business trip. If the spouse's presence on the trip serves a legitimate business purpose, and the spouse's travel expenses are reimbursed by the church under an accountable arrangement (described above) then the reimbursements represent a nontaxable fringe benefit. If these two requirements are not met, the reimbursements represent taxable income to the minister or staff member.

▲ **CAUTION.** *If either of these conditions is not met, then a church's reimbursement of a nonemployee spouse's travel expenses will represent taxable income to the minister or other staff member. The same applies to children who accompany a minister or staff member on a business trip. Further, the IRS may assert that a church's failure to report the reimbursement of the spouse's expenses as taxable income to an employee meeting the definition of a disqualified person (see above) makes the reimbursement an "automatic" excess benefit triggering intermediate sanctions, as noted previously in this chapter.*

➤ TAX SAVINGS TIP. If a church does not reimburse the travel expenses of a pastor's spouse who accompanies the pastor on a business trip, then the spouse may be able to deduct travel expenses as a charitable contribution (assuming that the spouse's presence on the trip serves a legitimate charitable purpose). Some conditions apply.

Expense documentation – practical suggestions

Busy church pastors and leaders can find the expense documentation requirements of federal tax law burdensome and frustrating. At the same time, failure to comply with them can result in very severe penalties being assessed against the pastor or leader personally, in addition to a requirement that he/she repay the expenses to the church. Accordingly, church leaders should develop practical, workable systems that allow them to provide the necessary documentation in a timely manner. If the pastor or other leader has an administrative assistant or equivalent, the assistant is often familiar with the leader's calendar and appointments and can assist in providing the required documentation.

Technology (software/applications) can also aid compliance in this area. For example, some newer applications allow an executive to take a snapshot of a receipt with his/her smart phone and jot a few notes that provide the required documentation in a very efficient manner. Some applications actually read the information on the receipt and then create and email an expense report to a user-selected email address. A popular example of such an application is Expensify (*expensify.com*). Such applications may also be used to track automobile mileage. Whatever the method, church leaders should make the effort to avoid the potentially severe penalties that can apply to inadequately documented expenses.

Church-owned vehicles

Churches should consider the advantages of acquiring an automobile for employees' church-related travel. Here's why: If a church purchases a car, and the church board adopts a resolution restricting use of the car to church-related activities, then the employee reports no income or deductions, and better yet, there are no accountings, reimbursements, allowances, or recordkeeping requirements. This assumes that the car is, in fact, used exclusively for church-related purposes, and the conditions specified in the income tax regulations are satisfied.

Commuting is always considered to be a personal use of a car, and so this procedure would not be available if a church allowed an employee to commute to work in a church-owned vehicle. Fortunately, the income tax regulations permit certain church employees who use a church-owned vehicle exclusively for business purposes except for commuting to receive all of the benefits associated with business use of a church-owned vehicle, if certain additional conditions are met.

Most churches that provide a staff member with a car do not consider either of these alternatives. Rather, they simply allow the employee to use the vehicle and impose no limitations on personal use. This arrangement results in taxable income to the staff member, whether the staff member is a minister or a lay employee.

Self-employment tax

There is one provision in the tax code that has caused more confusion for ministers and church treasurers than any other, and it is this: Ministers are always treated as self-employed for Social Security with regard to services they perform in the exercise of their ministry. This is true even if they are employees for federal income tax reporting purposes. This is sometimes referred to as the "dual tax status" of ministers.

Social Security benefits are financed through two tax systems. Employers and employees each pay Social Security and Medicare (sometimes collectively referred to as "FICA") taxes up to a specified amount. Self-employed persons pay the "self-employment tax" up to a specified amount. Note that self-employed workers are responsible for paying their entire Social Security tax liability, while employees pay only half (their employer pays the other half).

5

Compensation and Benefits

143

⦿ **KEY POINT.** Ministers always are treated as self-employed for Social Security with respect to services performed in the exercise of their ministry, and so they do not pay Social Security and Medicare taxes. Rather, they pay the self-employment tax with respect to church compensation, unless they have filed a timely application for exemption from Social Security taxes (and received back a copy of their exemption application from the IRS marked "approved"). As a result, ministers must be familiar with the self-employment tax rules. So must lay church employees who work for a church that filed a timely exemption from Social Security coverage (Form 8274), since they are considered self-employed for Social Security.

⦿ **KEY POINT.** Many churches pay some or all of their pastor's self-employment taxes.

⦿ **KEY POINT.** Housing allowances and the fair rental value of parsonages are includable in self-employment earnings for Social Security purposes.

▲ **CAUTION.** *Many churches withhold the employees' share of Social Security and Medicare taxes from ministers' compensation, and then pay the employer's share. In other words, they treat their minister as an employee for Social Security. This is understandable, especially when the church treats the minister as an employee for purposes of federal income taxation. But, it is always incorrect for a church to treat a minister as an employee for Social Security with respect to services performed in the exercise of ministry.*

Ministers may exempt themselves from self-employment taxes with respect to services performed in the exercise of ministry if several requirements are met. Among other things, the exemption application (IRS Form 4361) must be filed by the due date of a minister's federal tax return (Form 1040) for the second year in which he or she had net self-employment earnings of $400 or more, any part of which derived from the performance of ministerial duties. In most cases, this means the form is due by April 15 of the third year of ministry. Also, the minister must be opposed on the basis of religious convictions to accepting Social Security benefits.

As a self-employed person for Social Security, a minister computes self-employment taxes on Schedule SE of Form 1040.

Health insurance

Prior to the enactment of the Affordable Care Act ("Obamacare"), many employers provided health benefits for their employees by paying health insurers directly for the cost of private health insurance, or by reimbursing employees for the substantiated cost of insurance premiums. The amounts paid by employers under such arrangements were a nontaxable fringe benefit under section 106 of the tax code, which states that, with some exceptions, "gross income of an employee does not include employer-provided coverage under an accident or health plan."

The IRS affirmed the tax-free status of these arrangements in a 1961 ruling in which it concluded that if an employer reimburses an employee's substantiated premiums for non-employer sponsored medical insurance, the payments are excluded from the employee's taxable income under section 106. *IRS Revenue Ruling 61-146.* The IRS added that this exclusion also applies if the employer pays the premiums directly to the insurance company.

> **EXAMPLE.** A church does not have a group health plan for its employees. Instead, employees purchase their own health insurance through private insurers, and the church reimburses employees who substantiate the amount of the health insurance premium they paid. Prior to the Affordable Care Act, the employer's reimbursement of insurance premiums under such an arrangement was a nontaxable fringe benefit, subject to some conditions.

> **EXAMPLE.** Same facts as the previous example, except that the church paid the insurance companies directly for the cost of health insurance premiums on policies secured by their employees. Prior to the Affordable Care Act, the employer's payment of insurance premiums under such an arrangement was a nontaxable fringe benefit, subject to some conditions.

Are these common and longstanding arrangements affected by the Affordable Care Act? Can employers continue to treat their payment of the health insurance premiums of employees under individual health insurance policies as a nontaxable fringe benefit? If they pay some or all of the premiums of their employees' private health insurance are its payments a nontaxable fringe benefit as in prior years? And what about churches that drop their health coverage in favor of what they assume will be a lower cost alternative of paying some or all of their employees' premiums for insurance coverage purchased on a state exchange? Is this a nontaxable fringe benefit?

In late 2013, the IRS and Departments of Labor and Health and Human Services addressed these questions directly in an official notice. *IRS Notice 2013-54.* The Notice concludes that two of the Affordable Care Act's "market reforms" apply to all "group health plans," with a few exceptions, and it defines group health plans to *include* plans under which "an employer reimburses an employee for some or all of the premium expenses incurred for an individual health insurance policy . . . or arrangements under which the employer uses its funds to directly pay the premium for an individual health insurance policy covering the employee" (collectively, an "employer payment plan").

The Affordable Care Act contains several "reforms" of the insurance market (the "market reforms") that apply to "group health plans" effective January 1, 2014. The market reforms include:

- *The "annual dollar limit prohibition."* A group health plan may not establish any annual limit on the dollar amount of benefits for any individual.
- *"The preventive services requirement."* Employer-sponsored group health plans must provide certain preventive services without imposing any cost-sharing requirements for these services on employees.

The Notice concludes that in most cases employer payment plans will fail to meet these market reforms and therefore will be unlawful under the Affordable Care Act because they typically impose limits on benefits in violation of the annual dollar limit prohibition. The Notice explains:

A group health plan, such as an employer payment plan, that reimburses employees for an employee's substantiated individual insurance policy premiums must satisfy the market reforms for group health plans. However the employer payment plan will fail to comply with the annual dollar limit prohibition because (1) an employer payment plan is considered to impose an annual limit up to the cost of the individual market coverage purchased

through the arrangement, and (2) an employer payment plan cannot be integrated with any individual health insurance policy purchased under the arrangement.

⊙ **KEY POINT.** A group health plan that violates one of the market reforms is subject to a penalty in the form of an excise tax of $100 per day per affected individual.

Are there any exceptions to these rules? Is there any way for churches to continue paying for employees' health insurance through private insurers or state exchanges as a nontaxable fringe benefit? The Notice mentions three possibilities:

- The market reforms do not apply to a group health plan that has fewer than two participants who are current employees on the first day of the plan year.
- The market reforms do not apply to a group health plan with regard to "excepted benefits" which are defined to include disability income, dental and vision benefits, long-term care benefits, and certain health FSAs. As a result, these plans are not necessarily prohibited for failing to comply with the Affordable Care Act's market reforms.
- Another option that may allow some churches to continue to pay employee insurance premiums on a pre-tax basis is to participate in the "SHOP" (Small Business Health Options Program) marketplace. The SHOP marketplace makes it possible for small employers to provide qualified health plans to their employees. Some conditions apply. For 2014, the SHOP marketplace is open to employers with 50 or fewer full-time-equivalent employees (FTEs). You may qualify for tax credits if you use SHOP. The small business health care tax credit that many churches received in the past is only available for 2014 for plans purchased through the SHOP marketplace.

⊙ **KEY POINT.** The notice acknowledges that "employers may establish payroll practices of forwarding post-tax employee wages to a health insurance issuer at the direction of an employee without establishing a group health plan if the standards of the Department of Labor regulation at 2510.3-1(j) are met."

HRAs, FSAs, and HSAs

IRS Notice 2013-54 specifies that the Affordable Care Act's market reforms apply to certain types of group health plans, including health reimbursement arrangements (HRAs), health flexible spending arrangements (health FSAs), in addition to the employer payment plans described above.

HRAs

The Notice concludes that "standalone" HRAs are no longer permitted by the Affordable Care Act due to their failure to comply with the market reforms. But there are two exceptions:

- HRAs that are "integrated" with other coverage as part of a group health plan are allowed if the other coverage complies with the annual dollar limit prohibition. In such a case, the fact that benefits under the HRA by itself are limited does not fail to comply with the annual dollar limit prohibition because the combined benefit satisfies the requirements. The requirements for integration are explained in *Notice 2013-54.*
- In the case of a "standalone" HRA that is limited to *retirees*, the exemption for plans with less than two employees means that the retiree-only HRA is not subject to the annual dollar limit prohibition.

FSAs

A health FSA is not subject to the annual dollar limit market reform but only if it is offered through a "cafeteria plan" that is subject to the separate annual limitation under section 125 of the tax code. Employees electing coverage under a health FSA typically elect to enter into a salary reduction agreement. For plan years beginning after 2012, the amount of the salary reduction is limited to $2,500 (indexed annually for plan years beginning after 2013). There is no similar limitation on a health FSA that is not part of a section 125 plan, and as a result "a health FSA that is not offered through a section 125 plan is subject to the annual dollar limit

prohibition and will fail to comply with the annual dollar limit prohibition."

IRS Notice 2013-54 states:

The market reforms do not apply to a group health plan in relation to its provision of benefits that are excepted benefits. Health FSAs are group health plans but will be considered to provide only excepted benefits if the employer also makes available group health plan coverage that is not limited to excepted benefits and the health FSA is structured so that the maximum benefit payable to any participant cannot exceed two times the participant's salary reduction election for the health FSA for the year (or, if greater, cannot exceed $500 plus the amount of the participant's salary reduction election). Therefore, a health FSA that is considered to provide only excepted benefits is not subject to the market reforms. If an employer provides a health FSA that does not qualify as excepted benefits, the health FSA generally is subject to the market reforms, including the preventive services requirements. Because a health FSA that is not excepted benefits is not integrated with a group health plan, it will fail to meet the preventive services requirements.

HSAs

Health Savings Accounts were created by Congress in 2003 as a way to manage health costs by giving consumers an incentive to lower their medical expenses. This was done by limiting eligibility to persons with high deductible health insurance who would then use the savings in premium dollars to invest in an HSA, with the balance in their HSA being accessible to pay qualified health expenses. Unlike FSAs, any balance in an HSA at year-end is not forfeited. It rolls over to succeeding years. Further, beginning at age 65, persons can use their HSA balance to pay for any expenses, including non-medical expenses. So, an HSA can augment retirement savings.

The Affordable Care Act does not prohibit HSAs, but it does impact them in various ways, including the following:

- The penalty for making HSA distributions that are not used for qualified medical expenses increases from 10 to 20 percent for those under the age of 65.
- You can receive tax-free distributions from your HSA to pay or be reimbursed for qualified medical expenses you incur after you establish the HSA. Qualified medical expenses are those expenses that would generally qualify for the medical and dental expenses itemized deduction on your federal tax return. Also, non-prescription medicines (other than insulin) are not considered qualified medical expenses for HSA purposes. A medicine or drug will be a qualified medical expense for HSA purposes only if the medicine or drug requires a prescription, is available without a prescription (an over-the-counter medicine or drug) and you get a prescription for it, or is insulin.
- Beginning in 2014, all non-grandfathered health insurance coverage in the individual and small group markets will cover essential health benefits (EHB), which include items and services in 10 statutory benefit categories, such as hospitalization, prescription drugs, and maternity and newborn care, and are equal in scope to a typical employer health plan. In addition to offering EHB, non-grandfathered health insurance plans must provide consumers with "minimum value," meaning that the plan provides a minimum "actuarial value" of 60 percent of mandated expenses. This level of coverage is designated as a "bronze" plan. There are also silver, gold, and platinum plans that cover higher percentages of costs. The problem is that persons eligible for an HSA must be covered under a high deductible health plan (HDHP), and such plans may not cover the

minimum 60 percent of healthcare costs since the high deductible generally means that the employee is picking up a larger share of medical expenses.

◉ **KEY POINT.** Churches that offer (1) health reimbursement arrangements (HRAs), including HRAs integrated with a group health plan; (2) group health plans under which an employer reimburses an employee for some or all of the premium expenses incurred for an individual health insurance policy, or arrangements under which the employer uses its funds to directly pay the premium for an individual health insurance policy covering the employee; (3) health flexible spending arrangements (health FSAs); or (4) a health savings account, should have them reviewed by legal counsel or a tax professional to ensure that they either comply with the Affordable Care Act's market reforms, or qualify for an exception.

Other forms of insurance

The cost of group term life insurance bought by an employer for its employees ordinarily is not taxable to the employees so long as the amount of coverage does not exceed $50,000 per employee. Generally, life insurance can qualify as group term life insurance only if it is available to at least ten full-time employees. However, there are some exceptions to this rule. For example, the ten full-time employee rule does not apply if (1) an employer provides the insurance to all full-time employees who provide satisfactory evidence of insurability, (2) insurance coverage is based on a uniform percentage of pay, and (3) evidence of insurability is limited to a medical questionnaire completed by the employee that does not require a physical examination.

Other kinds of insurance premiums paid by the church on behalf of a minister or lay church employee ordinarily represent taxable income. For example, the cost of premiums on a whole life or universal life insurance policy paid by a church on the life of its minister (and naming the minister's spouse and children as beneficiaries) ordinarily must be reported as income to the minister.

Retirement accounts

Most ministers (and some lay staff members) participate in some form of retirement plan. Such plans often are sponsored either by the local church, or by a denomination or agency with which the church is affiliated. Church employees covered by certain kinds of plans can choose to have part of their pay set aside each year (through salary reductions) in the retirement fund, rather than receiving it as income. Amounts set aside by the employing church under these plans may be excludable from gross income for tax purposes. These amounts are sometimes called "elective deferrals" because the employee elects to set aside the money, and tax on the money is deferred until it is taken out of the account. This option is available to ministers or lay employees who are covered by tax-sheltered annuities ("403(b) plans"), simplified employee pensions (SEPs), and some other plans.

Payments made by an employing church to an employee's tax-sheltered annuity, SEP, and some other plans, and funded out of church funds rather than through a reduction in an employee's compensation, may also be excluded from the employee's gross income for tax purposes under certain circumstances. There are limits on how much an employee can elect to contribute into such plans, and on how much the employing church can contribute out of its own funds. Of course, ministers and lay workers (whether employees or self-employed for income tax purposes) can also contribute to an IRA.

➤ RECOMMENDATION. If a church has not established or contributed to a retirement plan for its staff members, then it should consider doing so, or at least ensuring that staff members are participating in an adequate alternative (particularly in the case of ministers who have exempted themselves from Social Security). Further, if staff members are participating in a retirement plan, then the end of the year is a good time to determine how contributions to the plan will be funded (i.e., through employee contributions, salary reductions, or church contributions) and in what amounts.

Works made for hire

It is common for church employees to compose music or write books or articles in their church office during office hours. What is often not understood is that such persons do not necessarily own the copyright to the works they create. While the one who creates a work generally is its author and the initial owner of the copyright in the work, section 201(b) of the Copyright Act specifies that "in the case of a work made for hire, the employer or other person for whom the work was prepared is considered the author ... and, unless the parties have expressly agreed otherwise in a written instrument signed by them, owns all of the rights comprised in the copyright."

The copyright law defines "work made for hire" as "a work prepared by an employee within the scope of his or her employment." There are two requirements that must be met: (1) the person creating the work is an employee, and (2) the employee created the work within the scope of his or her employment. Whether or not one is an employee will depend on the same factors used in determining whether one is an employee or self-employed for federal income tax reporting purposes. However, the courts have been very liberal in finding employee status in this context, so it is possible that a court would conclude that a work is a work made for hire even though the author reports federal income taxes as a self-employed person.

The second requirement is that the work must have been created within the scope of employment. This requirement generally means that the work was created during regular working hours, on the employer's premises, using the employer's staff and equipment. This is often a difficult standard to apply. As a result, it is desirable for church employees to discuss this issue with the church leadership to avoid any potential misunderstandings.

Section 201(b), quoted above, allows an employer and employee to agree in a signed, written instrument that copyright ownership in works created by the employee within the scope of employment does not belong to the employer. This should be a matter for consideration by any church having a minister or other staff member who creates literary or musical works during office hours, on church premises, using church staff and church equipment (e.g., computers, printers, paper, library, secretaries). The services of an attorney will be needed to draft an appropriate instrument, assuming that the church desires to divest itself of copyright ownership in a particular work made for hire. An attorney also will be able to explain the potential tax ramifications of such an instrument, which, if handled incorrectly, may include jeopardy to the church's tax-exempt status and the possible application of intermediate sanctions to the employee and members of the church board.

Qualified Tuition Reductions ("QTR")

Many churches operate elementary or secondary schools, and charge reduced tuition to certain school employees. For example, assume that a church operates an elementary school, charges annual tuition of $4,000, but only charges tuition of $500 for the children of school employees and charges no tuition at all for the child of Pastor Eric (the church's senior minister and president of the school). Such "tuition reductions" are perfectly appropriate. Further, section 117(d) of the federal tax code specifies that they will not necessarily result in taxable income to the school employees. In other words, the church or school may not need to report the tuition reductions as taxable income.

However, section 117(d) also provides that "highly compensated employees" cannot exclude qualified tuition reductions from their income unless the same benefit is available on substantially similar terms to other employees. The term "highly compensated employee" is defined to include any employee who was paid compensation for the previous year in excess of a specified amount that is adjusted annually for inflation.

If, in the example cited above, Pastor Eric is a highly compensated employee, then the church would have to include $4,000 (the entire amount of the tuition reduction) in Pastor Eric's reportable income since he is a highly compensated employee and the benefit available to him is not available on substantially similar terms to other employees. However, this will not affect other school employees who are not "highly compensated." They will be able to exclude tuition reductions from their income.

○ **KEY POINT.** The IRS has ruled that tuition reductions are tax-free only for school employees, and so if a church operates a private school, only employees who perform duties on behalf of the school qualify for this benefit. If the school offers tuition reductions to church employees who perform no duties for the school, these reductions are a taxable fringe benefit.

Loans to ministers

Churches often make loans to ministers to enable a minister to pay for housing or some other major purchase. In some cases the church charges no interest or a low rate far below the prevailing market rate of inter-est. These loans can create problems for a number of reasons. Consider the following:

- Many state nonprofit corporation laws prohibit loans to officers and directors. No church should consider making any loan (even at a reasonable rate of interest) to a minister who is an officer or director of the church without first confirming that such loans are permissible under state law.
- No-interest or low-interest loans to ministers may be viewed as "inurement" of the church's income to a minister. As noted above, this can potentially jeopardize the church's tax-exempt status.
- For loans of $10,000 or more (or for loans of lower amounts where an intent to avoid taxes exists), a church must value the benefit to a minister of receiving a no-interest or low-interest loan and add this amount to the minister's reportable income. The point is this—even if loans to ministers are allowed under your state's nonprofit corporation law, the church must recognize that no-interest and low-interest loans of $10,000 or more will result in income to a minister that must be valued and reported on the minister's Form W-2 and Form 1040. Failure to do so could result in prohibited "inurement" of the church's income to a private individual, jeopardizing the church's tax-exempt status.

➤ OBSERVATION. Some ministers and lay employees never fully repay a loan made to them by their church. The forgiveness of debt ordinarily represents taxable income to the debtor. As a result, if a church makes a loan to a minister or other staff member and the debt is later forgiven by the church, taxable income is generated in the amount of the forgiven debt.

Voluntary withholding

Ministers' compensation is exempt from income tax withholding whether a minister reports income taxes as an employee or as self-employed. While it is true that the tax code requires *every* employer, including churches and religious organizations, to withhold federal income taxes from employee wages, there are some exceptions to this rule. One exception is wages paid for "services performed by a duly ordained, commissioned, or licensed minister of a church in the exercise of his ministry." Therefore, a church need not withhold income taxes from the salary of a minister who is an employee for income tax reporting purposes. Further, since the withholding requirements only apply to the wages of *employees*, a church should not "withhold" taxes from the compensation of a minister (or any other worker, such as a part-time custodian) who reports his or her income taxes as a *self-employed* person.

The IRS maintains that a church and a minister-employee may agree voluntarily that federal income taxes be withheld from the minister's wages, but this is not required. Some ministers find voluntary withholding attractive since it eliminates the guesswork, quarterly reports, and penalties associated with the estimated tax procedure (which applies automatically if *voluntary withholding* is *not* elected). A minister-employee who elects to enter into a voluntary withholding arrangement with his or her church need only file a completed Form W-4 (employee's withholding allowance certificate) with the church. The filing of this form is deemed to be a request for voluntary withholding. Voluntary withholding arrangements can be terminated unilaterally by either a minister or the church, or by mutual consent. Alternatively, a minister can stipulate that the voluntary withholding arrangement will terminate on a specified date. In such a case, the minister must give the church a signed statement setting forth the date on which the voluntary withholding is to terminate; the minister's name and address; and a statement that he wishes to enter into a voluntary withholding arrangement with his or her employer. This statement must be attached to a completed Form W-4. The voluntary withholding arrangement will terminate automatically on the date specified.

But what about a minister's self-employment taxes? Ministers who have not exempted themselves from Social Security coverage are required to pay the self-employment tax (Social Security tax for self-employed persons). Can a church "withhold" the self-employment tax from a minister-employee's wages? The answer is yes. *IRS Publication 517* ("Social Security and Other Information for Members of the Clergy") states that "if you perform your services as an employee of the church (under the common law rules), you may be able to enter into a voluntary withholding agreement with your employer, the church, to cover any income *and self-employment tax* that may be due." A church whose

minister has elected voluntary withholding (and who is not exempt from Social Security taxes) simply withholds an additional amount from each paycheck to cover the minister's estimated self-employment tax liability for the year. The additional amount withheld to cover self-employment taxes must be reported (on the minister's W-2 form and the church's 941 forms) as additional income tax withheld, and not as "Social Security taxes" (or "FICA" taxes). The minister should amend his or her W-4 (withholding allowance certificate) by inserting on line 6 the additional amount of tax to be withheld. The excess income tax withheld is a credit against tax that the minister claims on his or her federal income tax return, and it in effect is applied against the minister's self-employment tax liability. Further, it is considered to be a timely payment of the minister's self-employment tax obligation, and so no penalties for late payment of the quarterly estimates will apply.

➤ RECOMMENDATION. Churches should apprise ministers that they may enter into a voluntary withholding arrangement. For many ministers, such an arrangement will be preferable to the estimated tax procedure. This procedure requires ministers to estimate their income tax and self-employment tax liability for the year prior to April 15 and then to pay one-fourth of the total estimated tax liability on or by April 15, June 15, September 15, and the following January 15. These quarterly payments are accompanied by a "payment voucher" that is contained in IRS Form 1040-ES. Some ministers find the estimated tax procedure inconvenient and undesirable (it is often hard to budget for the quarterly payments).

Special occasion gifts

It is common for ministers (and in some cases lay employees) to receive special occasion gifts during the course of the year. Examples include Christmas, birthday, and anniversary gifts. Churches and church employees often do not understand how to report these payments for federal tax purposes. The general rule is this—if the "gifts" are funded through members' contributions to the church (i.e., the contributions are entered or recorded in the church's books as cash received and the members are given charitable contribution credit) then the distribution to the recipient should be reported as taxable compensation and included on his or her W-2 and Form 1040. The same rule applies to special occasion "gifts" made to a minister or lay employee by the church out of the general fund. Members who contribute to special occasion offerings may be able to deduct their contributions if (1) the offering was authorized in advance by the church board; (2) the contributions are to the church and are entered or recorded in the church's books as cash received; and (3) they are able to itemize deductions on Schedule A (Form 1040). Churches should be prepared to report such "gifts" to a minister or lay employee as taxable income on Form W-2. Of course, members are free to make personal gifts to ministers and lay employees, such as a card at Christmas accompanied by a check or cash. Such payments may be tax-free gifts to the recipient (though they are not deductible by the donor). These same rules apply to other kinds of special occasion gifts as well.

It is common for churches to make generous retirement gifts to retiring ministers (and in some cases lay employees). Do these gifts represent taxable income to the recipient? To the extent that the recipient is an employee (or would be classified as an employee by the IRS), there is little doubt that the "gift" would constitute taxable income since section 102(c) of the tax code specifies that "any amount transferred by or for an employer to or for the benefit of an employee" is not excludable from taxable income by the employee as a gift, other than certain employee achievement awards and insignificant holiday gifts. This conclusion is reinforced by the narrow definition of the term *gift*. The Supreme Court has noted that "a gift... proceeds from a detached and disinterested generosity... out of affection, respect, admiration, charity, or like impulses.... The most critical consideration ... is the transferor's intention." *Commissioner v. Duberstein, 363 U.S. 278, 285 (1960).* The Court also observed that "it doubtless is the exceptional payment by an employer to an employee that amounts to a gift," and that the church's characterization of the distribution as a "gift" is "not determinative—there must be an objective inquiry as to whether what is called a gift amounts to it in reality."

● **KEY POINT.** Intermediate sanctions, discussed earlier in this chapter, may apply to a special occasion or retirement gift that results in unreasonable compensation to the recipient, or that is not reported as taxable income regardless of the amount involved. Church leaders must be sure to consider this possibility when considering such a gift.

Bargain sales

Occasionally, a church will sell property to a staff member at a price that is below market value. To illustrate, some churches "sell" a parsonage to a retiring minister at a price well below the property's fair market value. Other churches may sell a car or other church-owned vehicle to a minister at a below-market price. The important consideration with such "bargain sales" is this—the "bargain" element (*i.e.*, the difference between the sales price charged by the church and the property's market value) must be reported as income to the minister on Form W-2. Churches should consider the tax consequences of such sales before approving them.

Director immunity

Most states have adopted laws that provide *uncompensated* officers and directors of most charitable organizations (including churches) with limited immunity from legal liability. The federal Volunteer Protection Act provides similar protection as a matter of federal law. The immunity provided under state and federal law only applies to uncompensated officers and directors. What does this have to do with compensation planning? Simply this—churches should consider adopting a resolution clarifying that a minister's annual compensation package is for ministerial duties rendered to the church, *and is not for any duties on the church board.* Like any other church officer or director, the minister serves without compensation. Such a resolution might qualify the minister for protection under the legal immunity law. It is worth considering.

Discretionary funds

It is a fairly common practice for a church to set aside a sum of money in a "discretionary fund" and give the senior minister the sole authority to distribute the money in the fund. In some cases, the minister has no instructions regarding permissible distributions. In other cases, the church establishes guidelines, but these often are oral and ambiguous. Many churches are unaware of the tax consequences of such arrangements. To the extent the minister has the authority to use any portion of the discretionary fund for his or her own personal use, then the entire fund must be reported as taxable income to the minister in the year it is funded. This is true even if the minister does not personally benefit from the fund. The mere fact that the minister *could* personally benefit from the fund is enough for

5

Compensation and Benefits

the fund to constitute taxable income. The basis for this result is the "constructive receipt" rule, which is explained in the income tax regulations as follows:

> *Income although not actually reduced to a taxpayer's possession is constructively received by him in the taxable year during which it is credited to his account, set apart for him, or otherwise made available so that he may draw upon it at any time, or so that he could have drawn upon it during the taxable year if notice of intention to withdraw had been given. However, income is not constructively received if the taxpayer's control of its receipt is subject to substantial limitations or restrictions.*

For a discretionary fund to constitute taxable income to a minister, the minister must have the authority to "draw upon it at any time" for his or her own personal use. This means that the fund was established without any express prohibition against personal distributions. On the other hand, if a discretionary fund is set up by a board resolution that absolutely prohibits any distribution of the fund for the minister's personal use, then the constructive receipt rule is avoided. In the words of the regulation, "income is not constructively received if the taxpayer's control of its receipt is subject to substantial limitations or restrictions." In order to avoid the reporting of the entire discretionary fund as taxable income to the minister, the fund should be established by a board or congregational resolution that prohibits any use of the fund by the minister for personal purposes. Further, the resolution should specify that the fund may be distributed by the minister only for needs or projects that are consistent with the church's exempt purposes (as set forth in the church's governing documents). For accountability purposes, a member of the church board should review all distributions from the discretionary fund to be sure that these requirements are met.

Severance pay

Many churches have entered into severance pay arrangements with a pastor or other staff member. Such arrangements can occur when a pastor or staff member is dismissed, retires, or voluntarily resigns. Church treasurers must determine whether severance pay is taxable so that it can be properly reported (on a W-2

and the church's 941 forms). Also, taxes must be withheld from severance pay that is paid to nonminister employees (and ministers who have elected voluntary withholding). Failure to properly report severance pay can result in substantial penalties for both a church and the recipient.

In most cases, severance pay represents taxable income to the recipient. There is one exception that will apply in some cases. The tax code excludes from taxable income "the amount of any damages received (whether by suit or agreement and whether as lump sums or as periodic payments) *on account of personal injuries or sickness*." According to this provision, severance pay that is intended to settle personal injury claims may be nontaxable. The term "personal injuries" is defined broadly by the IRS and the courts, and in some cases includes potential or threatened lawsuits based on discrimination and harassment.

◉ KEY POINT. The Tax Court has noted that "payments for terminating and canceling employment contracts are not payments for personal injuries."

◉ KEY POINT. The tax code specifies that the term "personal injury" does not include emotional distress.

Here are some factors to consider (based on actual cases) in deciding whether a severance payment made to a former employee represents taxable compensation or nontaxable damages in settlement of a personal injury claim:

(1) An amount paid to a former employee "to reward her for her past services and to make her severance as amicable as possible" is taxable compensation.
(2) An amount paid to a former employee under a severance agreement that contains no reference to a specific discrimination or other personal injury claim is taxable compensation.
(3) If an employer pays a former employee severance pay, and reports the severance pay on a Form W-2, this is strong evidence that the amount represents taxable compensation.
(4) If an employer continues one or more employee benefits (such as health insurance) as part of a severance agreement, this suggests that any

amount payable under the agreement represents taxable compensation.

(5) If an employer withholds taxes from amounts paid under a severance agreement, this "is a significant factor" in classifying the payments as taxable income. Of course, this factor will not be relevant in the case of ministers whose wages are not subject to withholding (unless they elect voluntary withholding).

(6) Referring to a payment as "severance pay" indicates that it is taxable compensation rather than nontaxable damages in settlement of a personal injury claim.

(7) Severance pay based on a former employee's salary (such as one year's salary) is more likely to be viewed as taxable compensation rather than nontaxable damages in settlement of a personal injury claim.

(8) To be nontaxable, severance pay must represent "damages" received in settlement of a personal injury claim. The IRS has noted that this language requires more than a settlement agreement in which a former employee "waives" any discrimination or other personal injury claims he or she may have against an employer. If the employee "never filed a lawsuit or any other type of claim against [the employer] ... the payment cannot be characterized as damages for personal injuries" since "there is no indication that personal injuries actually exist."

● **KEY POINT.** Section 409A of the tax code imposes strict requirements on most nonqualified deferred compensation plans (NQDPs). IRS regulations define an NQDP to include any plan that provides for the deferral of compensation. This definition may be broad enough to include some severance agreements and many other kinds of church compensation arrangements. Any church or other organization that is considering a severance agreement with a current employee (or any other arrangement that defers compensation to a future year) should contact an attorney to have the arrangement reviewed to ensure compliance with both section 409A and the final regulations. Such a review will protect against the substantial penalties the IRS can assess for noncompliance. It also will help clarify whether a deferred compensation arrangement is a viable option in light of the limitations imposed by section 409A and the final regulations.

Income "splitting"

Some ministers have attempted to "split" their church income with their spouse. This often is done to qualify the spouse for Social Security or other benefits or to avoid the Social Security "annual earnings test" (which reduces Social Security benefits to retired employees who are under "full retirement age" who earn more than an amount prescribed by law). For income splitting arrangements to work, the courts have required proof that the spouse is an employee of the church. This means that the spouse performs meaningful services on behalf of the church. The courts have pointed to a number of factors indicating that a spouse is *not* an employee:

(1) The spouse did not receive a paycheck.
(2) The spouse was not employed elsewhere.
(3) The spouse's "compensation" was designed to provide a tax benefit (such as an IRA contribution), and lacked any economic reality.
(4) Neither the church nor the minister documented any of the services the spouse performed.
(5) Neither the church nor the minister could explain how the spouse's "salary" was determined.
(6) There was no employment contract between the church and the minister's spouse.
(7) No taxes were withheld from the spouse's "salary."
(8) The spouse's income was not reported on the church's employment tax returns (Forms 941).
(9) There was no evidence that wages were actually paid to the spouse, or that any employment contract existed, or that the spouse was treated as an employee.

The courts generally have been skeptical of attempts by taxpayers to shift income to a spouse. The message is clear—ministers should not attempt to obtain tax benefits by shifting income to a spouse unless there is economic reality to the arrangement.

Chapter 6

Managing Liquidity and Financial Position

PHILOSOPHY OF LIQUIDITY AND FINANCIAL POSITION

As with budgeting (addressed in Chapter 1), a church's management of liquidity and financial position begins with a philosophical assessment. Some churches, for example, intentionally choose to operate with little or no cash reserves because their leaders believe such a practice results in daily dependence on God to supply the church's needs. Such a philosophy is based on their views of Scripture. Churches that adhere to such a philosophy often believe it is appropriate to spend all money soon after it arrives to carry out the work of the church. An example of the scriptural support used by churches that follow this philosophy is God's providing for the Israelites when they wandered in the wilderness after their exodus from Egypt. God provided daily manna from heaven and instructed the Israelites not to save any of the manna from one day to the next (other than on the day before the Sabbath), so that they would depend daily on God for their sustenance.

Other churches adhere to the philosophy that maintaining a reasonable level of cash reserves and maintaining strong liquidity is an act of biblical stewardship. Churches that adhere to this philosophy also cite scriptural examples, such as Joseph instructing Pharaoh to prepare for a seven-year famine by storing grain, and the scriptural command in Malachi to bring the tithes into the "storehouse." Churches in this camp believe that financial stability and viability are essential traits for a church to do its work consistently and reliably. Some churches support the idea of having resources to provide for contingencies by citing the fact that David picked up "five smooth stones" for his sling on the way to see Goliath, instead of just one.

During the Great Recession that began to affect the U.S. economy so severely in late 2008, churches with little or no cash reserves felt the most immediate, severe effects. In fact, many churches that had significant debt outstanding and that had little or no cash reserves found themselves in immediate financial peril. A significant number of churches were unable to pay their debt obligations and lost their church facilities in foreclosure or its equivalent. Failure to honor a debt obligation certainly presents scriptural challenges for any church leader.

From a practical perspective, any number of unexpected developments can occur that could present cash flow challenges to a church. For example, if a well-respected leader of the church left, or committed some discreditable act, then attendance and financial support of the church could significantly and immediately suffer. A sudden downturn in the economy like the one that occurred in 2008, brought on by the outbreak of war, a stock market collapse, or any other unpredictable event, could have a similar impact.

Part of effective stewardship involves having a viable and stable ministry. If church leaders are frequently focused on addressing cash flow challenges or related concerns, they will focus less on their ministry objectives.

For churches with significant outstanding debt, healthy cash reserves and financial position are essential in supporting the church's ability to honor its debt obligations—and failure by a church to honor its debt obligations can adversely affect the credibility, witness, and mission of a church and its leaders. A church with the philosophy of maintaining no significant cash reserves should not incur significant debt obligations.

References to "cash reserves" herein refer not only to cash maintained in a bank and similar accounts, but also to investments in liquid marketable securities that may be readily converted to cash.

PHILOSOPHY OF DEBT

Whether it is permissible or advisable for a church to enter into a debt obligation depends upon the church's philosophy about debt and financial position. Churches' philosophies about debt are often based on Scripture. Many churches enter into debt obligations, considering it permissible to do so as long as each church carefully and wisely plans for the ability to honor its debt obligations. Some churches believe they should not incur debt obligations, and the references to debt and its management herein are not intended to disrespect their positions.

PHILOSOPHY OF CASH FLOW SURPLUSES

As addressed much more fully in Chapter 1 (Budgeting), the authors support the idea that positive cash flows from the church's operations support healthy cash reserves and financial position. A church that intends to maintain a healthy financial position cannot, by definition, do so without cash flow surpluses. Many church leaders express their desire to maintain healthy cash reserves and financial position, but then operate in a manner that doesn't support that objective. If a church spends all of its cash revenue each year, then that church cannot improve its liquidity or cash reserves no matter how much its leaders may say they want to.

Improving a church's liquidity and cash reserves requires intentional effort as an essential part of the planning and budgeting process. That effort must include planning to spend less than what the church receives in cash revenues. For a church that has been following the habit of spending all of its cash receipts annually, the transition can be challenging. If the church's revenues are growing, the church may be able to make progress in this area by slowing or stopping spending increases as revenues rise. For churches whose revenues are not growing significantly, the transition will require the church to pursue additional revenue (through additional giving or from alternative revenue sources), employ expense reductions, or both.

For information about alternative revenue sources and their implications, see Chapter 4 (Other Revenue Sources). If expense reductions are necessary, they may be in areas of "overhead" (administrative and supporting activities), in ministry program areas, or in a combination of the two. Churches are often very reluctant to curtail a ministry program—especially one that seems to be doing good work. It is also painful and personal when expense reductions involve employee layoffs or terminations.

We all know that churches want to do as many things as they can to carry out their missions … and that there are always more needs and more ideas for ministries than churches can carry out. Obviously, there is a limit to how much any church can spend on carrying out its mission. The absolute limit is the amount of money that comes into the church. The church will either allow that limit to be its boundary or it will choose to impose a more disciplined boundary that is within the absolute limit. Only when the church imposes the more disciplined boundary will it make progress in im-

proving its liquidity and financial position. Either way, there will still be unmet needs and unfulfilled desires to carry out ministry.

TARGETING AND ACHIEVING DESIRED FINANCIAL POSITION

While positive cash flows and surpluses have merit, pursuing them should be part of a broader, but specific plan. The church should have specific, targeted objectives for achieving a desired financial condition as well as a timeframe for doing so. This combination provides a roadmap for the church's leaders in planning and budgeting. Adopting specific, targeted objectives addresses the reasonable question that some may have about the church's budget surpluses: *To what end is the church generating these surpluses?* An appropriate response is "To achieve the church's specific objectives for liquidity and financial position."

We hear from expert financial advisors continuously that individuals should have a financial plan with specific objectives. "Get out of debt," "Build cash reserves," and other phrases are ubiquitous parts of such plans. Interestingly, churches do not commonly have specific financial objectives or a roadmap for accomplishing them.

Once the church is philosophically on board with maintaining reasonable cash reserves and an improved financial position, and has determined that it is willing to take the steps to achieve those objectives, the next step is to define what the church considers to be appropriate cash reserves and a desired financial condition. The church should have specific targets. For example, the church may establish that its target for cash reserves is six months of cash operating expenses. The church may also state its objective of reducing its debt from $5 million to $3 million. These are merely examples. The point is that the targets should be specific. By setting specific targets, the church knows precisely why and to what extent it is pursuing cash flow surpluses.

Once the financial targets are defined, the church should establish what it considers to be a reasonable timeframe for achieving the objectives. For a church that is a long way from achieving its objectives, it is wise not to attempt to get from "Point A" to "Point B" overnight. Depending on the circumstances, the process of reaching the church's targets may take a number of years. If the church believes its journey from Point A to Point B will be long-term, it is important for the church to establish annual benchmarks or milestones (interim targets) to facilitate the monitoring and assessment of progress.

For example, assume the church has one month's cash operating expenses as a cash reserve and it plans to achieve a six-month reserve. Assume the church decides to achieve its target over a five-year period, by increasing the reserve by one month's operating expenses each year. The church establishes milestones for the end of each year accordingly. At the end of Year 1, the church should have two months of operating expenses in its cash reserves. At the end of Year 2, it should have three months, and so on, until the end of Year 5, when it should have six months of operating expenses in reserves, assuming the church has been able to follow its plan.

RECOMMENDED LIQUIDITY AND FINANCIAL POSITION OBJECTIVES

Church leaders may desire to improve their financial position and liquidity and to establish appropriate targets, but they may not have a sense for what the targets should be. What constitutes "reasonable" cash reserves and "sound" financial position?

The recommendations provided herein are general in nature and may not be appropriate for some churches, depending on the individual facts and circumstances. Churches should obtain counsel from advisors with significant professional financial experience in establishing their individual targets and objectives.

Baseline refers to a level that represents the minimum position for establishing healthy liquidity and financial position. *Strong refers to a level where financial position and liquidity should be more than adequate in most circumstances.* The term "cash" as it relates to reserves and balances is intended to include liquid marketable investment securities.

Operating cash reserves

Note: *The recommended levels are based on the assumption that the church already maintains cash, including liquid marketable securities, adequate to cover all donor-restricted and designated net assets. Recommended reserves and bal-*

ances are levels in excess of the amounts required to cover such items.

> Baseline: Three months of operating cash expenses plus current liabilities

> Strong: At least six months of operating cash expenses plus current liabilities

Debt service reserves (for churches with mortgage or other long-term debt)

> Baseline: Six months of debt service costs (principal and interest payments)

> Strong: At least one year of debt service costs

Note: *If a lender requires maintenance of minimum debt service reserves, the actual use of the lender-required reserves will typically create an event of default on the loan if the use of the funds causes the reserve balance to decrease below the required minimum. Accordingly, the church should maintain debt service reserves above and beyond the level required by a lender if the church wishes to be able to use the funds without defaulting on the loan. See below for more information about debt service reserves.*

Debt level

> Baseline: Total liabilities should not exceed 2.5 times the church's unrestricted net assets.

> Strong: Total liabilities are less than 2 times the church's unrestricted net assets.

Loan-to-value ratio

> Baseline: Debt should not exceed 70 percent of the current market value of the underlying collateral property.

> Strong: Debt is less than 65 percent of the current market value of the collateral property.

Debt service

> Baseline: Annual debt service payments (principal and interest) do not exceed 15 to 20 percent of the church's annual cash operating expenses.*

> Strong: Annual debt service payments do not exceed 10 percent of the church's annual cash operating expenses.*

*To the extent that debt service payments are made from operating expenses. Debt service payments funded by special gifts or separate funds, such as a building fund or debt service fund, would not be counted in this calculation.

Average age of accounts payable invoices

Baseline: Accounts payable invoices should not generally be more than 30 days old if the church is paying its bills in a timely manner. Accordingly, the average age of accounts payable invoices should not exceed about 25 days. If the average age of accounts payable invoices increases much beyond 25 days, the church's leadership should consider that a warning sign of potential cash flow issues.

Strong: The average age of accounts payable invoices is not more than 15 days.

Other benchmarks, ratios, industry data, and so on

The authors consider the benchmarks described above to be among the most important for churches to monitor and pursue for sound liquidity and financial position. Churches may find other measurements useful in their financial operations, as well as operations. In some cases, comparisons of a church's data with industry data may be useful, such as when comparing the church's salaries for key positions to information in salary surveys such as the *Compensation Handbook* published by Christianity Today (ChurchLawAndTaxStore.com). In other cases, industry data may have limited usefulness, since churches are as unique as the individuals who comprise them. For example, it might be interesting to know how a particular church stacks up against a peer group in the area of missions expense as a percentage of the operating budget or annual giving per family. However, individual churches have widely varying philosophies about such matters as missions spending and the socioeconomic demographics of a particular church will have a dramatic effect on per-family giving.

Even if the peer group to which a church compares itself is extraordinarily homogeneous, the fact that a group of churches, for example, spends four percent on average of its budget on missions means just that. It doesn't necessarily mean that such a spending level is appropriate for a particular church. Such a determination would be based on the philosophy, mission, and objectives of the particular church. The same even can be said about broad areas, such as personnel expense as a percentage of operating expenses. While churches generally tend to spend between 40 percent and 50 percent of their budgets on personnel, individual practices and philosophies vary widely. Some churches, for example, believe in engaging volunteers heavily and others espouse the approach of employing people to carry out most duties.

Accordingly, a church interested in tracking financial measurements and benchmarks may find the most useful information by comparing the church's own numbers over time. For example, a church may find it valuable to track the percentage of its operating expenses spent on missions over a period of several years. Similarly, a church may find it helpful to track the cost of personnel expenses as a percentage of its budget from year to year in order to determine whether the percentage is trending higher or lower.

Whatever methods or measurements are employed, church leaders should assess the tools and benchmarks that will be most relevant and helpful given their church's unique identity.

INVESTMENT MANAGEMENT

Churches that maintain cash reserves sometimes choose to invest in marketable securities in order to pursue increased returns on their investments, especially given the low interest rates that are often paid by banks on deposit accounts. Churches that maintain investment portfolios must take care to invest prudently.

6

Managing Liquidity and Financial Position

THE UNIFORM PRUDENT MANAGEMENT OF INSTITUTIONAL FUNDS ACT

At the time this publication went to press, every state in the United States, except Pennsylvania, had adopted a version of the Uniform Prudent Management of Institutional Funds Act (UPMIFA), a model law developed by the Uniform Law Commission. UPMIFA establishes legal requirements for nonprofit organizations, including churches in most states, related to the investment and management of "institutional funds." The term "institutional funds" is defined very broadly and, for all practical purposes, includes virtually all cash and investments maintained by a church or other nonprofit organization.

According to the Uniform Law Commission,

> UPMIFA requires investment "in good faith and with the care an ordinarily prudent person in a like position would exercise under similar circumstances." It requires prudence in incurring investment costs, authorizing "only costs that are appropriate and reasonable." Factors to be considered in investing are expanded to include, for example, the effects of inflation. UPMIFA emphasizes that investment decisions must be made in relation to the overall resources of the institution and its charitable purposes. No investment decision may be made in isolation, but must be made in light of the fund's entire portfolio, and as a part of an investment strategy "having risk and return objectives reasonably suited to the fund and to the institution." A charitable institution must diversify assets as an affirmative obligation unless "special circumstances" dictate otherwise. Assets must be reviewed within a reasonable time after they come into the possession of the institution in order to conform them to the investment strategy and objectives of the fund. Investment experts, whether in-house or hired for the purpose, are held to a standard of care consistent with that expertise.[1]

Note that each state with an enacted version of UPMIFA may have modified or adapted the model law in ways that are unique to that state. Accordingly, when evaluating the provisions of UPMIFA for a church in a particular state, the church should consult that state's specific laws. The model version of UPMIFA includes the following general requirements, which are generally consistent among the states that have adopted UPMIFA, for the investment and management of any institutional fund:

(1) In managing and investing an institutional fund, the following factors, if relevant, must be considered:
   (a) General economic conditions;
   (b) The possible effect of inflation or deflation;
   (c) The expected tax consequences, if any, of investment decisions or strategies;
   (d) The role that each investment or course of action plays within the overall investment portfolio of the fund;
   (e) The expected total return from income and the appreciation of investments;
   (f) Other resources of the institution;
   (g) The needs of the institution and the fund to make distributions and to preserve capital; and
   (h) An asset's special relationship or special value, if any, to the charitable purposes of the institution.

(2) Management and investment decisions about an individual asset must be made not in isolation but rather in the context of the institutional fund's portfolio of investments as a whole and as a part of an overall investment strategy having risk and return objectives reasonably suited to the fund and to the institution.

(3) Except as otherwise provided by law other than this [act], an institution may invest in any kind of property or type of investment consistent with this section.

(4) An institution shall diversify the investments of an institutional fund unless the institution reasonably determines that, because of special circumstances, the purposes of the fund are better served without diversification.

---

1   See tinyurl.com/UPMIFASummary.

(5) Within a reasonable time after receiving property, an institution shall make and carry out decisions concerning the retention or disposition of the property or to rebalance a portfolio, in order to bring the institutional fund into compliance with the purposes, terms, and distribution requirements of the institution as necessary to meet other circumstances of the institution and the requirements of this [act].

(6) A person that has special skills or expertise, or is selected in reliance upon the person's representation that the person has special skills or expertise, has a duty to use those skills or that expertise in managing and investing institutional funds.

INVESTMENT PHILOSOPHY

Before a church decides on the specific investments to be included in its portfolio, the church's leadership must first agree on a philosophy with respect to the church's investing activities. A church's investment philosophy should be expressed in general terms, should be in writing, and should be officially approved by the church's governing body.

In adopting an investment philosophy, the church's primary considerations are its investment objectives and its risk tolerance. For example, church leaders may express their desire for moderate growth and income potential together with low volatility and low risk of significant decreases in value. It is important for church leaders to clearly articulate their investment objectives and risk tolerance and to arrive at a clear consensus regarding these matters.

INVESTMENT POLICY

Once the church's leaders have adopted an appropriate statement reflecting its investment philosophy, the church should adopt a more specific document that describes in more detail the nature of the investments to be held by the church and the allocation of the church's investment assets to particular categories of investments. Such a document is commonly referred to as an investment policy.

Unless the church has leaders with significant investment expertise participating directly in the process, the church may wish to engage the services of an investment advisor or consultant in developing an appropriate investment policy. The investment policy should conform to the objectives and risk tolerance expressed by the church in its investment philosophy statement described above. The investment policy will apply the principles from the investment philosophy statement to specific assets – commonly, in the form of asset allocation parameters. For example, an investment policy statement may dictate the percentage of the church's investment portfolio to be invested in asset categories such as growth equities, value equities, government debt securities, corporate debt securities, real estate securities, commodities, international investments, and so on. It is also common for investment policy statements to provide more specificity in each of these categories. For example, the policy may provide for specific levels of investment in short-term, intermediate-term, and long-term debt securities. Once an investment policy is drafted, it should be approved by the church's governing body to ensure consistency with the church's investment objectives and risk tolerance.

In addition to addressing the matters described in the preceding paragraph, the church's investment policy should also include provisions designed to remind those responsible for the church's investments of the requirements of applicable law, such as UPMIFA. Accordingly, some churches include certain UPMIFA requirements in their investment policy document—a practice recommended by the authors. Additionally, the church's investment policy document should be reviewed and approved by the church's legal counsel before it is adopted in its final form.

ASSET MANAGEMENT

A church must decide how it will manage and oversee the investment process. Some churches form an investment committee to oversee the process. Others delegate the responsibility to a finance committee or its equivalent. Some churches have their governing body (or board) oversee the process directly. If a church utilizes a committee to oversee the investment process, the committee's charter should clearly state the committee's role and reporting responsibilities. Regardless of whether a committee is used or not, the church's governing body (or board) should maintain an appropriate awareness and exercise appropriate oversight of the process.

The process of managing the individual investments maintained by a church in its portfolio requires significant and continuous attention in order to ensure that the portfolio is managed in conformity with applicable laws and in conformity with the church's investment philosophy and investment policy. If the church's investment policy requires investments to be allocated among various asset categories, the management process also includes ensuring that the portfolio is "rebalanced" from time to time to conform to the asset allocation model adopted in the investment policy.

Because of the legal implications and related risks associated with asset management, most churches with significant investment portfolios engage external professional investment managers to oversee and manage their investment portfolios. Most churches do not have the expertise or capacity in-house to manage a significant investment portfolio in conformity with applicable laws, well-developed statements of investment philosophy, and investment policy. For particularly large investment portfolios, a church may wish to engage the services of more than one investment manager. Such an approach not only diversifies risk with respect to the investment management process, but also creates an opportunity to evaluate the performance of each manager against that of the other.

When using an external investment manager, it is important for the church to periodically evaluate the manager's performance. One of the most effective ways of evaluating an investment manager's performance is to compare the total return of the individual investments with appropriate benchmarks for investment returns in the applicable categories of investment. For example, the parties may agree that an appropriate benchmark for evaluating the church's investment in domestic growth equity securities is the S&P 500 index. The benchmarks should be agreed upon in advance between the church's leaders and the investment manager, and results should be evaluated periodically. Given modern technology for investment performance reporting, such an analysis is typically available on a monthly basis, along with regular investment performance reports.

USE AND MANAGEMENT OF DEBT

Debt financing is like a chainsaw. It can be a very useful tool in specific circumstances, but it can also cause lethal injury if used unwisely. In the church arena, there are circumstances in which the use of debt financing can be helpful and wise and there are circumstances in which the use of debt financing is inappropriate and dangerous.

There are generally two circumstances in which the use of debt financing by a church may be appropriate. One is when a church needs financing to fund the acquisition, construction, improvement, or refinancing of its long-lived furniture, equipment, or facilities. The other is when a church needs temporary financing to cover short-term, seasonal variations in cash flow. Even in these two circumstances, the specific conditions must be appropriate for debt financing.

There are many circumstances in which the use of debt financing by a church is unwise, inappropriate, and dangerous. It is *not* appropriate to use debt financing in the following circumstances:

- To finance operating costs or non-capital outlays. (A working capital line of credit may be useful if cash flows are truly seasonal and funds for repayment are reasonably assured. However, an unexpected downturn or shortfall in revenue is probably the worst possible reason to incur debt financing.)
- When cash flows are not growing or at least stable. (A church should never enter into debt financing if its cash flows are declining—even if current cash flows cover the required debt service. The church must determine the reasons for the downward trend and address that satisfactorily before it should consider debt financing.)
- When personal guarantees are required. (Requiring personal guarantees of church leaders in connection with church debt would be an extraordinary requirement in today's market. If a lender were to impose such a requirement, it is likely an indicator that either the borrower does not have satisfactory capacity to obtain a loan under ordinary market terms or the lender does not operate with an appropriate level of professionalism.)

- When the lender will not offer the church market rates and terms. (Above-market interest rates and highly restrictive terms are indicators that a lender perceives the church's credit risk as higher than normal. A higher than normal credit risk means, of course, a higher risk that the church may not be able to satisfactorily service its debt obligations.)

Following are some comments by nationally prominent church lenders regarding the use of debt financing by churches:

> *Strong, effective board oversight and leadership accountability are—by far—the greatest contributors to healthy financial choices and faithful loan performance.*
>> Mark Holbrook
>> President and CEO
>> Evangelical Christian Credit Union

> *The most common challenge a church encounters when it is pursuing approval of a mortgage loan is the lack of adequate recent cash flow.*
>> Dan Mikes
>> National Division Manager Religious Institution Banking
>> Bank of the West

> *The most important attribute that makes a church a strong candidate for a mortgage loan is a need driven by growth and vision.*
>> Scott Rolfs
>> Managing Director
>> Head of Religion Division
>> Ziegler Investment Banking

Working Capital Loans

Churches with highly seasonal variations in cash flow sometimes utilize working capital loans to bridge the temporary gaps in cash flow in order to maintain stable financial operations. Working capital loans are often made in the form of lines of credit, which allow the church to draw and repay amounts with flexibility within the maximum limit approved by the bank. Working capital loans are typically made by lenders only to the most creditworthy borrowers, and only in scenarios where there is a history of seasonal or cyclical cash flows creating reasonable assurance that the amounts bor-

rowed will be repaid in the future. As mentioned previously, working capital loans should never be utilized to fund unexpected downturns in revenue or operating expense shortfalls unless the church has specific and reliable reasons to believe that near-term cash flows will be adequate to allow the church to repay the debt.

Working capital loans may have specific maturity dates or, in some cases, they are due "on demand," which means that the bank may require repayment at its demand at any time. Working capital loans typically require minimum payments equal to the monthly interest charge on the outstanding balance. Principal payments are typically flexible until maturity. In some cases, lenders will require that a working capital line of credit be paid down to a zero balance for a minimum period of time at least once annually.

Furniture and Equipment Financing

Churches sometimes use debt financing to acquire furniture and equipment with long-term lives. Examples may include a major audio system for the church, a new air-conditioning system, new sanctuary seating, vehicles, and so on. Furniture and equipment loans are typically term loans with fixed interest rates and fixed payments that amortize the loan over a period of 3 to 7 years. In evaluating whether to utilize debt financing to acquire such assets, a church should consider whether it has alternative means for funding the acquisition of those assets and whether it has adequate cash flows to service the payments that will be required by the new financing. If a church has a stable history of generating cash flows that are more than adequate to service such debt, then the use of furniture and equipment financing may be appropriate.

Mortgage Financing

The most significant type of debt financing utilized by churches in the United States is mortgage financing incurred for the purpose of acquiring, constructing, improving, or refinancing church facilities. When it comes to mortgage financing, lending professionals generally agree that the best candidates for borrowing are those churches who need the financing to support larger facilities or new facilities driven by the church's growth. The need to provide for growth is arguably the "healthiest" reason a church may pursue new mortgage debt. In addition to borrowing to support growth-driven expansion, borrowing to refinance existing debt to achieve more favorable terms (especially a lower interest rate) can also be a healthy reason for a church to pursue a new mortgage. However, refinancing for the purpose of extending and reducing payments is often not a healthy scenario.

The Five C's of Credit in Church Mortgage Financing

Lending institutions often refer to "the Four C's of Credit." Interestingly, while there is some commonality among those who cite the Four C's, different institutions cite different "C's," and some refer to five rather than four. The C's most commonly cited are: Character, Capacity, and Collateral.

Based on professional experience and communications with numerous church lenders over the years, the authors hereby advance *The 5 C's of Church Mortgage Financing* as follows:

Character. The integrity and acumen of the church's leaders, and the quality of the church's accounting books and records. Character also includes the quality of the church's governing body (board) and the manner in which the governing body exercises oversight with respect to the church's activities.

Cash flow. A stable history of positive cash flow which clearly supports, in a well-documented manner, the church's ability to honor the proposed debt obligations.

Cash reserves. Cash and investment balances sufficiently significant to provide the church with flexibility and time to adapt in the event that the church experiences unexpected difficulty in servicing the debt from regular operating cash flows.

Collateral. Assets underlying the debt which have a market value significantly in excess of the debt amount and which are pledged to satisfy the debt in the event that the church is unable to repay.

Contingency plan. A plan that church leaders develop in advance addressing how it will adapt to ensure the church's ability to honor its debt ob-

ligations in the event of a sudden or unexpected downturn in revenue or other financial challenge.

Let's take a look at each of these Five C's in more detail.

Character

The starting point for a borrowing-and-lending relationship between a church and a financial institution is *trust*. The lender must believe that the church's leaders are people of integrity; that they are capable leaders; that they have an adequate command of their church's operations and financial condition; that the church's books and records are adequate, timely, and reliable; and that the church has a genuine intent and ability to honor the terms of any proposed debt agreement.

Additionally, the lender must have a sense that the church is well-governed. The governing body (board) of the church has a legal, fiduciary duty to exercise due care and prudence in the oversight of the church's activities—both financial and operational. Character in this context involves healthy, rigorous, and proactive engagement by the church's governing body to ensure that the church and its leaders operate within well-developed policies and parameters and that it stays "on mission" with respect to its activities. These responsibilities of the governing body must be carried out with appropriate independence and without improper conflicts of interest.

While it may seem that addressing the topic of character and integrity in the context of church leadership may be unnecessary, unfortunately that is not the case. Churches and ministries in America have experienced numerous high-profile examples of failed integrity and morality by those who lead them. At the time this publication went to press, Dan Busby, president of the Evangelical Council for Financial Accountability (ECFA), was completing the writing of a new book on the topic of integrity for church and ministry leaders. The anticipated book is *TRUST: The Firm Foundation for Kingdom Fruitfulness*, ECFAPress, 2015. The authors highly recommend that church leaders consider Mr. Busby's commentary on the topic.

Cash flow

When considering a mortgage loan, a lender is looking for documented *history* of the church's ability to make the proposed debt payments, *not* a commitment from the church that it will raise revenues or decrease expenses in the future in order to be able to make the payments. In making that assessment, lenders typically calculate a ratio commonly referred to as the "debt service coverage ratio (DSCR)." While lenders most assuredly assess the church's DSCR in the loan approval process, the church may not realize how this method of cash flow assessment is calculated. The DSCR is typically calculated as follows:

> Most recent year's change in unrestricted net assets + depreciation expense + interest expense
> *Divided by*
> Next year's required debt payments (principal and interest)
>
> *(Some variations in the details of the DSCR calculation vary from lender to lender and from church to church, based on specific facts and circumstances.)*

The idea behind this ratio is to determine whether the cash available from operations is adequate to make the proposed debt payments. Some lenders will accept a DSCR as low as approximately 1.1. However, many lenders require a DSCR of 1.25 or higher. In the opinion of the authors, a healthy DSCR will be at least 1.25 and a strong DSCR will significantly exceed 1.25. Some lenders will stipulate as a requirement of the loan agreement that a minimum DSCR be maintained in each year that the loan is in place.

Cash reserves (for debt service)

As addressed previously in this chapter, the authors suggest that a church with long-term mortgage debt should maintain healthy operating cash reserves as well as a cash debt service reserve equal to at least six months of required debt payments (principal and interest). The church will maintain a stronger financial position by having a debt service reserve equal to at least one year of

required debt payments. The larger the church's debt service reserve balance, the more time the church will have in the event of an unexpected downturn in revenue or other financial challenge to adapt to the situation while still being able to make the required debt payments.

Some lenders will stipulate as a condition of making a mortgage loan that a church maintain a minimum balance in a cash debt service reserve account at all times while the loan is outstanding. While such a requirement of the lender may seem to have the advantage of forcing the church to maintain a debt service reserve as described in the preceding paragraph, when the debt service reserve requirement is a contractual part of the loan, the concept is a bit more complicated.

When a church maintains a debt service reserve on its own (without a contractual requirement), the church can actually use a portion of the debt service reserve if necessary to maintain consistent operating cash flows. However, when the debt service reserve is contractual, the church cannot spend the reserve balance below the required minimum without triggering an event of default under the terms of the loan. For this reason, if a church has a contractually required minimum debt service reserve as part of its loan terms, the church should maintain an additional debt service reserve above and beyond the contractual minimum. This will ensure that the church has funds that it can actually use in the event they are needed without triggering an event of default under the terms of the loan.

A Special Word about the Importance of Cash Reserves for Debt Service

A church that is building or acquiring new property using debt financing typically puts significant cash equity into the property to reduce the amount of debt needed and to establish an appropriate loan-to-value ratio. While having substantial equity in its real estate is an advantage, in the opinion of the authors, maintaining an adequate debt service reserve is a higher priority than increasing equity in the real estate. In other words, it may be more advantageous to put less cash equity into a property in order to maintain an adequate cash reserve for debt service, assuming that the resulting loan-to-value ratio is appropriate. An adequate debt service reserve can provide much-needed flexibility and can assist in continuing to make debt payments in the event of an unexpected adverse financial development. Equity in the property does not offer this advantage.

Collateral

Church mortgage lenders typically require collateral in the form of the church's real estate as a condition of making a real estate-related loan. Commonly, lenders require that the loan amount not exceed 70% of the market value of the real estate that collateralizes the loan. There are occasional exceptions. In some cases, lenders require the loan-to-value ratio to be even lower than 70%. The loan-to-value ratio measurement is typically made at the beginning of the loan relationship and is not typically re-evaluated during the term of the loan unless there are unusual circumstances. An independent appraisal of the church's real estate is typically required to corroborate the value of the property.

Regardless of whether a lender requires a maximum loan-to-value ratio, a borrowing church should avoid entering into a loan relationship where there is not adequate collateral to satisfy payment of the loan in the event that the church is unable to pay. In the event a church is unable to make its required debt payments and no other solution is available, the lender may be required to foreclose on the church's property. While foreclosure on a church's property is certainly an unfortunate event, the situation is made worse when the proceeds from foreclosure do not adequately cover the balance owed by the church to the bank. In such cases, a lender may pursue the church's other assets to make up the deficiency.

Contingency plan

Church leaders should develop a plan in advance addressing how it will adapt to ensure the church's ability to honor its debt obligations in the event of a sudden or unexpected downturn in revenue or other financial challenge. While no one enjoys thinking about what bad things can happen, prudence dictates that it is wise to prepare for unexpected developments and to have a plan.

Suppose, for example, that a high-profile church learns that its popular pastor has been engaged in moral misconduct and is then terminated from his position. Such a church may experience a significant decline in attendance and financial giving. If the church has significant mortgage debt outstanding, such a development can create immediate and significant financial challenges. The church will need to adapt by reducing expenses and possibly in other ways. Unexpected developments can certainly come in forms other than the moral failure of a church's leader. Other possibilities include the sudden and unexpected death or disability of the church's pastor; an act of misconduct by a person serving the church involving a child, a counselee, or another person; and so on.

A church's contingency plan in this context need not be particularly detailed. It can be a helpful exercise to simply develop a list (in order of priority) of the expenses that would be cut in the event of a significant unexpected development that adversely affects the church's revenue stream.

A church often can insure its risk in the event of the unexpected death or disability of its senior pastor or any other leader whose death or disability could lead to a significant downturn in the church's revenues. Insurance providing this type of coverage is commonly referred to as "key-man" insurance. Key-man life insurance is readily available (and typically, at a fairly reasonable cost) in the marketplace, assuming that the church leader is in good health and is otherwise insurable. Key-man disability insurance provides coverage in the event that the church leader is no longer able to perform his or her customary services for the church. Disability insurance coverage may be available in the form of a lump-sum payment or a stream of monthly or annual payments. Availability and cost of disability insurance varies significantly. However, key-man disability insurance is typically significantly more expensive than key-man life insurance. Insurance professionals often cite statistics stating that a person is more likely to become disabled early in life than to die. Church leaders should take these factors into consideration if they have significant mortgage debt and if the church's revenue stream could be significantly harmed by the unexpected death or disability of one or more of the church's leaders. In some cases, lenders will require a church to maintain key-man life insurance in a particular minimum amount during the term of a mortgage loan. In rare cases, the lender may require a church to submit a leadership succession plan.

MORTGAGE DEBT OPTIONS AND TERMS

Church mortgages come in many varieties. In some cases, a church may have the opportunity to choose from among various options made available by the lender. Following is a discussion of some of the more significant options and terms that are commonly addressed in the church mortgage lending process.

Fixed or variable?

Long-term fixed rate church mortgages are a very rare breed in the bank lending marketplace—for all practical purposes, they are extinct. If a church is part of a denomination that has a denominational church lending organization, that denominational lending organization may offer longer-term fixed rate church mortgages to churches within the denomination. Churches that do not have such an option and are interested in a true, long-term fixed rate mortgage may wish to consider bond financing as an alternative to bank debt (bond financing is addressed in more detail below). However, banks and other traditional lenders will often offer a church the option of a loan with a variable interest rate or a loan with an interest rate that is fixed for a period commonly ranging from three to five years (the actual number of years in this range for which a lender will fix the rate varies by lender and by scenario). Banks and other traditional lenders very rarely offer fixed interest rates for periods in excess of five years, but it does happen on occasion. For short-term fixed-rate loans, the loans typically either mature at the end of the fixed-rate term or they "reprice," meaning that a new interest rate is set at that time based on current market rates. A fairly common arrangement is a 10-year loan with an interest rate that is fixed for the first five years and is then adjusted to a new fixed rate (based on market conditions at that time) that applies to the second five-year period of the loan.

In deciding whether a variable rate is appropriate for a particular church, church leaders should assess their appetite for interest rate risk as well as their perception about the future of interest rates. In the years since the Great Recession began in late 2008, the vast majority of borrowers who have made assumptions about future interest rates have been wrong in their assumptions. Nonetheless, a loan with a variable interest rate does carry interest rate risk based on changing market conditions. In some cases, banks will offer a variable rate with a floor and a ceiling, meaning that the rate will not go below a particular percentage, nor will it exceed a particular percentage. Such arrangements can be helpful for a church in limiting its ultimate risk. In evaluating the possibility of a variable rate loan, the church should consider the history of the particular rate, including highs and lows.

Variable interest rates for church mortgages are based on an "index rate," which is typically either the bank's "prime rate," (sometimes referred to as the "base rate") or "LIBOR," the London Inter-Bank Offered Rate.[2] The bank's prime rate, while technically set by each bank, is generally the same as the prime rate used by banks across the United States, and is often the same as the prime rate published in The *Wall Street Journal* each business day. The prime rate changes periodically based on market conditions. LIBOR is a benchmark rate that some of the world's leading banks charge each other for short-term loans.[3] LIBOR typically changes much more frequently than the prime rate, and can change daily. LIBOR is typically expressed in one-month, three-month, and six-month rates in the context of variable-interest-rate mortgages.

6

Managing Liquidity and Financial Position

---

2   Occasionally, lenders utilize a different variable-rate index, such as the Five-Year Treasury Constant Maturity Index, an index published by the Federal Reserve Board based on the average yield of a range of Treasury securities adjusted to the equivalent of a five-year maturity. (See bankrate.com.)

3   Investopedia: investopedia.com/terms/l/libor.asp.

LIBOR rates are published daily in *The Wall Street Journal* and numerous other sources.

When the prime rate is used as the index in a variable-rate mortgage, the most creditworthy borrowers can commonly borrow at the prime rate or less. Borrowers whose financial position or other attributes are not as strong may be quoted rates in excess of the prime rate.

When LIBOR is used, lenders commonly use the one-month LIBOR rate, and because the rate is so low (as of the date of this writing, the one-month LIBOR rate was less than one-quarter of one percent), LIBOR-based variable church mortgage rates are always stated as some percentage in excess of the LIBOR rate. The authors have seen variable rates as low as one-month LIBOR +1.5% for extraordinarily strong borrowers.

A fixed interest rate loan offers the security of knowing the interest rate that will apply during the loan's term. Fixed-rate loans also offer protection from rising interest rates. Invariably, however, the fixed rate offered by a church lender is significantly higher than the variable rate available at the inception of the loan. Accordingly, churches must evaluate the pros and cons of these factors. A church may consider the fixed-rate option to be its best choice, since the interest rate will not increase during the term of the fixed rate, and the church believes that it can refinance the loan in the event that rates significantly decline. In recent years, however, church lenders have more frequently begun to impose prepayment penalties in connection with fixed-rate loans. Sometimes, these prepayment penalties are substantial. As a result, a church with a fixed-rate loan that has a significant prepayment penalty may not be able to economically refinance the loan in the event interest rates decline significantly. While prepayment penalties for fixed-rate loans are more common than has historically been the case, they are, in the authors' experience, still relatively uncommon. A church considering a fixed-rate loan should carefully review the loan documents for prepayment penalty provisions and should avoid such provisions if at all possible.

Hedging Variable Interest Rate Risk

In response to lenders' reluctance to offer long-term fixed-rate mortgages, and the desire by borrowers for such mortgages, the financial marketplace offers various financial instruments designed to help borrowers mitigate their interest rate risk while allowing lenders to continue making variable rate loans. These financial instruments are "hedging instruments," and they come in a variety of forms. The most common form of hedging instrument used by churches in today's lending marketplace is an "interest rate swap" contract.

An interest rate swap contract ("swap") is an agreement between the borrower (the church) and an investment banking firm (typically affiliated with the lender) in which the investment banking firm agrees to accept fixed interest payments from the borrower and to make variable interest payments to the lender. In other words, the borrower "swaps" the variable rate actually written into the loan agreement with a fixed rate that is accepted by the investment banking firm. A swap contract is a separate agreement from the loan documents and, accordingly, does not necessarily tie directly to the terms of the loan. In many cases, however, a swap agreement is drafted to align with the terms of the loan, including payment dates and principal balances, so as to have the effect of creating a fixed rate of interest on what is actually a variable rate loan. The advantage of a swap agreement to the borrower is that the interest cost related to the loan is fixed for the duration of the swap. The duration of the swap is a negotiable item, and it may or may not align with the maturity date of the loan. In some cases, a lender may require that the terms of a swap align with those of the related loan. Swaps are available with a variety of terms and a church considering such an arrangement should discuss it thoroughly with its lender, its financial advisors, and its legal counsel.

Since an interest rate swap contract is a separate contractual agreement from the loan itself, the swap itself has a value at any given time. The value to the borrower (the church) may be positive or negative depending on current market conditions. From a practical perspective, what this means is that if the borrower wishes to terminate the swap at any time, the borrower will either pay the investment banking firm to terminate the arrangement or the borrower will receive money from the investment banking firm in exchange for terminating the arrangement. Borrowers must understand this attribute of a swap. In a declining interest rate environment, the value of a swap will decrease and may go negative—substantially negative, which would mean that the church would be required to pay a substantial sum in order to terminate the swap. In a rising interest rate environment, the value of a swap will increase and may be positive, which would mean that the church would receive money from the investment banking firm if it were to terminate the swap.

Swap agreements are complex documents and the detailed provisions are not likely to be well understood by people who do not practice substantially in the investment banking arena. Accordingly, if the amounts of money involved are substantial, a church faced with terminating a swap agreement may wish to obtain an opinion from an independent party as to the value of the swap, whether positive or negative. There is a current market of professionals who offer such services.

During the Great Recession, as interest rates declined significantly and remained low for a sustained period of time, many churches who entered into swap agreements regretted that decision. However, the future of interest rates remains uncertain and the market will determine the popularity of swap arrangements in the years ahead.

Loan covenants

Loan agreements virtually always contain certain conditions that the borrower agrees to meet or maintain during the term of the loan. These provisions are often referred to as "loan covenants." Loan covenants vary substantially from lender to lender and from loan to loan.

Financial Covenants

One category of loan covenants frequently found in church loans is "financial covenants"—covenants stating that the church will maintain certain specific financial benchmarks during the term of the loan. The three most common financial covenants written into church loan agreements are: a minimum cash reserves covenant, a debt service coverage ratio covenant, and a debt-to-net assets covenant.

Minimum Cash Reserves Covenant

As mentioned above in "The Five C's of Credit in Church Mortgage Financing," some lenders will stipulate, as a condition of making a mortgage loan, that a church maintain a minimum balance in a cash debt service reserve account at all times while the loan is outstanding. The amount of the required reserves is a matter of professional judgment and discretion applied by the lender, and is typically equal to several months of debt payments.

Important Note about Cash Reserves Covenants

While a cash reserves covenant imposed by the lender may seem to have the favorable effect of forcing the church to maintain a debt service reserve, when the debt service reserve requirement is a contractual part of the loan, special consideration is required. When a church maintains a debt service reserve on its own (without a contractual requirement), the church can actually use a portion of the debt service reserve if necessary to maintain consistent operating cash flows. However, when the debt service reserve is contractual, the church cannot spend the reserve balance below the required minimum without triggering an event of default under the terms of the loan—which, at a minimum, will require a waiver or approval by the lender. For this reason, if a church has a contractually required minimum debt service reserves covenant, the church should maintain an additional debt service reserve above and beyond the contractual minimum in order to ensure that the church has funds that it can actually use in the event that they are needed without triggering an event of default under the terms of the loan.

Debt Service Coverage Covenant

As mentioned above in "The Five C's of Credit in Church Mortgage Financing," lenders will assess the church's debt service coverage ratio (DSCR) in the loan approval process, regardless of whether the DSCR is expressed as an ongoing covenant in the loan agreement. The DSCR is typically calculated as follows:

Most recent year's change in unrestricted net assets + depreciation expense + interest expense
Divided by
Next year's required debt payments (principal and interest)

(Some variations in the details of the DSCR calculation vary from lender to lender and from church to church, based on specific facts and circumstances.)

The idea behind this ratio is to determine whether the cash available from operations is adequate to make the proposed debt payments. Some lenders will accept a DSCR as low as 1.1. However, many lenders require a DSCR of 1.25 or higher.

Important Note about DSCR Covenants

Given the fact that the DSCR calculation is made annually, is based on a particular year's cash flows, and does not take into consideration prior year cash flows or assets available to service debt, it is possible for a church to be in a very strong financial position and still violate a DSCR covenant. For example, assume that a church receives substantial unexpected contributions in a given year and does not spend any of those additional funds

during that year. For the year in which the substantial contributions are received, the church is likely to have a very large DSCR—well within compliance of the loan covenant. Assume that in the following year, the church spends one half of the unexpected contribution funds on a missions-related project, resulting in a net loss for that year (the funds were received in the prior year). Regardless of the fact that the church still has one half of the unexpected contributions in its accounts, the loss incurred during Year Two could cause the church to violate a DSCR covenant in that year.

While the authors, of course, encourage churches to maintain a strong financial position, for the reasons described above, the authors encourage churches to avoid having DSCR covenants in their loan agreements if possible. In the event a church finds itself in potential violation of a DSCR covenant for reasons like those described above, the church should pursue a waiver of the covenant from its lender in light of the unusual circumstances.

Debt-to-Net Assets Covenant

The debt-to-net assets covenant is typically defined as the ratio of the church's debt or total liabilities to the church's unrestricted net assets balance as of each year-end. The idea behind this covenant is to ensure that the church's total debt or liabilities do not exceed the church's overall equity in its assets beyond a certain level. The debt-to-net assets ratio is typically expressed as a maximum and, if present, is typically in a range of 2.0 to 3.0.

Evaluating Financial Covenants in General

The lender may impose financial covenants other than those described above. For any financial covenants that a lender proposes to be included in the loan agreement, a church should carefully evaluate the covenant requirements, definitions, measurement methods, and measurement dates and have reasonable assurance that the church will be able to comply with the requirements on an ongoing basis during the term of the loan. The church should run "what-if" scenarios to evaluate the likelihood of compliance with financial covenants in different situations.

Nonfinancial Covenants

A church loan agreement may include a variety of nonfinancial covenants. Some of the more common nonfinancial covenants included in church loans are:

- a requirement that the church submit audited financial statements annually within a certain period after each year-end;
- a requirement that the church submit internally prepared interim financial reports (e.g., quarterly);
- a requirement that the church maintain its entire banking relationship with the lending bank (which requires moving the relationship if it is not already with the lending bank);
- a stipulation that the church will not incur any new debt without the lender's approval;
- a stipulation that the church will not enter into any new long-term lease agreements without the lender's approval;
- a limit on the amount of capital expenditures that the church can make without the lender's approval;
- a stipulation that the church will not make any significant change in the nature or scope of its operations without the lender's approval;
- a stipulation that the church will maintain its federal tax-exempt status.

The importance of engaging legal counsel to assist with debt financing

Mortgages and other loan documents are complex contractual agreements with many terms and provisions that can have significant implications for a church. In addition to loan covenant provisions such as those described above, loan documents typically contain numerous other legally significant provisions that can affect a church's costs or options in the future, depending on the circumstances that arise. It may be tempting for church leaders to view the many provisions in loan documents as simply "boilerplate" provisions that "are probably non-negotiable" or "are probably in all loan documents," and, thus, to pay little

attention to them. Numerous churches have taken such an approach, only to deeply regret it later when circumstances arise that bring to light the dramatic significance of provisions that they had deemed to be "boilerplate."

Accordingly, churches should have their own legal counsel review all mortgage and other loan documents before they are signed to ensure that the church's interests are adequately considered. (While the lending institution may have legal counsel involved in the loan document preparation process, the bank's legal counsel does not represent the interests of the church.) Additionally, a church should never assume that *any* provision in a lender-prepared loan document is non-negotiable. Banks and other lending organizations frequently make changes to loan documents based on requests made by borrowers or their legal counsel.

TAX-EXEMPT FINANCING FOR CHURCH-OPERATED PRIVATE SCHOOLS

Due to developments in federal and state law in recent years, it has become possible in many states for church-operated private schools to obtain tax-exempt financing for their facilities. While the details of these arrangements are outside the scope of this publication, the authors would like readers to be aware of this possibility. Churches that operate or control private schools may wish to consider tax-exempt financing if they qualify. While tax-exempt financing is somewhat complex in nature, it typically offers interest rates that are substantially below those that are otherwise available to churches and schools in the marketplace. The authors are aware of circumstances in which tax-exempt financing has saved church-operated schools hundreds of thousands of dollars per year in interest costs. Interested churches should consult their lenders and legal counsel with specific experience in tax-exempt financing for private schools.

BOND FINANCING

As an alternative to financing provided by bankers and other traditional lenders, churches sometimes turn to bond financing to provide funds for real property acquisition, construction, improvement, or refinancing. With bond financing, investors hold the church's debt.

The church's bonds are sold to the investors either by the church directly or by a bond underwriting firm.

Bond financing is sometimes used in order to permit a church to establish a truly long-term fixed interest rate for its debt without a prepayment penalty. Bond financing is also used in some cases by churches that are not able to obtain credit from traditional lenders in other ways.

Church bond issues are generally issued on either a "firm" underwriting or a "best efforts" basis. A firm underwriting is a bond issue in which the bond under-writer guarantees the sale of all of the bonds, ensuring that the church will receive the full proceeds of the bond issue, net of applicable costs. As the term implies, a best efforts bond issue is one in which "best efforts" are made to sell the bonds with no guarantee as to what portion of the bonds will be sold and the amount of proceeds the church will receive.

Issuing bonds is a complex legal process and should only be undertaken under the advice of highly experienced and competent legal counsel who is knowledge-able about federal and state securities law as well as church bond law. Because of the complexity involved in issuing bonds, there are typically substantial up-front costs associated with a church bond issue. The church must consider the advantages provided by a church bond issue as compared with traditional borrowing in light of the higher up-front costs.

SECURITIES LAWS

As the first part of this chapter demonstrates, there are a variety of ways that churches can obtain financing. Depending on the types of financing a church may pursue, securities laws may be an important factor for churches and their legal counsel to consider. Securities laws are particularly relevant in connection with church bond financing.[4] Laws regulating the sale of securities have been enacted by the federal government and by all 50 states,[5] and the term *security* is defined very broadly by such laws—so broadly that it includes certain types of church financing efforts, including the issuing of bonds or the securing of other types of financing. Any church that wishes to engage in such

activities must consider the applicability of these laws under the advice of legal counsel.

Securities laws were enacted to protect the public against fraudulent and deceptive practices in the sale of securities and to provide full and fair disclosure to prospective investors. To achieve these purposes, most securities laws impose the following conditions on the offer and sale of securities:

(1) Registration of proposed securities with the federal or state government in advance of sale
(2) Filing of sales and advertising literature with the federal or state government
(3) Registration of agents and broker dealers who will be selling the securities
(4) Prohibition of fraudulent practices

Certain limited exemptions apply to churches and religious organizations with respect to certain aspects of federal and state securities laws.[6] However, certain provisions, such as antifraud provisions, apply without exception.

⊙ **KEY POINT.** All securities laws subject churches and other religious organizations to the antifraud requirements. Churches therefore must not assume that any securities that they may offer are automatically exempt from registration or regulation. Church securities always will be subject to some degree of regulation. The question in each case is how much.

It is important to observe that most states require that persons who sell or offer to sell securities be registered with the state securities commission. Registration involves submitting a detailed application and, in most cases, the successful completion of a securities law examination. A few states that exempt the securities of religious organizations from registration do not exempt persons selling or offering to sell such securities from the salesman registration requirements.

⊙ **KEY POINT.** There are two additional considerations that churches should consider before offering securities. First, some securities may be regulated under state and federal banking law. For example, it is possible that the issuance

---

4   Securities Act of 1933, 15 U.S.C. §§ 77a 77aa.
5   Nearly 40 states have enacted all or significant portions of the Uniform Securities Act.

6   Most states accept the uniform Form U 4 prepared by the National Association of Securities Dealers. See generally § 4-07, supra.

of "demand notes" (notes redeemable by investors "on demand") would violate state and federal banking laws. Demand notes are basically deposit arrangements which may trigger banking regulation. Second, complex accounting principles apply to some securities programs. It is essential for churches to work with a CPA firm with experience in representing nonprofit organizations that issue securities.

In a leading case, the federal Securities and Exchange Commission (SEC) brought an action in federal court seeking to enjoin a church and its leader from violating the antifraud provisions of the Securities Act of 1933.[7] The church solicited funds through investment plans consisting essentially of the sale of interest bearing notes to the general public. The notes were promoted through advertising literature extolling the security of the investment. For example, one advertisement stated in part:

> You may be a Christian who has committed his life into the hands of God, but left his funds in the hands of a floundering world economy. Financial experts everywhere are predicting a disaster in the economy. They say it is only a matter of time. . . . God's economy does not sink when the world's economy hits a reef and submerges! Wouldn't it be wise to invest in His economy?

The SEC argued that the church had defrauded investors by such representations when, in fact, it had a substantially increasing operating deficit that had jumped from $42,349 to $203,776 in the preceding three years. This fact was not disclosed to investors.

The church argued that religious organizations are protected from the reach of securities laws by the First Amendment. In rejecting this contention, the court observed: "Defendants constantly emphasize that they are engaged in 'God's work.' No court has ever found that conduct, by being so described, is automatically immunized from all regulation in the public interest."[8] The court quoted with approval the United States Supreme Court's earlier observation that "[n]othing we have said is intended even remotely to imply that, under the cloak of religion, persons may, with impunity, commit

frauds upon the public."[9] The court found it irrelevant that investors had a "religious" motivation, that most investors were "believers," and that the church did not intend to defraud or deceive anyone.

A number of churches and other religious organizations have been investigated by the SEC and by state securities commissions. In most cases, the investigation was prompted by the complaint of an investor.[10]

Churches that violate state securities laws face a variety of potential consequences under state and federal securities laws. These include investigations, hearings, subpoenas, injunctions, criminal actions, cancellation of sales, suits for monetary damages by aggrieved investors, monetary fines, and revocation of an exemption, or registration, of securities.

⊙ **KEY POINT.** It is important to recognize that "good faith" (a lack of an intention to deceive, or lack of knowledge that a particular transaction is either fraudulent or otherwise in violation of securities law) does not necessarily protect against liability. To illustrate, some courts have ruled that the sale of unregistered securities in violation of state securities law is punishable despite the innocent intentions of the seller.[11] However, civil lawsuits by investors alleging fraud in the sale of securities must demonstrate an actual intent to deceive or defraud.[12]

EXAMPLE. A church issues $200,000 in 10-year promissory notes to its members and spends all of the proceeds on a new education

---

7 Securities and Exchange Commission v. World Radio Mission, Inc., 544 F.2d 535 (1st Cir. 1976).

8 Id. at 539 n.7.

9 Id. at 537 n.3, quoting Cantwell v. Connecticut, 310 U.S. 296, 306 (1940). The court was "surprised . . . by defendants' recitation of the parable of the servants entrusted with their master's talents. We do not question the parable, but insofar as it indicates a duty to make loans, it is to make profitable ones. A servant contemplating lending to a possibly shaky enterprise would do well to note the final verse." Id. at 538 n.6.

10 See, e.g., In the Matter of Keep the Faith, Inc., Ariz. Corp. Com., Dec. 54503 (April 25, 1985) (issuer incorrectly stated that its securities program did not involve a donation and did not disclose material information to investors, including the interest rate and term of the securities, and the background and financial condition of the issuer); In the Matter of Johnson Financial Services, Inc., Ga. Securities Div., No. 50-84-9500 (August 6, 1984) (salesperson falsely represented that he was working with a Presbyterian church to help sell its bonds, that he was a licensed salesperson, and that the church bonds he was offering earned 18 percent "tax free" for years); In the Matter of Tri-County Baptist Church, Mich. Corp. and Secs. Bureau, No. 84-32-S (June 11, 1984) (church failed to maintain an escrow account for proceeds of bond sales and did not apply proceeds as described in prospectus).

11 Moerman v. Zipco, Inc., 302 F. Supp. 439 (E.D.N.Y. 1969), aff'd, 422 F.2d 871 (2nd Cir. 1970); Trump v. Badet, 327 P.2d 1001 (Ariz. 1958).

12 The United States Supreme Court so held in Ernst & Ernst v. Hochfelder, 425 U.S. 185 (1976). While the Ernst decision dealt only with proof of an intent to deceive under the antifraud provisions of federal securities law, the decision has been held to apply by implication to private actions under the antifraud provisions of state securities laws. See, e.g., Greenfield v. Cheek, 593 P.2d 293 (Ariz. 1978).

6

Managing Liquidity and Financial Position

building. The failure to establish a "sinking fund" out of part of the proceeds received from the sale of these securities, and out of which the securities will be repaid at maturity, constitutes securities fraud. This is a good example of how churches can unwittingly engage in securities fraud.

EXAMPLE. A church issues 10-year, 10 percent promissory notes to several of its members. No prospectus, offering circular, or other literature is filed with the state securities commission or made available to investors. The failure to provide prospective investors with a prospectus (also called an "offering circular") constitutes securities fraud. Once again, this illustrates how churches can innocently commit securities fraud.

EXAMPLE. A church plans to issue $300,000 in promissory notes. It composes a prospectus describing much of the financial background of the church. The prospectus also contains the following four statements: (1) "The membership of the church has increased during each of the past 10 years, so it can be expected that membership growth will continue to occur." (2) "These securities have been exempted from registration by the state securities commission and thus you are assured that they have been carefully studied and approved by the state." (3) "A copy of this prospectus shall at all times be maintained in the church office for the benefit of any prospective investor." (4) "Interest on these obligations is guaranteed." Each of these statements may constitute securities fraud.

EXAMPLE. Same facts as the previous question. The church decides not to include the following information in its prospectus out of a concern that this information might make the church's securities less attractive: (1) A lawsuit is pending against the church alleging malpractice on the part of the pastor. (2) The total dollar value of securities to be offered. (3) A statement that no sinking fund reserve exists. (4) A statement that for two of the past five years the church's expenses exceeded revenues. Omitting any of this information from the church's prospectus may constitute securities fraud.

CASE STUDY. The Virginia Division of Securities investigated a church's securities program, and concluded that the church violated state securities law by selling unregistered securities in the form of bonds called "Certificates of Faith," and using unregistered agents in the sale of the securities. The church entered into a settlement offer with the Division, which required it to make a rescission offer to all bondholders including an explanation for the reason for the rescission offer. The church also agreed to offer only securities that are registered under the Virginia Securities Act or are exempted from registration, and to offer and sell such securities only through agents who are

registered under the Virginia Securities Act or who are exempted from registration.[13]

CASE STUDY. A church began selling to investors what it called "certificates of deposit." The pastor allegedly told potential purchasers that the certificates of deposit would be used to finance the improvement or expansion of the church and to build a retirement complex. He represented or caused others to represent that the church would pay certificate holders between 12 and 16 percent interest on a quarterly basis and that interest payments would continue until the maturity of the certificate (five years after the date of issuance). He further promised that, when the certificate matured, the investor would be entitled to repayment of the principal plus the balance of any outstanding interest. The pastor further informed investors that they would not have to pay income taxes on the interest payments they received from the church and that the investment was safe because it was backed by the assets of the church. The church raised over $1.6 million from the sale of the certificates to 90 investors, 27 of whom were church members. The pastor took a significant portion of the certificate proceeds for his personal use. Among other things, he purchased four airplanes, a house for his mother, sports cars and passenger trucks, and made a down payment on his daughter's house. The pastor resigned when his actions were uncovered, and the church filed for bankruptcy protection.

The pastor was later prosecuted for 12 counts of securities fraud under federal law, including the following: (1) He "converted approximately $900,000 of certificate funds to the personal benefit of himself and family members." (2) He represented or caused others to represent that the church would pay certificate holders between 12 and 16 percent interest on a quarterly basis and that interest payments would continue until the maturity of the certificate (five years after the date of issuance). (3) He promised that when the certificate matured, the investor would be entitled to repayment of the principal plus the balance of any outstanding interest. (4) He told investors that they would not have to pay income taxes on the interest payments they received from the church. (5) He told investors that their investments were safe because they were backed by the assets of the church. (6) At no time did the pastor tell investors that the money from the sale of certificates was to be used for the personal expenses of the pastor and his family. The pastor was convicted on all counts and sentenced to prison.

A federal appeals court affirmed the pastor's conviction, and an increase in his sentence to the "aggravating" circumstance that he breached a position of trust. The court concluded, "Because [the pastor] was the church's financial decision maker, church-member

---

13 *Commonwealth of Virginia v. Unity Christ Church, 1996 WL 392586 (Va. Corp. Com. 1996).*

investors and church personnel trusted him to be the sole, unsupervised manager of the church's finances. This position of trust allowed the pastor to control the church's bank accounts and misapply the certificate funds clandestinely. Because he was the church's pastor and spiritual leader, his congregation undoubtedly trusted him to further the church's religious mission. His position of trust allowed him to use his authority to mislead church-member investors into believing that the church needed the certificate funds for building projects and to persuade them to invest their money for the good of the church and its endeavors. The trial court therefore correctly determined that the pastor occupied and abused a position of trust."[14]

PROTECTING CHURCHES AND CHURCH MEMBERS FROM INVESTMENT FRAUD

Many churches, and church members, have been victimized by investment fraud. This section will assist church leaders in protecting church assets, and the assets of church members, from such scams.

EXAMPLE. A church raises $250,000 for its building fund, but it is still years away from reaching the goal specified by the congregation before construction can begin. This year the pastor meets Jon, an "investment expert," who seems very knowledgeable about investment opportunities. Jon claims that he can turn the 1 percent return the church is earning on its building fund in a local bank to 30 percent or even 50 percent. The pastor is skeptical at first, but begins to see Jon as an answer to prayer. "Within just a few years, we will be able to begin construction on our new sanctuary," he muses. The pastor is also impressed by Jon's description of a "high yield investment program" involving international banks. The pastor invites Jon to make a presentation to the church board. Jon assures the board that the investment program only involves the "top ten world banks." The board is impressed, and votes to turn over the investment of the church's building fund to Jon. Within a few months, Jon suggests that the pastor promote the investment program to members of the congregation. With the pastor's encouragement, many church members invest their own funds in Jon's program. After several months, the pastor, board, and individual investors begin to wonder when they will receive their 50 percent return on their investments. Jon assures them that it is only a matter of time. A year passes, and still no earnings have been reported. Federal investigators contact the pastor and explain that Jon was engaged in a multi-million dollar securities scam, and that there is little chance that the church, or the individual investors, will ever receive back their invested funds, much less any earnings. The pastor is devastated, as is the church board. Some church members invested

their life savings in what they believed was a blessing from God. Several members begin blaming the pastor and board.

Sound unbelievable? It shouldn't. Investment scams have victimized many churches and church members, and no church is immune. This section will explain the most common forms of securities fraud, provide several examples from real life, address the fiduciary duty of church leaders to invest church funds prudently, and provide practical steps that church leaders can take to minimize, if not eliminate, this risk.

Investment fraud is a risk not only to churches, but also to church members. Church leaders who familiarize themselves with the information in this section not only will be protecting their church, but they also will be protecting members from scams.

Let's begin with a simple principle that will protect churches and church members against most investment scams—"if it sounds too good to be true, it is." In the pages that follow you will be introduced to several tragic cases of securities fraud involving churches and church members. In every one of these cases, the tragedy could have been avoided through heeding this simple principle.

COMMON INVESTMENT SCAMS

The kinds of investment scams that have victimized churches and church members are too numerous to mention. Here are some common and recurring ones.

Pyramid schemes

In the classic "pyramid" scheme, participants attempt to make money solely by recruiting new participants into the program. The hallmark of these schemes is the promise of sky-high returns in a short period of time for doing nothing other than handing over your money and getting others to do the same.

The Federal Trade Commission offers the following advice about pyramid schemes:

Steer clear of multilevel marketing plans that pay commissions for recruiting new distributors. They're actually illegal pyramid schemes. Why is pyramiding dangerous? Because plans that

14 *United States v. Lilly, 37 F.3d 1222 (7th Cir. 1994).*

pay commissions for recruiting new distributors inevitably collapse when no new distributors can be recruited. And when a plan collapses, most people (except perhaps those at the very top of the pyramid) end up empty-handed.

If you're thinking about joining what appears to be a legitimate multilevel marketing plan, take time to learn about the plan before signing on.

What's the company's track record? What products does it sell? How does it back up claims it makes about its product? Is the product competitively priced? Is it likely to appeal to a large customer base? What up-front investment do you have to make to join the plan? Are you committed to making a minimum level of sales each month? Will you be required to recruit new distributors to be successful in the plan?

Use caution if a distributor tells you that for the price of a "start-up kit" of inventory and sales literature—and sometimes a commitment to sell a specific amount of the product or service each month—you'll be on the road to riches. No matter how good a product and how solid a multilevel marketing plan may be, expect to invest sweat equity as well as dollars for your investment to pay off.

Ponzi schemes

Ponzi schemes are a type of illegal pyramid scheme named for Charles Ponzi, who duped thousands of New England residents into investing in a postage stamp speculation scheme back in the 1920s. Ponzi thought he could take advantage of differences between U.S. and foreign currencies used to buy and sell international mail coupons. Ponzi told investors that he could provide a 40 percent return in just 90 days compared with 5 percent for bank savings accounts. Ponzi was deluged with funds from investors, taking in $1 million during one three-hour period. Though a few early investors were paid off to make the scheme look legitimate, an investigation found that Ponzi had only purchased about $30 worth of the international mail coupons.

A Ponzi scheme is closely related to a pyramid because it revolves around continuous recruiting, but in a Ponzi

scheme, the promoter generally has no product to sell and pays no commission to investors who recruit new "members." Instead, the promoter collects payments from a stream of people, promising them all the same high rate of return on a short-term investment. In the typical Ponzi scheme there is no real investment opportunity, and the promoter just uses the money from new recruits to pay obligations owed to longer-standing members of the program. This is often called "robbing Peter to pay Paul." In fact some law enforcement officers call Ponzi schemes "Peter-Paul" scams.

Both Ponzi schemes and pyramids are quite seductive because they may be able to deliver a high rate of return to a few early investors for a short period of time. Yet, both pyramid and Ponzi schemes are illegal because they inevitably must fall apart. No program can recruit new members forever. Every pyramid or Ponzi scheme collapses because it cannot expand long enough to satisfy current and new investors. When the scheme collapses, most investors find themselves at the bottom, unable to recoup their losses.

Ponzi schemes continue to work on the "rob-Peter-to-pay-Paul" principle, as money from new investors is used to pay off earlier investors until the whole scheme collapses. Many churches and church members have been defrauded out of funds by investing in such schemes.

○ **KEY POINT.** Here's a good common sense rule to follow when evaluating investment options: "If it looks too good to be true, don't touch it."

Another definition of a Ponzi scheme is "a fraudulent investment scheme in which money contributed by later investors generates artificially high dividends for the original investors, whose example attracts even larger investments."[15]

Nigerian investment scams

Nigerian advance-fee fraud has been around for decades, but now seems to have reached epidemic proportions. According to the Federal Trade Commission (FTC), some citizens receive dozens of offers a day from supposed Nigerians politely promising big profits in exchange for help moving large sums of money out

---

15 *Black's Law Dictionary* 1180 (7th ed.1999).

of their country. Apparently, many compassionate consumers are continuing to fall for the convincing sob stories, the unfailingly polite language, and the unequivocal promises of money. These advance-fee solicitations are scams, according to the FTC.

Here is a typical scenario. Claiming to be Nigerian officials, businesspeople, or the surviving spouses of former government officials, con artists offer to transfer millions of dollars into your bank account in exchange for a small fee. If you respond to the initial offer, you may receive "official looking" documents. Typically, you're then asked to provide blank letterhead and your bank account numbers, as well as some money to cover transaction and transfer costs and attorney's fees. You may even be encouraged to travel to Nigeria or a border country to complete the transaction. Sometimes, the scam promoters will produce trunks of dyed or stamped money to verify their claims. Inevitably, though, emergencies come up, requiring more of your money and delaying the "transfer" of funds to your account; in the end, there aren't any profits for you to share, and the promoter has vanished with your money.

Incredibly, many church members, and some churches, have fallen victim to Nigerian investment scams. If you're tempted to respond to an offer, the FTC suggests you stop and ask yourself two important questions:

> *Why would a perfect stranger pick you, also a perfect stranger, to share a fortune with?*

> *Why would you share your personal or business information, including your bank account numbers or your company letterhead, with someone you don't know?*

The U.S. State Department cautions against traveling to the destination mentioned in the letters. According to State Department reports, people who have responded to these "advance-fee" solicitations have been beaten, subjected to threats and extortion, and in some cases, murdered.

● **KEY POINT.** If you receive an offer via email from someone claiming to need your help getting money out of Nigeria (or any other country, for that matter) forward it to the FTC at uce@ftc.gov. If you have lost money to one of these schemes, call your local Secret Service field office.

Prime bank scams

Prime bank scams are yet another investment scam that has been perpetrated against churches and church members. Here is how the SEC describes these scams:

> *Lured by the promise of astronomical profits and the chance to be part of an exclusive, international investing program, many investors have fallen prey to bogus "prime bank" scams. These fraudulent schemes involve the use of so-called "prime" bank, "prime" European bank or "prime" world bank financial instruments, or other "high yield investment programs" ("HYIP"s). Persons who promote these schemes often use the word "prime" (or a synonymous phrase, such as "top fifty world banks") to cloak their programs with an air of legitimacy. They seek to mislead investors by suggesting that well regarded and financially sound institutions participate in these bogus programs. But prime bank and other related schemes have no connection whatsoever to the world's leading financial institutions or to banks with the word "prime" in their names.*

How do prime bank scams work? Here is the SEC explanation:

> *Prime bank programs often claim investors' funds will be used to purchase and trade "prime bank" financial instruments on clandestine overseas markets in order to generate huge returns in which the investor will share. However, neither these instruments, nor the markets on which they allegedly trade, exist. To give the scheme an air of legitimacy, the promoters distribute documents that appear complex, sophisticated, and official. The sellers frequently tell potential investors that they have special access to programs that otherwise would be reserved for top financiers on Wall Street, or in London, Geneva, or other world financial centers. Investors are also told that profits of 100 percent or more are possible with little risk.*

The SEC warns that nonprofit organizations are often targeted by the promoters of these scams, and that promoters have demonstrated "remarkable audacity, advertising in national newspapers, such as *USA Today* and the *Wall Street Journal.*" Some promoters avoid using the term "Prime Bank note," and tell prospective investors that their programs do not involve prime bank instruments in an effort to demonstrate that their programs are not fraudulent. Regardless of the terminology, the basic pitch, that the program involves trading in international financial instruments, remains the same, and investors should continue to be vigilant against such fraud.

The SEC has provided the following warning signs of prime bank or other fraudulent bank-related investment schemes.

Excessive guaranteed returns. These schemes typically offer or guarantee spectacular returns of 20 percent to 200 percent *monthly*, absolutely risk free! Promises of unrealistic returns at no risk "are hallmarks of prime bank fraud."

Fictitious financial instrument. Despite having credible-sounding names, the supposed "financial instruments" at the heart of any prime bank scheme simply do not exist. Exercise caution if you've been asked to invest in a debt obligation of the top 100 world banks, Medium Term Bank Notes or Debentures, Standby Letters of Credit, Bank Guarantees, an offshore trading program, a roll program, bank-issued debentures, a high yield investment program, or some variation on these descriptions. Promoters frequently claim that the offered financial instrument is issued, traded, guaranteed, or endorsed by the World Bank or an international central bank.

Extreme secrecy. Promoters claim that transactions must be kept strictly confidential by all parties, making client references unavailable. They may characterize the transactions as the best-kept secret in the banking industry, and assert that, if asked, bank and regulatory officials would deny knowledge of such instruments. Investors may be asked to sign nondisclosure agreements.

Exclusive opportunity. Promoters frequently claim that investment opportunities of this type are by invitation only, available to only a handful of special customers, and historically reserved for the wealthy elite.

Claims of inordinate complexity. Investment pitches frequently are vague about who is involved in the transaction or where the money is going. Promoters may try to explain away this lack of specificity by stating that the financial instruments are too technical or complex for "non-experts" to understand.

You should be especially watchful for prime-bank related schemes promoted over the Internet.

Illustrative cases

Summarized below are several actual cases of investment scams that have victimized churches and church members. Many involve variations of Ponzi or pyramid schemes.

CASE STUDY. A promoter (Jerry) of a "Ponzi" style investment scheme pled guilty to 17 counts of securities fraud and mail fraud in connection with the fraudulent sale of securities to several church members. Jerry's leadership position in the church caused some victims to trust him. A number of his victims commented that he manipulated their faith to gain access to their money. For example, one victim testified that "the church out there where we went, where Jerry went, endorsed him highly, the pastor did. I trusted the pastor, and thus, we trusted Jerry." Another victim described how Jerry prayed with her just before he showed her fraudulent layouts for his purported developments. A letter from a former church member contained the following description of Jerry's activities:

> Jerry was constantly being praised from the pulpit as an "anointed Christian businessman," with visiting prophets prophesying about his future successes and blessings from God. His later legal problems were called demonic attacks by these same people. . . . Normally I could spot someone like Jerry a mile away, but believing the church's active promotion of him; I turned off my internal alarms. . . . Jerry skillfully manipulated my faith in God to his advantage, looking me in the eye while praying to God to bless the investment, all the while stealing my life savings. . . . To summarize, Jerry is an expert at using people's faith in God as a means of getting to their savings, reaching through their souls to pick their pockets, taking not only their savings but also their faith.

Jerry used his victims' faith to target investors. A brochure printed by the church invited parishioners to invest with Jerry, announcing that "in almost every case, our plan will be able to at least match or outperform your current yields, and at the same time earn dividends for our church and its future. These funds will become the backbone of our plan to build the church campus and retire all debt within five years." In soliciting parishioners' investments, Jerry announced:

> We can take . . . individuals who have $200 dollars in a savings account or $200,000 in mutual funds, and we can allow you to retain the principal, but you use that interest . . . to help build God's kingdom, and also receive the same rate that you're receiving currently from the bank. . . . I consider it a real honor and a privilege to be able to be an elder of this church and to be able to take part . . . in a vision that . . . will allow us to quadruple in size and when we finally get this facility, we're going to be able to minister to so many more people.

A federal appeals court affirmed Jerry's guilt, but ordered a trial court to reconsider the length of his prison sentence.[16]

CASE STUDY. A church hired a treasurer (Steve) as a compensated employee. Steve was responsible for the church's bookkeeping, payment of bills, and had a general responsibility for the church's financial accounting. At the time he became treasurer, he was employed as a loan officer by a local bank. Steve invested a large amount of the church's funds with an investment firm. He later testified that he wanted to become a "hero" by investing the church's money in stocks and securities and thereby increasing the church's funds. Steve urged the investment firm to invest the church's funds in speculative stock. Over the next few years, the value of the church's portfolio plummeted, creating a financial crisis for the church. Steve confessed that he had invested the church's funds in speculative investments, and that most of the investments had "failed." Church board members occasionally signed "authorization" forms giving Steve the authority to invest the church's funds. But the board exercised insufficient oversight over Steve's activities to ascertain the true status of church funds. The church later sued the investment firm for malpractice and securities fraud.[17]

CASE STUDY. An investment advisor (John) derived his income through various social contacts, including his church. He lured several church members into investing in commodities and a gold mine. John received 5 percent of each person's investment to cover "personal expenses," plus 25 percent of all profits. As an inducement to investing with him, John "personally guaranteed" a 25 percent return over the first year. If an account failed to perform sufficiently, he would pay the guaranteed return from his personal assets. No risks were explained to the

investors, who were generally unsophisticated. Rather than receive any return after the first year, the investors were informed that John's practices had caused the loss of "a substantial portion of their investment." No guarantee was forthcoming from John at that time but he assured investors that he was withdrawing their funds and transferring them to another commodities broker who would "recover" their original investment plus the guaranteed amount within a "relatively short period of time." Other than a partial return of funds to a select few, the investors received nothing, but were convinced by John to leave their remaining funds in his control with the promise that he would recover their original investment plus much more by investing their funds in a gold mine in Arizona. John informed all of the investors there was "the possibility of becoming as financially independent as you want" and that he "had spent years and thousands of dollars acquiring financial information." In fact, the investors lost virtually all of their investments.[18]

CASE STUDY. A religious ministry operated and marketed a "double-your-money" scheme called the "Faith Promises Program." The ministry used a bank as a major depository and source of financial services while operating the Ponzi scheme. Eventually, the Ponzi scheme swindled more than 15,000 victims out of an estimated $500 million. Many of the founders of the scheme were convicted for a variety of federal offenses. The ministry filed for bankruptcy protection. Several investors later sued the ministry's bank, claiming that it was responsible for the ministry's fraud on the basis of negligence and breach of fiduciary duty. A court ruled that the relationship of the ministry to the bank was a fiduciary one, but not the relationship between individual investors and the bank and therefore the bank was not liable to the investors for the ministry's fraud. The court concluded, "To hold the bank liable in this situation, essentially, would be to instill on banking institutions the power to regulate what their customers do with their money, a power this court cannot and will not establish. As such, the bank had no duty to disclose any material facts to the investors, even if it had knowledge of such facts."[19]

CASE STUDY. A business representing itself as a nondenominational, nonsectarian international Christian ministry (formed in the Dutch Antilles Island of Aruba) placed the following advertisement in an entrepreneur magazine with a nationwide circulation: "Need extra income? [We] would like to show Christian families how working together they can become debt free. Call [a toll-free telephone number] and request the Christian program." Persons who responded to the ad were mailed literature that offered financial assistance through participation in a monthly fund-raising project. By providing others with "love gifts" in the amount of $30, $60, or $100 per month, a participant became eligible to receive monetary "gifts of love" from a "3 wide x 7 level deep network." Of the monthly payments,

16 *United States v. Luca, 183 F.3d 1018 (9th Cir. 1999).*
17 *Yellowstone Conference of the United Methodist Church v. Davidson, 741 P.2d 794 (Mont. 1987).*
18 *Stokes v. Henson, 265 Cal. Rptr. 836 (Cal. App. 1990).*
19 *O'Halloran v. First Union National Bank, 205 F.Supp.2d 1296 (M.D. Fla. 2002).*

30 percent went to the ministry and 70 percent was for "love gifts" to be forwarded to earlier participants in the program. New participants recruited and sponsored other participants, creating an upline of up to seven levels. A participant received a portion of the monthly "love gifts" payments made by those in one's upline. A participant became eligible to receive "love gifts" from others by making monthly payments and by sponsoring others to join the program. The literature represented that it was possible for a participant to receive $10,800 per month from this program. The program was also promoted through radio ads to Kansas residents who needed extra income through a "Christian program." In response to these advertisements, approximately 30 Kansas residents sent for information about the program. The Kansas securities commission concluded that the program was a security, and that it violated securities law in the following ways: (1) neither the securities nor those selling them had been registered; and (2) investors were not informed that the ministry had been issued a cease-and-desist order by the state securities commission a few years earlier. The commissioner ordered the ministry to discontinue any further offers or sales of its program to residents of Kansas unless the securities are registered in advance.[20]

CASE STUDY. A securities dealer offered for sale and sold securities in a local church's mortgage bond investment program. The offering materials for such securities contained a letter which indicated that the bonds were "A" rated when, in fact, they had not received any independent rating. The Texas securities commission determined that this representation was misleading, and it ordered the dealer to discontinue any further references to "ratings" unless it obtained an independent rating from a recognized securities rating agency. It also ordered the dealer to pay a fine, and make "rescission offers" to all persons who invested in any securities accompanied by materials containing the misleading representation.[21]

CASE STUDY. In 2001 the SEC filed charges against two companies relating to a fraudulent trading scheme that raised approximately $22 million from at least 50 investors, many of whom were members of the same religious denomination. According to the SEC, the defendants fraudulently offered and sold unregistered securities in an "international bank-related financial instrument trading program" that was completely fictitious. The defendants promoted their trading program under various names, including Swiss Asset Management, Wall Street South, and Resource F. The SEC claimed that the companies' agents solicited investors using misrepresentations that the investment involved high-quality debt instruments of very large international banks, that the investors' principal was never at risk and could be returned after one year, and that

investors would receive profits of approximately 4 percent to 5 percent every month (or 48 percent to 60 percent annually).

During the initial stages of the fraud, investors received monthly payments that the defendants represented were "profits" on their investment. However, monthly payments to investors eventually stopped. Despite numerous requests, no investors received the return of their investment. Further, since the cessation of monthly payments, promoters regularly sent letters to investors making excuses for the cessation of payments, and making the false statements that trading and monthly payments would resume soon. These letters included a request that investors contribute money to purported "legal efforts" to obtain the return of investors' funds.

A federal court entered an order barring certain officers of the defendants from engaging in further fraudulent activity and freezing their assets to ensure that assets were preserved to pay investors their lost principal.

CASE STUDY. The SEC filed a lawsuit in federal court seeking to halt an ongoing nationwide affinity fraud, primarily targeting African-American churches, conducted by an individual (the defendant) through a bogus company. The SEC alleged that the defendant engaged in a deliberate scheme to defraud investors by making false and misleading statements in connection with the unregistered offer and sale of securities in the form of investment contracts in a "church funding project." The defendant raised at least $3 million from over 1,000 investing churches located throughout the United States. The SEC claimed that through various promotional means, including a website, the defendant's presentations at group meetings and religious conferences, telephone solicitations, mailings, and a commissioned sales force, the defendant solicited churches to invest in the church funding project by falsely promising huge financial returns. Specifically, for each investment of $3,000, the defendant promised to pay a return of $500,000. He told investors that his company would fund the promised returns from a pool of money it received for this purpose from four sources—profit-making corporations, federal government grants, other Christian institutions, and profits from a series of worldwide Christian-based resorts to be built and run by a "sister corporation." In fact, the defendant did not have any commitments from profit-making corporations or other institutions to fund this project, and he built no resorts. As a result of this scam, the defendant has outstanding commitments to investors of at least $500 million. The SEC asked the court to permanently enjoin the defendant from selling securities, and also sought an asset freeze, disgorgement of profits, civil penalties, and an order preventing the destruction of documents.

CASE STUDY. In 2001 the SEC sued an individual (the defendant) alleging that he defrauded a church out of $900,000. The SEC claimed

---

20 *In the Matter of Agape International Ministries, 1995 WL 582034 (Kan. Sec. Com. 1995).*

21 *In the Matter of California Plan of Church Finance, Inc., 1997 WL 403287 (Tex. State Securities Board 1998).*

that the defendant used his investment advisory firm to misappropriate hundreds of thousands of dollars in "soft dollar credits" generated by securities transactions made on the church's behalf in an account that the defendant created with a broker-dealer. Soft dollar credits are created when an investment adviser and a broker-dealer enter into an arrangement in which a percentage of commissions are used to pay for products and services, such as research, that help the adviser in making investment decisions. Because soft dollar credits are generated by commissions paid by the advisory client, they are assets of the client. Soft dollar arrangements are permissible under the securities laws if there is appropriate disclosure to the client about the products and services for which the soft dollars will be used, as well as disclosure that the client may pay higher commission rates as a result of the soft dollar arrangement.

The SEC alleged that as part of the scheme to misappropriate soft dollar credits, the defendant submitted over 100 invoices to the broker-dealer for payments with soft dollars that had been generated by trading in the church's account. Many of the invoices were in the name of a "shell entity" the defendant controlled, and falsely indicated that it had provided services that were payable with soft dollars. The broker-dealer paid hundreds of thousands of dollars to this shell company based on these false invoices. The defendant personally picked up these payments from the broker-dealer and deposited them into bank accounts that he controlled. He then withdrew the majority of the funds for his personal use.

The SEC claimed that the church was not informed that its soft dollars were being used for the defendant's personal benefit, and that the defendant violated his fiduciary duty of "best execution" for his client's securities trades by fraudulently setting the commissions paid by the church at a rate that was approximately five times higher than the average rate charged for soft dollar transactions at the time. The SEC also charged that the defendant "churned" the church's endowment account, frequently causing the church to accumulate large positions of stock in a company only to sell the entire position weeks later at a similar price. These actions were taken to generate additional soft dollar credits, which the defendant then misappropriated.

The SEC asked a federal court to grant injunctive relief, disgorgement of improperly obtained benefits, plus civil penalties. This case was settled by the parties, with the defendant agreeing to pay back $1.2 million (all but $300,000 was waived based on his financial inability to pay).

Reducing the Risk of Investment Fraud—SEC Recommendations

As you read through the cases summarized above, you may be amazed that anyone could have fallen for these scams. But the truth is that in each case church members and leaders found the investment scheme to be legitimate, and did not realize that they were being victimized. Are there specific steps that church members and leaders can take to reduce the risk of financial fraud? Fortunately, the answer is yes. A first step is to be familiar with the four specific kinds of investment fraud described above (pyramid schemes, Ponzi schemes, Nigerian investments, and prime bank investments). A second step is to review the actual cases summarized above. Third, review the following recommendations from the SEC:

If it sounds too good to be true, it is

High-yield investments tend to involve extremely high risk. Never invest in an opportunity that promises "guaranteed" or "risk-free" returns. Words like "guarantee," "high return," "limited offer," or "as safe as a C.D." are a red flag. No financial investment is "risk free" and a high rate of return means greater risk. Watch out for claims of astronomical yields in a short period of time. Be skeptical of "off-shore" or foreign investments. And beware of exotic or unusual sounding investments, especially those involving so-called "prime bank" securities. Compare promised yields with current returns on well-known stock indexes. Any investment opportunity that claims you'll get substantially more could be highly risky. And that means you might lose money.

"Guaranteed returns" aren't

Every investment carries some degree of risk, and the level of risk typically correlates with the return you can expect to receive. Low risk generally means low yields, and high yields typically involve high risk. If your money is perfectly safe, you'll most likely get a low return. High returns represent potential rewards for folks who are willing to take big risks. Most fraudsters spend a lot of time trying to convince investors that extremely high returns are "guaranteed" or "can't miss." Don't believe it.

Check out the company before you invest

If you've never heard of a company, broker, or adviser, spend some time checking them out before you invest. Most public companies make electronic filings with the SEC that can be inspected on the SEC website (sec.gov). Some smaller companies don't have to register their securities offerings with the SEC, so always check with your state securities regulator. You'll find that telephone number in the government section of your phone book. Or call the North American Securities Administrators Association (NASAA). Many online investment scams involve unregistered securities. One simple phone call can make the difference between investing in a legitimate business or squandering your money on a scam.

Your state securities department can tell you whether the person pushing the investment opportunity has a disciplinary history by checking the Central Registration Depository (CRD). You can also obtain a partial disciplinary history by contacting the Financial Industry Regulatory Authority's toll-free public disclosure hotline at (800) 289-9999 or by visiting its website, finra.org.

If a promoter only lists a P.O. box, you'll want to do a *lot* of work before investing your money.

If it is that good, it will wait

Scam artists usually try to create a sense of urgency, implying that if you don't act now you'll miss out on a fabulous opportunity. But savvy investors take time to do their homework before investing. If you're being pressured to invest, especially if it is a once-in-a-lifetime, too-good-to-be-true opportunity that you "just can't miss," just say "no." Your wallet will thank you.

Understand your investments

Scam artists frequently use a lot of big words and technical-sounding phrases to impress you. But have faith in yourself. If you don't understand an investment, don't buy it. If a salesman isn't able to explain a concept clearly enough for you to understand, it isn't your fault. Don't make it your problem by buying.

Beauty isn't everything

Don't be fooled by a pretty website—it is remarkably easy to create one.

Is the person offering the securities licensed?

Find out if the person or firm selling the investment needs to be licensed. Call your state securities regulator and ask whether the person or firm is licensed to do business in your state and whether they have a record of complaints or fraud.

Be especially skeptical of investing via the Internet

You should be skeptical of investment opportunities you learn about through the Internet. When you see an offering on the Internet (whether it's on a company's website, in an online newsletter, on a message board, or in a chat room) you should assume it's a scam until you've done your homework and proven otherwise. Get the facts before you invest, and only invest money you can afford to lose.

Be skeptical of offshore investment opportunities

Watch out for offshore scams and investment opportunities in other countries. When you send your money abroad, and something goes wrong, it's more difficult to find out what happened and to locate your money.

Call the SEC

If you have any doubts about an investment opportunity, call the SEC or your state securities department. You can get the telephone numbers by visiting their websites.

10 Questions to Ask Before You Invest

The SEC suggests that prospective investors ask the following 10 questions before investing funds:

1. Is the investment registered with the SEC and the state where I live?

2. Is the person recommending this investment licensed with my state securities agency? Is there a record of any complaints about this person or the firm he or she works for?

3. How does this investment match my investment objectives?

4. Will the sales representative send me the latest reports that have been filed on this company?

5. What are the costs to buy, hold, and sell this investment? How easily can I sell?

6. Who is managing the investment? What experience do they have? Have they made money for investors before?

7. What is the risk that I could lose the money I invest?

8. What return can I expect on my money? When?

9. How long has the company been in business? Is it making money, and if so, how? What is its product or service? What other companies are in this business?

10. How can I get more information about this investment, such as audited financial statements, annual and quarterly reports, and a prospectus?

Chapter 7

Maintaining Sound Internal Control

A BIBLICAL EXAMPLE OF INTERNAL CONTROL

The Bible provides a clear example of internal control in 2 Corinthians 8:18–21:

> And we are sending along with him the brother who is praised by all the churches for his service to the gospel. What is more, he was chosen by the churches to accompany us as we carry the offering, which we administer in order to honor the Lord himself and to show our eagerness to help. We want to avoid any criticism of the way we administer this liberal gift. For we are taking pains to do what is right, not only in the eyes of the Lord but also in the eyes of man.

The passage above describes the concept of *dual control* (described in more detail later in this chapter) and also conveys an appropriate "tone at the top" expression of desire to operate with integrity in the context of church offerings.

THE CONCEPT OF INTERNAL CONTROL

The Committee of Sponsoring Organizations of the Treadway Commission (COSO) is the body generally recognized in the United States as the primary source of authority and guidance related to the topic of internal control. Guidance provided by COSO is used by financial institutions, publicly traded companies, government agencies, and many other types of organizations in establishing and maintaining systems of internal control. COSO is a joint initiative of the American Accounting Association, the American Institute of CPAs, Financial Executives International, The Association of Accountants and Financial Professionals in Business, and The Institute of Internal Auditors. COSO has developed an "integrated framework" for internal control which is updated periodically.

COSO defines internal control as:

> A process, effected by an entity's board of directors, management, and other personnel, designed to provide reasonable assurance regarding the achievement of objectives relating to operations, reporting, and compliance.

COSO's integrated framework for internal control states that internal control consists of five integrated components:

- *Control environment.* The control environment is the set of standards, processes, and structures that provide the basis for carrying out internal control across the organization.
- *Risk assessment.* Risk assessment involves a dynamic and iterative process for identifying and assessing risks to the achievement of objectives.
- *Control activities.* Control activities are the actions established through policies and procedures that help ensure management directives are carried out to mitigate risks to the achievement of objectives.
- *Information and communication.* Relevant and quality information must be communicated in a continual, iterative process of obtaining, providing, and sharing.
- *Monitoring activities.* Monitoring activities consist of ongoing and separate evaluations to ascertain whether each of the components of internal control is present and functioning.[1]

More information about COSO and its integrated framework for internal control is available at COSO.org.

PRACTICAL APPLICABILITY OF INTERNAL CONTROL FOR CHURCHES

Following is a practical working definition of internal control with respect to a church's financial matters:

> The system of checks and balances necessary to protect the church from intentional or unintentional acts that could cause a loss of the church's financial assets or that could result in misreporting of the church's financial information.

This chapter will focus on internal control matters that are most relevant and most commonly addressed by churches in the United States. Accordingly, the focus here is on internal control matters related to:

---

1   Committee of Sponsoring Organizations of the Treadway Commission, Internal Control – Integrated Framework, Executive Summary, May 2013, available at www.coso.org.

- Safeguarding of assets, particularly in connection with cash transactions;
- Relevant and timely financial reporting; and
- Compliance with applicable laws and regulations.

"TONE AT THE TOP"

The COSO integrated framework referred to above addresses the **control environment** of an organization. The control environment includes an organization's culture and what COSO refers to as the "tone at the top." The idea is that an organization has a particular culture among its leaders with respect to issues related to internal control and similar matters. While many organizations have leaders that desire to operate with complete integrity and in compliance with applicable laws, not all organizations are blessed with such leaders. The tone at the top of an organization has a significant effect on the nature, extent, and quality of an organization's internal control.

If there were ever a type of organization that should be known for its steadfast commitment to integrity and to maintaining sound internal control, it should be the church. After all, if a church and its leaders do not have a genuine desire to operate with integrity and a desire to comply with applicable law, that church has a much more fundamental problem than its internal control. While in the minds of many, the previous sentence may go without saying, the sad reality is that some churches are led by people who do not share such ideals and who often pay little respect to sound internal control, operating with financial integrity, and compliance with applicable law. For any church official reading this publication and addressing the topic of internal control in his or her church, the tone at the top is the starting point and it may also be the endpoint. If your church is led by people who do not respect sound internal control, financial integrity, and legal compliance, you should find a different church—quickly. The remainder of this chapter on internal control assumes the church's leaders have a genuine desire to operate with integrity.

ADEQUATE STAFFING AND FINANCIAL EXPERTISE: AN IMPORTANT PRIORITY

A church with the right attitude regarding financial integrity and compliance still will find internal control difficult if it does not have adequate staffing and financial expertise. In order for a church to maintain accurate financial records and implement appropriate safeguards, the church must have people with the knowledge and capacity to carry out such objectives. Churches sometimes struggle in this area—and many times, this struggle is caused by the church's unwillingness to incur the financial costs necessary to hire the right people and use the right outside help to maintain adequate capacity and expertise to address financial matters well.

Having adequate capacity in financial administration and oversight should be a high priority for any church. Church leaders who place a low priority on financial administration invariably find themselves dealing with frequent financial and administrative challenges—challenges that are often an impediment to the growth and influence of the church. Church leaders who place a low priority on financial administration sometimes have a "blind spot" with respect to this issue, not understanding that having strong and sound financial administration is like having a strong and sound foundation for a building. With a strong foundation, a large building may be built with confidence. But if the foundation is thin and weak, the building may easily collapse. Rarely, if ever, does a large, growing, effective, and dynamic church operate for long with a low priority on the quality of its financial administration.

Part of having adequate capacity in financial administration is having talented and knowledgeable accounting and finance staff. Churches should be selective in hiring accounting and finance staff. Care should be taken to ensure that accounting and finance employees have the talent and ability to perform their duties with excellence. In addition to checking references, churches should find other ways to evaluate the talents and abilities of prospective employees. If the church has a relationship with a knowledgeable CPA, the church may consider asking the CPA to interview a candidate for employment to discuss accounting matters. Another option is to require candidates to complete assessment exams for accounting and financial matters. Once hired, employees must be regularly evaluated to address the quality of their work. The church must address situations where employees are not performing in an excellent manner by requiring them to improve or by replacing them. Many churches struggle in this area, taking the position that "grace and mercy" should be applied to justify retaining poorly performing employees. The experiences of highly effective churches, however, consistently reveal that the "greater good" is to do what it takes to the best of our ability to administer the Lord's church with excellence.

SCREENING FINANCE AND ACCOUNTING EMPLOYEES

In addition to seeking finance and accounting employees with talent and ability, churches must also ensure that its employees are people of high moral character. Many churches require their employees to affirm adherence to a particular statement of faith or doctrine. Churches also must check references provided by prospective employees and volunteers for finance and accounting positions.

It is also essential to perform criminal background checks on all employees or volunteers who are involved in the financial administration of the church. However, background checks must be performed with screenings specifically related to the jobs and duties that the individual will perform if selected, due to federal antidiscrimination laws. Churches should consult their legal counsel for advice regarding policies for obtaining and using criminal background checks in connection with employment decisions. To go deeper on background screening, check out the resources on ChurchLawandTaxStore.com.

Many employers obtain credit history reports for finance and accounting employees, in addition to criminal background checks. Such a practice is wise. The theory behind obtaining a credit history report is that if an individual is experiencing significant financial challenges, he or she may be unusually tempted to engage in improper activities. In determining whether to obtain credit history reports for its finance and accounting employees, a church should evaluate applicable law under the advice of its legal counsel. The laws of some states govern how credit history reports may be used by employers, and also mandate procedures that employers must follow in obtaining and using such reports.

Criminal and credit background checks should be periodically updated for existing employees. A church may hire an employee with no criminal record, but unless the church periodically updates its background checks, the church may not be aware if an employee subsequently engaged in criminal activity.

INSURANCE COVERAGE FOR EMPLOYEE DISHONESTY

A church should maintain adequate insurance coverage for the risk of employee theft or fraud. In determining an appropriate level of coverage, the church should take into consideration the cash balances it maintains in bank accounts, investment accounts, and similar assets. Typically, such coverage is relatively inexpensive and adds an element of protection against the risk of misappropriation or embezzlement.

Insurance coverage for employee dishonesty is not, however, a substitute for sound internal controls. Some church leaders may have the view that if the church has insurance coverage for employee dishonesty, it has little need to put significant internal controls in place. There are serious flaws in such logic. First, it is irresponsible to ignore a risk merely because the risk is insured. It is possible that an insurance company may challenge a claim made by a church that is irresponsible in maintaining basic internal control. Second, and perhaps more importantly, the church must realize that it can only make a claim against its insurance policy if it is aware that a loss has occurred. In a church where internal controls are inadequate, the church may experience significant losses without knowing the losses occurred. Finally, insurance coverage for employee dishonesty has limits. A significant loss that occurs over an extended period of time can easily exceed any reasonable level of insurance coverage.

PROTECTING CASH TRANSACTIONS

Cash transactions are the most important area of internal control for the financial activity of churches. Internal control over cash transactions may be defined as the processes and systems designed to reduce the risk that embezzlement or misappropriation could occur and not be detected in a timely manner.

Prevention or detection?

Not all misappropriation, embezzlement, or fraud can be prevented. While internal control should serve to reduce the risk that such activities could occur, it is impossible to design a practical system that can completely prevent such improper activities. Accordingly, internal control must be designed to reduce the risk that an impropriety could occur and not be detected in a timely manner.

For example, consider an accounts payable clerk who has access to a church's blank check stock for writing checks to vendors. Even if the accounts payable clerk is not an authorized signer on the church's bank account (which she should not be), she could create a check payable to herself or to a fictitious vendor and forge the signature of one or more authorized signers. It would be very difficult to design a practical system that would completely prevent such a possibility. However, a sound internal control system should reduce the risk that the accounts payable clerk could perpetrate such a fraud without being detected in a timely manner.

What are cash transactions?

At the outset, it is important to note that, for the purposes of this chapter, the term "cash" refers to money in any form, including currency, electronic transfers, checks, or any other form of money. Church leaders sometimes make the mistake of thinking that internal control is only important with respect to currency transactions.

For example, when addressing internal control over the receipt of offerings and contributions, some church leaders take the position that since the vast majority of their offerings and contributions come in the form of checks or electronic transfers, there is little need for concern about internal control. Few things could be further from the truth. Sadly, there are numerous ways that ill-intentioned people may convert checks to their own use or divert the destination of electronic transfers. Specific instructions on how such misappropriations can occur are beyond the scope of this chapter. Suffice it to say, however, that conversion of all forms of money to improper use is relatively simple in the absence of adequate internal control.

Does internal control represent a distrust of the individuals involved?

Churches sometimes justify a lack of internal control based on the premise that the church employees, and others who are involved in financial administration, are trustworthy people. One would certainly hope that the church trusts the people it has vested with the responsibilities of financial administration. Imagine the alternative. Of course the church trusts its people. Maintaining sound internal control is not a practice based on distrust. During the Cold War, Ronald Reagan was known for his expression, "Trust but verify," when addressing the global reduction in nuclear arms. The concept of "trust but verify" sums up a healthy view of internal control as it relates to the integrity of the church's finance and accounting team.

Church leaders are sometimes wary of implementing internal controls for fear that doing so will cause the people in charge of financial administration to perceive that the church does not trust them. If the people in charge of financial administration are actually financially savvy, not only will they not harbor that viewpoint, they will typically argue just the opposite. The fact that they are trustworthy is the reason that implementing sound internal control is welcome.

Internal control is for individual protection as well

Sound internal control not only serves to safeguard the assets of the church, it also serves to protect individuals from false accusations or suspicion.

> **EXAMPLE** Mildred, the bookkeeper, has signatory authority over the church's checking account, keeps all the books and records, produces the financial reports, reconciles the bank account, and processes the weekly offerings for deposit alone. One day, someone in the church accuses the church of mishandling offerings and says that money has been taken from the offering and not accounted for.
>
> What defense will Mildred have? Very little, if any.
>
> On the other hand, if the church's practices required two people to accompany the offerings at all times, through the point at which a deposit was fully prepared and a log or other record was made of the items in the deposit, Mildred would have a very strong defense. In reality, if such practices were followed, it is unlikely that such an accusation would even be made. In the absence of such practices, regardless of whether any improper conduct occurred, it will be difficult, if not impossible, for Mildred to avoid suspicion.

Lead us not into temptation

Sound internal control over cash transactions also reduces opportunity for people to engage in impropriety or embezzlement, due to the likelihood of being detected. Placing someone in a position in which they could perpetrate a fraud or embezzlement without detection is clearly unwise and represents poor stewardship. Regardless of how trustworthy a church may consider its people, it should never place people in the path of temptation.

KEY PRINCIPLES OF INTERNAL CONTROL FOR CASH TRANSACTIONS

Specific internal controls related to cash transactions should be developed and maintained based on an understanding of certain key principles. Three primary applicable principles are:

- Segregation of duties with people and systems;
- Dual control; and
- Appropriate oversight and monitoring.

Segregation of duties: people

Certain duties with respect to cash transactions and related activities are not compatible and should not be carried out by one person. (For this purpose, members of the same family should be considered one person.) A lack of appropriate segregation of duties creates an environment in which there is a greater risk that misappropriation, embezzlement, or fraud could occur and not be detected in a timely manner.

As a general rule, it is ideal to separate duties that involve the following roles with respect to cash:

- *Authorization of cash disbursements.* The authorization to make cash disbursements involves the authority to commit the church to making expenditures, purchases, contractual commitments, or other similar actions. Authorization to make cash disbursements is usually vested in the top leadership of a church.
- *Custody or control over cash.* Custody over cash can be in the form of physical possession (e.g., handling of offerings received during a worship service) or signatory authority over bank accounts, investment accounts, and other cash accounts.
- *Accounting responsibilities.* Accounting responsibilities include the responsibility to maintain the books and records of the church. Including (but not limited to) the church's general ledger,

contribution records, accounts payable, accounts receivable, payroll, financial statements, and other reports and financial records related to cash transactions.

While separating duties related to all three of the categories of responsibility described above is ideal, the size and makeup of many churches sometimes makes it difficult to fully separate the responsibility for authorization of cash disbursements from control over cash. For example, a church's executive pastor or business administrator is often vested with the authority to approve or authorize spending commitments, purchases, and contractual commitments. The executive pastor or business administrator is also often vested with signatory authority over the church's bank accounts. Such arrangements are common and do not necessarily present significant weaknesses in internal control, so long as other appropriate safeguards are in place. In reality, a church's executive pastor, business administrator, or equivalent official is typically in the best position to know whether a disbursement is proper and whether a check or other instrument authorizing the disbursement is appropriate.

While combining the duties of authorizing cash disbursements and signatory authority over cash accounts may be permissible in some circumstances, it is never permissible or acceptable to combine the duties of custody or control over cash with accounting responsibilities that involve cash transactions. For example, it is not appropriate for the church's primary accountant to have physical custody of cash or to have signatory authority over any of the church's bank accounts.

Segregation of duties: systems

In addition to applying the proper segregation of duties to the assigned roles of individuals, the church's financial accounting software system should be configured in a manner that requires adherence to the segregation principles described above.

Properly configuring the financial accounting software system involves assigning user rights to individuals in a manner that aligns with their duties. User rights should permit employees to perform the duties to which they are assigned and should not permit them to perform other incompatible duties or functions. For example, a person responsible for handling incoming funds should not have the ability to enter or modify accounting data related to incoming funds or to general accounting. As another example, a person with signatory authority over the church's bank accounts should not have the ability to enter or modify accounting data related to expenses, disbursements, or to general accounting.

A detailed analysis of the topic of assigning and maintaining system user rights in a church's financial accounting software applications is beyond the scope of this chapter, but following are some key principles for churches to consider in this important area:

(1) An application that allows for multiple levels of user rights will have an "administrator" role, which is the role of assigning user rights to individual users.

(2) The administrator role may also permit the master administrator to allow other users to have administrative rights—permitting them to also assign or change user rights. Having more than one user with administrative rights is generally not a good practice.

(3) Ideally, the person with administrative rights (we will refer to this person as the "administrator") will be a person who has no financial authority, meaning no control or custody over assets (including no signatory authority) and no accounting or financial reporting responsibilities.

(4) The person vested with the responsibility to determine how user rights should be assigned (we will refer to this person as the "authorizer") will be different from the administrator. The authorizer should be a person in a position of executive authority with knowledge about the financial operations of the church, but not a person with direct accounting or financial reporting responsibilities. The authorizer should not have user rights that permit the entry or modification of system data—the authorizer may have "read-only" access.

(5) The authorizer will carefully consider the roles and duties of individual users, and will authorize the assignment of individual user rights. The authorization should be in writing and should be communicated to the administrator, who will physically implement the assignment of user rights pursuant to the instructions of the

authorizer. The administrator and authorizer will retain the written authorization of user rights as an important record. Modifications to user rights must be approved by the authorizer in writing and communicated to the administrator in the same manner that applies to the assignment of user rights. The administrator and authorizer should retain records of user rights modifications as important records.

(6) Some applications may allow for "profiles," which are bundles of user rights that are typically assigned to persons with a particular role. For example, some applications may have a user rights profile labeled "accountant" with user rights deemed by the application publisher to be appropriate for most accountants in an organization. An authorizer must take care with using pre-bundled profiles to ensure that all of the rights assigned to a particular person are appropriate. Software publishers may not adequately consider internal control matters in their creation of bundled user profile options, regardless of how they may be labeled.

(7) Some financial software applications allow for user rights to include the ability to delete or modify a previously posted transaction or entry. Such a feature is dangerous and should never be permitted in a sound internal control environment. When assigning user rights, no user should have the ability to delete or modify an individual transaction, record, or entry once it is posted or entered into the system. (A previous mistake should be corrected by posting a new entry so that a proper record of the postings may be maintained.) The church's financial software application should maintain a permanent log or record of all activity, entries, or modifications.

(8) Users should not have rights to perform functions within the system for which they are not assigned, regardless of whether such functions are incompatible with their duties or not. For example, the church business administrator, executive pastor, or treasurer should not, normally, have rights that would permit data entry or data modification. It would be common and appropriate in most circumstances for such individuals to have "read-only" access.

7

Maintaining Sound Internal Control

191

(9) The church's human resources processes should include removing a user's access rights to the system immediately upon termination.

(10) As a matter of policy, all users should be advised to report to their supervisors any variations from the church's policies in this area or any other anomalies that may be cause for concern.

Dual control

The practice of dual control relates to having at least two unrelated people working together when handling "live" funds. A lack of dual control in circumstances where it is warranted creates an environment in which there is a greater risk that misappropriation, embezzlement, or fraud could occur and not be detected in a timely manner.

Most commonly, dual control is practiced in churches in connection with the collection of physical offerings. Physical offerings may be collected during a worship service, from collection receptacles, through the mail, or by other means. Dual control may also be practiced when currency is used for operating purposes (e.g., on an international missions trip, when carrying out disaster relief, or in similar circumstances.)

Appropriate oversight and monitoring

In addition to the principles of segregation of duties and dual control, church leaders must engage in adequate oversight and monitoring of the church's financial affairs. That includes carefully reviewing financial reports, reconciliations, and other records. This responsibility also includes monitoring to verify that policies, procedures, and internal controls which are supposed to be in place are, indeed, in place and being carried out by those who are responsible. See Chapter 8 – Audits for more information about oversight and monitoring.

SPECIFIC INTERNAL CONTROLS OVER CASH TRANSACTIONS

Following are a number of recommended internal controls that should be applied to cash transaction activities. Cash transaction activities may be generally divided into three categories:

- Receipts (including storage);
- Disbursements; and
- Reconciliation.

Receipts

Physical collection

Cash receipts obtained by physical collection (from worship services, receptacles, mail, and so on) should be handled under dual control at all times, up through the point at which a deposit is prepared and a log is made of the items being deposited. The deposit documents and the log should be signed off by the two or more people who are handling and processing the funds. The log or detailed record of items deposited should be securely provided to separate persons with accounting responsibilities.

As a general rule, the people physically handling funds and preparing the deposit should be separate from the people who post deposits to the accounting records or to donor records. The use of electronic scanners to gather data from checks for the purpose of assisting with the posting of contributions to donor records, or for the purpose of depositing the funds in the bank, does not negate this principle or the need to exercise dual control throughout the process. Care should be taken to ensure that the church's process would not permit someone to misappropriate a check or currency while still having the contribution represented by that check or currency posted to a donor's contribution records. Proper reconciliation of amounts posted to donor records to amounts deposited will reduce such risks.

The concept of dual control should be applied from the very moment church officials have access to funds. For example, if offerings are collected in a worship service, the ushers or stewards who collect the funds should never physically be in a location where they cannot be seen by others. The ushers or stewards should gather together in plain sight of the congregation, and then at least two of them should accompany the offering to the place where it is stored or further processed. If contributions are collected from receptacles, such receptacles should be locked and should only be accessed by two people working together. The keys to such receptacles should be stored in a manner that requires at least two people working together to retrieve them.

For cash receipts received by mail, such items should be segregated from other mail and processed under dual control.

As mentioned above, the people who physically collect and process cash receipts should be separate from those who have accounting responsibilities for the church.

In recent years, churches have begun to add additional elements of physical security as part of the process of receiving and processing cash receipts. For example, some churches use security guards, police officers, armored courier services, security surveillance cameras, and other safeguards that help reduce the risk of theft—or even robbery or burglary. Churches are wise to consider such measures in light of the increasing frequency of crimes in this area. It is not difficult to understand how the church's people or funds could be vulnerable, if it is known that funds are processed in a certain location following a certain schedule and then transported predictably to a specific location. Many banks now offer armored car service pickups to facilitate church deposits.

When processing checks for deposit, checks should be restrictively endorsed immediately upon their receipt. This is true, even if the church uses electronic scanners and makes deposits through the "remote capture" services offered by their bank. Restrictively endorsing checks makes it more difficult for the checks to be misappropriated.

Storage

Deposits of cash receipts should be made immediately after funds are received and processed. When immediate deposit is not possible, funds should be stored in a safe and secure manner that requires dual control for access. For example, the church could use a safe that requires both a key and a combination to open it. No one person should have both a key and the combination to the safe. In recent years, safe manufacturers have added security features, such as biometric devices, to reduce the risk of unauthorized access. Regardless of the security features, a safe or other storage device should not permit one person to access it alone.

Electronic collection

In recent years, donors have increasingly adopted the practice of making contributions to their churches electronically. Electronic contributions may be made through ACH transactions from their bank accounts or by credit or debit card transactions initiated through the Internet or at kiosks provided by the church.

Electronic collection of cash receipts greatly reduces the risk of misappropriation and fraud. However, there are important considerations to keep in mind in safely accepting cash receipts electronically.

When a church utilizes a service provider, such as a merchant processing firm, to facilitate electronic transactions via the Internet, the church should take care to ensure that the service provider itself maintains appropriate internal controls and security measures to conduct its activities. Practically, there is virtually no way to assess a service provider's controls other than to determine whether the service provider has obtained a report on its internal controls from an independent certified public accounting firm. The report that the church should seek from a service provider is referred to as a "SOC 1" report, and it should include an opinion on the effectiveness of the organization's internal control with respect to processing transactions. There are two types of SOC 1 reports—cleverly labeled "Type 1" and "Type 2." A Type 1 report does not provide an opinion on the effectiveness of the organization's internal control. A Type 2 report does. Churches that engage in significant and material electronic transactions utilizing an online merchant processing firm should insist that their service provider produce a SOC 1 Type 2 report. The SOC 1 Type 2 report should contain a favorable opinion regarding the organization's internal control over the processing of transactions.

Not all service providers in this arena obtain independent assessments of their internal control and therefore, not all service providers can produce the type of report described above. Some service providers will bristle at such a demand. Church leaders are wise to seek a service provider that regularly obtains such a report and can provide it.

Note that the type of report described above is a report on the organization's internal control. Some service providers who do not have a SOC 1 report will point to the fact that they have Payment Card Industry Data Security Standards (PCI DSS) certification. These standards are mandatory for the payment card industry and relate to data security. While data security is important, internal control over electronic cash transactions involves much more than simple data security. PCI DSS credentials alone are not adequate to establish that an organization maintains effective internal control over its processing of transactions. The SOC 1 Type 2 report is intended to address the service provider's overall system of internal control for processing transactions.

EXAMPLE A church used a service provider to process online contributions. Donors submitted their credit and debit card information along with information about the amounts they wished to contribute to the church. The church was contacted one day by a donor who stated that he had not received an acknowledgment for his online contributions to the church. Upon investigating the matter, the church determined that it had not received the online contributions the donor claimed to have made. Charges, however, were posted to the donor's credit card account. Upon further investigation, the church learned that several hundred thousand dollars of online contributions made by its donors had been diverted due to the inadequate internal controls and processes maintained by its service provider.

Other cautions about credit and debit card processing arrangements

When a church establishes an agreement with a debit or credit card processing organization, the church must tell the service provider what bank account should be used to transfer funds from donor debit or credit cards. Churches must ensure that the person authorized to enter into the agreement or to make changes to the agreement does not also have accounting responsibilities. The risk in this area relates to the possibility that a church official could designate an unauthorized account, such as his or her own, as the destination for processed funds. If the individual with the authority to make such changes also has accounting responsibilities, there is a greater risk that such a scheme might not be detected in a timely manner.

It is wise to maintain a separate bank account for the purpose of receiving deposits from merchant processing companies. A separate account can facilitate reconciliation to the records provided from the merchant processing firm. Additionally, monitoring of the separate account by an independent official can reduce the risk of impropriety by identifying unusual activity.

One other important point should be made regarding processing receipts from credit or debit card transactions. The ability to accept contributions or purchases made by debit or credit cards, whether online, by telephone, or in person, often carries with it the ability to issue credits or refunds to cardholders. The ability to issue a credit or refund to a cardholder is the same as the ability to disburse the church's funds. Accordingly, merchant processing account activity should be monitored by an independent official for the possibility of unauthorized credits issued to cardholders. For example, an employee working in the church bookstore might issue a credit to his own credit card account. More sophisticated merchant processing systems will only allow credits to accounts for which there has been a recent corresponding debit and only an amount that does not exceed the corresponding debit. Churches should question their service providers regarding such security measures and appropriately monitor account activity for impropriety.

Disbursements

Segregation of duties

One of the most important internal control principles that should be applied in the area of cash disbursements is that no one individual should have duties or authority that would permit him or her to initiate and complete a cash disbursement in its entirety. For example, the person who prepares checks for payment to vendors should not be an authorized signer on the church's bank account and vice versa. Authorized signers should not have access to blank check stock. Electronic disbursements from the church's bank account should require participation or approval by more than one individual. This principle reflects the concept of segregation of duties.

Controlled review of bank activity

Another key rule that churches should apply in the arena of cash disbursements is that a person with signatory authority should perform a controlled review of bank statements or bank activity to verify the propriety of all disbursements. Controlled review refers to a review of banking activity performed in a manner that ensures that the reviewer is analyzing unaltered documentation.

An example of a controlled review is a review of bank statements received from the bank that are still sealed in their original envelopes when delivered to the reviewer. Another example of a controlled review is a review of cash disbursements activity online on the bank's website. Both approaches permit the reviewer to analyze information directly as it comes from the bank and reduces the risk that the reviewer analyzes altered or fraudulent documentation. The review should include an analysis of all canceled check images, as well as information about all other debits (or reductions) in the church's bank account.

Don't forget PayPal

In performing a review of bank activity for the purpose of vetting disbursements, church leaders should consider all monetary accounts in which activity could be conducted, including those that may be "off the radar" accounts, such as PayPal accounts, virtual currency accounts, and so on.

Positive pay services

Another way that a church can reduce the risk of unauthorized disbursements is to utilize "positive pay" services offered by its bank—especially if the service includes "payee verification." With a bank's positive pay service, the bank only pays checks or debits that are preauthorized by the bank customer (the church). The church sends the bank and electronic file listing the checks that have been authorized for payment. The bank then compares checks that are presented to it for payment against the list provided by the church. If a check presented for payment does not match the file provided by the church, the bank reports it to the church as an exception, and the church then has an opportunity to determine whether the check is valid or not. Basic positive pay services typically do not include verification of the name of the payee—only the check number and the amount of the check.

The enhancement of payee verification reduces the risk of a fraudulent disbursement that may be recorded in the church's books as having been made to a payee who is different from the actual payee indicated on the check. In order to establish the greatest protection in using positive pay, the person reviewing and submitting the positive pay file to the bank should be someone who is knowledgeable about authorized vendors and disbursements and who is someone other than an accounts payable or other accounting person.

Cloud-based paperless accounts payable applications

As is more fully described in Chapter 2, in recent years cloud-based paperless accounts payable applications have become increasingly popular. An example of such a service is Bill.com. In addition to providing significant efficiencies, electronic accounts payable manage-

ment systems generally facilitate improved internal control by requiring multiple individuals to provide approvals in connection with disbursements (assuming the application has been properly set up with segregated user rights).

For example, such an application offers "roles," such as the accountant role, with duties that align with the principle of segregation of duties. An accountant, for example, would not be permitted to execute a "pay" command.

Another feature that enhances internal control is that such systems do not produce physical checks to be signed by the church's employees and mailed or delivered from the church's office. Instead, disbursements are either made electronically through the ACH system or checks are actually cut and mailed by the service provider directly to the vendors. Cloud-based paperless accounts payable management systems offer significant advantages over traditional paper-check-based systems. The applications integrate with a number of accounting software applications.

Application to payroll

While the internal control practices described above are explained primarily in terms of disbursements to vendors, the same principles should apply with respect to payroll disbursements. Segregation of duties should apply in the area of payroll such that no one person is responsible for all phases of payroll processing.

For example, it would be inappropriate for a single person to maintain personnel records, to input information about pay rates into the payroll processing system, prepare the payroll, and authorize or make payroll disbursements without any other independent review. Even though vesting one person with the authority to perform all the duties described above would represent a lack of segregation of duties, such arrangements are common in churches.

A relatively practical way to apply segregation of duties in the payroll arena is to require a controlled review of payroll information for each payroll after the fact. If an outside payroll service is used, the reviewer should obtain payroll information related to each payroll directly from the payroll service provider, either by receiving the information in an unopened package or by reviewing the information directly online. The reviewer should be a person who is knowledgeable about the church's employees and pay rates, and should not be a member of the payroll staff or the accounting team. Such a review is designed to reduce risks that include, but are not limited to, unauthorized modification of pay rates and payment to fictitious employees.

Reconciliation

It should go without saying that a church's bank accounts and investment accounts should be reconciled in a timely manner after the end of each month (at a minimum). An ordinary bank account reconciliation should be performed by an appropriate member of the accounting team, and not by any person who has

Horror Story

The pastor of Oak Tree Church, a church that did not follow the procedures described above, received a call from the church's bank one morning. "Pastor," the voice on the line said, "the church's account is overdrawn and you need to deposit funds to cover the deficit."

"What? That can't be!" exclaimed the pastor.

"We have plenty of money in our account!" he continued. "I have a financial report right here in front of me that says we have over $100,000 in our account. There must be an error in your records."

The pastor's confidence quickly faded when the banker said, "Sir, you haven't had that much money in your account in at least a year."

When he went to the bank to get more information, that pastor learned the horrible truth: He and the other church leaders had been deceived by their bookkeeper. For months, the bookkeeper covered up an irregularity in the accounting records by producing financial reports showing a cash balance that far exceeded the actual amount in the bank. Because no one ever verified the accuracy of the information in the reports, the deception continued until the church was literally out of money.

(This scenario is real, based on a real occurrence – the name of the church has been changed.)

signing authority with respect to the accounts or other custody or control over the funds.

Review of reconciliation

Once account reconciliation is performed, sound internal control dictates that the reconciliation be reviewed by an appropriate official who does not have accounting responsibilities. Ideally, this official is a person with authority and knowledge about the church's financial activities—particularly disbursements.

One step further

To adequately close the loop of internal control with respect to cash and investment activity and the church's financial reporting, one final key step in the reconciliation process should be performed regularly by an appropriate high-level church official. That is, making a comparison of the cash and investment balances as determined by the reviewed reconciliations described above, with the balances reported in financial reports provided to the church's financial oversight body (finance committee, board, and so on).

EXAMPLE Elm Street Church has two bank accounts and one investment account. The church's bookkeeper performs a monthly reconciliation of all three accounts. The original bank statements and reconciliations are provided to the church's treasurer, who reviews the reconciliations for propriety. The treasurer also compares the reconciled balances for all three accounts to the cash and investment balances reported in the financial reports provided to the church's finance committee. The treasurer signs off on a log indicating that he performs this step each month.

SAFEGUARDING OF ASSETS OTHER THAN CASH

Internal control encompasses safeguarding other types of assets in addition to cash. While internal controls over cash transactions likely warrant the most attention to detail in a church's system of internal control, controls related to other assets should be considered as well. If a church maintains significant assets of a type that may be vulnerable to theft, the church should consider applying appropriate internal control measures to protect the assets. Common examples of non-cash assets that may be particularly vulnerable to theft in a church would be:

- Food-service inventories;
- Bookstore inventories; and
- Electronic and media equipment.

If such assets are significant, the church should apply accounting procedures to track the inflow and outflow of such items. The accounting records for such assets should be maintained by someone other than the people who have custody or control over the assets. Additionally, accounting team members can perform analytical procedures to identify anomalies in inventory levels or related items.

For electronic and media equipment or other similar assets used by the church in its operations, the church should consider maintaining an inventory record of such items that includes a description of the item, its cost, the date it was acquired, the location at which the asset is to be kept, and the name of the person or persons responsible for the asset.

Additional protection may be afforded by using serially numbered tags affixed to the assets, where the serial numbers correspond to entries in the asset inventory records. Periodic inspections should be made to ensure that the assets are still on hand and in their proper locations. Some churches fail to maintain an inventory of their vulnerable non-cash assets because they believe that such an inventory must be maintained for all furniture, fixtures, and equipment. But that is not true. The church may choose to inventory only those items that it considers vulnerable, such as electronic or media equipment. Applying such an approach can make the task of maintaining inventory records for such items much more manageable.

RELEVANT AND TIMELY FINANCIAL REPORTING

In a healthy internal control environment, financial statements and reports are produced for church leadership on a regular and timely basis. The financial reports should be complete and correct, allowing church officials to review them and inquire about unexpected or unusual items. Timely production of relevant financial information facilitates a healthy review process and is essential in maintaining sound internal control. Sometimes, a church's finance or accounting team may get behind in its work and months may pass during which financial reports are not produced and reviewed. This is a most unhealthy scenario, and church leaders should take action to restore proper procedures when such events occur.

To enhance internal control and to facilitate a healthy review process, those who prepare financial reports should proactively highlight or otherwise identify and explain unusual items, fluctuations, and so on. In a healthy reporting process, members of the accounting team do not wait for questions that they know will or should be asked by those who will review the reports.

The financial reporting process, further described in Chapter 2, should be clearly defined to include:

- Specific financial reports;
- Specific due dates for the reports; and
- A defined distribution list for the reports.

COMPLIANCE WITH APPLICABLE LAWS AND REGULATIONS

Pastor Church & Law, 4th Edition, and the annual *Church and Clergy Tax Guide,* both published by Christianity Today (ChurchLawAndTaxStore.com) provide comprehensive information about laws and regulations that apply to churches in the United States.

With respect to laws and regulations generally, a church can employ practices to reduce the risk of non-compliance or legal controversy. Following are some healthy practices that can help reduce such risks:

- Hire and use legal counsel to review and address items, such as:
  - The church's governing documents (articles of incorporation and bylaws);
  - The church's board-approved policies (employment policies, child- safety policies, transportation policies, and so on);
  - Significant contractual agreements (before they are executed); and
  - Other important documents.

- Conduct a "legal audit" in which an attorney assesses the church's compliance with a variety of laws and regulations, and provides a report to the church's leadership on his or her findings.

- Hire knowledgeable, capable, and business-savvy people to lead the administrative operations of the church.
- Hire qualified tax counsel, such as a CPA firm or a law firm knowledgeable in the area of church and clergy tax law, to perform an assessment of the church's compliance with significant aspects of the tax laws. Such an assessment should be followed by a report to the church's leadership of the findings and recommendations of the tax counsel.

EMBEZZLEMENT

Embezzlement of church funds is a very serious offense, both legally and scripturally. Acts 5:1-11 contains the following account:

Now a man named Ananias, together with his wife Sapphira, also sold a piece of property. With his wife's full knowledge he kept back part of the money for himself, but brought the rest and put it at the apostles' feet. Then Peter said, "Ananias, how is it that Satan has so filled your heart that you have lied to the Holy Spirit and have kept for yourself some of the money you received for the land? Didn't it belong to you before it was sold? And after it was sold, wasn't the money at your disposal? What made you think of doing such a thing? You have not lied to just to human beings but to God." When Ananias heard this, he fell down and died. And great fear seized all who heard what had happened. Then some young men came forward, wrapped up his body, and carried him out and buried him. About three hours later his wife came in, not knowing what had happened. Peter asked her, "Tell me, is this the price you and Ananias got for the land?" "Yes," she said, "that is the price." Peter said to her, "How could you conspire to test the Spirit of the Lord? Listen! The feet of the men who buried your husband are at the door, and they will carry you out also." At that moment she fell down at his feet and died. Then the young men came in and, finding her dead, carried her out and buried her beside her hus-band. Great fear seized the whole church and all who heard about these events.

The definition of embezzlement varies slightly from state to state, but in general, it refers to the wrongful conversion of property that is lawfully in your possession. The idea is that someone has legal control or custody of property or funds, and then decides to convert the property or funds to his or her own personal use.

Most people who embezzle funds insist that they intended to pay the money back and were simply "borrowing" the funds temporarily. Intent to pay back embezzled funds is not a defense to the crime of embezzlement. The crime is complete when the embezzler misappropriates the church's funds to his or her own personal use. As one court has noted:

The act of embezzlement is complete the moment the official converts the money to his own use even though he then has the intent to restore it. Few embezzlements are committed except with the full belief upon the part of the guilty person that he can and will restore the property before the day of accounting occurs. There is where the danger lies and the statute prohibiting embezzlement is passed in order to protect the public against such venturesome enterprises by people who have money in their control.

One can only imagine how many such schemes actually work without anyone knowing about it.

What if the embezzled funds are returned? The crime of embezzlement has occurred even if the embezzled funds in fact are paid back. Of course, it may be less likely that a prosecutor will prosecute a case under these circumstances. And even if the embezzler is prosecuted, this evidence may lessen the punishment. But the courts have consistently ruled that an actual return of embezzled funds does not purge the offense of its criminal nature or absolve the embezzler from punishment.

HOW EMBEZZLEMENT OCCURS

Let's look at a few cases of actual embezzlement of church funds to see how it can occur.

CASE 1 An usher collected offerings each week in the church balcony, and pocketed all loose bills while carrying the offering plates down a stairway to the main floor. Church officials later estimated that he embezzled several thousands of dollars over a number of years, before being caught.

CASE 2 The same two persons counted church offerings for many years. Each week they removed all loose coins and currency (not in offering envelopes) and split it between them. This practice went on for several years, and church officials later estimated that the two had embezzled tens of thousands of dollars.

CASE 3 A church left its Sunday offering, along with the official count, in a safe in the church office until Monday. On Monday morning a church employee deposited the offering. The employee ignored the official counts, and deposited the offering less loose coins and currency (which she retained). The deposits were never checked against the offering counts.

CASE 4 A church child care director embezzled church funds by issuing herself paychecks for the gross amount of her pay (before deductions for tax withholding). The church withheld taxes and paid them to the government, but her paychecks reflected the gross amount of her pay.

CASE 5 A pastor had the sole authority to write checks on the church's checking account. He used church funds to pay for several personal expenses, amounting to thousands of dollars each year, until his actions were discovered.

CASE 6 A church bookkeeper's responsibilities included managing the church's bank account, maintaining financial records, and handling the church's finances. A few years after she started working at the church, she began to misappropriate church funds by issuing unauthorized checks to herself, her personal creditors, and other individuals. According to the church's investigation, she embezzled nearly $560,000 over an eight-year period. The embezzlement was eventually discovered, and the bookkeeper was arrested and charged with grand theft. She pled guilty to misappropriating the funds and was convicted of grand theft and sentenced to a ten-year prison term.[2]

CASE 7 A minister received an unauthorized kickback of 5 percent of all funds paid by a church to a contractor who had been hired to build a new church facility. The minister received over $80,000 from this arrangement, in exchange for which he persuaded the church to use the contractor. The minister's claim that the $80,000 represented a legal and nontaxable "love offering" was rejected by a federal court

that found the minister guilty of several felony counts. This arrangement was not disclosed to the church board, and obviously amounted to an unauthorized diversion of church funds back to the minister.

CASE 8 A volunteer church treasurer began using church funds to pay a number of personal debts, including his mortgage, his cell phone bill, a car loan, and other personal expenses. On several occasions, he made the checks payable to himself and indicated "payroll" on the checks. After the end of his two-year term as treasurer, his successor discovered the discrepancies in the church's accounts. It was later determined that 142 checks, worth $82,130, had been "written outside the scope" of the former treasurer's authority and for his personal benefit. The church informed the police, and the former treasurer was charged with five separate counts of embezzlement.[3]

CASE 9 Two deacons were responsible for collecting offerings from church members, depositing the funds into the church's bank account, and paying for authorized maintenance and repairs to the church building and facilities. Both deacons were authorized to sign checks individually, without the safeguard of requiring two signatories. They were not, however, authorized to make expenditures without the approval of the members, which was determined at meetings held after church services. Over the course of six months, one of the deacons (the "defendant") wrote checks totaling $1,600 to himself, with no documentation showing that he used the funds to pay for expenditures authorized by the congregation. When the other deacon became aware of the defendant's behavior, he notified law enforcement officials. An investigation was initiated that resulted in the indictment of the defendant for embezzlement. The jury found him guilty, and he was sentenced to a ten-year term of imprisonment and ordered to pay restitution in the amount of $2,255.[4]

CASE 10 A church administrator embezzled over $350,000 from his church. He wrote unauthorized checks to himself and others from the church's accounts, and used the church's credit card on over 300 occasions to purchase personal items. Police officers were called and he made a full confession. The church secured a $1 million civil judgment against him. He was prosecuted and convicted on four felony counts including forgery and theft, and was sentenced to 32 years in prison based on "aggravated circumstances" (the large amount of money that had been stolen, the care and planning that went into the crimes and their concealment, the fact that a great number of checks were stolen and unauthorized credit card charges made, and breach of trust). Several years earlier, the administrator embezzled a large

3   *Bragg v. Commonwealth,* 593 S.E.2d 558 (Va. App. 2004).
4   *Coleman v. State,* 947 So.2d 878 (Miss. 2006) (the verdict was reversed on appeal due to a technicality).

Magpusao v. Magpusao, 265 B.R. 492 (M.D. Fla. 2001).

amount from a prior church employer. However, that church chose not to initiate criminal charges, believing that he had learned his lesson.[5]

CASE 11 A woman (the "defendant") was employed as a church's office manager from 1993 until 2000. During that period, she misused church funds for her personal gain, using checks from the church's general fund account and the pastor's discretionary account on which she was a signatory. The defendant forged signatures and falsified endorsements on checks. She also made out checks to herself, and various individuals and entities, which she cashed. Many of the checks were cashed at a supermarket next door to the church. The defendant also misused the church's funds and the pastor's name in other ways for her financial benefit. Her activities enabled her to misappropriate $450,000 of church funds. The defendant's misconduct was eventually discovered, and she was charged with several crimes. She pled guilty to 28 counts of forgery; three counts of mail fraud; one count of bank fraud; and one count of making a false statement on a credit

---

[5] *Kemp v. State, 887 N.E.2d 102 (Ind. App. 2008).* A state appeals court, calling the offenses "undeniably despicable," reduced the sentence from 32 to 16 years based on the "mitigating factors" of no prior criminal record and a full confession.

Churches That Take Steps To Prevent Embezzlement

- Remove a source of possible temptation from church employees and volunteers who work with money.

- Protect the reputation of innocent employees and volunteers who otherwise might be suspected of financial wrongdoing when financial irregularities occur.

- Avoid the unpleasant task of confronting individuals who are suspected of embezzlement.

- Avoid the risk of congregational division that often is associated with cases of embezzlement—with some members wanting to show mercy to the offender and others demanding justice.

- Reduce the risk of having to tell donors that some of their contributions have been misappropriated by a church employee or volunteer.

- Reduce the damage to the reputation and stature of its leaders who otherwise may be blamed for allowing embezzlement to occur.

- Create a "culture of accountability" with regard to church funds.

---

application. She received a sentence of 15 years, which included an upward adjustment (pursuant to federal sentencing guidelines) for misrepresenting that she was acting on behalf of her church.[6]

CASE 12 A church's chief financial officer (the "defendant") embezzled $850,000 in church funds, mostly by arranging increases in the church's line of credit at a local bank. His technique was simple. As chief financial officer he had access to digital versions of the signatures of at least four of the church's officers. He used these to create phony corporate resolutions bearing the officers' signatures and authorizing increased borrowing. His deeds eventually came to light after he was terminated on other grounds, and he was charged with several financial crimes including aggravated identity theft (one for each of the officers), bank and wire fraud, making a false statement on a loan application, four counts of tax evasion, and first-degree fraud. The defendant was tried and convicted on 12 counts in federal district court, and sentenced to 97 months in prison. The district court judge also ordered the defendant to pay $850,000 in restitution to the church. Upon completion of his prison term, the defendant will be placed on five years of supervised release. During that time, the judge has ordered that he not work in any capacity handling the finances of any other church or organization. The defendant's conviction and sentencing was affirmed on appeal by a federal appeals court.[7]

RESPONDING TO ALLEGATIONS OF EMBEZZLEMENT—IN GENERAL

Sometimes a person who has embezzled church funds will voluntarily confess—usually out of a fear that he or she is about to be "caught." But in many cases the embezzler does not confess—at least initially. Discrepancies or irregularities may occur which cause church leaders to suspect this person. Consider the following case studies.

CASE 1 The same person has counted church offerings for many years. The pastor inadvertently notices that offerings are always higher when this person is absent (due to illness, business, or vacation).

CASE 2 Church officials noticed that a church bookkeeper was living a higher standard of living than was realistic given her income.

CASE 3 Church offerings have remained constant, or increased slightly, despite the fact that attendance has increased.

---

6   *U.S. v. Reasor, 541 F.3d 366 (5th Cir. 2009).*

7   *710 F.3d 434 (D.C. Cir. 2013).*

CASE 4 A church treasurer notices that a church official with sole signature authority on the church checking account has purchased a number of expensive items from unknown companies without any documentation to prove what was purchased and why.

Church leaders often are unsure how to address suspected cases of embezzlement. Often the suspected embezzler is a trusted member or employee, and church leaders are reluctant to accuse such a person without irrefutable evidence that he or she is guilty. The pastor may confront the person about the suspicion, but in many cases the individual will deny any wrongdoing--even if guilty. This compounds the frustration of church officials, who do not know how to proceed.

Here are several steps that church leaders can take to help resolve such difficult cases:

1. *Confront the suspected embezzler.* The pastor and at least one other church leader should inform the person that the church has evidence indicating that he or she has embezzled church funds. Seek a confession. Inform the person that if no one confesses, the church will be forced to call in a CPA firm to confirm that embezzlement has occurred, and to identify the probable embezzler.

Embezzlement is a criminal offense. Depending on the amount of funds or property taken, it may be a felony that can result in a sentence in the state penitentiary. This obviously would have a devastating impact on the embezzler, and his or her family. If the evidence clearly indicates that a particular member or employee has embezzled church funds, but this person denies any wrongdoing, inform him or her that the church may be forced to turn the matter over to the police for investigation and prosecution.

Embezzlers never report their illegally obtained "income" on their tax returns. Nor do they suspect that failure to do so may subject them to criminal tax evasion charges. In fact, in some cases it is actually more likely that the IRS will prosecute the embezzler for tax evasion than the local prosecutor will prosecute for the crime of embezzlement. If the evidence clearly indicates that a particular member or employee has embezzled church funds, but this person denies any wrongdoing, inform him or her that the church may be forced to turn the matter over to the IRS for investigation and possible prosecution.

2. *Have a local CPA conduct an audit to establish that embezzlement has occurred, and provide an estimate of how much was embezzled.* If the suspected embezzler denies any wrongdoing (or if embezzlement is suspected but it is not clear who is guilty), church leaders should consider hiring a local CPA firm to look for evidence of embezzlement. There is a good possibility that the embezzlement will be detected, and that the perpetrator will be identified.

Many church leaders have found that turning the investigation over to a CPA firm is much more acceptable than conducting the investigation internally. The CPA firm is completely objective, and ordinarily will not know the suspected embezzler. Further, few church members will object to the church hiring a CPA firm to detect wrongdoing and help establish a sound system of internal control.

Church leaders who suspect embezzlement should consider hiring a "certified fraud examiner." CFEs are typically CPAs with specialized training in identifying and quantifying embezzlement. They can provide a church with the best evidence of whether embezzlement occurred, how it occurred, and how much was taken. Check with the Association of Certified Fraud Examiners for a CFE in your area.

➤ TIP: CPAs can also help the church establish a strong system of internal control to reduce the risk of embezzlement in the future.

3. *Contacting the police or local prosecutor.* If the suspected embezzler does not confess, or if embezzlement is suspected but it is not clear who is guilty, church leaders must consider turning the matter over to the police or local prosecutor. This is a very difficult decision, since it may result in the prosecution and incarceration of a member of the congregation.

4. *The embezzler confesses.* In some cases the embezzler eventually confesses. Often, this is to prevent the

church from turning the case over to the IRS, the police, or a CPA firm. Embezzlers believe they will receive "better treatment" from their own church than from the government. In many cases they are correct. It is astonishing how quickly church members will rally in support of the embezzler once he or she confesses—no matter how much money was stolen from the church. This is especially true when the embezzler used the embezzled funds for a "noble" purpose, such as medical bills for a sick child. Many church members demand that the embezzler be forgiven. But should church leaders join in the outpouring of sympathy? Should the matter be dropped once the embezzler confesses?

These are questions that each church will have to answer for itself, depending on the circumstances of each case. *Before forgiving the embezzler and dropping the matter, church leaders should consider the following points:*

(1) *A serious crime has been committed, and the embezzler has breached a sacred trust.* The church should insist, at a minimum, that the embezzler must:
- Disclose how much money was embezzled.
- Make full restitution by paying back all embezzled funds within a specified period of time.
- Immediate and permanent removal from any position within the church involving access to church funds.
- *Closely scrutinize and question the amount of funds the embezzler claims to have taken. Remember, you are relying on the word of an admitted thief. Is it a realistic amount? Is it consistent with the irregularities or discrepancies that caused church leaders to suspect embezzlement in the first place? If in doubt, consider hiring a local CPA to review the amount the embezzler claims to have stolen.*

(2) *In many cases the embezzler will insist that he or she is not able to pay back the embezzled funds.* This presents church leaders with a difficult decision, since the embezzler has received unreported taxable income from the church. The embezzler should be informed that the embezzled funds must either be returned within a specified time, or a promissory note must be

signed promising to pay back the embezzled funds within a specified period of time. The embezzler should be informed that failure to agree to either alternative will force the church to issue him or her a 1099 (or a corrected W-2 if the embezzler is an employee) reporting the embezzled funds as taxable income. Failure to do so will subject the church to a potential penalty (up to $10,000) for aiding and abetting in the substantial understatement of taxable income under section 6701 of the tax code.
- *An embezzler's biggest problem ordinarily will not be with the church or even with the local prosecutor. It will be with the IRS for failure to report taxable income. There are only two ways to avoid trouble with the IRS: (1) the embezzler pays back the embezzled funds, or (2) the church reports the embezzled funds as taxable income on a 1099 or corrected W-2.*

(3) *Church leaders must also remember that they owe a fiduciary obligation to the church and that they are stewards of the church's resources.* Viewing the offender with mercy does not necessarily mean that the debt must be forgiven and a criminal act ignored. Churches are public charities that exist to serve religious purposes, and they are funded entirely out of charitable contributions from persons who justifiably assume that their contributions will be used to further the church's mission. These purposes may not be served when a church forgives and ignores cases of embezzlement.

(4) *Debt forgiveness.* In some cases, employees who embezzle funds will agree to pay them back, when confronted, if the church agrees not to report the embezzlement to the police or the IRS. Does this convert the embezzled funds into a loan, thereby relieving the employee and the church of any obligation to report the funds as taxable income in the year the embezzlement occurred? The answer is no. Intent to pay back embezzled funds is not a defense to the crime of embezzlement.
- There is another problem with attempting to re-characterize embezzled funds as a loan. If the church enters into a loan agreement with the embezzler, this may require congregational approval. Many church bylaws require

congregational authorization of any indebtedness, and this would include any attempt to reclassify embezzled funds as a loan. Of course, this would have the collateral consequence of apprising the congregation of what has happened.

RESPONDING TO ALLEGATIONS OF EMBEZZLEMENT—TAX COMPLIANCE

Church leaders often are confused regarding their tax obligations in the event of a known or suspected case of embezzlement. Here is a checklist of relevant considerations:

(1) Embezzled funds constitute taxable income to the embezzler. The embezzler has a legal duty to report the full amount of the embezzled funds as taxable income on his or her tax return, whether or not the employer reports the embezzled funds as taxable income on the employee's W-2 or 1099. If funds were embezzled in prior years, then the employee will need to file amended tax returns for each of those years to report the illegal income, since embezzlement occurs in the year the funds are misappropriated.

    (a) IRS Publication 525 states: "Illegal income, such as stolen or embezzled funds, must be included in your income on line 21 of Form 1040, or on Schedule C (Form 1040) or Schedule C-EZ (Form 1040) if from your self-employment activity."

(2) Federal law does not require employers to report embezzled funds on an employee's W-2, or on a Form 1099. This makes sense, since in most cases an employer will not know how much was stolen. How can an employer report an amount that is undetermined? Embezzlers are not of much help here. This means that any attempt by an employer to report embezzled funds on an employee's W-2 or 1099 will almost always represent a gross understatement of what was taken.

(3) In rare cases, an employer may be able to determine the actual amount of embezzled funds as well as the perpetrator's identity. In such a case, the full amount may be added to the employee's W-2, or it can be reported on a Form 1099 as miscellaneous income. But remember, do not use this option unless you are certain that you know the amount that was stolen as well as the thief's identity.

(4) In most cases, employers do not know the actual amount of embezzled funds. The embezzler's "confession" is unreliable, if not worthless. Reporting inaccurate estimates on a W-2 or 1099 will be misleading. Also, if you report allegedly embezzled funds on an employee's W-2 or 1099 without proof of guilt, this may expose the church to liability on the basis of several grounds. One of these is section 7434 of the tax code, which imposes a penalty of the greater of $5,000 or actual damages plus attorney's fees on employers that willfully file a fraudulent Form 1099.

(5) Employers that cannot determine the actual amount of funds that an employee embezzled, or the employee's identity, will not be penalized by the IRS for failing to file a W-2 or 1099 that reports an estimate of the amount stolen.

(6) Employers that are certain of the identity of the embezzler, and the amount stolen, may be subject to a penalty under section 6721 of the tax code for failure to report the amount on the employee's W-2 or 1099. This penalty is $50, or up to the greater of $100 or 10 percent of the unreported amount in the case of an intentional disregard of the filing requirement. For employers that are certain how much was stolen, and who intentionally failed to report it, this penalty can be substantial. To illustrate, let's say that church leaders know, with certainty, that a particular employee embezzled $100,000, but they choose to forgive the person and not report the stolen funds as taxable income. Since this represents an intentional disregard of the filing requirement, the church is subject to a penalty of up to 10 percent of the unreported amount, or $10,000. But note that there is no penalty if the failure to report is due to reasonable cause, such as uncertainty as to how much was embezzled, or the identity of the embezzler.

(7) If the full amount of the embezzlement is not known with certainty, then church leaders have the option of filing a Form 3949-A ("Information Referral") with the IRS. Form 3949-A is a form that allows employers to report suspected

illegal activity, including embezzlement, to the IRS. The IRS will launch an investigation based on the information provided on the Form 3949-A. If the employee in fact has embezzled funds and not reported them as taxable income, the IRS may assess criminal sanctions for failure to report taxable income.

➤ TIP. In many cases, filing Form 3949-A with the IRS is a church's best option when embezzlement is suspected.

THE CONSEQUENCES OF EMBEZZLEMENT

Persons who embezzle church funds face a number of consequences. Some of them may come as unpleasant surprises. Here are four of them.

(1) *Felony conviction.* Embezzling church funds is a felony in most states, and conviction can lead to a term in a state penitentiary. The definition of embezzlement varies slightly from state to state, but in general it refers to the wrongful conversion of property that is lawfully in your possession. The idea is that someone has legal control or custody of property or funds, and then decides to convert the property or funds to his or her own personal use.

◉ KEY POINT. It does not matter that the embezzler intended to pay back the embezzled funds. This intent in no way justifies or excuses the crime. The crime is complete when the funds are converted to one's own use—whether or not there was intent to pay them back.

◉ KEY POINT. Sometimes an embezzler, when caught, will agree to pay back embezzled funds. This does not alter the fact that the crime of embezzlement has occurred. Of course, it may be less likely that a prosecutor will prosecute the case under these circumstances. And even if the embezzler is prosecuted, this evidence may lessen the punishment. But the courts have consistently ruled that an actual return of embezzled property does not purge the offense of its criminal nature or absolve the embezzler from punishment for his or her wrongdoing. Also, note that church officials seldom know if all embezzled funds are being returned. They are relying almost entirely on the word of the thief.

(2) *Tax evasion.* In many cases the embezzler's biggest concern is not the possibility of being prosecuted for the crime of embezzlement. Rather, it is the possibility of being prosecuted by the IRS for tax evasion. Embezzlers never report their illegally obtained "income" on their tax returns. Nor do they suspect that failure to do so may subject them to criminal tax evasion charges. In fact, in some cases it is actually more likely that the IRS will prosecute the embezzler for tax evasion than the local prosecutor will prosecute for the crime of embezzlement.

CASE STUDY. A church accountant embezzled $212,000 in church funds. His scheme was to divert to his own use several designated offerings, and to inflate the cost of equipment that he paid for with his own funds and that the church later reimbursed at the inflated amounts. The accountant not only was found guilty of embezzlement, but he was also convicted of tax evasion because he failed to report any of the embezzled money as taxable income. He was sentenced to a two year prison term, followed by two years of probation.

(3) *Recovery of property purchased with embezzled funds.* Here's a real shocker—persons who receive property purchased by the embezzler with embezzled funds may be required to return the property to the church.

CASE STUDY. A church bookkeeper embezzled several thousand dollars by issuing checks to a fictitious company. He opened an account in the name of a fictitious company, issued church checks to the company for services that were never performed, and then deposited the checks in the fictitious company's account. He later withdrew the funds and purchased two automobiles, which he gave to a friend. A court ruled that the friend had to give the cars back to the church, since they had been purchased with embezzled church funds. The point here, as noted by the court, is that one who acquires property with embezzled church funds may be required to transfer the property to the church.

(4) *Insurance company lawsuits.* As if the three consequences summarized above are not enough, embezzlers face an additional consequence—they may be sued by an insurance company that pays a claim based on the embezzlement. Many churches purchase insurance to cover financial losses due to theft or embezzlement. Insurance companies that pay out claims based on such losses are free to sue the persons responsible.

CASE STUDY. A court ruled that an insurance company that paid out $26,000 to a charity because of an act of embezzlement could sue the embezzler for the full amount that it paid.

CONFIDENTIALITY AND PRIVILEGED COMMUNICATIONS

Sometimes ministers learn of embezzlement through a confession by the embezzler in the course of confidential counseling. This presents the minister with a dilemma—either protect the confidentiality of the confession and refuse to disclose it, or ignore confidentiality and disclose the confession. This dilemma is compounded by the fact that some ministers have been sued for disclosing confidential information without the consent of the other person. Embezzlers may claim that they confessed their crime to their minister in confidence and in the course of spiritual counseling, with no thought that the minister would disclose the information to others.

Ministers who disclose confidential information without permission risk being sued for breaching their duty of confidentiality. When an employee or volunteer approaches a minister and confesses to embezzling church funds, there normally will be an expectation that the minister will keep that information in confidence. There is no sign above the minister's desk that says, "Warning: Confessions of criminal activity will be promptly shared with the board or with the civil authorities."[8] Ministers who violate this expectation need to understand that they face potential legal liability for doing so—unless they have the employee's permission, in writing.

Ministers who receive a confidential confession of embezzlement from a church employee or volunteer should not disclose this information to others, including the church board, without the person's written permission. If the embezzler does not consent to the disclosure of the confession, and refuses to meet with the board, the minister should not disclose the information to any other person. Disclosure under these circumstances could result in a lawsuit being brought against the minister and church.

Does this mean that the minister should drop the matter? Not necessarily. The minister is free to gather independent evidence that embezzlement occurred, so long as this is done without disclosing the confession. For example, the minister could persuade the church board to hire a CPA to conduct an audit of the church's financial records. Such a procedure may reveal that embezzlement has occurred. The minister also should attempt to persuade the embezzler to confess to the board.

Closely related to the concept of confidentiality is the clergy-penitent privilege. Ministers cannot be compelled to disclose in court the contents of confidential communications shared with them in the course of spiritual counseling.

CASE STUDY. Late one night, a church treasurer arranged a meeting with her priest after informing him that she "had done something almost as bad as murder." The treasurer, after requesting that their conversation be kept confidential, informed the priest that she had embezzled $30,000 in church funds. The priest, with the permission of the treasurer, sought the assistance of the church board. The board decided that the embezzlement had to be reported to the local police. The treasurer was later prosecuted for embezzling church funds, and she was convicted and sentenced to four months in jail despite the fact that she fully repaid the church prior to her trial. She appealed her conviction on the ground that it had been based on her confidential statements to the priest which, in her opinion, were "penitential communications" that were privileged against disclosure in court. The appeals court concluded that the statements made by the church treasurer to the priest were not privileged since they involved a "problem-solving entreaty" by the treasurer rather than "a request to make a true confession seeking forgiveness or absolution—the very essence of the spiritual relationship privileged under the statute." That is, the treasurer sought out the priest not for spiritual counseling, but to disclose her embezzlement and to seek his counsel on how to correct the problem. The court also emphasized that the treasurer had "released" the priest from his assurance of confidentiality by consenting to his disclosure of the facts of the case to the church board members.[9]

INFORMING THE CONGREGATION

Church leaders often refuse to disclose to the congregation any information about an incident of embezzlement for fear of being sued for defamation. This concern is understandable. However, serious problems can occur when the pastor or church board dismisses a long-term employee or volunteer for embezzlement

---

See *Lightman v. Flaum, 687 N.Y.S.2d 562 (Sup. 1999),* in which the court observed: "It is beyond peradventure that, when one seeks the solace and spiritual advice and guidance of a member of the clergy, whether it be a priest, rabbi or minister, on such sensitive, personal matters as those involved in our case, this is not done as a prelude to an announcement from the pulpit."

9   *People v. Edwards, 284 Cal. Rptr. 53 (Cal. App. 1988).*

and nothing is disclosed to the membership. Church leaders under these circumstances often are accused of acting arbitrarily, and there is a demand for an explanation. Refusal to respond to such demands may place the church leadership in an even worse light.

There is a possible answer to this dilemma. Many states recognize the concept of "qualified privilege." This means that statements made to others concerning a matter of common interest cannot be defamatory unless made with malice. Statements are made with malice if they are made with knowledge that they are false, or with a reckless disregard as to their truth or falsity. In the church context, this privilege protects statements made by members to other members concerning matters of common interest. Such communications cannot be defamatory unless malice is proven. Church leaders who decide to disclose why an embezzler was dismissed can reduce the legal risk to the church and themselves by following a few basic precautions:

- Only share information with active voting members of the church—at a membership meeting or by letter. The qualified privilege does not apply if the communication is made to non-members.
- Adopt procedures that will confirm that no non-member received the information.
- Limit your remarks to factual information and do not express opinions.
- Prepare in advance a written statement that is communicated with members, and that is approved in advance by an attorney.

⊙ **KEY POINT.** In some cases, it is helpful to obtain a signed confession from an individual who has been found guilty or who has confessed. If the individual consents to the communication of the confession to church members, then you can quote from the confession in a letter that is sent to members of the congregation, or in a membership meeting. Be sure that this consent is in writing.

⊙ **KEY POINT.** One court ruled that a church could be sued for defamation for sharing suspicions regarding a church treasurer's embezzlement with members in a congregational meeting. The court concluded that the treasurer should have been investigated and dismissed by the board, without informing the congregation. While no other court has reached a similar conclusion, this case suggests that

church leaders should disclose cases of embezzlement to the church membership only if (1) absolutely necessary (for example, to reduce congregational unrest), and (2) an attorney is involved in making this decision.

AVOIDING FALSE ACCUSATIONS

In some cases it is not certain that embezzlement has occurred, or that a particular individual is guilty. A church must be careful in how it proceeds in these cases to avoid possible liability for defamation or emotional distress.

CASE STUDY. A church's senior pastor believed that certain members of the church board (including the chairman) diverted $94,000 of church funds earmarked for a remodeling project to other uses. He expressed his concerns at meetings of the church board, and to the entire congregation at a special business meeting. He informed the congregation that he wanted an "accounting" of the funds to determine if they had been used improperly, and he insisted that the board chairman resign his position. The chairman claimed that the pastor's acts amounted to a "false accusation" that he and other board members had embezzled church funds. The pastor retained an attorney who wrote the board chairman a letter demanding that he "immediately cease and desist from [his] unlawful threats, harassment, blackmail and extortion of the pastor." The attorney's letter continued:

> It is a disgrace that a man who holds himself out to be a Christian engages in such conduct. You are upset that the pastor has requested an accounting of the church monies which you have controlled for years and, rather than provide the information, you have launched a personal attack on him. The only conclusion one can reach from such behavior is that you have, in fact, embezzled money from the church. The pastor has referred this matter to the appropriate church board as well as governing bodies. We are confident that they will pursue actions against you to recover all church property.

The deposed board chairman sued the church for defamation. A trial court dismissed the lawsuit and a state appeals court affirmed the trial court's ruling. It noted that the pastor's expressing concerns about the use of designated church funds was not defamatory, and the attorney's letter that accused the board chairman of "embezzlement" was not defamatory since it was protected by the "litigation privilege" (good faith statements made in contemplation of litigation generally cannot be defamatory). *Miller v. Second Baptist Church, 2004 WL 1161653 (Cal. App. 2004).*[10]

---

10 *Miller v. Second Baptist Church, 2004 WL 1161653 (unpublished decision, Cal. App. 2004).*

EXAMPLE. A church convened a special business meeting at which the church treasurer was accused of embezzling church funds. Following this meeting the treasurer was shunned by church members who viewed her as guilty. This case is tragic, since the treasurer had been a long and devoted member of the church. Her life was ruined by the allegation, and she had to leave the church. It was later proven that she was completely innocent. She later filed a lawsuit, accusing the pastor and members of the church board of defamation. A court agreed with her, and awarded her a substantial verdict. The court pointed out that the accusation of embezzlement was based on flimsy evidence and could have easily been refuted with any reasonable investigation. The court concluded that church leaders are liable for defamation if they charge a church worker with embezzlement without first conducting a good faith investigation. The court also pointed out that the charges should not have been disclosed to the congregation, but rather, should have been discussed among the church board and a decision made at that level on whether or not to dismiss the treasurer.

This second case study provides church leaders with very helpful guidance in handling suspicions of embezzlement. Do not rush to judgment. Conduct a deliberate and competent investigation, and let the church board resolve the issue without involving or informing the congregation, if possible. In some cases, congregational outrage may occur following the dismissal of an embezzler by the pastor or church board, especially if nothing is communicated to the congregation about the basis for the action. In these cases the board may decide that the membership must be informed. If so, refer to the above discussion on "Informing the Congregation."

THE EMPLOYEE POLYGRAPH PROTECTION ACT

The federal Employee Polygraph Protection Act (EPPA) prohibits employers from requiring or requesting any employee or job applicant to take a lie detector test, or from discharging, disciplining, or discriminating against an employee or prospective employee for refusing to take a test or for exercising other rights under the Act.

However, the Act contains limited exemptions where polygraph tests (but no other lie detector tests) may be administered, subject to certain restrictions. One exception allows employers to ask employees to submit to a polygraph exam if they are suspected of theft and there is an ongoing investigation. Here are the details of this exception:

[This Act] shall not prohibit an employer from requesting an employee to submit to a polygraph test if—

(1) The test is administered in connection with an ongoing investigation involving economic loss or injury to the employer's business, such as theft, embezzlement, misappropriation, or an act of unlawful industrial espionage or sabotage;

(2) The employee had access to the property that is the subject of the investigation;

(3) The employer had a reasonable suspicion that the employee was involved in the incident or activity under investigation; and

(4) The employer executes a statement, provided to the examinee before the test, that—(A) sets forth with particularity the specific incident or activity being investigated and the basis for testing particular employees, (B) is signed by a person (other than a polygraph examiner) authorized to legally bind the employer, (C) is retained by the employer for at least 3 years, and (D) contains at a minimum—(i) an identification of the specific economic loss or injury to the business of the employer, (ii) a statement indicating that the employee had access to the property that is the subject of the investigation, and (iii) a statement describing the basis of the employer's reasonable suspicion that the employee was involved in the incident or activity under investigation.[11]

➤ TIP. Know the details of the "ongoing investigation" exception. Under very limited circumstances, you can request that an employee take a polygraph exam if you suspect the employee of theft and you are conducting an ongoing investigation. Do not rely on this exception without fully complying with all of the requirements quoted above. Also, consult with legal counsel to be sure the exception is available to you.

CASE STUDY. A church board suspects the church's volunteer treasurer of embezzling several thousands of dollars of church funds. The treasurer is called into a board meeting, and is told "you can clear your name if you submit to a polygraph exam." Does this conduct violate the

---

11 29 U.S.C. § 2006(d).

Employee Polygraph Protection Act? Possibly not. The Act only protects "employees," and so a volunteer treasurer presumably would not be covered. However, if the treasurer receives any compensation whatsoever for her services, or is a "prospective employee," then the Act would apply. Because of the possibility that volunteer workers may in some cases be deemed "employees," you should not suggest or request that they take a polygraph exam without the advice of legal counsel.

CASE STUDY. Same facts as the previous example, except that the church suspects a full-time secretary of embezzlement. Can it suggest that the secretary take a polygraph exam? Only if all the requirements of the "ongoing investigation" exception apply. These include: (1) the test is administered in connection with an ongoing investigation involving economic loss or injury to the employer's business, such as theft or embezzlement; (2) the employee had access to the property that is the subject of the investigation; (3) the employer had a reasonable suspicion that the employee was involved in the incident or activity under investigation; and (4) the employer executes a statement, provided to the examinee before the test, that—(A) sets forth with particularity the specific incident or activity being investigated and the basis for testing particular employees, (B) is signed by a person (other than a polygraph examiner) authorized to legally bind the employer, (C) is retained by the employer for at least 3 years, and (D) contains at a minimum—(i) an identification of the specific economic loss or injury to the business of the employer, (ii) a statement indicating that the employee had access to the property that is the subject of the investigation, and (iii) a statement describing the basis of the employer's reasonable suspicion that the employee was involved in the incident or activity under investigation.

The EPPA provides that an employer that violates the Act is liable to the employee or prospective employee for "such relief as may be appropriate, including, but not limited to, employment, reinstatement, promotion, and the payment of lost wages and benefits." A court may also award damages based on "emotional distress," and punitive damages.

KEY POINT. Damages awarded for violating the Employee Polygraph Protection Act may not be covered under a church's liability insurance policy. This is another reason for church leaders to assume that the Act applies to their church, and to interpret its provisions prudently.

OTHER CONSIDERATIONS

Church leaders who become aware of a case of embezzlement should consider a few additional points:

- Be sure to notify your insurance agent, and ask if your church has insurance to cover embezzled funds.
- When should you notify the embezzler? That is a difficult question that will depend on the facts and circumstances of each case. One thing is clear—as soon as the embezzler is confronted, you must immediately seize his or her church computer and deny any further access to his or her office without one or two church employees or board members being present to ensure that no materials are removed. No access to the computer should be allowed, to prevent the destruction of evidence, and the computer should be transferred to an off-site location. Ask an attorney, CPA, or certified fraud examiner (CFE) for recommendations concerning when and how to notify the embezzler.
- When you confront the embezzler, it is helpful to have a printed confession available for the embezzler to sign. The confession not only should include a confession, but also an authorization for the pastor to share the confession with anyone he or she chooses, including staff members and the congregation.
- Cases of embezzlement raise a number of complex legal and tax issues. Our recommendation is that you retain an attorney, CPA, or CFE to assist you in responding to these issues.

7

Chapter 8

Audits and Other Financial Accountability Activities

INTRODUCTION

The term "audit" can—and does—mean many different things to different people in different contexts. The *Merriam-Webster Dictionary* defines the term "audit" as, "a complete and careful examination of the financial records of a business or person; a careful check or review of something." Wikipedia offers an alternative definition—"a planned and documented activity performed by qualified personnel to determine by investigation, examination, or evaluation of objective evidence, the adequacy and compliance with established procedures, or applicable documents, and the effectiveness of implementation." These formal definitions and others like them center on a common theme—an audit is a process designed to facilitate accountability.

For our purposes, the term "audit" and references to other accountability activities are used to refer to activities conducted or contracted by a church for the purposes of addressing:

- The reliability of financial statements or reports;
- Whether the church has vulnerabilities in internal controls, tax compliance, or legal matters; and,
- Whether certain aspects of a church's operations are being carried out as intended or expected.

FINANCIAL ACCOUNTABILITY

Financial accountability should be of utmost interest to any church and its leaders. In the context of handling money, Paul writes in 2 Corinthians 8:21, "For we are taking pains to do what is right, not only in the eyes of the Lord but also in the eyes of man." The highest and best reason for a church to have an external audit is to facilitate the church's financial integrity and accountability, and to increase the likelihood that significant internal control deficiencies, tax compliance vulnerabilities, or similar matters will come to the attention of the church's leadership.

In its report dated December 2012, the Commission on Accountability and Policy for Religious Organizations, sponsored by ECFA (Evangelical Council for Financial Accountability), stated the following regarding churches and financial accountability:

...[C]hurches should verifiably demonstrate their commitment to proper oversight and accountability. Freedom of religion requires, however, that they be free to choose oversight and accountability measures that fit their own religious polity and doctrine. Independent accreditation by a bona fide accrediting organization is one option for voluntarily demonstrating such a commitment. Robust and meaningful financial oversight by a denominational organization is another method for churches that are part of a hierarchical structure. Independent religious groups unaffiliated with any larger organization may choose to be governed by independent board members, obtain outside audits or legal reviews, and create internal checks and balances such as special committees empowered to review the organization's affairs or to approve certain decisions, or pursue other options. The methods for achieving and verifiably demonstrating accountability are as varied as the religious communities they are meant to protect. Whatever the method, churches should be able to articulate to their adherents, members, congregants, supporters, and other stakeholders how they demonstrate proper oversight and accountability.

External and internal audits

Churches tend to utilize internal and external audits and other accountability processes in ways that correlate to the size of the church. Smaller churches tend to utilize informal internal accountability processes performed by members of the church's governing body, its finance committee, or by volunteers. Larger churches (annual revenues exceeding $2 million) commonly engage external auditors. Very large church organizations (annual revenues in the tens of millions of dollars) often engage external auditors as well as maintaining a regular, formal internal audit function by employing an internal auditor on staff or contracting with a vendor for formal internal audit services.

External audits and other CPA-performed engagements

Churches may have external audits performed as a condition of acquiring a loan or seeking other funding. Lending institutions and funders often require audited financial statements. A church that has an external audit performed solely for the purpose of complying with a contractual or funding obligation may see little value in the audit beyond the church's contractual obligation.

Only Certified Public Accountants (CPAs) and CPA firms are uniquely licensed under state law throughout the United States to render opinions and provide certain other services with respect to an organization's financial statements. It is a violation of state law for anyone other than a CPA or a CPA firm to provide assurance or attestation with respect to an organization's financial statements. Churches should be careful when seeking an external audit to ensure that the person or firm being engaged is licensed or legally authorized to practice as a CPA or CPA firm.

The highest quality external audits for churches are those provided by independent CPAs or CPA firms with extensive and reputable experience serving churches and other religious nonprofit organizations. Firms with such experience should be able to help the church identify issues that are common to the church and religious nonprofit sectors and warrant attention.

In addition to independent external audits, CPA firms offer other levels of service with respect to a church's financial statements and/or operating activities. Below is a description of the primary levels of engagement and includes commentary on the relative value and usefulness of each.

AUDIT

An audit is the highest level of assurance a CPA firm can provide with respect to a church's financial statements. Audited financial statements provide the church's governing body with the auditor's opinion as to whether the financial statements are presented fairly, in all material respects, in conformity with the method of accounting utilized. The opinion offers reasonable but not absolute assurance with respect to the financial statements to which it applies.

In an audit, the CPA firm should obtain an understanding of the organization's internal control and assess fraud risk as it relates to the financial statements. The firm should also corroborate the amounts and disclosures

included in the financial statements by obtaining audit evidence through inquiry, physical inspection, observation, third-party confirmations, examination, analytical procedures, and other procedures.

A properly performed audit should result in the following reports, at a minimum:

- An opinion on the financial statements;
- Financial statements and related disclosures;
- A report addressing any material weaknesses or significant deficiencies in internal control identified by the CPA firm in performing the engagement *(a church should request its auditor to issue a report addressing internal control regardless of whether the auditor identifies material weaknesses or significant deficiencies in the course of the audit)*; and,
- A report to those charged with oversight of the church regarding certain matters related to the audit process itself, such as the independence of the auditors, sensitive items in the financial statements, and difficulties performing the engagement.

Commentary

A well-performed audit conducted by a CPA firm with extensive reputable experience serving churches and religious organizations should yield significant value to a church and its leaders. An audit results in an opinion on the financial statements by the CPA, providing reasonable assurance that the financial statements are fairly stated (assuming the audit test work supports such a conclusion). No other level of engagement provides a comparable level of assurance regarding the church's financial statements. The other levels of engagement described below are substantially less in scope than an audit.

Additionally, in an audit, the CPA is required to obtain an understanding of the church's internal control and assess the risk of material misstatements, including the risk of fraud, in the financial statements to the extent necessary to perform the audit. In the event that the auditor identifies material weaknesses or significant deficiencies in the church's internal control, the auditor is required to report such matters to the church's leadership. The auditor's report addressing internal control can be one of the most valuable products of the independent external audit process. A well-performed audit that identifies weaknesses in a church's internal controls can help the church improve its systems, processes, and protocols to reduce the risk of improprieties and financial misstatements in the future.

Finally, if the CPA firm performing the audit has extensive experience addressing tax and operational matters for churches and religious organizations, the CPA firm may utilize the audit process to identify other vulnerabilities, such as tax compliance risks, or opportunities, such as tax exemptions not fully utilized by the church. When a firm provides such value-added commentary to a church for which it is performing an audit, the overall value received by the church in an audit process is enhanced further.

While an independent external audit provides the most value to the church of all of the types of engagements a CPA firm may provide, an audit is also typically the most costly type of engagement. Accordingly, churches considering having an independent external audit must weigh the value of the services to be received with the overall cost. For this reason, it is more common for larger churches (typically, those with annual revenues of $2 million or more) to have independent external audits than it is for smaller churches to do so.

See Sample Audit Report on page 220

REVIEW

Financial statements reviewed by the CPA provide the church's governing body with comfort that the CPA is not aware of any material modifications that should be made to the financial statements for the statements to be in conformity with the method of accounting utilized. A review is substantially less in scope than an audit, and does not require obtaining an understanding of internal control, assessing the risk of fraud, or testing the church's records.

In a review engagement, the CPA firm performs procedures (primarily analytical procedures and inquiries)

that will provide a reasonable basis for obtaining limited assurance that there are no material modifications that should be made to the financial statements.

A properly performed review should result in the following reports:

- A review report expressing limited assurance on the financial statements.
- Financial statements and related disclosures.

Note that a review does not result in a report addressing the church's internal control, since a CPA firm performing a review is not required to obtain an understanding of the church's internal control as part of conducting the engagement.

Commentary

A review of a church's financial statements has limited value, and is often obtained by a church in scenarios where the church is contractually required to obtain a review or an audit of its financial statements and the church does not wish to incur the cost of an audit. A review provides the church's governing body with "limited assurance" regarding the reliability of the financial statements. The CPA firm conducting a review is not required to obtain an understanding of the church's internal control, nor is the CPA firm required to perform any specific tests of the underlying documentation supporting the church's financial statements. As a result, a review engagement typically does not involve any report to the church with respect to its internal control, tax compliance matters, or other potential operational risks or vulnerabilities. If a church wishes to engage a CPA firm for the purpose of obtaining assurance with respect to the financial statements *and* to obtain information about weaknesses in the church's internal control, a review engagement is not adequate for such purposes. A church should carefully evaluate the value being received before entering into engagement to have a review of its financial statements.

See Sample Review Report on page 221

COMPILATION

A compilation represents *the most basic level of service* a CPA firm may provide that includes a report with respect to an organization's financial statements. In a compilation engagement, the CPA assists management in presenting financial information in the form of financial statements without undertaking to obtain or provide any assurance with respect to the financial statements. In a compilation, the CPA firm is required to have an understanding of the industry in which the client operates, obtain knowledge about the client, read the financial statements, and consider whether the financial statements appear appropriate in form and free from obvious material errors.

A compilation does not contemplate performing inquiry, analytical procedures, or other procedures ordinarily performed in a review; or obtaining an understanding of the organization's internal control, assessing fraud risk, or testing of accounting records. Compiled financial statements may be prepared without disclosures (notes to the financial statements). The compilation report provides no assurance whatsoever with respect to the financial statements.

A properly performed compilation typically results in the following reports:

- A compilation report expressing no assurance on the financial statements.
- Financial statements and (if applicable) related disclosures.

Commentary

A compilation is the *simplest and lowest cost engagement option* involving a church's financial statements in which a report is issued by a CPA firm. A compilation is often vernacularly described within the accounting profession as "taking the client's financial information, without checking or testing it, and putting it into the format of proper financial statements." That description, while simple, reasonably summarizes the nature of a compilation engagement. Typically, the CPA firm assists the church in preparing financial statements in the format required for the particular method of accounting used. The CPA

firm uses the church's financial information to do so, but the firm does not test the information as it would in an audit, nor does it perform analytical procedures and inquiries as it would in a review. While it is true that a compilation results in a report from the CPA, the report specifically states that the CPA provides no assurance with respect to the financial statements.

There are multiple reasons that churches may engage CPA firms to perform compilations of their financial statements. In many cases, the reason revolves around the lack of ability or capacity of the church's staff to prepare proper financial statements in conformity with an applicable method of accounting. By engaging a CPA firm to perform a compilation, the church essentially contracts with the CPA firm to prepare the church's financial statements in a proper format. The compiled financial statements may be used for internal purposes, which may include financial reporting to the church's congregation. Sometimes, a compilation of the church's financial statements is obtained in response to a requirement by the church's lender as a condition of making a loan to the church. (A compilation may be an acceptable level of financial statement engagement for a lender when the loan amount is small. Typically, the larger the loan amount, the higher the level of financial statement engagement a lender may require.)

Given the fact that a CPA firm provides no assurance with respect to the financial statements in a compilation engagement, a church should not expect or depend on a compilation engagement to address the reliability or accuracy of the church's financial statements. The church most certainly should not have the impression that a compilation engagement will help the church identify any internal control deficiency that may exist, tax compliance risks that may exist, or other vulnerabilities. While a compilation may serve a useful purpose, such as one or more of those described above, its value is severely limited—a fact churches should take into consideration when considering such an engagement.

See Sample Compilation Report on page 222

OUTSOURCED ACCOUNTING SERVICES (WITH OR WITHOUT COMPILATION)

A church also may outsource its accounting and financial reporting processes to an accounting firm. In outsourced accounting arrangements, the accounting firm takes on the role normally performed by the church's internal accounting staff. Various service providers offer various forms of outsourced accounting. Historically, outsourced accounting services tended to be in the form of after-the-fact bookkeeping services. In recent years, some accounting firms have begun to offer live or real-time outsourced accounting services in which the accounting firm takes on the role of day-to-day processing of transactions and accounting records. Depending on state law, it may be possible for some service providers that are not CPA firms to provide certain outsourced accounting services. In some states, such services may not be referred to as "accounting" services unless they are provided by a CPA firm. Churches interested in engaging a firm other than a CPA firm to provide outsourced accounting services should ensure that the firm is properly licensed to provide the required services.

If outsourced accounting services are provided by a CPA firm, such services may (by mutual agreement) include the production of financial statements with a compilation report by the CPA firm. Depending on the nature of the services provided by the CPA firm, the CPA firm may not be independent with respect to the church's financial statements. Professional standards governing the accounting profession permit a CPA firm to issue a compilation report with respect to an organization's financial statements, even if the CPA firm is not independent with respect to the organization. In such cases, the lack of independence must be disclosed in the compilation report.

Commentary

Churches wishing to simplify their internal responsibilities for financial administration may find that outsourcing the accounting function to a CPA firm or other service provider allows the church's leaders to focus more on mission and program-related activities and less on administrative matters. In some cases, the cost of such an arrangement may be less than if the church were to perform the services

internally. If a church does outsource its accounting and internal financial reporting responsibilities and can also benefit from a compilation report on its financial statements, the church can engage a CPA firm to perform the outsourced services and include a compilation of the appropriate financial statements. Such an arrangement may be appropriate in cases where a lender or other third party requires compiled financial statements.

Agreed-upon Procedures

Another type of engagement for which a church may involve a CPA firm is an agreed-upon procedures engagement. As the term implies, the CPA performs certain procedures agreed upon by the client through an agreement specifically describing the procedures to be performed. A church may engage a CPA to perform procedures that are important to the church for some reason or that help the church assess its practices in certain areas. Professional standards provide significant freedom for the CPA in designing an agreed-upon procedures engagement.

The CPA firm performing the agreed-upon procedures will provide a report of the results of the procedures performed. Professional standards governing the accounting profession provide, however, that the reported results are to represent the objective outcomes of the procedures performed. The CPA firm does not provide an opinion regarding the procedures performed or regarding the items or matters that are subjected to the procedures. For example, it would be inappropriate under professional standards for a CPA to include in an agreed-upon procedures report language such as, "therefore, we believe the cash balance as of December 31 is reasonable," or "accordingly, the procedures related to reconciling contributions revenue are being correctly followed by the church's staff." An example of appropriate language in an agreed-upon procedures report related to year-end cash balances follows:

We inspected the original bank statement as of December 31, 20XX, and compared the ending balance per the bank statement to the balance per bank on the church's bank reconciliation report as of the same date without exception. We identified deposits in transit on the church's bank reconciliation as of De-

cember 31 individually in excess of $1,000, and traced the items to the church's original January bank statement, noting that all items cleared the bank within the first five days of January without exception. Further, we identified debits to the church's bank account as reported in the first 10 days of January on the church's original January bank statement, and traced those in excess of $500 to the church's December 31 reconciliation report, without exception.

[Note that the language in the example provided above does not include qualitative assessments with respect to the procedures performed. For example, the CPA does not use the words "reasonable" or "opinion" in this language. He or she merely describes the procedures performed and objectively states that they were performed "without exception." Had there been exceptions, the CPA would specifically describe the exceptions noted. An agreed-upon procedures engagement does not result in an assessment of the quality of an item nor an opinion with respect to it.]

Following are examples of procedures that a church may agree with a CPA firm to perform in connection with the church's financial operations. (Note that these are merely a couple of examples. The church and the CPA may agree to a variety of procedures provided that they can be performed objectively and reported on objectively. Specific dates and other parameters, or their basis of selection, must be described in order for the CPA to perform the procedures objectively.)

- Compare the cash balance per bank as reported in the original bank statement to the balance used by the church in performing its year-end bank account reconciliation. Trace deposits in transit reported on the church's bank account reconciliation in excess of a certain amount to clearing the bank within a certain number of days as noted on the original bank statement for the following month. Trace debits clearing in the original bank statement for the first 10 days of the following month to the outstanding debits reported by the church in its year-end bank rec-

onciliation report. Describe any exceptions that are identified.
- For three separate months randomly selected by the CPA, compare the amounts recognized as contributions revenue in the church's general ledger with the amounts included in the church's donor contribution database for the same period. Identify the reason and basis provided by the church's staff for any difference in excess of $1,000 for a particular month and report same.

Commentary

Given the constraints that apply to an agreed-upon procedures engagement under the professional standards that govern the accounting profession, the process of planning and specifically tailoring an agreed-upon procedures engagement to meet the particular needs of a church can be intricate and tedious. Further, since an agreed-upon procedures engagement results in an objective report describing the specific outcomes of the procedures and not an opinion or other qualitative assessment, the report may have limited value for the church. For example, if procedures such as those described above were performed for a church and the CPA firm identified two deposits in transit that did not clear within the specified time and three debits that did not appear as outstanding debits on the church's bank reconciliation, the agreed-upon procedures report would simply note that fact, along with the amounts and other descriptive information regarding the items identified. An agreed-upon procedures engagement does not provide assurance regarding the items tested, nor does it involve making corrections to the church's accounting records or financial statements.

Agreed-upon procedures engagements may be useful when a church has certain elements or practices for which it wishes to have independently performed procedures to address or test. In reality, such situations are rare.

Churches should also be careful when considering an agreed-upon procedures engagement to address whether the CPA firm has the experience necessary to plan and perform the engagement properly. For example, while the professional standards prohibit a CPA firm from making qualitative statements or providing an opinion with respect to procedures performed in an agreed-upon procedures engagement, some CPA firms unwittingly violate the standards and issue reports using terms such as "reasonable," "in our opinion," or other similar verbiage.

Advisory Services

In addition to the various levels of service described above for which a church may engage an accounting firm, a church may also consider engaging a firm to provide advisory services with respect to certain aspects of its financial operations. Advisory services engagements provided by CPA firms may take many forms, but they generally involve a formal agreement to provide informal advice to the church with respect to a particular area of the church's financial operations. Examples of areas for which the church may wish to engage a CPA firm to provide advisory services include, but are not limited to, the following:

- Internal control matters;
- Tax compliance matters;
- Efficiencies in financial operations;
- Accounting treatment for certain transaction types;
- Business-oriented commentary on proposed transactions;
- Risk management; and,
- Board governance.

Along these lines, some churches choose to engage law firms to provide what is sometimes referred to as a "legal audit." The nature of such engagements will vary, but they generally involve an assessment by the law firm of the church's compliance with, and risks associated with, various activities of the law.

Commentary

A good, regular, and proactive working relationship with a CPA firm and a law firm can be a great source of help to church leaders as they address business, financial, risk, and legal matters. Such working relationships are common among larger churches that use their professional advisors as sounding boards in a proactive manner to facilitate and reduce the risk associated with significant new transactions, initiatives, and policy matters.

Internal Audits

Internal audits and similar activities may be conducted in a variety of ways. In some cases, a church's board members, or finance committee members, or equivalent perform the tasks. In other cases, volunteer supporters of the church perform the duties. In larger settings, the church may contract an individual or a firm to perform procedures and in very large church organizations, an internal auditor may be employed by the organization.

The purposes of internal audits often vary significantly from the purpose of an external audit. As noted above, external audits are primarily focused on addressing the reliability of the church's financial statements. Internal audits, however, may be designed to address either financial or operational matters. For example, an internal audit may be performed to assess a church's compliance with its own operational policies in areas such as internal control, human resources, child safety, transportation safety, or other areas of significant interest (and potential risk) to the church.

Regardless of who leads and carries out an internal audit process for a church, certain attributes should exist with respect to any internal audit activity in order for the activity to be useful and credible:

- An internal audit process should be overseen by a person or group [the oversight body] that is independent with respect to the issues being addressed.
- The person or group performing the internal audit procedures and issuing the related reports [the internal auditor] should also be independent with respect to the issues being addressed.
- The internal auditor should report directly to the oversight body and not to the church's management. While the internal auditor will certainly interact with the church's management and employees in performing audit procedures, the internal auditor must issue and present reports directly to the oversight body in order for an internal audit process to maintain credibility.

○ **KEY POINT.** If an internal auditor is an employee of the church, he or she is subject to the church's applicable employment and other policies. With respect to such matters, an employee-internal auditor is subject to the authority of the church's management, so long as management's oversight does not interfere with, or impede the objectivity of, the internal auditor's work and reporting responsibilities.

- The oversight body should establish and formally approve specific objectives of the internal audit process, the methodologies to be used, and the timing and nature of the reports to be issued.
- The internal auditor should conduct the internal audit procedures and prepare the related reports pursuant to the objectives and methodologies approved by the oversight body described in the preceding sentence.
- The internal auditor's reports should provide an *objective* description of the internal auditor's findings. The quality and credibility of an internal auditor's reports can be severely compromised when the internal auditor's report goes beyond reporting objective findings to drawing personal conclusions or making subjective statements of opinion regarding the matters subject to the audit.

EXAMPLE. An internal auditor notes in his report that he observed certain children's classrooms being supervised by only one adult in violation of the church's two-adult protocol. This note, in and of itself, is objective. However, if the internal auditor also adds a subjective statement such as, "These violations jeopardized the safety of our church's children," or "The teachers responsible for these violations should be disciplined," the credibility and objectivity of the internal auditor's report would be compromised. Further, such statements could increase the church's legal risks.

REPORT OF INDEPENDENT ACCOUNTANTS

The Governing Body

Elm City Church, Inc.

City, State

We have audited the accompanying financial statements of Elm City Church, Inc. ("the Church"), which comprise the statement of financial position as of December 31, 20XX, and the related statements of activities and cash flows for the year then ended, and the related notes to the financial statements.

Management's Responsibility for the Financial Statements

Management is responsible for the preparation and fair presentation of these financial statements in accordance with accounting principles generally accepted in the United States of America; this includes the design, implementation, and maintenance of internal control relevant to the preparation and fair presentation of financial statements that are free from material misstatement, whether due to fraud or error.

Auditor's Responsibility

Our responsibility is to express an opinion on these financial statements based on our audit. We conducted our audit in accordance with auditing standards generally accepted in the United States of America. Those standards require that we plan and perform the audit to obtain reasonable assurance about whether the financial statements are free from material misstatement.

An audit involves performing procedures to obtain audit evidence about the amounts and disclosures in the financial statements. The procedures selected depend on the auditor's judgment, including the assessment of risk of material misstatement of the financial statements, whether due to fraud or error. In making those risk assessments, the auditor considers internal control relevant to the Church's preparation and fair presentation of the financial statements in order to design audit procedures that are appropriate in the circumstances, but not for the purpose of expressing an opinion on the effectiveness of the Church's internal control. Accordingly, we express no such opinion. An audit also includes evaluating the appropriateness of accounting policies used and the reasonableness of significant accounting estimates made by management, as well as evaluating the overall presentation of the financial statements.

We believe that the audit evidence we have obtained is sufficient and appropriate to provide a basis for our audit opinion.

Opinion

In our opinion, the financial statements referred to above present fairly, in all material respects, the financial position of Elm City Church, Inc. as of December 31, 20XX, the changes in its net assets, and its cash flows for the year then ended in accordance with accounting principles generally accepted in the United States of America.

SIGNATURE

City, State

Month Day, 20XX

Standard Review Report

REVIEW REPORT OF INDEPENDENT ACCOUNTANTS

The Governing Body

Elm City Church, Inc.

City, State

We have reviewed the accompanying statement of financial position of Elm City Church, Inc. ("the Church") as of December 31, 20XX, and the related statements of activities and cash flows for the year then ended. A review includes primarily applying analytical procedures to management's financial data and making inquiries of Church management. A review is substantially less in scope than an audit, the objective of which is the expression of an opinion regarding the financial statements as a whole. Accordingly, we do not express such an opinion.

Management is responsible for the preparation and fair presentation of the financial statements in accordance with accounting principles generally accepted in the United States of America and for designing, implementing, and maintaining internal control relevant to the preparation and fair presentation of the financial statements.

Our responsibility is to conduct the review in accordance with Statements on Standards for Accounting and Review Services issued by the American Institute of Certified Public Accountants. Those standards require us to perform procedures to obtain limited assurance that there are no material modifications that should be made to the financial statements. We believe that the results of our procedures provide a reasonable basis for our report.

Based on our review, we are not aware of any material modifications that should be made to the accompanying financial statements in order for them to be in conformity with accounting principles generally accepted in the United States of America.

SIGNATURE

City, State

Month Day, 20XX

COMPILATION REPORT OF INDEPENDENT ACCOUNTANTS

The Governing Body

Elm City Church, Inc.

City, State

We have compiled the accompanying statement of financial position of Elm City Church, Inc. ("the Church") as of December 31, 20XX, and the related statements of activities and cash flows for the year then ended. We have not audited or reviewed the accompanying financial statements and, accordingly, do not express an opinion or provide any assurance about whether the financial statements are in accordance with accounting principles generally accepted in the United States of America.

Management is responsible for the preparation and fair presentation of the financial statements in accordance with accounting principles generally accepted in the United States of America and for designing, implementing, and maintaining internal control relevant to the preparation and fair presentation of the financial statements.

Our responsibility is to conduct the compilation in accordance with Statements on Standards for Accounting and Review Services issued by the American Institute of Certified Public Accountants. The objective of a compilation is to assist management in presenting financial information in the form of financial statements without undertaking to obtain or provide any assurance that there are no material modifications that should be made to the financial statements.

SIGNATURE

City, State

Month Day, 20XX

Chapter 9

Tax Law Compliance: A Priority for Financial Management

INTRODUCTION

Federal, state, and local governments have enacted a variety of tax laws to finance the costs of government. The primary sources of federal revenue are individual and corporate income taxes and Social Security taxes. Other federal taxes include unemployment, estate, and excise taxes. State and local governments often impose income, sales, and property taxes and provide employment security through unemployment taxes.

The applicability of any of these various taxes to churches depends upon the following factors: (1) whether the statute that imposes the tax specifically exempts churches; (2) if churches are exempt, whether all conditions to exempt status have been satisfied; and (3) whether a tax that purports to apply to churches is permissible under state and federal constitutions.

Any discussion regarding church finance must include a careful review of these numerous tax laws, since the applicability of any of these laws to churches inevitably will affect their financial activities. This chapter will review the status of churches under the following laws:

      (a) federal income taxes
      (b) federal payroll tax reporting
      (c) Social Security
      (d) unemployment taxes
      (e) state income taxes
      (f) state sales taxes
      (g) state property taxes
      (h) IRS examinations

FEDERAL INCOME TAXES

Church leaders must understand requirements for exemption, the recognition of exemption, the loss of exemption, and the church audit procedures act in order to have a full understanding of the effects of federal income taxes on church finances. Below is an analysis of these four issues.

Requirements for exemption

Section 501(a) of the tax code exempts organizations described in section 501(c) from federal income taxation. Section 501(c)(3) lists several exempt organizations, including "corporations . . . organized and

operated exclusively for religious, charitable . . . or educational purposes."

This section exempts churches from federal income taxation. Note that the exemption is conditioned upon the following six factors: (1) the church is a corporation; (2) the church is organized exclusively for exempt purposes; (3) the church is operated exclusively for exempt purposes; (4) none of the church's net earnings benefit any private individuals; (5) the church does not engage in substantial efforts to influence legislation; and (6) the church does not intervene or participate in political campaigns. These six factors will be considered separately.

Factor 1 - Church as a corporation

While section 501(c)(3) would appear to exempt only those churches that are incorporated, the IRS maintains that unincorporated churches are eligible for exemption. The IRS *Internal Revenue Manual* states that "the typical nonprofit association formed under a constitution or bylaws, with elective officers empowered to act for it, would be treated as a corporation." *IRM § 7.25.3.2.3 (1999).*

Factor 2 - Organized exclusively for exempt purposes

To be exempt from federal income tax, a church must be organized exclusively for exempt purposes. This requirement is referred to by the IRS as the "organizational test" of tax-exempt status.

The income tax regulations state that an organization will be deemed to be organized exclusively for exempt purposes only if its articles of incorporation limit the purposes of the organization to one or more of the exempt purposes listed in section 501(c)(3) of the tax code and do not empower the organization to engage, other than as an insubstantial part of its activities, in activities that are not in furtherance of one or more exempt purposes. *Treas. Reg. 1.501(c)(3)-1(b)(1)(i).* Note that the regulations require these limitations to appear in an exempt organization's articles of incorporation, and not in its bylaws.

A church's purposes may be as broad as, or more specific than, the purposes stated in section 501(c)(3) (cited above). But in no event will a church be considered organized exclusively for one or more exempt purposes if its articles of incorporation recite purposes broader than the purposes stated in section 501(c)(3). *Treas. Reg. 1.501(c)(3)-1(b)(1)(iv).* The fact that the actual operation of a church whose purposes are broader than those stated in section 501(c)(3) is exclusively in furtherance of one or more exempt purposes will not be sufficient to permit the church to satisfy the organizational test. Similarly, a church whose purposes are broader than those stated in section 501(c)(3) will not meet the organizational test as a result of statements or other evidence that its members intend to operate it solely in furtherance of one or more exempt purposes. In summary, a church can be organized for purposes other than religious if such purposes are among those listed in section 501(c)(3).

The income tax regulations specify that an organization is not organized exclusively for exempt purposes unless its assets are dedicated to an exempt purpose, and that an organization's assets will be presumed to be dedicated to an exempt purpose if, upon dissolution, the assets would, by reason of a provision in the organization's articles of incorporation, be distributed to another exempt organization.

The IRS has drafted the following paragraphs, which if inserted in a church's articles of incorporation, will indicate compliance with the organizational test:

> Said corporation is organized exclusively for charitable, religious, and educational . . . purposes, including, for such purposes, the making of distributions to organizations that qualify as exempt organizations under section 501(c)(3) of the Internal Revenue Code, or the corresponding section of any future federal tax code.

> No part of the net earnings of the corporation shall inure to the benefit of, or be distributable to its members, trustees, officers, or other private persons, except that the corporation shall be authorized and empowered to pay reasonable compensation for services rendered and to make payments and distributions in furtherance of the purposes set forth [herein]. No substantial part of the activities of the corporation shall be the carrying on of propaganda, or otherwise attempting to influence legislation, and the corporation shall not participate in, or intervene in (including the pub-

lishing or distribution of statements) any political campaign on behalf of any candidate for public office. Notwithstanding any other provision of these articles, the corporation shall not carry on any other activities not permitted to be carried on (a) by a corporation exempt from federal income tax under section 501(c)(3) of the Internal Revenue Code, or corresponding section of any future federal tax code, or (b) by corporation, contributions to which are deductible under section 170(c)(2) of the Internal Revenue Code, or corresponding section of any future federal tax code.

> Upon the dissolution of the corporation, assets shall be distributed for one or more exempt purposes within the meaning of section 501(c)(3) of the Internal Revenue Code, or corresponding section of any future federal tax code, or shall be distributed to the federal government, or to a state or local government, for a public purpose. Any such assets not so disposed of shall be disposed of by the Court of Common Pleas of the county in which the principal office of the corporation is then located, exclusively for such purposes or to such organization or organizations, as said Court shall determine, which are organized and operated exclusively for such purposes. *IRS Publication 557. See also Revenue Procedure 82-2.*

Factor 3 - Operated exclusively for exempt purposes

To be exempt from federal income taxes, section 501(c)(3) of the tax code requires that a church be "operated exclusively" for exempt purposes. This requirement is referred to as the operational test. The regulations specify that an organization will be regarded as operated exclusively for one or more exempt purposes only if it engages primarily in activities that accomplish one or more of the exempt purposes specified in section 501(c)(3) and if no more than an insubstantial part of its activities are not in furtherance of an exempt purpose.

Factor 4 - No inurement of net earnings to private individuals

In order to be tax exempt under section 501(c)(3) of the tax code, no part of a church's net earnings may personally benefit an insider, and the church must not provide a substantial "private benefit" to anyone. The

9

Tax Law Compliance: A Priority for Financial Management

related concepts of personal benefit (inurement) and private benefit are summarized below.

A church is not entitled to exemption from federal income taxes if any part of its net earnings inures or accrues to the benefit of a private individual other than as reasonable compensation for services rendered or as distributions in direct furtherance of the church's exempt purposes. The IRS construes this requirement as follows:

> Churches and religious organizations, like all exempt organizations under IRC section 501(c)(3), are prohibited from engaging in activities that result in inurement of the church's or organization's income or assets to insiders (i.e., persons having a personal and private interest in the activities of the organization). Insiders could include the minister, church board members, officers, and in certain circumstances, employees. Examples of prohibited inurement include the payment of dividends, the payment of unreasonable compensation to insiders, and transferring property to insiders for less than fair market value. The prohibition against inurement to insiders is absolute; therefore, any amount of inurement is, potentially, grounds for loss of tax-exempt status. In addition, the insider involved may be subject to excise tax. See the following section on Excess benefit transactions. Note that prohibited inurement does not include reasonable payments for services rendered, payments that further tax-exempt purposes, or payments made for the fair market value of real or personal property. *IRS Publication 1828.*

The IRS *Internal Revenue Manual* lists several examples of unreasonable compensation, including the withdrawal of an exempt organization's earnings by an officer under the guise of salary payments; receipt of less than fair market value in sales of property; and inadequately secured loans to an officer.

The IRS also has found private inurement in each of the following situations:

- A church, consisting mostly of family members and conducting few, if any, religious services, that paid rent on a residence for the church's "ministers," paid for a church car that was used by church members,

and purchased a "church camp" for church members. *Riemers v. Commissioner, 42 T.C.M. 838 (1981).*

- A religious denomination whose assets could be distributed to members upon dissolution. *General Conference of the Free Church of America v. Commissioner, 71 T.C. 920 (1979).*
- A church that made cash grants of 20 percent of its income to officers and other individuals based on no fixed criteria and with no provision for repayment. *Church in Boston v. Commissioner, 71 T.C. 102 (1978).*
- A church that received almost all of its income from its minister and, in turn, paid back 90 percent of such income to the minister in the form of living expenses. *People of God Community v. Commissioner, 75 T.C. 127 (1980).*
- A church comprised of three minister-members that paid each minister a salary based on a fixed percentage of the church's gross receipts. *New Life Tabernacle v. Commissioner, 44 T.C.M. 309 (1982).*
- A church that paid an unreasonable and excessive salary to its pastor. *United States v. Dykema, 666 F.2d 1096 (7th Cir. 1981); Unitary Mission Church v. Commissioner, 74 T.C. 507 (1980).*
- The founder of a church, who was paid 10 percent of the church's gross income, received a residence and car at the church's expense, and received loans and unexplained reimbursements from the church. The court held that an organization's net earnings may inure to the benefit of a private individual in ways other than excessive salaries, such as loans. The court also emphasized that the tax code specifies that "no part" of the net earnings of a religious organization may inure to the benefit of a private individual, and therefore the amount or extent of benefit is immaterial. *The Founding Church of Scientology v. United States, 412 F.2d 1197 (Ct. Cl. 1969), cert. denied, 397 U.S. 1009 (1970).* See also *Church of the Chosen People v. United States, 548 F. Supp. 1247 (D. Minn. 1982); Truth Tabernacle v. Commissioner, 41 T.C.M. 1405 (1981).*

Closely related to but distinguishable from inurement is the concept of private benefit. The IRS defines private benefit as follows:

> An IRC section 501(c)(3) organization's activities must be directed exclusively toward charitable, educational, religious, or other exempt purposes.

Such an organization's activities may not serve the private interests of any individual or organization. Rather, beneficiaries of an organization's activities must be recognized objects of charity (such as the poor or the distressed) or the community at large (for example, through the conduct of religious services or the promotion of religion). Private benefit is different from inurement to insiders. Private benefit may occur even if the persons benefited are not insiders. Also, private benefit must be substantial in order to jeopardize tax-exempt status. *IRS Publication 1828.*

Note the following two important distinctions between inurement and private benefit:

(1) Inurement applies to insiders; private benefit applies to anyone receiving benefits from a public charity.

(2) Inurement involves any use of a charity's resources for the private benefit of an insider, regardless of amount; private benefit must be substantial in order to jeopardize tax-exempt status.

Factor 5 - No substantial efforts to influence legislation

Section 501(c)(3) of the tax code exempts from federal income taxation a church or religious organization organized and operated exclusively for exempt purposes and "no substantial part of the activities of which is carrying on propaganda, or otherwise attempting to influence legislation, and which does not participate in, or intervene in (including the publishing or distributing of statements), any political campaign on behalf of any candidate for public office."

Note that there are two distinct limitations. First, churches may not engage in substantial efforts to influence legislation. Second, churches may not participate or intervene in any political campaign, even to an insubstantial degree. The first of these limitations is addressed here in Factor 5. The second limitation is addressed in Factor 6 below.

Legislative limitations

The income tax regulations, interpreting the legislative activity limitation, provide that neither a church nor any other organization can be exempt from federal income taxation if its charter empowers it "to devote more than an insubstantial part of its activities to attempting to influence legislation by propaganda or otherwise," or if "a substantial part of its activities is attempting to influence legislation by propaganda or otherwise." *Treas. Reg. §1.501(c)(3)-1(c)(3)(ii).*

The regulations further provide that

an organization will be regarded as attempting to influence legislation if the organization (a) contacts, or urges the public to contact, members of a legislative body for the purpose of proposing, supporting, or opposing legislation; or (b) advocates the adoption or rejection of legislation. The term "legislation". . . includes action by the Congress, by any State legislature, by any local council or similar governing body, or by the public in a referendum, initiative, constitutional amendment, or similar procedure. An organization will not fail to meet the operational test merely because it advocates, as an insubstantial part of its activities, the adoption or rejection of legislation.

This language helps clarify the meaning of "legislation" and "attempts to influence legislation" but does not define the critical term "substantial."

The regulations also provide that an organization cannot be exempt if it has the following two characteristics:

(a) Its main or primary objective or objectives (as distinguished from its incidental or secondary objectives) may be attained only by legislation or a defeat of proposed legislation; and (b) it advocates, or campaigns for, the attainment of such main or primary objective or objectives as distinguished from engaging in nonpartisan analysis, study, or research, and making the results thereof available to the public. In determining whether an organization has such characteristics, all the surrounding facts and circumstances, including the articles and all activities of the organization, are to be considered. *Treas. Reg. § 1.501(c)(3)-1(c)(iii).*

The regulations also provide that "the fact that an organization, in carrying out its primary purpose, advocates social or civic changes or presents opinion on controversial issues with the intention of molding public opinion or creating public sentiment to an acceptance of its views does not preclude such organization from qualifying under section 501(c)(3) so long as it [does not violate any of the regulations quoted above]." *Treas. Reg. § 1.501(c)(3)-1(d)(2).*

The IRS *Internal Revenue Manual* provides the following additional information regarding the limitation on legislative activities:

> Attempts to influence legislation are not limited to direct appeals to members of the legislature (direct lobbying). Indirect appeals to legislators through the electorate or general public (indirect or "grass roots" lobbying) also constitute attempts to influence legislation. Both direct and indirect lobbying are nonexempt activities subject to the IRC 501(c)(3) limitation on substantial legislative action. . . . Whether a communication or an appeal constitutes an attempt to influence legislation is determined on the basis of the facts and circumstances surrounding the communication in question. . . . Attempting to influence legislation includes requesting that an executive body support or oppose legislation. Attempting to influence legislation does not include appearing before a legislative committee in response to an official request for testimony. . . . Study, research, and discussion of matters pertaining to government and even to specific legislation, may, under certain circumstances, be educational activities rather than attempts to influence legislation. This is so where the study, research, and discussion do not serve merely as a preparatory stage for the advocacy of legislation. (Of course, the primary inquiry is the purpose of the study, research, or discussion.) *IRM § 7.25.3.17.1 (1999).*

Attempts to influence legislation that are less than a substantial part of the organization's activities will not deprive it of exemption. Whether a specific activity of an exempt organization constitutes a "substantial" portion of its total activities is a factual issue, and there is no simple rule as to what amount of activities is substantial. The earliest case on this subject, *Seasongood v. Commissioner*, held that attempts to influence legislation that constituted 5 percent of total activities were not substantial. *Seasongood* provides only limited guidance because the court's view of activities to measure is no longer supported by the weight of precedent. Further, it is not clear how the court arrived at the 5 percent figure. Most courts have not attempted to measure activities by percentage or have stated that a percentage test is not conclusive. *IRM § 7.25.3.17.2 (1999).*

The Christian Echoes case

The one case in which a religious organization's tax-exempt status was revoked because of political activities was *Christian Echoes National Ministry, Inc. v. United States*, 470 F.2d 849 (10th Cir. 1972). Christian Echoes was a religious organization founded to disseminate conservative Christian principles through radio and television broadcasts and literature. Publications and broadcasts appealed to the public to react to a wide variety of issues in specific ways, including: (1) write their representatives in Congress in order to influence political decisions; (2) work in politics at the precinct level; (3) support a constitutional amendment restoring prayer in the public schools; (4) demand a congressional investigation of the biased reporting of major television networks; (5) demand that Congress limit foreign aid spending; (6) discourage support of the World Court; (7) cut off diplomatic relations with communist countries; (8) reduce the federal payroll and balance the federal budget; (9) stop federal aid to education, socialized medicine, and public housing; (10) abolish the federal income tax; (11) withdraw from the United Nations; and (12) restore stringent immigration laws. The organization also attempted to influence legislation by molding public opinion on the issues of firearms control, the Panama Canal treaty, and civil rights legislation.

In 1966 the IRS notified the organization that its exemption was being revoked for three reasons: (1) it was not operated exclusively for charitable, educational, or religious purposes; (2) it had engaged in substantial activity aimed at influencing legislation; and (3) it had directly and indirectly intervened in political campaigns on behalf of candidates for public office. Christian Echoes filed suit in federal court, challenging the IRS action, and a federal district court ruled in its favor. This ruling was reversed by a federal appeals court.

The federal appeals court began its opinion by observing that "tax exemption is a privilege, a matter of grace rather than right," and that the limitations on exempt status set forth in section 501(c)(3) of the tax code are valid restrictions on the privilege. The limitations on political activity "stem from the congressional policy that the United States Treasury should be neutral in political affairs and that substantial activities directed to attempts to influence legislation or affect a political campaign should not be subsidized." The court emphasized that prohibited legislative activity was not limited to attempts to influence specific legislation before Congress. Quoting the income tax regulations (excerpted above), the court concluded that efforts to influence legislation must be interpreted much more broadly and include all indirect attempts to influence legislation through a "campaign to mold public opinion." The fact that specific legislation is not mentioned is irrelevant.

The court rejected the "5 percent test" applied by a federal appeals court in a previous case as a measure of substantial legislative activities, noting that "a percentage test to determine whether the activities were substantial obscures the complexity of balancing the organization's activities in relation to its objectives and circumstances." *Seasongood v. Commissioner, 227 F.2d 907 (6th Cir. 1955) (5 percent of an organization's time devoted to lobbying was not substantial).*

Christian Echoes' contention that revocation of its tax-exempt status violated the constitutional guaranty of religious freedom was rejected by the court. Rejecting the notion that the guaranty of religious freedom "assures no restraints, no limitations and, in effect, protects those exercising the right to do so unfettered," the court concluded that the limitations on political activities set forth in section 501(c)(3) of the tax code were constitutionally valid.

From the perspective of many churches, the *Christian Echoes* decision is unsatisfactory for at least three reasons. First, the court gave an excessively broad definition of the term "attempts to influence legislation," including within that term indirect attempts to mold public opinion despite the income tax regulations' statement (quoted above) that an organization's exempt status is not jeopardized if it, in carrying out its primary purpose, "advocates social or civic changes or presents opinion on controversial issues with the inten-

tion of molding public opinion or creating public sentiment to an acceptance of its views." Second, the court rejected the 5 percent test for determining whether legislative activity is substantial but replaced it with an ambiguous "balancing test." Churches can never know in advance whether their legislative activities are substantial under the *Christian Echoes* standard. Third, the court gave insufficient weight to the constitutional guaranty of religious freedom.

The United States Supreme Court refused to review the *Christian Echoes* case, and it has not directly addressed the issue of the validity of the limitations on church political activity.

In summary, churches will jeopardize their tax-exempt status by engaging in substantial efforts to influence legislation. Whether particular efforts are "substantial" will depend upon a balancing of the facts and circumstances of each case. As a result, churches have no clear standard to guide them. Nevertheless, it is clear that certain activities would be insubstantial, such as the circulation of a few petitions each year addressing legislative issues. Also, it ordinarily is the exempt organization itself that must engage in the legislative activities, not individual members. To illustrate, the IRS has ruled that a university's exempt status was not jeopardized by the legislative activities of a student newspaper. *Revenue Ruling 72-513.*

The limitation on legislative activity may violate the constitutional right of churches to exercise their religion. The *Christian Echoes* decision rejected such a claim, but no other federal court has addressed this issue since the *Christian Echoes* decision. In 1970 the Supreme Court observed that the "adherents of particular faiths and individual churches frequently take strong positions on public issues including . . . vigorous advocacy of legal or constitutional positions. Of course, churches as much as secular bodies and private citizens have that right." *Walz v. Tax Commission, 397 U.S. 664 (1970).*

⦿ **KEY POINT.** The *Christian Echoes* ruling is binding only in the tenth federal circuit (which includes the states of Colorado, Kansas, New Mexico, Oklahoma, Utah, and Wyoming). In addition, in 1976 Congress took the extraordinary step of refusing to approve or disapprove of the *Christian Echoes* decision.

The IRS Tax Guide for Churches and Religious Organizations

The IRS has published a *Tax Guide for Churches and Religious Organizations* (the "Guide"). *IRS Publication 1828.* The Guide notes that "a church or religious organization will be regarded as *attempting to influence legislation* if it contacts, or urges the public to contact, members or employees of a legislative body for the purpose of proposing, supporting, or opposing legisla-

tion, or if the organization advocates the adoption or rejection of legislation."

On the other hand, some lobbying activities will not jeopardize a church's exempt status: "Churches and religious organizations may, however, involve themselves in issues of public policy without the activity being considered lobbying. For example, churches may conduct educational meetings, prepare and distribute educational materials, or otherwise consider public

Political Campaign Activities By Churches
An Analysis of Selected Activities

Campaign activity	Impact on tax-exempt status	Basis
Contributions to political campaign funds.	Prohibited	IRS *Tax Guide for Churches and Religious Organizations*
Public statements of position (verbal and written) in favor of or in opposition to candidates for office—in official church publications and at official church functions.	Prohibited	IRS *Tax Guide for Churches and Religious Organizations*
Providing a nonpartisan forum for all candidates to address the church.	Permitted	IRS *Tax Guide for Churches and Religious Organizations*
Public comments made by ministers and other church employees in connection with political campaigns, not made at church facilities or in church publications and accompanied by statement that the comments are strictly personal and are not intended to represent the church.	Permitted	IRS *Tax Guide for Churches and Religious Organizations*; Jimmy Swaggart Ministries settlement with IRS; Revenue Ruling 2007-41
A church invites all candidates for a political office to address the congregation and informs the congregation before each candidate's speech that the views expressed are those of the candidate and not the church and that the church does not endorse any candidate.	Permitted	*Revenue Ruling 74-574*; IRS *Tax Guide for Churches and Religious Organizations*
A church invites only one candidate in a political campaign to address the congregation.	Prohibited	*Revenue Ruling 2007-41*
The church provides an opportunity for a candidate to speak in a noncandidate capacity (for example, as a member of the church, public figure, or expert in a nonpolitical field) without providing equal access to all political candidates for the same office. The church ensures that the candidate speaks in a noncandidate capacity; no reference is made to the person's candidacy; the church mentions the capacity in which the candidate is appearing (without mentioning the person's political candidacy); and no campaign activity occurs.	Permitted	IRS *Tax Guide for Churches and Religious Organizations*
A church distributes a compilation of voting records of all members of Congress on major legislative issues involving a wide range of subjects; the publication contains no editorial opinion, and its contents and structure do not imply approval or disapproval of any members or their voting records.	Permitted	*Revenue Ruling 78-248*
A church distributes a voter guide containing questions demonstrating a bias on certain issues.	Prohibited	*Revenue Ruling 78-248*
The endorsement of candidates.	Prohibited	Int. Rev. News Release IR-96-23
Campaign activities by employees within the context of their employment.	Prohibited	*FSA 1993-0921-1*
A church fails to "disavow" the campaign activities of persons under "apparent authorization" from the church by repudiating those acts "in a timely manner equal to the original actions" and taking steps "to ensure that such unauthorized actions do not recur."	Prohibited	*FSA 1993-0921-1*

policy issues in an educational manner without jeopardizing their tax-exempt status."

Only substantial lobbying activity will jeopardize a church's exempt status. The tax code does not define the term "substantial." The Guide clarifies that

> whether a church or religious organization's attempts to influence legislation constitute a substantial part of its overall activities is determined on the basis of all the pertinent facts and circumstances in each case. The IRS considers a variety of factors, including the time devoted (by both compensated and volunteer workers) and the expenditures devoted by the organization to the activity, when determining whether the lobbying

activity is substantial. Churches must use the substantial part test since they are not eligible to use the expenditure test described in the next section.

Factor 6 - No intervention or participation in political campaigns

The participation by churches and church leaders in political campaigns is an American tradition. Common examples include

- inviting candidates to speak during worship services;
- distributing "voter education" literature reflecting candidates' views on selected topics;
- voter registration activities;

Political Campaign Activities By Churches (cont'd.)
An Analysis of Selected Activities

Campaign activity	Impact on tax-exempt status	Basis
Engaging in fund-raising on behalf of a candidate.	Prohibited	Int. Rev. News Release IR-96-23
Neutral voter registration drives.	Permitted	*11 C.F.R. § 111.4(c)(4)*
Newspaper ads urging voters to vote for or against a candidate.	Prohibited	*Branch Ministries, Inc. v. Commissioner, 99-1 USTC ¶50,410 (D.D.C. 1999), aff'd, Branch Ministries v. Rossotti, 2000 USTC ¶50,459 (D.C. Cir. 2000)*
Church websites that contain information either supporting or opposing candidates for public office.	Prohibited	*Revenue Ruling 2007-41*
Church websites containing a link to candidate-related material, if the facts and circumstances indicate that one or more candidates are being supported or opposed.	Prohibited	*Revenue Ruling 2007-41*
A minister who is well-known in the community attends a press conference at a political candidate's campaign headquarters and states that the candidate should be reelected. The minister does not say he is speaking on behalf of his church. His endorsement is reported on the front page of the local newspaper, and he is identified in the article as the minister of his church.	Permitted	*Revenue Ruling 2007-41*
The Sunday before the November election, a minister invites a political candidate to preach to her congregation during worship services. During his remarks the candidate states, "I am asking not only for your votes, but for your enthusiasm and dedication, for your willingness to go the extra mile to get a very large turnout on election day." The minister invites no other candidate to address her congregation during the campaign.	Prohibited	*Revenue Ruling 2007-41*
A church maintains a website that includes biographies of its ministers, times of services, details of community outreach programs, and activities of members of its congregation. A member of the congregation is running for a seat on the town council. Shortly before the election, the church posts the following message on its website: "Lend your support to your fellow parishioner in Tuesday's election for town council."	Prohibited	*Revenue Ruling 2007-41*

- enlisting volunteers for a particular candidate's campaign;
- collecting contributions for a particular candidate; and,
- statements by ministers during worship services either supporting or opposing various candidates.

Unfortunately, it is not well understood that these kinds of activities, as well-meaning as they may be, jeopardize a church's exemption from federal income taxation. This is because section 501(c)(3) of the tax code prohibits tax-exempt organizations (including churches) from any intervention or participation in political campaigns on behalf of or in opposition to any candidate for public office.

The income tax regulations interpreting the limitation on political campaign intervention provide that neither a church nor any other organization can be exempt from federal income taxation if its charter empowers it "directly or indirectly to participate in, or intervene in (including the publishing or distributing of statements), any political campaign on behalf of or in opposition to any candidate for public office."

The regulations further provide:

> The term "candidate for public office" means an individual who offers himself, or is proposed by others, as a contestant for an elective public office, whether such office be national, state, or local. Activities which constitute participation or intervention in a political campaign on behalf of or in opposition to a candidate include, but are not limited to, the publication or distribution of written or printed statements or the making of oral statements on behalf of or in opposition to such a candidate. *Treas. Reg. 1.501(c)(3)-1(c)(3)(iii).*

This regulation provides some clarification. In particular:

- A candidate for public office includes local, state, and national candidates;
- The prohibited intervention or participation in a political campaign can be satisfied either by the making of oral statements or by the publishing or distribution of written statements;

- Statements made in opposition to as well as on behalf of a particular candidate are prohibited.

The application by the courts and the IRS of the ban on campaign activities by churches and other public charities is summarized in the chart below.

RECOGNITION OF EXEMPTION

Before 1969 there was no legal requirement that an organization file with the IRS an application for tax-exempt status. Rather, an organization was automatically exempt if it met the requirements set forth in section 501(c)(3) of the tax code. In general, those requirements are as follows: (1) the organization is organized exclusively for exempt (e.g., religious, charitable, educational) purposes; (2) the organization is operated exclusively for exempt purposes; (3) none of the organization's net earnings inures to the benefit of any private individuals; (4) the organization does not engage in substantial efforts to influence legislation; and (5) the organization does not intervene or participate in political campaigns. Although many organizations voluntarily applied for IRS recognition of exempt status by filing a Form 1023 (Application for Recognition of Exemption) under Section 501(c)(3) of the tax code, many did not.

The Tax Reform Act of 1969 added section 508 to the tax code. This section stipulated that after October 9, 1969, no organization, with a few exceptions, would be treated as exempt unless it gave notice to the IRS, in the manner prescribed by regulation, that it was applying for recognition of exempt status under section 501(c)(3). This is commonly referred to as the "508(a) notice." The income tax regulations state that the 508(a) notice is given by submitting a properly completed Form 1023 to the appropriate IRS district director.

Section 508(c) and the income tax regulations state that the following organizations are exempted from the 508(a) notice requirement and therefore are not required to file a Form 1023 to be exempt from federal income tax:

- churches, interchurch organizations of local units of a church, conventions and associations of churches, or integrated auxiliaries of a church, such as a men's or women's organization, religious seminary, mission society, or youth group;

• any organization that is not a private foundation and the gross receipts of which in each taxable year are normally not more than $5,000; and,

• subordinate organizations covered by a group exemption letter.

The recognition of the exempt status of an organization without the need for complying with the section 508(a) notice requirement of course assumes that all of the prerequisites contained in section 501(c)(3) of the tax code have been satisfied.

The IRS maintains that although such organizations are not required to file a Form 1023 to be exempt from federal income taxes or to receive tax-deductible charitable contributions, they may "find it advantageous to obtain recognition of exemption." *IRS Publication 557*. Presumably, such organizations might voluntarily wish to obtain IRS recognition of tax-exempt status in order to assure contributors who itemize their deductions that donations will be tax-deductible.

The IRS publishes a cumulative listing (*Publication 78*) of organizations that have been determined to be exempt from federal income tax, the contributions to which are tax-deductible. Contributions made to an organization whose name does not appear in *Publication 78* may be questioned by the IRS, in which case the contributor would have to substantiate the deductibility of his or her contributions by demonstrating that the organizations met the requirements of section 501(c)(3) and was exempt from the notice requirements. Similarly, some potential contributors may be reluctant to contribute to a religious organization not listed in *Publication 78*.

Group exemptions

Each year, tens of thousands of organizations file individual applications with the IRS for recognition of tax-exempt status. But for more than 70 years, the IRS has also had procedures permitting certain affiliated organizations to obtain recognition of their exemption on a group basis rather than by filing separate applications. Under the group procedure, an organization (called the central organization) submits a request for recognition of exemption for a group of organizations that are affiliated with it and under its general supervision or control (called the subordinate organizations).

If the IRS grants this request, the central organization is authorized to add other similar subordinates to the group as well as to delete subordinates that no longer meet the group exemption requirements. As a result of the group exemption procedure, subordinate organizations covered by group exemptions are relieved from filing their own individual applications for recognition of exemption with the IRS.

Currently, there are more than 4,300 group exemptions covering some 500,000 subordinate organizations. These statistics do not include church group exemptions because they are not required to file annual information reports with the IRS regarding additions and deletions of subordinate organizations from their group exemptions. Some church group exemptions cover thousands and even tens of thousands of subordinate organizations. The IRS Advisory Committee on Tax Exempt and Government Entities (ACT) estimates that there are 100,000 to 150,000 churches covered by group exemptions. About 700 of the more than 4,300 nonreligious central organizations holding group exemptions elect to file group Form 990 information returns on behalf of some or all of their subordinate organizations.

The group exemption procedure has simplified the process for obtaining exempt status for hundreds of thousands of organizations over the years. However, there have been some significant changes in the law over the years that are not reflected in the current group exemption procedure that dates back to *IRS Revenue Procedure 80-27* in 1980 (see chart on page 240).

LOSS OF EXEMPTION

A church's exemption may be revoked or modified by a ruling or determination letter sent to it or by a revenue ruling or other statement published in the Internal Revenue Bulletin. The revocation or modification may be retroactive if the church omitted or misstated a material fact or operated in a manner materially different from that originally represented. *Treas. Reg. § 601.201(n)(6)(i)*. In any event, revocation or modification ordinarily will take effect no earlier than the time at which the church received written notice that its exemption ruling or determination letter might be revoked or modified.

Loss of a church's exempt status would have a variety of negative consequences, including some or all of the following:

- The church's net income would be subject to federal income taxation;
- The church's net income would be subject to income taxation in many states;
- Donors no longer could deduct charitable contributions they make to the church;
- The church would be ineligible to establish or maintain 403(b) tax-sheltered annuities;
- The church could lose its property tax exemption under state law;
- The church could lose its sales tax exemption under state law;
- The church could lose its exemption from unemployment tax under state and federal law;
- The church's status under local zoning law may be affected;
- The church could lose its preferential mailing rates;
- The church could lose its exemption from registration of securities under state law;
- Nondiscrimination rules pertaining to various fringe benefits (including an employer's payment of medical insurance premiums) would apply;
- A minister's housing allowance may be affected in some cases;
- The exempt status of ministers who opted out of Social Security may be affected in some cases;
- The significant protections available to a church under the Church Audit Procedures Act would not apply;
- The exemption of the church under the state charitable solicitation law may be affected;
- The exemption of the church from the ban on religious discrimination under various federal and state employment discrimination laws may be affected;
- The exemption of the church from the public accommodation provisions of the Americans with Disabilities Act may be affected.

Clearly, any activity that jeopardizes a church's exemption from federal income taxation is something that must be taken seriously.

Group Exemption Requirements

Req	Action
1	"[C]entral organization . . . must establish that the subordinates to be included in the group exemption letter are affiliated with it."
2	"[C]entral organization . . . must establish that the subordinates to be included in the group exemption letter are . . . subject to its general supervision or control."
3	"[C]entral organization . . . must establish that the subordinates to be included in the group exemption letter are . . . all exempt under the same paragraph of section 501(c) of the tax code."
4	"[C]entral organization . . . must establish that the subordinates to be included in the group exemption letter are . . . not private foundations."
5	"[C]entral organization . . . must establish that the subordinates to be included in the group exemption letter are . . . all on the same accounting period."
6	"[E]ach subordinate must authorize the central organization to include it in the application for the group exemption letter."
7	The application for a group exemption must include "a sample copy of a uniform governing instrument (charter, trust indenture, articles of association, etc.) adopted by the subordinates."
8	The application for a group exemption must include "a detailed description of the purposes and activities of the subordinates."
9	The application for a group exemption must include "an affirmation that . . . the purposes and activities of the subordinates are as set forth" in requirements 8 and 9.
10	The application for a group exemption must include "a list of subordinates to be included in the group exemption letter."
11	The application for a group exemption must include "the information required by *Revenue Procedure 75-50*" (pertaining to racially nondiscriminatory policies of schools).
12	The application for a group exemption must include "a list of the . . . employer identification numbers of subordinates to be included in the group exemption letter."
13	"[T]he central organization must submit with the exemption application a completed Form SS-4 on behalf of each subordinate not having" an employer identification number.
14	Each year the central organization must provide the IRS with lists of "(a) subordinates that have changed their names or addresses during the year, (b) subordinates no longer to be included in the group exemption letter because they have ceased to exist, disaffiliated, or withdrawn their authorization to the central organization, and (c) subordinates to be added to the group exemption letter."

THE CHURCH AUDIT PROCEDURES ACT

⊙ **KEY POINT.** The Church Audit Procedures Act provides churches with a number of important protections in the event of an IRS inquiry or examination. However, there are some exceptions.

Section 7602 of the tax code gives the IRS broad authority to examine or subpoena the books and records of any person or organization for the purposes of (1) ascertaining the correctness of any federal tax return, (2) making a return where none has been filed, (3) determining the liability of any person or organization for any federal tax, or (4) collecting any federal tax. This authority has been held to apply to churches. *See, e.g., United States v. Coates, 692 F.2d 629 (9th Cir. 1982); United States v. Dykema, 666 F.2d 1096 (7th Cir. 1981); United States v. Freedom Church, 613 F.2d 316 (1st Cir. 1979).*

In 1984 Congress enacted the Church Audit Procedures Act to provide churches with important protections when faced with an IRS audit. The Act's protections are contained in section 7611 of the tax code. Section 7611 imposes detailed limitations on IRS examinations of churches. The limitations can be summarized as follows.

Church tax inquiries

Section 7611 refers to church tax inquiries and church tax examinations. A church tax inquiry is defined as any IRS inquiry to a church (with exceptions noted below) for the purpose of determining whether the organization qualifies for tax exemption as a church or whether it is carrying on an unrelated trade or business or is otherwise engaged in activities subject to tax. An inquiry is considered to commence when the IRS requests information or materials of a type contained in church records.

The IRS may begin a church tax inquiry only if

- an appropriate, high-level Treasury official reasonably believes, on the basis of written evidence, that the church is not exempt (by reason of its status as a church), may be carrying on an unrelated trade or business, or is otherwise engaged in activities subject to taxation; and,

- the IRS sends the church written inquiry notice containing an explanation of the following: (1) the specific concerns which gave rise to the inquiry, (2) the general subject matter of the inquiry, and (3) the provisions of the tax code that authorize the inquiry and the applicable administrative and constitutional provisions, including the right to an informal conference with the IRS before any examination of church records, and the First Amendment principle of separation of church and state.

The limitations of section 7611 are illustrated by the following examples:

EXAMPLE. First Church receives substantial rental income each year from several residential properties it owns in the vicinity of the church. The IRS has learned of the rental properties and would like to determine whether the church is engaged in an unrelated trade or business. It sends the church an inquiry notice in which the only explanation of the concerns giving rise to the inquiry is a statement that "you may be engaged in an unrelated trade or business." This inquiry notice is defective, since it does not specify the activities which may result in unrelated business taxable income.

EXAMPLE. The IRS receives a telephone tip that First Church may be engaged in an unrelated trade or business. A telephone tip cannot serve as the basis for a church tax inquiry, since such an inquiry may commence only if an appropriate high-level Treasury official reasonably believes, on the basis of written evidence, that a church is not tax-exempt, is carrying on an unrelated trade or business, or otherwise is engaged in activities subject to taxation.

EXAMPLE. The IRS sends First Church written notice of a church tax inquiry on March 1. On March 10 of the same year it sends written notice that it will examine designated church records on April 15. The examination notice is defective. While it was sent at least 15 days before the beginning of the examination, it was sent less than 15 days after the date the inquiry notice was sent. The church's only remedy is a stay of the examination until the IRS sends a valid examination notice.

EXAMPLE. An IRS inquiry notice does not mention the possible application of the First Amendment principle of separation of church and state to church audits. Such a notice is defective. A church's only remedy is a stay of the inquiry until the IRS sends a valid inquiry notice.

EXAMPLE. An IRS examination notice specifies that the religious activities of First Church will be examined as part of an investiga-

9

235

tion into a possible unrelated business income tax liability. Such an examination is inappropriate, since the religious activities of a church may be examined by the IRS under section 7611 only to the extent necessary to determine if a church is, in fact, a bona fide church entitled to tax-exempt status.

EXAMPLE. The IRS sends First Church written notice of a church tax inquiry on August 1. As of October 20 of the same year, no examination notice had been sent. The church tax inquiry must be concluded by November 1.

EXAMPLE. Four years ago the IRS conducted an examination of the tax-exempt status of First Church. It concluded that the church was properly exempt from federal income taxation. This year the IRS commences an examination of First Church to determine if it is engaged in an unrelated trade or business and if it has been withholding taxes from nonminister employees. Such an examination is not barred by the prohibition against repeated examinations within a five-year period, since it does not involve the same or similar issues.

EXAMPLE. First Church knowingly fails to withhold federal income taxes from wages paid to its nonminister employees despite its knowledge that it is legally required to do so. The limitations imposed upon the IRS by section 7611 do not apply.

EXAMPLE. The IRS commences an examination of a separately incorporated private school that is controlled by First Church. The limitations of section 7611 do not apply.

Church tax examinations

The IRS may begin a church tax examination of the church records or religious activities of a church only under the following conditions: (1) the requirements of a church tax inquiry have been met; and (2) an examination notice is sent by the IRS to the church at least 15 days after the day on which the inquiry notice was sent, and at least 15 days before the beginning of such an examination, containing the following information: (a) a copy of the inquiry notice, (b) a specific description of the church records and religious activities which the IRS seeks to examine, (c) an offer to conduct an informal conference with the church to discuss and possibly resolve the concerns giving rise to the examination, and (d) a copy of all documents collected or prepared by the IRS for use in the examination, and the disclosure of which is required by the Freedom of Information Act.

Church records

Church records (defined as all corporate and financial records regularly kept by a church, including corporate minute books and lists of members and contributors) may be examined only to the extent necessary to determine the liability for, and amount of, any income, employment, or excise tax.

Religious activities

Religious activities may be examined only to the extent necessary to determine whether an organization claiming to be a church is, in fact, a church.

Deadline for completing church tax inquiries

Church tax inquiries not followed by an examination notice must be completed no later than 90 days after the inquiry notice date. Church tax inquiries and church tax examinations must be completed no later than two years after the examination notice date. The 2-year limitation can be suspended (1) if the church brings a judicial proceeding against the IRS; (2) if the IRS brings a judicial proceeding to compel compliance by the church with any reasonable request for examination of church records or religious activities; (3) for any period in excess of 20 days (but not more than 6 months) in which the church fails to comply with any reasonable request by the IRS for church records; or (4) if the IRS and church mutually agree.

⊙ **KEY POINT.** A federal appeals court ruled that the revocation of a church's tax-exempt status by the IRS could not be challenged on the ground that the IRS's examination of the church exceeded the two-year limit imposed by the Church Audit Procedures Act. The court noted that the Act specifies that "no suit may be maintained, and no defense may be raised in any proceeding . . . by reason of any noncompliance by the [IRS] with the requirements of this section." *Music Square Church v. United States, 2000-2 USTC ¶50,578 (Fed. Cir. 2000).*

Written opinion of IRS legal counsel

The IRS can make a determination, based on a church tax inquiry or church tax examination, that an organization is not a church that is exempt from federal income taxation, or that is qualified to receive tax-deductible contributions, or that otherwise owes any income, employment, or excise tax (including the unrelated business income tax), only if the appropriate regional legal counsel of the IRS determines in writing that there has been substantial compliance with the limitations imposed under section 7611 and approves in writing of such revocation of exemption or assessment of tax.

Statute of limitations

Church tax examinations involving tax-exempt status or the liability for any tax other than the unrelated business income tax may be begun only for any one or more of the three most recent taxable years ending before the examination notice date. For examinations involving unrelated business taxable income, or if a church is proven not to be exempt for any of the preceding three years, the IRS may examine relevant records and assess tax as part of the same audit for a total of six years preceding the examination notice date. For examinations involving issues other than revocation of exempt status or unrelated business taxable income (such as examinations pertaining to employment taxes), no limitation period applies if no return has been filed.

Limitation on repeat inquiries and examinations

If any church tax inquiry or church tax examination is completed and does not result in a revocation of exemption or assessment of taxes, then no other church tax inquiry or church tax examination may begin with respect to such church during the five-year period beginning on the examination notice date (or the inquiry notice date if no examination notice was sent) unless such inquiry or examination is (1) approved in writing by the Assistant Commissioner of Employee Plans and Exempt Organizations of the IRS, or (2) does not involve the same or similar issues involved in the prior inquiry or examination. The five-year period is suspended if the two-year limitation on the completion of an examination is suspended.

Exceptions

The limitations on church tax inquiries and church tax examinations do not apply to

- inquiries or examinations pertaining to organizations other than churches (the term "church" is defined by section 7611 as any organization claiming to be a church, and any convention or association of churches; the term does not include separately incorporated church-affiliated schools or other separately incorporated church-affiliated organizations);
- any case involving a knowing failure to file a tax return or a willful attempt to defeat or evade taxes;
- criminal investigations;
- the tax liability of a contributor to a church, or inquiries regarding assignment of income to a church or a vow of poverty by an individual followed by a transfer of property. *See, e.g., St. German of Alaska Eastern Orthodox Catholic Church v. Commissioner, 840 F.2d 1087 (2nd Cir. 1988); United States v. Coates, 692 F.2d 629 (9th Cir. 1982); United States v. Life Science Church of America, 636 F.2d 221 (8th Cir. 1980); United States v. Holmes, 614 F.2d 895 (5th Cir. 1980); United States v. Freedom Church, 613 F.2d 316 (1st Cir. 1979);*
- the tax liability of pastors and other church staff members. *See, e.g., Thomas F. v. Commissioner, 101 T.C.M. 1550 (2011); Pennington v. U.S. 2010 WL 417410 (W.D. Tex. 2010);*
- routine IRS inquiries, including (1) the filing or failure to file any tax return or information return by the church; (2) compliance with income tax or FICA tax withholding; (3) supplemental information needed to complete the mechanical processing of any incomplete or incorrect return filed by a church; (4) information necessary to process applications for exempt status, letter ruling requests, or employment tax exempt requests; or (5) confirmation that a specific business is or is not owned by a church.

Application to excess benefit transactions

For many years, the IRS asked Congress to provide a remedy other than outright revocation of exemption that it could use to combat excessive compensation paid by exempt organizations. In 1996 Congress responded by enacting section 4958 of the tax code. Section 4958 empowers the IRS to assess intermediate sanctions in the form of substantial excise taxes against insiders (called "disqualified persons") who benefit from an excess benefit transaction.

Section 4958 also allows the IRS to assess excise taxes against a charity's board members who approved an excess benefit transaction. These excise taxes are called "intermediate sanctions" because they represent a remedy the IRS can apply short of revocation of a char-

9

Tax Law Compliance: A Priority for Financial Management

ity's exempt status. While revocation of exempt status remains an option whenever a tax-exempt organization enters into an excess benefit transaction with a disqualified person, it is less likely that the IRS will pursue this remedy now that intermediate sanctions are available.

The tax regulations specify that

> the procedures of section 7611 will be used in initiating and conducting any inquiry or examination into whether an excess benefit transaction has occurred between a church and a disqualified person. For purposes of this rule, the reasonable belief required to initiate a church tax inquiry is satisfied if there is a reasonable belief that a section 4958 tax is due from a disqualified person with respect to a transaction involving a church. *Treas. Reg. 53.4958-8(b).*

Remedy for IRS violations

If the IRS has not complied substantially with (1) the notice requirements, (2) the requirement that an appropriate high-level Treasury official approve the commencement of a church tax inquiry, or (3) the requirement of informing the church of its right to an informal conference, the church's exclusive remedy is a stay of the inquiry or examination until such requirements are satisfied.

The fact that the IRS has authority to examine church records and the religious activities of a church or religious denomination does not necessarily establish its right to do so. The courts have held that an IRS summons or subpoena directed at church records must satisfy the following conditions to be enforceable:

Issued in good faith

Good faith in this context means that (1) the investigation will be conducted pursuant to a legitimate purpose; (2) the inquiry is necessary to that purpose; (3) the information sought is not already within the IRS's possession; and (4) the proper administrative steps have been followed. In *United States v. Powell, 379 U.S. 48 (1964)*, the United States Supreme Court held that in order to obtain judicial enforcement of a summons or subpoena, the IRS must prove "that the investigation will be conducted pursuant to a legitimate

purpose, that the inquiry may be relevant to the purpose, that the information sought is not already in the Commissioner's possession, and that the administrative steps required by the tax code have been followed." Powell did not involve an IRS examination of church records. In *United States v. Holmes, 614 F.2d 985 (5th Cir. 1980)*, a federal appeals court held that section 7605(c) narrowed the scope of the second part of the Powell test from mere relevancy to necessity in the context of church records, since it required that an examination of church records be limited "to the extent necessary." The "necessity test" should apply to church inquiries or examinations conducted under section 7611, since the same language is employed. *United States v. Church of Scientology, 90-2 U.S.T.C. ¶ 50,349 (D. Mass. 1990).*

No violation of the church's First Amendment right to freely exercise its religion

An IRS subpoena will not violate a church's First Amendment rights unless it substantially burdens a legitimate and sincerely held religious belief and is not supported by a compelling governmental interest that cannot be accomplished by less restrictive means. This is a difficult test to satisfy, not only because few churches can successfully demonstrate that enforcement of an IRS summons or subpoena substantially burdens an actual religious tenet, but also because the courts have ruled that maintenance of the integrity of the government's fiscal policies constitutes a compelling governmental interest that overrides religious beliefs to the contrary. *See, e.g., St. German of Alaska Eastern Orthodox Catholic Church v. Commissioner, 840 F.2d 1087 (2nd Cir. 1988); United States v. Coates, 692 F.2d 629 (9th Cir. 1982); United States v. Life Science Church of America, 636 F.2d 221 (8th Cir. 1980); United States v. Holmes, 614 F.2d 895 (5th Cir. 1980); United States v. Freedom Church, 613 F.2d 316 (1st Cir. 1979).*

No impermissible entanglement of church and state

See generally *United States v. Coates, 692 F.2d 629 (9th Cir. 1982); United States v. Grayson County State Bank, 656 F.2d 1070 (5th Cir. 1981); EEOC v. Southwestern Baptist Theological Seminary, 651 F.2d 277 (5th Cir. 1981)* (application of 1964 Civil

Rights Act's reporting requirements to seminary did not violate First Amendment).

Federal law provides that if the IRS wants to retroactively revoke the tax-exempt status of a church, it must show either that the church "omitted or misstated a material fact" in its original exemption application or that the church has been "operated in a manner materially different from that originally represented." *Treas. Reg. 601.201(n)(6)(i).*

Although IRS authority to examine and subpoena church records is broad, it has limits. To illustrate, one subpoena was issued against all documents relating to the organizational structure of a church since its inception; all correspondence files for a three-year period; the minutes of the officers, directors, trustees, and ministers for the same three-year period; and a sample of every piece of literature pertaining to the church. *United States v. Holmes, 614 F.2d 985 (5th Cir. 1980). See also United States v. Trader's State Bank, 695 F.2d 1132 (9th Cir. 1983)* (IRS summons seeking production of all of a church's bank statements, correspondence, and records relating to bank accounts, safe deposit boxes, and loans held to be overly broad). A court concluded that this subpoena was "too far reaching" and declared it invalid. It noted, however, that a "properly narrowed" subpoena would not violate the First Amendment. Another federal court that refused to enforce an IRS subpoena directed at a church emphasized that "the unique status afforded churches by Congress requires that the IRS strictly adhere to its own procedures when delving into church activities." *United States v. Church of Scientology of Boston, 739 F.Supp. 46 (D. Mass. 1990).*

The court also stressed that the safeguards afforded churches under federal law prevent the IRS from "going on a fishing expedition into church books and records."

FEDERAL PAYROLL TAX REPORTING

The Importance of Compliance
The most significant federal reporting obligation of most churches is the withholding and reporting of employee income taxes and Social Security taxes. These requirements apply, in whole or in part, to almost every church. Yet many churches do not comply with them because of unfamiliarity. This can trigger one or more of the penalties summarized in the chart on pages 236-37.

One of the most serious penalties is found in section 6672 of the tax code. This section specifies that "any person required to collect, truthfully account for, and pay over any [income tax or FICA tax] who willfully fails to collect such tax, or truthfully account for and pay over such tax, or willfully attempts in any manner to evade or defeat any such tax or the payment thereof, shall, in addition to other penalties provided by law, be liable for a penalty equal to the total amount of the tax evaded, or not collected, or not accounted for and paid over."

Stated simply, this section says that if an employer has failed to collect or pay over income and employment taxes, the trust fund recovery penalty may be asserted against those determined to have been *responsible and willful* in failing to pay over the tax. Responsibility and willfulness must both be established.

Responsibility
The IRS *Internal Revenue Manual* (IRM) states that responsibility is a matter of "status, duty, and authority," that "a determination of responsibility is dependent on the facts and circumstances of each case," and that "potential responsible persons" include an officer or employee of a corporation, or a corporate director. *IRM 5.7.3.3.1.* The IRM further clarifies that a responsible person has: (1) power to direct the act of collecting withheld taxes; (2) accountability for and authority to pay employment taxes; and (3) authority to determine which creditors will or will not be paid. The IRM lists the following "indicators of responsibility":

1. *The full scope of authority and responsibility is contingent upon whether the person had the ability to exercise independent judgment with respect to the financial affairs of the business. . . .*
2. *If a person has the authority to sign checks, the exercise of that authority does not, in and of itself, establish responsibility. Signatory authority may be merely a convenience.*

3. Persons with ultimate authority over financial affairs may generally not avoid responsibility by delegating that authority to someone else. . . .

4. Persons serving as volunteers solely in an honorary capacity as directors and trustees of tax-exempt organizations will generally not be considered responsible persons unless they participated in the day-to-day or financial operations of the organization and they had actual knowledge of the failure to withhold or pay over the trust fund taxes. This does not apply if it would result in there being no person responsible [for the section 6672 penalty].

To determine whether a person has the status, duty, and authority to ensure that employment taxes are paid, the IRM directs IRS agents to consider "the duties of the officers as set forth in the corporate bylaws as well as the ability of the individual to sign checks." In addition, agents are instructed to determine the identity of individuals who

- are officers, directors, or shareholders of the corporation;
- hire and fire employees;
- exercise authority to determine which creditors to pay;
- sign and file the excise tax or employment tax returns, such as Form 941 (Employer's Quarterly Federal Tax Return);
- control payroll and disbursements; and,
- make federal tax deposits.

IRS Policy Statement 5-14 specifies:

An employee is generally not a "responsible person" if the employee's function was solely to pay the bills as directed by a superior, rather than to determine which creditors would or would not be paid. However, if an employee . . . has significant control over making the company's other financial decisions about who to pay or has the ability to obtain financing for the company, then such an employee cannot avoid being responsible for the [section 6672 penalty] by

merely showing that [the employer] limited his discretion on the specific matter of paying taxes that the company owed.

Here are two examples that appear in the IRM (these are adapted for church use):

EXAMPLE. A church bookkeeper has check-signing authority, and she pays all of the bills the treasurer gives her. She is not permitted to pay any other bills, and when there are not sufficient funds in the bank account to pay all of the bills, she must ask the treasurer which bills to pay. The bookkeeper should generally not be held responsible for the section 6672 penalty.

EXAMPLE. An employee works as a clerical secretary in the office. She signs checks and tax returns at the direction of, and for the convenience of, a supervisor. She is directed to pay other vendors, even though payroll taxes are unpaid. The secretary is not a responsible person, because she works under the dominion and control of the owner or a supervisor and is not permitted to exercise independent judgment.

Willfulness

Willful means intentional, deliberate, voluntary, reckless, or knowing, as opposed to accidental. No evil intent or bad motive is required. To show willfulness, the IRS generally must demonstrate that a responsible person was aware, or should have been aware, of the outstanding taxes and either intentionally disregarded the law or was plainly indifferent to its requirements. A responsible person's failure to investigate or correct mismanagement after being notified that withholding taxes have not been paid satisfies the willfulness requirement.

Application to churches and other nonprofit organizations

Does the penalty imposed by section 6672 apply to churches and other nonprofit organizations? The answer is yes. In *Policy Statement 5-14* (part of the IRM), the IRS states:

In general, non-owner employees of the business entity, who act solely under the dominion and control of others, and who are not in a position to make independent decisions on behalf of the business entity, will not be asserted the trust fund recovery penalty. The penalty shall not be imposed on unpaid, volunteer members of any board of trustees or directors of an organization referred to in section 501 of the Internal Revenue Code to the extent such members are solely serving in an honorary capacity, do not participate in the day-to-day or financial operations of the organization, and/or do not have knowledge of the failure on which such penalty is imposed.

In order to make accurate determinations, all relevant issues should be thoroughly investigated. An individual will not be recommended for assertion if sufficient information is not available to demonstrate he or she was actively involved in the corporation at the time the liability was not being paid. However, this shall not apply if the potentially responsible individual intentionally makes information unavailable to impede the investigation. [Emphasis added.]

This language indicates that the IRS will not assert the 100 percent penalty against uncompensated, volunteer board members of a church who

- are solely serving in an honorary capacity;
- do not participate in the day-to-day or financial operations of the organization; and,
- do not have knowledge of the failure to withhold or pay over withheld payroll taxes.

Taxpayer Bill of Rights 2 (TBOR2)

Congress enacted the Taxpayer Bill of Rights 2 in 1996. This law contains four important limitations on the application of the penalty under section 6672:

1. Notice requirement

The IRS must issue a notice to an individual it has determined to be a responsible person with respect to unpaid payroll taxes at least 60 days prior to issuing a notice and demand for the penalty.

2. Disclosure of information if more than one person is subject to penalty

TBOR2 requires the IRS, if requested in writing by a person considered by the IRS to be a responsible person, to disclose in writing to that person the name of any other person the IRS has determined to be a responsible person with respect to the tax liability. The IRS is required to disclose in

writing whether it has attempted to collect this penalty from other responsible persons, the general nature of those collection activities, and the amount (if any) collected. Failure by the IRS to follow this provision does not absolve any individual from any liability for this penalty.

3. Contribution from other responsible parties

If more than one person is liable for this penalty, each person who paid the penalty is entitled to recover from other persons who are liable for the penalty an amount equal to the excess of the amount paid by such person over such person's proportionate share of the penalty. This proceeding is a federal cause of action and is separate from any proceeding involving IRS collection of the penalty from any responsible party.

4. Volunteer board members of churches and other charities

TBOR2 clarifies that the responsible person penalty is not to be imposed on volunteer, unpaid members of any board of trustees or directors of a tax-exempt organization to the extent such members are solely serving in an honorary capacity, do not participate in the day-to-day or financial activities of the organization, and do not have actual knowledge of the failure. However, this provision cannot operate in such a way as to eliminate all responsible persons from responsibility.

The precedent summarized above demonstrates that church officers and directors (and in some cases employees, such as administrators or bookkeepers) can be *personally liable* for the payment of income taxes and Social Security and Medicare taxes that they fail to withhold, account for, or pay over to the government. It does not matter that they serve without compensation, so long as they satisfy the definition of a "responsible person" and act willfully.

Many church officers and directors (and in some cases employees, such as administrators or bookkeepers) will satisfy the definition of a "responsible person," and such persons can be personally liable for unpaid payroll taxes if they act under the liberal definition of "willfully" described above. Clearly, church leaders must be knowledgeable regarding a church's payroll tax obligations and ensure that these obligations are satisfied.

APPLICATION OF PAYROLL REPORTING RULES TO MINISTERS

The application of the payroll reporting rules to ministers has created considerable confusion because of two rather simple rules that are often misunderstood. These two rules are explained below.

Self-employed status for Social Security

The first special rule is that ministers always are self-employed for Social Security with respect to services performed in the exercise of their ministry (with the exception of some government-employed chaplains). As a result, ministers pay the self-employment tax rather than the employee's share of Social Security and Medicare taxes—even if they report their federal income taxes as employees. It is incorrect for churches to treat ministers as employees for Social Security and to withhold the employee's share of Social Security and Medicare taxes from their wages. *IRC 3121(b)(8)(A)*.

Exemption from income tax withholding

The second special rule is that ministers' compensation is exempt from income tax withholding whether a minister reports his or her income taxes as an employee or as self-employed. While it is true that the tax code requires every employer, including churches and religious organizations, to withhold federal income taxes from employee wages, some exceptions to this rule are made. One exception is wages paid for "services performed by a duly ordained, commissioned, or licensed minister of a church in the exercise of his ministry." *IRC 3401(a)(9)*. Therefore, a church need not withhold income taxes from the salary of a minister who is an employee for income tax reporting purposes. Further, since the income tax withholding requirements only apply to the wages of *employees*, a church should not withhold taxes from the compensation of a minister (or any other worker) who is *self-employed*.

Voluntary withholding for minister-employees

The IRS maintains that a church and a minister-employee may agree voluntarily that federal income taxes be withheld from the minister's wages, but this is not required. Some ministers find voluntary with-

holding attractive because it eliminates the guesswork, quarterly reports, and penalties associated with the estimated tax procedure (which applies automatically if voluntary withholding is not elected).

Use of voluntary withholding may help to avoid underpayment penalties that may apply to ministers and other taxpayers whose estimated tax payments are less than their actual tax liability.

A minister-employee who elects to enter into a voluntary withholding arrangement with his or her church need only file a completed Form W-4 (employee's withholding allowance certificate) with the church. The filing of this form is deemed to be a request for voluntary withholding.

Voluntary withholding arrangements can be terminated unilaterally by either a minister or the church, or by mutual consent. Alternatively, a minister can stipulate that the voluntary withholding arrangement will terminate on a specified date. In such a case, the minister must give the church a signed statement setting forth the date on which the voluntary withholding is to terminate; the minister's name and address; and a statement that he or she wishes to enter into a voluntary withholding arrangement with his or her employer. This statement must be attached to a completed Form W-4. The voluntary withholding arrangement will terminate automatically on the date specified. Either the church or the minister may terminate a voluntary withholding arrangement before a specified or mutually agreed upon termination date by providing a signed notice to the other.

If a church and its minister voluntarily agree that income taxes will be withheld, a minister ordinarily will no longer be subject to the estimated tax requirements with respect to federal income taxes. But what about a minister's self-employment taxes? Ministers who have not exempted themselves from Social Security coverage are required to pay the self-employment tax (Social Security tax for self-employed persons). Can a church withhold the self-employment tax from a minister-employee's wages? The answer is yes. *IRS Publication 517* (Social Security and Other Information for Members of the Clergy) states that "if you perform your services as a common-law employee of the church and your salary is not subject to income tax withholding, you can enter into a voluntary withholding agreement with the church to cover any *income and [self-employment] tax that may be due*" (emphasis added).

A church whose minister has elected voluntary withholding (and who is not exempt from Social Security taxes) withholds an additional amount from each paycheck to cover the minister's estimated self-employment tax for the year, and then reports this additional amount as additional *income tax* (not FICA tax) withheld on its quarterly 941 forms. The minister should submit an amended Form W-4 to the church, inserting on line 6 an additional amount of income tax to be withheld that will be enough to cover projected self-employment taxes for the year. The excess income tax withheld is a credit against tax that the minister claims on his or her federal income tax return and is applied against the minister's self-employment tax liability. Further, it is considered to be a timely payment of the minister's self-employment tax obligation, so no penalties for late payment of the quarterly estimates will apply.

Voluntary withholding for self-employed ministers

A self-employed minister is free to enter into an unofficial withholding arrangement whereby the church withholds a portion of his or her compensation each week and deposits it in a church account, then distributes the balance to the minister in advance of each quarterly estimated tax payment due date. However, note that no Form W-4 should be used to initiate such unofficial withholding arrangements, and none of the withheld taxes should be reported to the IRS on the church's Forms 941.

Ministers who report their income taxes as self-employed persons should recognize that the use of a Form W-4 will almost guarantee that they will be deemed to be an employee by the IRS. Only ministers who report their income taxes as employees should use a Form W-4 to initiate (or amend) voluntary withholding.

CONSTITUTIONALITY OF CHURCH COMPLIANCE WITH PAYROLL TAX REPORTING

No withholding exemption exists for nonminister church employees. As a result, churches must be careful to follow the withholding requirements discussed below with respect to any nonminister employees (or to minister-employees who have elected voluntary withholding).

Does the imposition of these requirements upon churches violate the constitutional principle of separation of church and state? Every court that has addressed this question has said no. Consider the following two examples.

The Eighth Street Baptist Church case

A church withheld federal payroll taxes from the wages of its organist, pianist, choir director, janitor, and church clerk. It paid the withheld taxes to the government and then filed a refund claim with the IRS. It cited the following five reasons why it was not legally obligated to withhold payroll taxes from its employees: (1) a church cannot be made a trustee or collection agent of the government against its will; (2) the First Amendment prevents the IRS from requiring churches to withhold taxes from the wages of employees; (3) it was not the intent of Congress to require churches to withhold taxes from the wages of employees; (4) if withholding laws apply to churches, then churches would become "servants" of the federal government in violation of their constitutional right of religious freedom; and (5) church employees are exempt because they qualify for the exemption available to members of religious orders. The IRS rejected the church's request for a refund, and the church appealed the case to a federal court.

A federal district court in Kansas rejected all of the church's arguments. It noted that the tax code specifies that *all* wages are subject to withholding, with certain exceptions, and therefore the wages of church employees are subject to withholding unless a specific exception applies. The court concluded that the wages of nonminister church employees are not specifically exempted from the withholding requirements, and therefore a church is legally required to comply with the tax withholding requirements with respect to these employees. Note that the wages of ministers are exempted by law from tax withholding, as noted previously in this chapter, so churches are not required to withhold taxes from the wages of ministers who are being compensated for the performance of ministerial duties. The court also rejected the church's attempt to bring its employees under the exemption available to members of religious orders.

In rejecting the church's constitutional arguments, the court observed: "A taxing statute is not contrary to the provisions of the First Amendment unless it directly restricts the free exercise by an individual of his religion. We think it clear that, within the intendment of the First Amendment, the Internal Revenue Code, in imposing the income tax and requiring the filing of returns and the payment of the tax, is not to be considered as restricting an individual's free exercise of his religion." A federal court rejected a church's challenge to the constitutionality of the tax withholding requirements. *Eighth Street Baptist Church v. United States, 291 F. Supp. 603 (D. Kan. 1968), aff'd, 431 F.2d 1193(10th Cir. 1970); see also, Bethel Baptist Church v. United States, 822 F.2d 1334 (3rd Cir. 1987) Schultz v. Stark, 554 F. Supp. 1219 (D. Wis. 1983); Goldsboro Christian Schools, Inc. v. United States, 436 F. Supp. 1314 (D.S.C. 1976).*

The Indianapolis Baptist Temple case

A church stopped filing federal employment tax returns and withholding or paying federal employment taxes for its employees. Church leaders insisted that the government could not regulate an unincorporated "New Testament church." When IRS attempts to discuss the matter with church leaders failed, the IRS assessed $5.3 million in unpaid taxes and interest. The IRS asked a federal court to enter a judgment for the full $5.3 million and to foreclose on a tax lien the IRS had placed on the church's property.

The church claimed that the First Amendment guaranty of religious freedom prevented the IRS from applying payroll tax reporting requirements to churches opposed on religious grounds to complying with those requirements, and also prohibited the IRS from penalizing noncompliant churches for failing to comply.

The court rejected the church's position, noting that "neutral laws of general application that burden religious practices do not run afoul" of the First Amendment. Since federal employment tax laws are "neutral laws of general application" (they apply to a large class of employers and do not single out religious employers for less favorable treatment), they do not violate the First Amendment.

This case demonstrates that any attempt by a church to avoid compliance with federal payroll tax obligations (including the withholding and payment of income taxes and Social Security taxes) on the basis of the First Amendment will be summarily rejected by the civil courts. *Indianapolis Baptist Temple v. United States, 224 F.3d 627 (7th Cir. 2000).*

Conclusions

In summary, the wages of nonminister church employees are subject to withholding. This obligation cannot be avoided by labeling a church employee an independent contractor or self-employed, unless the person clearly fails the IRS common-law employee. Church secretaries, teachers, choir directors, preschool workers, and business managers almost always will satisfy the common-law employee test and therefore will be employees of the church (unless they represent temporary help secured from a local temporary help service). Church custodians who work full-time similarly will almost always be employees subject to withholding. However, a custodian who is paid by the job rather than by the hour, who decides when to work and how to perform his or her services, who works substantially less than full-time, and who is not subject to the control of the church with respect to the performance of his or her services, often may properly be characterized as self-employed. The effect of this is that no income taxes or Social Security taxes are withheld from the worker's compensation. Rather, he or she uses the quarterly estimated tax procedure to prepay and report taxes.

If a church worker satisfies the common-law employee definition, he or she will be an employee despite the church's characterization of the person as self-employed (although in a close case, such as the custodian described above, the written characterization of the worker as self-employed will be a relevant factor).

Obviously, if a church concludes that a particular worker is self-employed, it should issue the person a Form 1099-MISC rather than a Form W-2 at year end (assuming the person has received church compensation of at least $600 for the year). Churches should be careful in characterizing any worker as self-employed, since section 3509 of the tax code imposes a penalty on any employer that fails to withhold income taxes or Social Security taxes from the wages of a worker deemed to be self-employed but whom the IRS reclassifies as an employee.

THE 10-STEP APPROACH TO COMPLIANCE WITH FEDERAL PAYROLL TAX REPORTING RULES

Churches can comply with the payroll tax reporting rules by following 10 simple steps. Keep in mind that all 10 steps will not apply to every church. All (or most) of the 10 steps apply only if a church has nonminister employees to whom it pays wages or if its minister is an employee for income tax purposes and has requested voluntary withholding. Smaller churches with no nonminister employees will only be subject to a few of these steps. But regardless of a church's size, its payroll tax reporting obligations will be described by some or all of the following 10 steps.

These 10 steps are illustrated in comprehensive examples at the end of this chapter.

Step 1: Obtain an employer identification number (EIN) from the IRS

This number must be listed on some of the returns listed below. It is used to reconcile a church's deposits of withheld taxes with the Forms W-2 it issues to employees. The EIN is a nine-digit number that looks like this: 00-0246810.

The IRS *Tax Guide for Churches and Religious Organizations* contains the following statement about employer identification numbers:

Every tax-exempt organization, including a church, should have an Employer Identification Number (EIN), whether or not the organization has any employees. There are many instances in which an EIN is necessary. For example, a church needs an EIN when it opens a bank account, in order to be listed as a subordinate in a group ruling, or if it files returns with the IRS (e.g., Forms W-2, 1099, 990-T). An organization may obtain an EIN by filing Form SS-4, Application for Employer Identification Number, in accordance with the instructions.

Many pastors and church treasurers think their church has a special "tax exemption number" confirming that it is exempt from federal income tax. This is not the case. While in some states churches have "tax exemption numbers" for sales tax purposes, no corresponding number is issued by the IRS. The IRS *Tax Guide for Churches and Religious Organizations* notes that "the IRS does not assign a special number or other identification as evidence of an organization's exempt status."

Step 2: Determine whether each church worker is an employee or self-employed, and obtain each worker's Social Security number

In some cases it is difficult to determine whether a worker is an employee or self-employed. If in doubt, churches always should treat a worker as an employee, since substantial penalties can be assessed against a church for treating a worker as self-employed whom the IRS later reclassifies as an employee.

In general, a self-employed worker is one who is not subject to the control of an employer with respect to how a job is to be done. Further, a self-employed person typically is engaged in a specific trade or business and offers his or her services to the general public. The IRS and the courts have developed various tests to assist in classifying a worker as an employee or self-employed. Factors that tend to indicate employee status include the following:

- The worker is required to follow an employer's instructions regarding when, where, and how to work;
- The worker receives on-the-job training from an experienced employee;
- The worker is expected to perform the services personally and not use a substitute;
- The employer, rather than the worker, hires and pays any assistants;
- The worker has a continuing working relationship with the employer;
- The employer establishes set hours of work;
- The worker is expected to work full time;
- The work is done on the employer's premises;
- The worker must submit regular oral or written reports to the employer;
- The worker's business expenses are reimbursed by the employer;
- The employer furnishes the worker's tools, supplies, and equipment;
- The worker does not work for other employers;
- The worker does not advertise his or her services to the general public.

Not all of these factors must exist for a worker to be an employee. But if most of them do, the worker is considered an employee. Again—if in doubt, treat the worker as an employee.

Backup withholding

After determining whether a worker is an employee or self-employed, you must obtain the worker's Social Security number. A worker who does not have a Social Security number can obtain one by filing Form SS-5. If a self-employed worker performs services for your church (and earns at least $600 for the year) but fails to provide you with his or her Social Security number, the church is required by law to withhold a portion of the worker's compensation as backup withholding. The backup withholding rate is 28 percent of a worker's compensation.

A self-employed person can stop backup withholding by providing the church with a correct Social Security number. The church will need the correct number to complete the worker's Form 1099-MISC (discussed later in Step 10).

Churches can be penalized if the Social Security number they report on a Form 1099-MISC is incorrect, *unless* they have exercised "due diligence." A church will be deemed to have exercised due diligence if it has self-employed persons provide their Social Security numbers using Forms W-9. It is a good idea for churches to present self-employed workers (e.g., guest speakers, contract laborers) with a Forms W-9 and to "backup withhold" unless the worker returns the form. The church should retain each Form W-9 to demonstrate its due diligence.

The backup withholding requirements were designed to ensure that self-employed persons fully report their income. Without backup reporting, self-employed persons can often underreport their true income (without detection) by simply refusing to provide their Social Security numbers to employers. Of course, to avoid backup withholding, some self-employed persons may consider providing a false Social Security number. The IRS will discover such a scheme when it receives the Form 1099-MISC containing the false number. At such time the IRS will notify the church to commence backup withholding on any future payments to the individual (until a correct Social Security number is provided).

Two additional rules pertain to backup withholding and must be understood.

Form 945. All taxes withheld through backup withholding are reported to the IRS on Form 945. The Form 945 must be filed with the IRS by January 31 of the following year. However, if you made deposits on time, in full payment of the taxes for the year, you may file the return by February 10.

Depositing backup withholdings. Deposit all nonpayroll withheld federal income tax, including backup withholding, by electronic funds transfer. Combine all Form 945 taxes for deposit purposes. Do not combine deposits for Form 941 with deposits for Form 945. Generally, the deposit rules that apply to Form 941 also apply to Form 945. However, because Form 945 is an annual return, the rules for determining your deposit schedule (discussed below) are different from those for Form 941.

Two deposit schedules—monthly or semiweekly—are used to determine when you must deposit withheld income tax. These schedules tell you when a deposit is due after a tax liability arises (e.g., you make a payment subject to income tax withholding, including backup withholding). See the instructions to Form 941 and *Publication 15* for details. If your backup withholdings for the year are less than $2,500, you may enclose a check for the balance with your annual Form 945.

Step 3: Have each employee complete Form W-4

Form W-4 is used by employees to claim withholding allowances. A church will need to know how many withholding allowances each nonminister employee claims in order to withhold the correct amount of federal income tax. A withholding allowance lowers the amount of tax that will be withheld from an employee's wages.

Allowances generally are available for the employee, the employee's spouse, each of the employee's dependents, and in some cases for itemized deductions.

Ask all new employees to give you a signed Form W-4 when they start work. If an employee does not complete such a form, the church must treat the employee as a single person without any withholding allowances or exemptions. Employers must put into effect any Form W-4 that replaces an existing certificate no later than the start of the first payroll period ending on or after the 30th day after the day you received the replacement Form W-4. Of course, you can put a Form W-4 into effect sooner, if you wish.

Employers are not responsible for verifying the withholding allowances employees claim.

Step 4: Compute each employee's taxable wages

The amount of taxes a church should withhold from an employee's wages depends on the amount of the employee's wages and the information contained on his or her Form W-4. A church must determine the wages of each employee that are subject to withholding and Social Security and Medicare taxes. Wages subject to federal withholding include pay given to an employee for service performed. The pay may be in cash or in other forms. Measure pay that is not in money (such as property) by its fair market value. Wages include a number of items in addition to salary. Some of these items include:

- Bonuses;
- Christmas and special occasion offerings;
- Retirement gifts;
- "Love gifts" provided by the church to an employee;
- The portion of an employee's Social Security tax paid by a church;
- Personal use of a church-provided car;
- Purchases of church property for less than fair market value;
- Business expense reimbursements under a non-accountable business expense reimbursement arrangement;
- Imputed interest on no-interest and low-interest church loans;
- Most reimbursements of a spouse's travel expenses;
- Forgiven debts;
- Noncash compensation.

Step 5: Determine the amount of income tax to withhold from each employee's wages

The amount of federal income tax the employer should withhold from an employee's wages may be computed in a number of ways. The most common methods are the *wage bracket method* and the *percentage method*.

Wage bracket method

Under the wage bracket method, the employer locates an employee's taxable wages for the applicable payroll period (i.e., weekly, biweekly, monthly) on the wage bracket withholding tables in *IRS Publication 15 (Circular E)* and determines the tax to be withheld by using the column headed by the number of withholding allowances claimed by the employee on Form W-4. You can view a copy of *IRS Publication 15* on the IRS website (*irs.gov*).

Percentage method

Under the percentage method, the employer multiplies the value of one withholding allowance (derived from a table contained in *Publication 15*) by the number of allowances an employee claims on Form W-4, subtracts the total from the employee's wages, and determines the amount to be withheld from another table.

Both of these withholding options are explained fully in *Publication 15*.

Step 6: Withhold Social Security and Medicare taxes from nonminister employees' wages

Churches and their nonminister employees are subject to Social Security and Medicare taxes. The combined tax rate is 15.3 percent of each employee's wages. This rate is paid equally by the employer and employee, with each paying a tax of 7.65 percent of the employee's wages. Churches must withhold the employee's share of Social Security and Medicare taxes from the wages of nonminister employees and, in addition, must pay the employer's share of these taxes. This 7.65 percent rate is comprised of two components: (1) a Medicare hospital insurance (HI) tax of 1.45 percent, and (2) an "old-age, survivor and disability" (Social Security) tax of 6.2 percent.

The 1.45 percent tax rate applies to all wages, regardless of amount. The Social Security tax (the 6.2 percent tax rate) applies to wages up to an amount specified each year by the Social Security Administration. The employee's share of Medicare (HI) tax is increased by an additional tax of 0.9 percent on wages for certain high-income employees. This same additional HI tax (0.9 percent) applies to the HI portion of SECA tax on self-employment income in excess of the threshold amount specified by law.

The church must withhold the employee's share of Social Security and Medicare taxes from each wage payment. Simply multiply each wage payment by the applicable percentage above. Special tables in *IRS Publication 15* help compute this. Wages of less than $108.28 per year paid to a church employee are exempt from Social Security and Medicare taxes.

Step 7: Deposit withheld taxes

Deposit withheld income taxes and the employee's share of Social Security and Medicare taxes, along with the employer's share of Social Security and Medicare taxes, by electronic funds transfer using the Electronic Federal Tax Payment System (EFTPS.) If you do not want to use EFTPS, you can arrange for your tax professional, financial institution, payroll service, or other trusted third party to make deposits on your behalf.

Payment with return

You may make a payment of payroll taxes with Form 941 instead of depositing them if you accumulate less than a $2,500 tax liability during the quarter (line 10 of Form 941) and you pay in full with a timely filed Form 941. However, if you are unsure that you will accumulate less than $2,500, deposit under the appropriate rules so you will not be subject to penalties for failure to deposit.

When to deposit

Two deposit schedules (monthly or semiweekly) are used by most churches to determine when to deposit Social Security, Medicare, and withheld income taxes. These schedules tell you when a deposit is due after a tax liability arises (e.g., when you have a payday). Prior to the beginning of each calendar year, you must determine which of the two deposit schedules you are required to use. The deposit schedule you must use is based on the total tax liability you reported on Form 941 during a four-quarter "lookback period," discussed below. Your deposit schedule is not determined by how often you pay your employees or make deposits.

Lookback period. Your deposit schedule for a calendar year is determined from the total taxes reported on your Forms 941 (line 10) in a four-quarter lookback period. The lookback period begins July 1 of the second preceding year and ends June 30 of the previous year. If you reported $50,000 or less of taxes for the lookback period, you are a *monthly* schedule depositor; if you reported more than $50,000, you are a *semiweekly* schedule depositor.

Monthly deposit schedule. You are a monthly schedule depositor for a calendar year if the total taxes on Form 941 (line 10) for the four quarters in your lookback period were $50,000 or less. Under the monthly deposit schedule, deposit Form 941 taxes on payments made during a month by the 15th day of the following month. Monthly schedule depositors should not file Form 941 on a monthly basis.

Semiweekly deposit schedule. You are a semiweekly schedule depositor for a calendar year if the total taxes on Form 941 (line 10) during your lookback period were more than $50,000. Under the semiweekly deposit schedule, deposit Form 941 taxes on payments made on Wednesday, Thursday, and Friday by the following Wednesday. Deposit amounts accumulated on payments made on Saturday, Sunday, Monday, and Tuesday by the following Friday.

How to deposit

You must make electronic deposits of all depository taxes (such as employment taxes) using EFTPS. If you do not want to use EFTPS, you can arrange for your tax professional, financial institution, payroll service, or other trusted third party to make deposits on your behalf.

Deposit penalties

Penalties may apply if you do not make required deposits on time, if you make deposits for less than the required amount, or if you do not use EFTPS when required. The penalties do not apply if any failure to make a proper and timely deposit was due to reasonable cause and not to willful neglect. For amounts not properly or timely deposited, the penalty rates are (1) 2 percent for deposits made 1 to 4 days late; (2) 5 percent for deposits made 6 to 15 days late; (3) 10 percent for deposits made 16 or more days late; (4) 10 percent for deposits made at an unauthorized financial institution, paid directly to the IRS, or paid with your tax return; (5) 10 percent for amounts subject to electronic deposit requirements but not deposited using EFTPS; and (6) 15 percent for amounts still unpaid more than 10 days after the date of the first notice the IRS sent asking for the tax due or the day on which you receive notice and demand for immediate payment, whichever is earlier.

Step 8: File Form 941

Form 941 reports the number of employees and amount of Social Security and Medicare taxes and withheld income taxes that are payable. Form 941 contains a box on line 4 that is checked if wages and other compensation are not subject to Social Security or Medicare tax. This box should be checked if your church filed a timely Form 8274 with the IRS, exempting itself from the employer's share of Social Security and Medicare taxes. Form 941 is due on the last day of the month following the end of each calendar quarter.

Clergy wages

The wages of ministers who report their income taxes as employees are reported on line 2 along with the wages of nonminister employees. Do not include a minister's housing allowance on this line, since it will not be reported on the Form W-2 issued to the minister. However, ministers' wages are exempt from tax withholding, so no amount will be entered on line 3 with respect to minister employees unless they have elected voluntary tax withholding.

Ministers are always deemed to be self-employed for Social Security with respect to services performed in the exercise of ministry, so they do not pay the employee's share of Social Security or Medicare taxes, and their employing church does not pay the employer's share of these taxes. Instead, ministers pay the self-employment tax. As a result, no amount is entered on lines 5a through 5d.

Form 941-X

Use Form 941-X to correct errors on a Form 941 that you previously filed. Use Form 941-X to correct

- wages, tips, and other compensation;
- income tax withheld from wages and other compensation;
- taxable Social Security wages;
- taxable Medicare wages; and,
- credits for COBRA premium assistance payments.

When you discover an error on a previously filed Form 941, you must

- correct that error using Form 941-X;
- file a separate Form 941-X for each Form 941 that you are correcting; and,
- file Form 941-X separately. Do not file Form 941-X with Form 941.

If you did not file a Form 941 for one or more quarters, do not use Form 941-X. Instead, file Form 941 for each of those quarters. However, if you did not file Forms 941 because you improperly treated workers as independent contractors or nonemployees and are now reclassifying them as employees, see the instructions for line 23 of Form 941-X.

Report the correction of underreported and overreported amounts for the same tax period on a single Form 941-X unless you are requesting a refund or abatement. If you are requesting a refund or abatement and are correcting both underreported and overreported amounts, file one Form 941-X correcting the underreported amounts only and a second Form 941-X correcting the overreported amounts. You will use the adjustment process if you underreported employment taxes and are making a payment or if you overreported employment taxes and will be applying the credit to Form 941 for the period during which you file Form 941-X.

Step 9: Complete Forms W-2 and W-3

A Form W-2 must be issued to any employee to whom you paid wages. The form must be completed and issued to each employee by January 31 of the following year. However, if a worker's employment ends before December 31, you may issue a Form W-2 to the person at any time after the termination of employment.

By February 28 (March 31 if you file electronically), submit to the Social Security Administration copies of all Forms W-2 (Copy A) that you issued for compensation, along with the Form W-3 (transmittal form).

Employee retention of Forms W-2

It is a good practice for employees to keep copies of all Forms W-2 issued to them by their employer until they confirm that the earnings reported on their Forms W-2 correspond to the earnings credited to them on their Social Security Statement. The Social Security Statement is available on the Social Security website and is mailed to workers age 60 or older who are not Social Security recipients.

If earnings reflected on an employee's Social Security Statement are underreported, the easiest way to correct the record is for the employee to present copies of his or her Forms W-2 for the year in question to the nearest Social Security office. While proof of earnings is possible without Forms W-2, it is much more difficult and time-consuming.

Completing Form W-3

Any employer required to file Form W-2 must file Form W-3 to transmit Copy A of Forms W-2 to the Social Security Administration. Make a copy of Form W-3 and keep it and Copy D of Forms W-2 with your records for four years. Be sure to use Form W-3 for the correct year. Churches need to file Form W-3 even if they only issue one Form W-2. Form W-3 combines all of the data reported on the individual Forms W-2 issued by an employer. Form W-3 is due by the last day of February of the following year.

Step 10: Complete Forms 1099-MISC and 1096

A Form 1099-MISC must be issued to any nonemployee who is paid compensation of at least $600 during any year. Furnish Copy B of this form to the recipient by January 31 of the following year, and file Copy A with the IRS by the last day of February. If you file electronically, the due date for filing Copy A with the IRS is March 31. Form 1099-MISC is designed to induce self-employed persons to report their full taxable income.

The income tax regulations specify that *no Form 1099-MISC is required* with respect to various kinds of payments, including the following:

Payments of income required to be reported on Forms W-2 or 941. This means that a church should not issue a Form 1099-MISC to any worker who is treated as an employee for income tax and payroll tax reporting.

Payments to a corporation. The Affordable Care Act, enacted by Congress in 2010, contained a provision eliminating the long-standing exemption of payments to corporations from the Form 1099-MISC reporting requirement for payments made after 2012. This provision ignited a firestorm of protest. Congress responded by enacting the Comprehensive 1099 Taxpayer Protection and Repayment of Exchange Subsidy Overpayments Act of 2011, which repealed the Form 1099-MISC requirement for payments made to corporations. The exemption for payments to tax-exempt entities was not affected.

EXAMPLE. In 2014 a church hires a local landscaping contractor to provide landscaping services for the church for an annual fee of $5,000. The contractor is unincorporated and self-employed. The church is required to issue the contractor a Form 1099-MISC reporting the compensation paid to him. It sends a copy of the Form 1099-MISC to the IRS.

EXAMPLE. Same facts as the previous example, except that the contractor is incorporated. The church is not required to issue a Form 1099-MISC to a corporation, since it is assumed that the corporation will issue the appropriate form (W-2 or 1099) to the contractor.

EXAMPLE. A self-employed, incorporated evangelist conducts religious services at a church on two occasions during 2014 and is paid $500 on each occasion. The church also reimburses the evangelist's substantiated travel expenses under its accountable reimbursement plan. The church is not required to issue a Form 1099-MISC to the evangelist, since his ministry is incorporated and his corporation is tax-exempt. It is a good practice for churches to confirm an evangelist's representation that he or she is a tax-exempt corporation. This is easily done by (1) checking with the secretary of state's office in the state in which the evangelist is allegedly incorporated to confirm nonprofit corporate status (in most states this can be done via the secretary of state's website) and (2) confirming that the corporation is tax-exempt by searching the online directory of tax-exempt organizations on the IRS website.

Payments of bills for merchandise, telegrams, telephone, freight, storage, and similar charges. According to this exception, a church need not issue a Form 1099-MISC to the telephone company, UPS, or to vendors from which it purchases merchandise.

Travel expense reimbursements paid under an accountable reimbursement arrangement. According to this exception, a church need not report on a Form 1099-MISC the amount of travel and other business expense reimbursements that it pays to a self-employed worker under an accountable reimbursement arrangement (i.e., expenses are reimbursed only if they are substantiated as to amount, date, place, and business nature, and any excess reimbursements must be returned to the employer).

On the other hand, travel expense reimbursements (or advances) paid to a self-employed person without adequate substantiation are considered to be nonaccountable and must be reported as compensation on the Form 1099-MISC. An example of a nonaccountable reimbursement would be a monthly car allowance paid to a minister without any requirement that the minister substantiate that the allowances were used to pay for business expenses. Another common example of a nonaccountable reimbursement would be a church's reimbursement of a guest speaker's travel expenses based on the speaker's oral statement or estimate of the amount of the expenses (without any documentary substantiation).

Canceled debts

The forgiveness or cancellation of a debt represents taxable income to the debtor. However, the instructions to Form 1099-MISC specify that "a canceled debt is not reportable on Form 1099-MISC." The instructions clarify that only financial institutions are required to report a canceled debt as income, and this is done on Form 1099-C. Of course, if the debtor is an employee, the forgiven debt represents taxable income that should be added to the debtor's compensation that is reported on Form W-2.

Repairs

The instructions for Form 1099-MISC clarify that "payment for services, including payment for parts or materials used to perform the services" are reportable

as nonemployee compensation "if supplying the parts or materials was incidental to providing the service. For example, report the entire insurance company payments to an auto repair shop under a repair contract showing an amount for labor and another amount for parts, since furnishing parts was incidental to repairing the auto."

The $600 requirement

As noted above, churches need not issue a person a Form 1099-MISC unless the individual is paid $600 or more in compensation. Let's take a closer look at this rule.

Compensation of less than $600. There is no need to issue a Form 1099-MISC to persons paid less than $600 in self-employment earnings during the year.

Accountable reimbursements of business expenses. Since reimbursements under an accountable business expense reimbursement arrangement are not included in the reportable income of self-employed persons, it is reasonable to assume that such reimbursements should not count toward the $600 threshold for filing a Form 1099-MISC. Under an accountable reimbursement arrangement, an employer reimburses a worker's expenses only if the worker substantiates (with documentary evidence, including receipts for individual expenses of $75 or more) the amount, date, location, and business purpose of each reimbursed expense within a reasonable time. The instructions for Form 1099-MISC state that a "travel reimbursement for which the nonemployee did not account to the payer, if the . . . reimbursement totals at least $600" must be reported on the form. This implies that accountable reimbursements do not count toward the $600 filing amount.

Benevolence recipients

Should a church give recipients of benevolence distributions a Form 1099-MISC (for distributions of $600 or more for the year)? Ordinarily, the answer would be no, since the Form 1099-MISC is issued only to nonemployees who receive *compensation* of $600 or more from the church during the year. *IRS Revenue Ruling 2003-12; IRS Letter Rulings 9314014, 200113031.* To the extent that benevolence distributions to a particular individual represent a legitimate charitable distribution by the church (consistent with its exempt purposes), no Form 1099-MISC would be required. It would be unrealistic to characterize such distributions as compensation for services rendered when the individual performed no services for the church.

Backup withholding

Federal law requires that organizations (including churches) that are required to furnish a Form 1099-MISC to a self-employed worker must apply "backup withholding" if (1) the worker fails or refuses to furnish his or her Social Security number (or other taxpayer identification number), *or* (2) the IRS notifies you that the worker's Social Security number is incorrect, *or* (3) the IRS notifies you to apply backup withholding.

Backup withholding means that you must withhold a specified amount of total compensation from the paycheck of the self-employed person and report the withholdings on Form 945. These requirements are explained fully under Step 2, above. The backup withholding rate typically is 28 percent of annual compensation. Annual updates are provided through the annual *Church & Clergy Tax Guide* (ChurchLawAndTaxStore.com).

Corrected forms

If you issue a Form 1099-MISC with incorrect information, you should issue a corrected Form 1099-MISC.

SOCIAL SECURITY TAXES

Since the beginning of the Social Security program in 1937, the employees of churches and most other nonprofit organizations were exempted from mandatory coverage. The exemption was designed to encourage nonprofit organizations by freeing them from an additional tax burden that they ordinarily could not pass along to customers through price increases. Churches and other nonprofit organizations were permitted to waive their exemption by filing Forms SS-15 and SS-15a with the IRS.

In 1983, Congress repealed the exemption beginning in 1984. The repeal was criticized by some church leaders who viewed it as a "tax" on churches, in violation of the constitutional principle of separation of church and state. In 1984, Congress responded to this criticism by again amending the Social Security Act, this time to give churches a one-time irrevocable election to exempt themselves from Social Security coverage if they were opposed, for religious reasons,

to the payment of the employer's share of Social Security and Medicare taxes and if they filed an election with the IRS *prior* to the deadline for filing the first quarterly employer's tax return (Form 941) after July 17, 1984, on which the *employer's* share of Social Security and Medicare taxes is reported. Since a Form 941 is due on the last day of the month following the end of each calendar quarter (i.e., April 30, July 31, October 31, and January 31), the election deadline for churches in existence as of July 1984 and having at least one nonminister employee was October 30, 1984 (the day before the deadline for filing Form 941 for the quarter ending September 30). Churches either not in existence as of July 1984, or not having nonminister employees at that time, have until the day prior to the deadline for their first Form 941 to file an election (Form 8274).

Churches that have elected to exempt themselves from the employer's share of Social Security and Medicare taxes (by filing a timely Form 8274) can revoke their exemption. Temporary regulations issued by the Treasury Department specify that churches can revoke their exemption by filing a Form 941 (employer's quarterly tax return) accompanied by full payment of Social Security taxes for that quarter.

UNEMPLOYMENT TAXES

The following activities ordinarily are exempt from state unemployment taxes:

- service performed in the employ of a church, a convention or association of churches, or an organization that is operated primarily for religious purposes and that is operated, supervised, controlled, or principally supported by a church or convention or association of churches. The exemption is not limited to employees performing strictly religious duties;
- service performed in the employ of an unincorporated church-controlled elementary or secondary school;
- service performed in the employ of an incorporated religious elementary or secondary school if it is operated primarily for religious purposes and is operated, supervised, controlled, or principally

supported by a church or a convention or association of churches;

- service performed for an elementary or secondary school that is operated primarily for religious purposes and is not operated, supervised, controlled, or principally supported by a church or a convention or association of churches;
- service performed by a duly ordained, commissioned, or licensed minister of a church in the exercise of his ministry or by a member of a religious order in the exercise of duties required by such order.

STATE INCOME TAXES

Most states impose a tax on the gross income of corporations. Although nearly all the income of most religious organizations is in the form of gifts that generally are excludable from the organization's income, most states specifically exempt religious organizations from the tax on corporate income. Some state corporate income tax laws exempt any corporation that is exempt from federal income tax. Others specifically exempt various charitable organizations, including religious and educational organizations. A number of states impose a tax on the unrelated business income of exempt organizations.

STATE SALES TAXES

Most states impose a tax on the sale of tangible personal property or the rendering of various services for compensation. Religious organizations are exempt from sales taxes in most states, although the nature of the exemption varies from state to state. Sales made *to* religious organizations are exempted from sales taxes in many states. Some states exempt sales made *by* religious organizations, and others exempt sales *to or by* religious organizations. Many states that exempt sales of property made to religious organizations stipulate that the exemption is available only if the organization uses the purchased property for exempt purposes. Some states are even more restrictive, and some have no specific exemption for sales by or to religious organizations.

The exemption of religious organizations from state sales taxes is available only to nonprofit religious organizations and ordinarily is available only to those organizations that make application. One court ruled a

religious organization was properly denied an exemption from a state's sales tax, since it had refused to submit sufficient information with its exemption application to establish that it was, in fact, a religious organization. *First Lutheran Mission v. Department of Revenue, 613 P.2d 351 (Colo. 1980).*

The Texas Monthly case

In 1989 the United States Supreme Court ruled that a Texas law exempting religious periodicals from state sales tax violated the First Amendment's nonestablishment of religion clause. *Texas Monthly, Inc. v. Bullock, 109 S. Ct. 890 (1989).* From 1984 until 1987, Texas law imposed a sales tax upon all periodicals except those "published or distributed by a religious faith and that consist wholly of writings sacred to a religious faith." This law was challenged by a secular publisher, and the United States Supreme Court agreed that the Texas law violated the First Amendment.

The court's ruling is significant, since it probed the meaning of the First Amendment's language prohibiting the establishment of a religion. The court noted that the First Amendment nonestablishment of religion clause "prohibits, at the very least, legislation that constitutes an endorsement of one or another set of religious beliefs or of religion generally." It observed that the "core notion" underlying the First Amendment is that the government "may not place its prestige, coercive authority, or resources behind a single religious faith or behind religious faith in general, compelling nonadherents to support the practices or proselytizing of favored religious organizations and conveying the message that those who do not contribute gladly are less than full members of the community."

The court was quick to add that government policies that are designed to implement a broad secular purpose are not invalid merely because they incidentally benefit religion. For example, the court noted that it had previously upheld a New York property tax exemption law because it exempted a wide variety of charitable organizations including churches. *Walz v. Tax Commission, 397 U.S. 664 (1970).* The court concluded:

> Every tax exemption constitutes a subsidy that affects nonqualifying taxpayers, forcing them to become indirect and vicarious donors. Insofar

as that subsidy is conferred upon a wide array of nonsectarian groups as well as religious organizations in pursuit of some legitimate secular end, the fact that religious groups benefit incidentally does not [violate the First Amendment]. However, when government directs a subsidy exclusively to religious organizations . . . and that either burdens nonbeneficiaries markedly or cannot reasonably be seen as removing a significant state-imposed deterrent to the free exercise of religion, as Texas has done, it provides unjustifiable awards of assistance to religious organizations and cannot but convey a message of endorsement to slighted members of the community. This is particularly true where, as here, the subsidy is targeted at writings that promulgate the teachings of religious faith. It is difficult to view Texas' narrow exemption as anything but state sponsorship of religious belief.

The court emphasized that if Texas chose to grant a tax exemption to "all groups that contributed to the community's cultural, intellectual, and moral betterment, then the exemption for religious publications could be retained." The court specifically ruled that a statute exempting organizations created for "religious, educational, or charitable purposes" from the payment of state sales tax would be a "model" exemption statute.

The Jimmy Swaggart case

In 1990, the United States Supreme Court ruled unanimously that the state of California could tax the sale of religious literature by Jimmy Swaggart Ministries (JSM). *Jimmy Swaggart Ministries v. Board of Equalization, 110 S. Ct. 688 (1990)*. JSM is a religious organization organized "for the purpose of establishing and maintaining an evangelistic outreach for the worship of Almighty God . . . by all available means, both at home and in foreign lands," including evangelistic crusades, missionary endeavors, radio broadcasting, television broadcasting, and publishing. From 1974 to 1981 (the years in question), JSM conducted 23 crusades in California. At the crusades, JSM conducted religious services and sold religious books, tapes, records, and other religious merchandise. JSM also offered its products for sale through radio and television broadcasts and in its monthly magazine, *The Evangelist*.

In 1980 the state of California informed JSM that religious materials were not exempt from the state sales tax and requested that it register as a seller to facilitate the payment of the tax. California law imposes a 6 percent tax on the sale of most items of tangible personal property. Churches and other religious organizations are not exempted from this tax. State law also requires certain out-of-state sellers to collect a 6 percent "use tax" on sales of property to California residents. JSM responded that the constitutional guaranty of religious freedom exempted it from collecting or paying sales or use taxes.

In 1981 the state of California audited JSM and again asked it to register as a seller and to collect sales taxes on all sales made at its California crusades and to collect use taxes on mail-order sales to California residents. The state concluded that from 1974 through 1981 JSM sold religious merchandise valued at $240,000 at its California crusades, and religious merchandise valued at $1.7 million through mail-order sales to California residents. Both figures represented sales of merchandise with specific religious content—Bibles, Bible study manuals, printed sermons and collections of sermons, audiocassette tapes of sermons, religious books and pamphlets, and religious music in the form of songbooks, tapes, and records. Based on these sales figures, the state notified JSM that it owed sales and use taxes of $120,000 plus interest of $36,000 and penalties of $11,000. JSM did not contest the state's assessment of sales and use taxes on sales of nonreligious merchandise.

JSM challenged the tax assessments on the basis of the First Amendment's guaranty of religious freedom. The state rejected this defense, and JSM appealed to the state courts. Both a trial court and state appeals court ruled in favor of the state, and the state supreme court denied review. JSM appealed the case directly to the United States Supreme Court. The Supreme Court agreed that JSM's sales of religious literature have as "high a claim to constitutional protection" as more orthodox forms of religious exercise, but it disagreed that the constitutional guaranty of religious freedom was violated by the California sales tax. The court based its ruling on six considerations.

First, it noted JSM's "religious beliefs do not forbid payment of the sales tax" and accordingly that the tax "imposes no constitutionally significant burden on [JSM's] religious practices or beliefs."

Second, the court rejected JSM's claim that its position was supported by two previous Supreme Court decisions made in the 1940s involving city ordinances that prohibited home solicitations or the sale of literature without the payment of a license tax. The ordinances were invalid, since they "restrained in advance those constitutional liberties of press and religion and inevitably tended to suppress their exercise." In contrast, the California sales tax "is not imposed as a precondition of disseminating the message." The court further noted that in one of the two earlier cases, it had emphasized that "we do not mean to say that religious groups and the press are free from all financial burdens of government," and it affirmed that "a tax on the income of one who engages in religious activities or a tax on property used or employed in connection with those activities" would not violate the constitution. It concluded that "the tax at issue in this case is akin to a generally applicable income or property tax, which [the two previous decisions] state may constitutionally be imposed on a religious activity."

Third, the California sales tax was applied neutrally to all retail sales of tangible personal property (whether by for-profit or nonprofit organizations). Religious organizations were not "singled out for special and burdensome treatment."

Fourth, the sales tax "represents only a small fraction of any retail sale" and accordingly could not meaningfully affect JSM's religious beliefs or practices.

Fifth, the sales tax only requires religious organizations to collect the tax from customers and remit collected taxes to the state. They are not required to pay it themselves. Such "pass through" taxes pose no significant burden on religious beliefs or practices, the court concluded.

Sixth, the court rejected JSM's claim that the marginally higher price that customers would have to pay for its literature (because of the 6 percent sales tax) violated its religious freedoms by driving away potential customers unwilling to pay the higher prices. The court found this argument "not

constitutionally significant" because it considered the 6 percent sales tax to be marginal.

JSM alleged that taxing its sales would create an "excessive entanglement" between church and state, since it would require "on-site inspections of evangelistic crusades, lengthy on-site audits, examination of [its] books and records, threats of criminal prosecution, and layers of administrative and judicial proceedings."

The court rejected this claim, noting three considerations. First, any "administrative burden" was reduced by the fact that JSM "had a sophisticated accounting staff and had recently computerized its accounting." Second, requiring JSM to collect and remit sales and use taxes "does not enmesh government in religious affairs [and] contrary to [JSM's] contentions requires neither the involvement of state employees in, nor on-site continuing inspection of, [its] day-to-day operations." Third, applying the sales tax to the sale of religious materials "does not require the state to inquire into the religious content of the items sold or the religious motivation for selling or purchasing the items."

Finally, the court refused to consider JSM's claim that it did not have a sufficient presence in California to subject it to sales or use taxes on mail-order sales of religious literature to California residents. This claim was barred, the court concluded, because it had not been raised by JSM in its initial challenge to the state's assessment of taxes. Ordinarily, new issues cannot be raised before the Supreme Court.

STATE PROPERTY TAXES

The exemption of religious organizations from property taxes is a practice that dates back to ancient times. The Bible records that "Joseph established it as a law concerning land in Egypt . . . that a fifth of the produce belongs to Pharaoh. It was only the land of the priests that did not become Pharaoh's" (Genesis 47:26).

The emperor Constantine exempted churches from property taxes in the fourth century. Medieval Europe generally exempted church property from property taxes. This tradition of exemption was adopted by the American colonies. All 50 states presently recognize some form of exemption of religious organizations from property taxes. The exemption of church property from taxation has been challenged on a number of occasions on the ground that such exemptions violate the First Amendment's nonestablishment of religion clause. The Supreme Court historically viewed such challenges as frivolous. *Walz v. Tax Commission, 397 U.S. 664, 686 n.6 (1970)*. In 1970 the court upheld the constitutionality of New York's property tax exemption statute, which exempted property used exclusively for religious purposes.

Every state exempts from taxation buildings that are used exclusively as places of worship. Much variety exists, however, regarding the exemption of other forms of church-owned property. The exemption of some common forms of church-owned property is evaluated below.

Houses of religious worship

Little doubt exists regarding the exemption of buildings used exclusively for religious worship. Every state exempts such buildings from taxation. To illustrate, many state laws exempt "houses of religious worship." Others exempt "places used for religious worship" or "buildings for religious worship" or "property used exclusively for worship." Many states simply exempt all property used exclusively for religious purposes or religious worship. Such an exemption certainly is broad enough to include buildings used for religious worship.

Questions may arise, however, in several ways, including the following: (1) How much of the church-owned property surrounding the sanctuary is exempt? (2) What if a portion of the church property is rented or otherwise used for commercial or investment purposes? (3) If a portion of church-owned property is rented or otherwise used for nonexempt purposes, does the entire property lose its exempt status, or only the portion rented? (4) What if the sanctuary is under construction? Some or all of these questions may not be addressed in an exemption statute, and this can lead to confusion and even litigation. Each of these issues is discussed below.

Surrounding grounds

How much of the property surrounding a church sanctuary is exempt from taxation? Many statutes do not address this issue directly, but rather, exempt all property used exclusively for religious purposes. Some statutes simply state that the "grounds" or land adjacent or appurtenant to the sanctuary

are exempt, without any attempt to clarify how much land is contemplated by the exemption. Other statutes clarify that the land surrounding the sanctuary is exempt to the extent that it is reasonably necessary to the accomplishment of a church's purposes. A few statutes specify how much of a church's property is exempt. For example, one state constitution specifies that up to one-half acre is exempt in cities or towns, and up to two acres "in the country." Other state laws exempt church grounds up to 5 acres, 15 acres, 30 acres, and 320 acres.

Effect of rental income

Churches occasionally rent a portion of their property. Does this affect the exempt status of the property? Some statutes specify that church property is not eligible for exempt status if it is rented or otherwise used for commercial, investment, or other nonexempt purposes. The same result may be presumed under state laws exempting property that is used exclusively for religious purposes. Other states recognize the "partial exemption" rule, under which the rental of a portion of exempt property does not affect the exempt status of the entire property but only of that portion actually rented. This rule is summarized in the following subsection. A few courts have concluded that the existence of rental income does not necessarily affect the exempt status of church-owned property. *University Christian Church v. City of Austin, 724 S.W.2d 94 (Tex. App. 1986) (a church rented two of its parking lots)*.

Partial exemption

Many states recognize the "partial exemption" rule. Under this rule, property that is used in part for exclusively religious purposes is entitled to a partial exemption based on the percentage of use or occupancy that is devoted to an exempt use. The rule is based on statute in some states and upon judicial decisions in others. To illustrate, one state statute specifies:

> If any portion of the property which might otherwise be exempted under this section is used for commercial or other purposes not within the conditions necessary for exemption (including any use the primary purpose

of which is to produce income even though such income is to be used for or in furtherance of the exempt purposes) that portion of the premises shall not be exempt but the remaining portion of the premises shall not be deprived of the exemption if the remaining portion is used exclusively for purposes within the conditions necessary for exemption. In the event of an exemption of a portion of a building, the tax shall be assessed upon so much of the value of the building (including the land thereunder and the appurtenant premises) as the proportion of the floor space of the nonexempt portion bears to the total floor space of the building.

Another statute provides: "If any portion of such real property is not so used exclusively to carry out thereupon one or more of such purposes but is leased or otherwise used for other purposes, such portion shall be subject to taxation and the remaining portion only shall be exempt."

Several courts have recognized the principle of partial exemption. On the other hand, a few courts have ruled that if any part of a building is used for commercial purposes, the entire facility is subject to tax.

Property under construction

Is a church building under construction exempt from property taxes? Unfortunately, few statutes address this question directly. One statute specifies that "all grounds and buildings used or *under construction* by . . . religious institutions and societies" (emphasis added) are exempt from tax. Another statute specifies:

> [Church property] from which no revenue is derived shall be exempt though not in actual use therefore by reason of the absence of suitable buildings or improvements thereon if (a) the construction of such buildings or improvements is in progress or is in good faith contemplated by such corporation or association or (b) such real property is held by such corporation or association upon condition that the title thereto shall revert in case

any building not intended and suitable for one or more such purposes shall be erected upon such premises or some part thereof.

Leased property

Some churches lease the property they use for worship services and other activities. Does the fact that a church leases the property it uses qualify the property for exemption from tax? Most property tax exemption statutes only apply to property that is *owned* by a church or other specified charity. The fact that a church leases property does not ordinarily render the property exempt from tax. Some statutes refer to property that is used for religious purposes. Property leased by a church for religious purposes may qualify for exemption under such a statute.

Parsonages

A parsonage is a church-owned property used as a residence by a minister. Many states exempt such properties from taxation. Some states impose restrictions on the exemption. For example, a few states exempt parsonages only up to a specified dollar value, exempt only one parsonage for each church, or exempt the grounds surrounding a parsonage only up to a specified area. The exemption does not extend to residences owned by ministers themselves. To illustrate, one court ruled that a parsonage was no longer entitled to exemption after the church sold it to its minister. *Watts v. Board of Assessors, 414 N.E.2d 1003 (Mass. 1981).* The court concluded that the "parsonage" was owned by a private individual, not by the church, and therefore was not entitled to exemption.

A few courts have ruled that church-owned parsonages may be exempt from property taxation even though they enjoy no specific statutory exemption. For example, one court concluded that a church-owned parsonage that served various religious purposes, such as a meeting place for church groups and a place for providing religious services, including pastoral counseling, was exempted from taxation by the general exemption of property used exclusively for religious purposes. *Immanuel Baptist Church v. Glass, 497 P.2d 757 (Okla. 1972).* But several other courts have ruled that parsonages are taxable unless they are specifically exempted. *Salt Lake County v. Tax Commission ex rel. Good Shepherd Lutheran Church, 548 P.2d 630 (Utah 1976)*.

In general, to be exempt from property taxation, a parsonage must be actually and exclusively used as an integral part of the operations of the church rather than as a mere convenience to a minister. *Clinton Township v. Camp Brett-Endeavor, Inc., 1 N.J. Tax 54 (1980)*. To illustrate, one court concluded that a dwelling used for several hours a week by a clergyman for commercial purposes did not qualify for a property tax exemption. *Ballard v. Supervisor of Assessments, 306 A.2d 506 (Md. 1973)*. However, one court upheld the exemption of a parsonage even though the clergyman's wife engaged in a part-time interior designing business and occasionally used a bedroom for business purposes. *Congregation Beth Mayer, Inc. v. Board of Assessors, 417 N.Y.S.2d 754 (1979)*. In holding that a parsonage can meet the definition of "property used exclusively for religious purposes," one court observed that "a parsonage qualifies for an exemption even if it reasonably and substantially facilitates the aims of religious worship and religious instruction because the pastor's religious duties require him to live in close proximity to the church or because the parsonage has unique facilities for religious worship and instruction or is primarily used for such purposes." *McKenzie v. Johnson, 456 N.E.2d 73 (Ill. 1983)*.

Vacant land

Many churches own tracts of vacant land for purposes of recreation or future expansion. Are such properties exempt from taxation? Courts have come to both conclusions. The key decisions are summarized below.

Exemption recognized

EXAMPLE. A Colorado court ruled that two vacant lots owned by a church were exempt from property tax because they were used one day each year for religious purposes. The church in question owned two vacant lots—one near the church and the second some distance away. The church was the only user of the two lots, and it used each lot one day each year for activities it claimed were in furtherance of its religious mission. The church

hoped to construct structures on each lot for church use, but it lacked the funds to do so. A local tax assessor ruled that the lots did not qualify for exemption because the quantity and extent of the church's use was insufficient. The court disagreed. It concluded: "We note that property tax exemptions are determined on an annual basis . . . based on the use of the property in each tax year. Implicit in this scheme is the requirement that, in order for the property to qualify for tax exemption for that tax year, there be at least some actual use of the property for tax exempt purposes in that tax year. Apart from this minimal implicit requirement, however, we decline to hold . . . that any particular frequency or quantity of use religious in character is required to satisfy the foregoing . . . standards for exemption based on religious use." The court noted that while the tax assessor considered the church's use of the lots just one day each year to be insufficient for exemption, he "was unable to quantify the frequency or amount of such use that would be considered sufficient." *Pilgrim Rest Baptist Church v. PTA, 971 P.2d 270 (Colo. App. 1998)*.

EXAMPLE. A Florida court ruled that vacant land owned by a religious agency and used occasionally for religious purposes was exempt from property taxation. A denominational agency (the "church") purchased 2.5 acres of vacant land. After purchasing the land, the church used it occasionally for religious purposes. This use included prayer services on the property by small groups of church leaders and frequent visits to the property for site development planning and fund-raising. A tax assessor ruled that the "inaccessible, weed-covered lot" was not exempt and that the religious activities that occurred on the property were incidental. A state appeals court disagreed with the assessor's decision and ruled that the property was exempt from tax. The court concluded: "The record demonstrates that the church's property was used exclusively for religious purposes. There is no evidence that the property was used for any nonexempt purpose. Thus, the church's use of the property cannot be characterized as incidental." *Robbins v. Florida Conference Association of Seventh Day Adventists, 641 So.2d 893 (Fla. App. 3 Dist. 1994)*.

EXAMPLE. The Kentucky Supreme Court ruled that a 10-acre tract of largely vacant property that a church had acquired for future expansion was exempt from property taxation due to its occasional use for church purposes. A church purchased 10 acres of land, including two houses. The acreage was divided into two parcels, each consisting of approximately five acres, with a single family dwelling located on each parcel. It was the stated purpose of the church to build a new, larger facility on this property, as well as to provide for an activity center and other related church facilities as soon as finances allowed. The two houses were rented to individuals for residential purposes, with the rental income being used by the church building fund to service a mortgage on the property. The field on the side of these houses is used by the church for recreational purposes about once a year. On two occasions, the church has held an annual church picnic on the property. And while there have been no improvements or permanent structures erected by the church, a cross and bench were erected on a small portion of the property with permission of the tenants. This area is used for meditation by some of the parishioners.

The tax assessor determined that the property was subject to taxation. The church appealed to the state supreme court, claiming that the property was exempt on the basis of a provision in the state constitution exempting from taxation "property owned and occupied by . . . institutions of religion." The court, in concluding that the property was entitled to exemption, observed: "While the evidence does not indicate a continuous use of these grounds by [the church] it does support the finding of the trial court as to periodic use, such as horseshoe pitching, volleyball, softball, and tugs of war during the occasional outings by the church membership. There is also a portion used as a prayer and meditation area, including a bench and a large wooden cross. In essence, the congregation has used this property like a park, although not on either a daily or weekly basis. However, it would seem that it has been utilized by the church with the same frequency as many, if not most, churches use outdoor land that adjoins their main sanctuaries. Therefore, we find that substantial evidence supports the findings by the trial court that the land owned by the church, but not occupied by the tenants, is, in fact, occupied by the church for purposes of the Kentucky Constitution."

The court then made the following significant comment: "We recognize that churches are unique. For the most part, they are never 'occupied' in the conventional sense. A vast majority of properties owned by 'institutions of religion' such as churches, mosques, tabernacles, temples, and the like, are used for places of worship at specified times and may remain vacant for substantial periods during the week. We further recognize that adjacent facilities, such as activity buildings, gymnasiums, even shelters, may be owned by religious institutions, but perhaps utilized irregularly on an as needed basis. School buildings owned by religious institutions may, in fact, sit idle for a great deal of time. This would not preclude these buildings from being 'occupied'. . . . It is precisely for these reasons that we find that the trial court's findings were supported substantially by the evidence in this case as to the property not being rented out as residences."

EXAMPLE. The Supreme Court of Ohio ruled that a 21-acre tract of land owned by a church and used for recreational purposes qualified

for exemption from property taxation on the basis of charitable use. The property included two softball fields, a soccer field, and a jogging trail and was used by an estimated 3,000 community members per year at no charge. The court rejected the tax assessor's argument that merely holding the property open to the public and allowing various third parties to use it was not a charitable use and did not qualify the property for exemption. The court concluded: "If the use to which property is put otherwise qualifies as charitable, neither the fact of ownership by a religious organization nor the existence of religious motives in connection with the charitable use will defeat the claim of exemption." *The Chapel v. Testa, 950 N.E.2d 142 (Ohio 2011).*

Exemption denied

A number of courts have held that vacant land ordinarily is not used exclusively for religious purposes and does not qualify for exemption. This almost always will be the result if the land is used for commercial purposes (such as farming) or if no religious or charitable activities occur on the land or such uses are insignificant.

EXAMPLE. A Connecticut court ruled that an undeveloped tract of land owned by a church was not entitled to exemption from property taxation, since it was not used exclusively for religious purposes. The church property was an unimproved, wooded lot that contained no structures or buildings other than a volleyball court. The court noted that the state property tax law exempts property belonging to a religious organization that is not in actual use for religious purposes because of "the absence of suitable buildings and improvements thereon, if the construction of such buildings or improvements is in progress." Despite the church's assertion that the property was used for religious purposes, in that "prayer walks" were occasionally conducted on the property, the court ruled that the property was not exempt, because it "contains neither any building or other improvement used for charitable purposes, nor such improvements in the process of being constructed." *Grace n' Vessels of Christ Ministries, Inc. v. City of Danbury, 733 A.2d 283 (Conn. App. 1999).*

EXAMPLE. The Minnesota Tax Court ruled that there was insufficient support for the exemption of three church-owned wooded lots from property taxation to grant the church's motion for summary judgment in its favor. The church claimed that the lots were entitled to exemption because they were devoted to and reasonably necessary to the accomplishment of church purposes. It pointed out that the lots were used for prayer, reflection, and Christian education, including a Vacation Bible School. The court, in denying the church's request, noted that the only support for its position were "self-serving statements" about the actual use of the lots without an adequate factual basis. *Advent Evangelical Lutheran Church v. County of Ramsey, 2008 WL 3892374 (Minn. Tax Court 2008).*

EXAMPLE. The Utah Supreme Court ruled that a parcel of vacant land purchased by a church was not exempt from property taxes, despite the church's use of the land for occasional worship services. The land was purchased as a site for a new church building. The church maintained the land but did not begin construction of a new church building. However, the church did use the property for religious purposes. For approximately two hours each year, the church held religious services on the property. The court noted that state law exempts from property taxes "property used exclusively for religious purposes." It concluded that the land in question failed this test. It insisted that in order for land to be used exclusively for religious purposes, it must be "actually used or committed to a use that is exclusively religious." The church argued that the land was used exclusively for religious purposes even though it was used for religious services for only a few hours each year, since "for 8,758 hours out of the year the land is committed to no use at all." The court disagreed, noting that "property held for future development is being used." *Corporation of the Episcopal Church v. Utah State Tax Commission, 919 P.2d 556 (Utah 1996).*

Exclusive use

Many statutes exempt property used exclusively for religious purposes. An exclusive use generally is construed to mean a primary, inherent, or principal use, in contrast to secondary or incidental uses. The courts have ruled that the term "exclusively" does not necessarily mean "directly" or "immediately"; that a use that is incidental and reasonably necessary to an exempt use is properly exempted from tax; and that the exemption of property used exclusively for exempt purposes does not require constant activity or vigorous or obvious activity, but rather, requires that the property be devoted to no other use than that which warrants the exemption. If part of church-owned property is used for commercial purposes, the entire property cannot be considered to be used exclusively for religious purposes. However, as noted previously, some states recognize the partial exemption rule, under which only the portion of church-owned property that is used for nonexempt purposes is denied exempt status.

Application for exemption

The fact that a religious organization has received a determination letter from the IRS acknowledging that it is exempt from federal income taxation as an organization described in section 501(c)(3) of the tax code does not necessarily entitle the organization to a property tax exemption. It is important to recognize that in many states, property used for religious purposes is not automatically exempt from taxation. An application must be filed with local tax authorities in such states. Failure to do so will result in loss of exemption, at least for the current year.

EXAMPLE. The Minnesota Supreme Court ruled that a church's property was not exempt from property taxes, since it had not been acquired by the assessment date of July 1 as required by state law. The court rejected the church's arguments that an oral understanding to acquire the property plus the signing of a letter of intent with the seller satisfied the acquisition requirement. *Crossroads Church v. County of Dakota, 800 N.W.2d 608 (Minn. 2011).*

EXAMPLE. The Nebraska Supreme Court ruled that a church can be denied an exemption from real estate taxes as a result of its failure to file an application for exemption. *Indian Hills Church v. County Board of Equalization, 412 N.W.2d 459 (Neb. 1987).*

EXAMPLE. The Ohio Supreme Court concluded: "We regard as settled the general proposition that the taxable or exempt status of property should be determined as of the tax lien date, which is January 1 of whatever tax year is at issue." *Sylvania Church of God v. Levin, 888 N.E.2d 408 (Ohio 2008).*

EXAMPLE. The Oregon Tax Court ruled that a church's property was subject to taxation because it failed to file a timely exemption application, despite the fact that the tax assessor's office used an incorrect address to inform the church of the need to file a timely exemption application. The court acknowledged that the church did not receive notice of the exemption status change or the tax statements because the assessor sent the notices to the wrong address.

In rejecting the church's request that a property tax exemption be granted for prior years based on the assessor's failure to send notices to the correct address, the court observed: "It is not the county's obligation to search for the taxpayer. Instead, it is the taxpayer's responsibility to search the county and make sure its records are correct."

This case illustrates that in most jurisdictions it is the responsibility of the property owner to ensure that the local tax assessor's records contain a correct mailing address. Church leaders should not assume that church property will be entitled to exemption from tax if no exemption application is filed, even if the failure to apply for an exemption was due to the fact that the local assessor sent tax statements and related information to the wrong address. *Byzantine Catholic Bishop v. County Assessor, 2011 WL 4444186 (Ore. Tax 2012).*

Assessment date

In most states, property acquired by a church *after the tax assessment date* is not entitled to exemption for the current year, even though it is used exclusively for religious purposes.

To illustrate, under New Jersey law, the taxable or exempt status of any tract of property is determined as of the tax assessment date (October 1 of the preceding calendar year). A church purchased property on December 12 and used it immediately for exclusively religious purposes. The church applied for a tax exemption for that year but was informed that no exemption would be available, since the property was not owned by the church as of October 1. The church claimed that it was doctrinally opposed, on the basis of biblical passages, to paying taxes with funds obtained from tithes and contributions and that requiring the church to pay property taxes would violate the constitutional guaranty of religious freedom.

A state court acknowledged that "the free exercise of religious beliefs can be crushed and closed out by the sheer weight of the tribute which is exacted." However, it also noted that "it is equally well-settled that religious groups are not free from all financial burdens of government" and that "not all burdens on religion are unconstitutional." A state may "justify a limitation on religious liberty by showing that it is essential to accomplish an overriding governmental interest" and that there exists "no less restrictive means" of achieving the state's interest. *Bethany Baptist Church v. Deptford Township, 542 A.2d 505 (N.J. Super. 1988).*

EXAMPLE. A Pennsylvania court ruled that a church's property was entitled to exemption from the date the property was purchased, even though this was after the tax assessment date for the year, because a state law authorized the recognition of exemption for properties that were acquired and used for exempt purposes after the tax assessment date. *In re Jubilee Ministries International, 2 A.3d 706 (Pa. Cmwlth. 2010).*

EXAMPLE. A church purchased a parcel of land in March 1997. A local tax assessor later sued the church for unpaid property taxes. A court ruled that, under state law, the exempt status of property is determined on January 1 of each year, and since on January 1, 1997, the church did not own the property in question, it was not entitled to exemption. Many states have similar laws specifying that the tax status of property is determined on a specified date each year. It is for this reason that churches may have to pay property taxes for at least a portion of a year on newly acquired property, even if the property is immediately used for church purposes. *St. Joseph Orthodox Christian Church v. Spring Branch Independent School District, 2003 WL 1922580 (Tex. App. Houston 2003).*

Fees and special assessments

Does a state or local government have the authority to assess a fee or special assessment against church property in lieu of a direct tax? A few courts have addressed this question, with conflicting results.

EXAMPLE. A Florida appeals court ruled that churches can be required to pay special assessments only if their property is directly benefited. A county ordinance imposed special assessments against various property owners, including churches, to pay for fire and rescue services as well as storm-water management services. *Sarasota County v. Sarasota Church of Christ, 641 So.2d 900 (Fla. App. 2 Dist. 1994).*

EXAMPLE. A New Jersey appeals court ruled that an annual registration fee of $115 assessed against a church-operated school and childcare center was constitutionally permissible. The fee helped cover the cost of an annual inspection to determine compliance with state fire and safety regulations. The state appeals court observed: "If the primary purpose of a fee is to raise revenue, it is a tax. . . . In contrast to a tax, a fee is imposed under the government's police power to regulate [to promote the public health, safety, and welfare]. A fee is not judged a tax so long as the amount of the fee bears a reasonable relationship to the cost incurred by the government to regulate. If a fee's primary purpose is to reimburse the municipality for services reasonably related to development, it is a permissible regulatory exaction." *New Life*

Gospel Church v. Department of Community Affairs, 608 A.2d 397 (N.J. App. 1992).

EXAMPLE. A Wisconsin court ruled that a city could assess a fee against all utility customers, including churches, to pay for the cost of providing water in the event of a fire. A church refused to pay the additional fee, arguing that it amounted to an unconstitutional "tax" on religion in violation of the First Amendment.

A state appeals court observed that "the primary purpose of a tax is to obtain revenue for the government, while the primary purpose of a fee is to cover the expense of providing a service." It concluded that the additional charge added to utility customers' bills was a fee rather than a tax. *River Falls v. St. Bridget's Catholic Church, 513 N.W.2d 673 (Wis. App. 1994).*

EXAMPLE. A city ordinance exempted property "owned by any religious corporation actually dedicated and used exclusively as a place of public worship" from water and sewer charges. A city denied a church's request for exemption from these charges because the church property contained apartments for three staff members (the pastor, church business administrator, and a full-time teacher at a church-operated school). The city assessed $12,000 in back charges against the church and imposed a tax lien on the church's property. The church appealed. A state appeals court ruled that the exemption of religious corporations from water and sewer charges "should be interpreted as applying to all property used in furtherance of the corporation's purpose," and in this case "that would include the housing provided its pastor, teacher and administrator staff promoting the primary purpose of the institution." The court added that even if the staff members who were provided housing were not promoting the purposes of the church, the city should have granted a "partial exemption" for all of the church's property less the three apartments. The city's denial of any exemption was "legally wrong, arbitrary and capricious." *Bathelite Community Church v. Department of Environmental Protection, 797 N.Y.S.2d 707 (N.Y. Sup. Ct. 2004).*

EXAMPLE. An Illinois court ruled that a storm-drainage service charge based on the amount of a property owner's runoff surface was a fee, not a tax, that could be assessed against churches without violating a state law exempting churches from property taxation. *Church of Peace v. City of Rock Island, 2005 WL 1140427 (Ill. App. 2005).*

IRS EXAMINATIONS

A comprehensive review of church tax inquiries, church tax examinations, church records, religious activities, deadline for completing church tax inquiries, and so on … appears at the beginning of this chapter.

As noted at the beginning of this chapter, federal, state, and local governments have enacted a variety of tax laws to finance the costs of government. The applicability of any of these taxes to churches depends upon the following factors: (1) whether the statute that imposes the tax specifically exempts churches; (2) if churches are exempt, whether all conditions to exempt status have been satisfied; and (3) whether a tax that purports to apply to churches is permissible under state and federal constitutions.

It is a core principle of church finance that tax obligations and exemptions be understood and followed. Assisting church leaders in these basic and significant responsibilities is the purpose of this chapter.

Now, let's correctly explore the law in this area.

A church, like other 501(c)(3) organizations, must serve a public interest, rather than a private one, in order to establish and maintain its tax-exempt status. While nonprofit leaders and their advisors are generally aware of the "private inurement" prohibition and the prohibition of "excess benefit transactions" in federal tax law for 501(c)(3) organizations, there is less awareness and understanding of the prohibition of substantial "private benefit." While some people, on occasion, use the terms interchangeably, they are definitely not interchangeable. There are important distinctions between the private inurement prohibition (and the related excess benefit transaction prohibition) and the substantial private benefit prohibition. A little-known aspect of the substantial private benefit prohibition is the fact that an organization may violate the substantial private benefit prohibition, even if its transactions are at "fair value" terms or involve unrelated parties.

Private inurement and excess benefit transactions

Prior to 1996, if a nonprofit 501(c)(3) organization paid excessive compensation to its leaders or otherwise allowed its earnings to benefit private individuals (actions referred to as "private inurement"), the Internal Revenue Service (IRS) had only one enforcement tool available—revoking the organization's tax-exempt status. While revocation was appropriate in egregious cases, the measure was considered inappropriately harsh in many other situations. Revocation was also often viewed as an improper response, since it penalized the organization and, indirectly, the people who benefit from its charitable, religious, or educational mission, rather than the individuals who received the prohibited benefits or those who approved them.

In an effort to provide the IRS with more appropriate and effective options to administer the law, Congress adopted "intermediate sanctions" as part of the Taxpayer Bill of Rights in 1996. Now found in Section 4958 of the Internal Revenue Code, the intermediate sanctions law imposes excise tax penalties on individuals who receive an excess benefit from a 501(c)(3) organization, as well as organizational leaders who knowingly approve excess benefits.

An "excess benefit transaction" occurs when a 501(c)(3) organization makes a payment or provides an economic benefit to an organizational leader in which the payment or the value of the benefit exceeds the value of what the organization receives from the leader in exchange (including performance of services). Excessive or unreasonable compensation is an example of an excess benefit transaction. The amount by which a payment or benefit exceeds the value of what the organization receives in exchange is referred to as the "excess benefit amount."

Under current law, if a nonprofit leader (referred to in the law as a "disqualified person") receives an excess benefit, a two-tier penalty structure applies to that leader. First, a penalty of 25 percent of the excess benefit amount applies. Additionally, the leader must "correct" the excess benefit (generally by returning the value of the excess benefit to the nonprofit organization) within a specified timeframe. In the event that the excess benefit is not corrected in a timely manner, a second-tier penalty, equal to 200 percent of the excess benefit amount, applies to the leader.

Also under current law, nonprofit officers, board members, or their equivalent (referred to in the law as "orga-

nization managers") who knowingly approve an excess benefit transaction are individually subject to excise tax penalties as well—10 percent of the excess benefit amount, up to $20,000 for each excess benefit transaction.

The IRS may revoke the exempt status of an organization that engages in private inurement. However, Treasury Regulations provide that the IRS will consider the facts and circumstances of a violation and consider the significance and frequency of violations to determine whether revocation is appropriate.

Key elements of the private inurement and excess benefit transaction prohibitions

Private inurement or excess benefit transactions generally involve certain elements:

1. The transaction or arrangement must be between the organization and one of its insiders or leaders. As a general rule, it is not possible to engage in private inurement or an excess benefit transaction with a non-leader employee or with a party who is unrelated to the organization. Code Section 4958 specifically defines "disqualified persons" as organizational leader and parties related to

How Churches Can Still Help

Church leaders sometimes make the unfortunate mistake of refraining from helping specific people in need, or allowing steps to help those in need, due to an incorrect and misplaced fear of federal tax law. That fear sometimes is fueled by unnecessarily harsh or incorrect information provided by tax or legal professionals. Using terms such as "private inurement" or "private benefit," some attorneys, tax advisors, and authors incorrectly advise churches that they will "lose their tax-exempt status" if they engage in, or allow, certain activities, even though the truth may be quite different.

Let's establish from the outset one observable principle: There is no evidence that any church has ever lost its federal tax-exempt status for providing reasonable help, including financial help, to people in genuine need who are not leaders of the church. No matter how it was done. Period.

them. Case law with respect to the private inurement prohibition has generally held that a party must be an "insider" to the organization for the rule to apply.

2. The transaction must involve the 501(c)(3) organization transferring more value to the related party than the organization receives in exchange. Private inurement or excess benefit transactions do not generally exist when the terms of a transaction between a 501(c)(3) organization and a related party are at fair value, or at a higher value for the organization. For example, if an organization rents a building for use in its operations from one of its board members and pays the board member "fair rental value" for use of the property, the transaction would not ordinarily constitute an excess benefit transaction or private inurement.

Private benefit

Private inurement is a subset of private benefit but private benefit is a broader concept.

Federal tax regulations provide that an organization is not organized or operated exclusively for exempt purposes unless it serves a public, rather than private, interest. Thus, even if an organization has many activities that further exempt purposes, exemption may be precluded if it serves a private interest. Federal courts have ruled that the presence of private benefit, *if substantial in nature*, will destroy the exemption regardless of an organization's other charitable purposes or activities.[1]

The reason private benefit must rise to a "substantial" level in order to be problematic is very simple. All business and financial transactions confer some element of private benefit on one or more parties. Private benefit exists any time a party benefits from a transaction with a nonprofit 501(c)(3) organization. For example, when a church hires an unrelated vendor at fair market value to provide maintenance services for the organization's facilities, an element of private benefit occurs because the arrangement benefits the vendor. Payment of compensation by an organization to its employees provides some private benefit to the employees.

Accordingly, some amount of private benefit is inherent in the operations of any organization.

A 501(c)(3) organization crosses the line in the area of private benefit when such a benefit is **substantial**. As the IRS stated in its 1990 training materials for IRS agents, "In the charitable area, some private benefit may be unavoidable. The trick is to know when enough is enough."[2]

The IRS has also stated in its training materials that private benefit generally constitutes a benefit that is provided to a person or group other than the "charitable class" of people who are the ordinary beneficiaries of the organization's exempt activities (such as the needy, sick, homeless, spiritually lacking, and so on).[3]

Cases addressing private benefit have generally found that when an organization's activities substantially benefit people or groups other than the "charitable class," an organization does not qualify for 501(c)(3) exemption. An example is a nonprofit organization formed to promote interest and appreciation in classical music. When the IRS learned that a local for-profit radio station stood to benefit significantly from the organization's activities, the IRS denied 501(c)(3) status to the organization—even though the people who controlled the nonprofit organization were unrelated to the for-profit radio station.

CONCLUSION AND PRACTICAL CHURCH EXAMPLES – PEOPLE IN NEED

Church leaders can quickly discern whether a transaction or arrangement properly benefits appropriate individuals or parties. Here are three examples to help leaders understand the types of permissible arrangements they can establish:

EXAMPLE. The Wilson family attends Elm Church. A devastating home fire destroys most of their belongings and severely injures two of the family's three children. No member of the Wilson family is employed by the church or related to any leader of the church. The Wilson family's homeowners insurance policy did not cover all of its losses, nor did the policy cover the non-medical costs associated with meeting the needs of

1   See IRS EO CPE Text, 2001, "Private Benefit Under IRC 501(c)(3)" by Andrew Megosh, Lary Scollick, Mary Jo Salins and Cheryl Chasin.

2   IRS EO CPE Text, 1990, Overview of Inurement/Private Benefit Issues in IRC 501(c)(3).
3   See IRS EO CPE Text, 2001, "Private Benefit Under IRC 501(c)(3)" by Andrew Megosh, Lary Scollick, Mary Jo Salins and Cheryl Chasin.

the injured children. Many people at Elm Church want to help. The church's board decides to open a fund to meet the family's needs and allows people to give to the fund. The church obtains documentation supporting the amount of the Wilson family's needs and ensures that the assistance it provides the family does not exceed the documented need. The church informs its donors that any excess amounts contributed to the family's fund will be transferred to the church's general benevolence fund.

Does this activity by the church represent a violation of the private inurement, excess benefit transaction, or substantial private benefit prohibition?

No. Since the Wilsons are not leaders of the church or related to leaders of the church, it is not possible for any arrangement between the church and the Wilson family to constitute private inurement or an excess benefit transaction. Since people in need are part of the "charitable class" served by the church, the assistance provided by the church does not constitute substantial private benefit.

EXAMPLE. Assume the same facts as above, except that instead of the church establishing a fund to help the Wilson family, a few members of the church offer to give money to the church to help the Wilson family. The church members want to help anonymously by giving through the church. The givers realize they are not entitled to a charitable contribution deduction for their gifts because they are, in essence, gifts to the Wilson family and not to the church. The church is willing to accommodate the gifts for the Wilson family. The church accepts the gifts from the givers and transfers the funds to the Wilson family. In doing so, the church obtains documentation of the Wilson family's demonstrated financial need and ensures that the amount transferred does not exceed the need.

Does this activity by the church represent a violation of the private inurement, excess benefit transaction, or substantial private benefit prohibition?

No. Since the Wilsons are not leaders of the church or related to leaders of the church, it is not possible for any arrangement between the church and the Wilson family to constitute private inurement or an excess benefit transaction. Since people in need are part of the "charitable class" served by the church, the church's involvement does not constitute substantial private benefit. In fact, since the overall arrangement really represents a gift from the givers to the Wilson family, the church's assets are not significantly involved in the arrangement.

EXAMPLE. The Senior Adult Sunday School class of Elm Church learns that Sadie, the granddaughter of one of its class members, needs leg braces and her family cannot afford them. The Sunday school class decides to host a chicken dinner at the church to raise money for Sadie's leg braces. The class gives the event's net proceeds to Sadie's family to help pay for the braces. Sadie has no relationship to the church other than the fact that her grandmother is a member of the Sunday school class.

Does this activity by the church represent a violation of the private inurement, excess benefit transaction, or substantial private benefit prohibition?

No. Since Sadie is not a leader of the church or related to leaders of the church, it is not possible for any arrangement between the church and Sadie's family to constitute private inurement or an excess benefit transaction. Since Sadie is part of the "charitable class" served by the church (the needy), the church's involvement does not constitute substantial private benefit. In this case, the small and isolated nature of the activity to aid this person also strongly supports this conclusion.

Sadly, church leaders occasionally receive poor advice with respect to arrangements like the ones used in the Wilson family and Sadie examples above, causing them to stop the church or Sunday school class from conducting the activities to help.

But as noted above, there is no evidence that any church has ever lost its federal tax-exempt status for providing reasonable help—including financial help—to people in genuine need who are not leaders of the church. And without regard to that fact, imagine the public relations nightmare the IRS would face if it revoked a church's exempt status for helping such people. That is not a realistic possibility.

9

Tax Law Compliance: A Priority for Financial Management

Chapter 10

Insurance and Risk Financing

THE ROLE OF INSURANCE

Insurance is one of the most common, if not the most fundamental, devices that churches use to engage in risk management at the organizational level. In many cases, it is the only formal risk management strategy that leaders may focus on with any regularity, and that may occur only when the policy is up for renewal. Furthermore, most church leaders have little, if any, understanding of the nature of their insurance coverage, and may not even know the name of their insurance company.

Insurance plays an important risk management role in most organizations. It does not, however, prevent losses. Rather, insurance is a risk financing technique that provides funds for losses that the insurance policy covers. As such, insurance is not really a risk management strategy that addresses the broad concerns of both loss prevention and loss control. Rather, insurance is a means of transferring some or all of the costs associated with certain losses in exchange for the payment of a premium. For most churches and schools, the primary concern is to have enough insurance coverage to provide financial protection for those losses that they cannot or do not want to bear on their own.

When thinking about insurance, leaders should consider it within the broader scope of the church's risk financing strategy. Risk financing is but one aspect of an overall financial management strategy. Furthermore, a risk financing strategy should take into account the frequency and severity of the risks that the church faces, the potential financial consequences of those risks, the viable alternatives available for loss prevention, loss control, and risk financing, the financial capabilities of the church, and how leaders desire to use their financial resources. Each of these factors should impact decision making concerning the purchase of insurance.

FREQUENCY AND SEVERITY OF RISKS

Most churches need and desire insurance coverage for losses that have a high degree of severity regardless of the frequency. Examples include a fire that destroys a sanctuary or a lawsuit involving sexual misconduct. Both can require large amounts of money to recover from the loss that often exceed a congregation's financial ability. However, in both cases a congregation may

be able to sustain part of that financial burden, and in turn, that affects how much of the risk a congregation is willing to retain. From an insurance viewpoint, that may translate in increasing or decreasing the deductible amount a church carries with its property or liability coverage. In turn, that affects the amount of the premium. Losses with low severity create a different set of options. As the severity and frequency of a loss declines, leaders may decide to retain more of the financing needed to respond to the loss if it should occur. This leads to consideration of the second factor, the potential financial consequences of any given risk.

FINANCIAL CONSEQUENCES

As a general rule, churches transfer risks associated with catastrophic losses. From a practical standpoint, however, most leaders do not evaluate the financial risk associated with every loss. Rather, insurance is purchased that covers a wide range of property and liability losses. Church leaders, however, may not fully understand the degree to which certain risks are retained, the potential costs associated with these risks, and the limits of the policy or how much of the risk is actually being transferred by the purchase of insurance.

For example, a church may have $1 million of property coverage. However, the church building may have a true value of $1.5 million. In essence the church only has two-thirds of the value of the building insured. Suppose a fire occurs and creates $900,000 in damage. Church leaders may think they are fully covered since the church has insurance coverage of $1 million. However, if the insurance policy contains a coinsurance clause that requires the building to be insured to its full value, the insurance company is obligated to pay the church only two-thirds of the loss, or $600,000. In essence, the church is retaining one-third of any property loss because it only has insured the building for two-thirds of its value.

Or consider the following situation. A church is sued for a claim of sexual misconduct. The church has $1 million of liability coverage. However, the insurance company declines the claim, noting that the policy endorsements exclude coverage for sexual misconduct. Perhaps none of the church leaders carefully read the exclusions, or they read them but did not understand the potential risk of a sexual misconduct claim. Or in a similar case, the church has $100,000 for sexual misconduct, but the total costs associated with the claim exceed $200,000. The church is liable for amounts above the $100,000 limit. Church leaders may not have understood that such claims can exceed the limits of their policy.

The failure to understand what is not covered, the amount of coverage that is available (which is not necessarily the same thing as the limits of the policy), and the potential severity of a risk can be devastating to a church. To make good decisions concerning risk financing, church leaders need to understand the financial consequences of the risks they face, the nature of the insurance coverage they are buying, and the alternatives that should be considered in addition to insurance. In all cases, churches will want to establish certain thresholds of coverage that will protect them if a worst-case scenario should occur.

RISK FINANCING ALTERNATIVES

Since most churches put little thought into risk management to begin with, it follows that not much attention is given to the consideration of risk financing alternatives other than insurance. Part of the problem is that frequently no one on the church staff or in a position of leadership has the background in risk management or the time to analyze risk management issues. As a result, many leaders depend almost exclusively upon their insurance agent to guide them concerning these concerns. What alternatives should the church and its leaders consider with respect to insurance as the sole source of risk financing? Some of the more common ones are discussed below.[1]

Paying for losses out of cash flow

Some losses are minimal and the typical church can pay for small losses out of the weekly cash flow. The amount of discretionary money that is available from cash flow is one factor that a church should use in evaluating deductibles for both property and liability coverage. As the deductible increases, the premium decreases. The offset in the premium can be applied toward potential losses. Naturally, the lower premium is also offset by the retained risk that the church is as-

suming. However, retaining that risk may make sense based on the loss history.

Paying for losses out of cash reserves

The same principle holds true for paying losses out of savings as for paying out of cash flow. Churches can designate some portion of their savings as a reserve for potential losses. As the reserve increases in size, it enables a church to purchase insurance with higher deductibles. Those savings can be applied toward the cash reserve. Of course, the church is retaining higher levels of risk, but when this is done in an informed way, it can be the best choice from a financial management perspective.

Paying for losses using borrowed funds

Leaders can plan in advance to use borrowed funds to pay for specific levels of losses. To be safe, though, a line of credit should be established with a bank or other lender for that specific purpose. The terms of the loan should be clear in advance. To plan properly, church leaders need to know interest rates and repayment terms.

Transferring risks through contracts other than insurance

In addition to purchasing insurance or retaining risks, churches can also transfer certain risks through the use of noninsurance contracts. One way of transferring risk financing is through the use of indemnity agreements, sometimes referred to as hold harmless agreements. For example, suppose a church sponsors a trip to a foreign country to help build a new church building. The church may require that each adult participant on that trip sign an agreement to hold the church harmless with respect to any losses that the individual may incur on the trip. Or a church may require that an outside group that uses church facilities indemnify the church for any losses that may occur during the use of the facilities by the outside group. Indemnification does not lower the risk of a particular loss. Rather, it transfers a financial responsibility if the loss should occur.

One of the problems of these contracts is enforcement. Contracts can be poorly written or legally invalid. Sometimes the party with whom the church enters into an agreement may not be able to fulfill the terms of the contract. When used appropriately and done right, however, indemnification agreements can be important devices for transferring financial burdens associ-

1 For a detailed discussion of these options see George L. Head, et. al., *Essentials of Risk Financing*, Third Edition (Malvern, PA: Insurance Institute of America, 1996).

ated with specific risks. Church leaders should always use the services of a competent attorney in preparing indemnification or hold harmless agreements.

FINANCIAL CAPABILITIES

To make an informed decision concerning risk financing, leaders need to examine the financial capabilities of the church based upon the factors that have been discussed above. Questions that require an answer include the following:

- How much discretionary money does the church have available from its cash flow that can be devoted to risk financing?
- How much money is available from savings that can be set aside for risk financing?
- How much credit can the church obtain and afford to pay for potential future losses?
- How much of a financial burden with respect to risk financing can the church afford to retain?
- What financial burdens can the church shift through contracts other than insurance?

FINANCIAL GOALS

Each church will have unique risk financing needs. They will also have different financial capabilities and goals. In establishing financial goals with respect to risk financing, one starting point is to determine two factors: (1) how much risk financing is needed for property, and (2) how much risk financing is needed for liability. Of the two, the property amount is easier to calculate because it can be derived from an objective analysis of church assets. Liability, on the other hand, is difficult to calculate with accuracy. Many factors affect potential liability, including the nature of the alleged offense, the degree of culpability, the actual harm to others, the available defenses, the jurisdiction of the case, the potential for a settlement, the means of settlement, and the potential perspective and values of a jury if a case goes to trial. While precedent can be used as a basis for analysis, it is not always a good guide.

Many churches now carry $2 million or more of liability coverage. However, that figure is somewhat misleading because some claims are not typically covered under a church's general liability policy. For example,

coverage for sexual misconduct, directors and officers, and employment practices usually require separate policies. Then the amounts of liability coverage available may vary from one company to another.

Based on their best judgment, leaders should establish threshold levels of risk financing for both property and liability coverage. Then, using a table such as the one below, a determination can be made on how the risk financing will occur. In every case, insurance will play a dominant role in providing catastrophic coverage.

1. Total risk financing needed: $_____

   Should equal the sum of the following:

2. amount from cash flow (per year):* $_____

3. amount from savings: $_____

4. amount available from line of credit: $_____

5. amount from insurance: $_____

   * takes into account payments if line of credit is also used.

How a church determines the amounts for lines 2-5 will depend upon many factors. Some will have a sizeable cash flow with discretionary money as well as savings that they may dedicate to risk financing. Others with the same financial means may be unwilling to devote any extra funds to risk financing other than what is needed to meet the church's deductible on its insurance policy. Another church may have no savings or extra funds available at all. It may have no choice but to be fully dependent on insurance.

A church's philosophy of ministry affects its financial goals and risk financing should fit into that philosophy by maintaining consistency with the financial goals of the institution. However, that process may not be as simple as it first appears. As a church adjusts it deductibles, premiums are affected. One task that each institution faces is to establish a balance between overall costs and benefits. Churches that want primarily catastrophic insurance coverage will retain higher levels of risk, and correspondingly should have the financial means available to pay for losses as needed. Leaders must also bear the emotional cost of bearing those risks. Churches that want to transfer as much of the financial burden as possible will have low deductibles and must be willing to pay higher insurance premiums for that benefit. In addition, they also get the peace of mind that comes with the insurance coverage. It is not that one approach is better; each simply reflects different philosophies and strategies regarding financial management.

THE INSURANCE CONTRACT

Most church insurance policies follow a similar format and structure that includes declarations, common conditions, and specific forms for each line of coverage. The declarations contain basic information about the policy, including the name of the insured, the inception and termination date of the policy, the policy number, and the amount of the premium. The common conditions include information that applies to several categories of coverage, such as property and liability. That way the information does not have to be repeated for each line of coverage that is purchased. Finally, forms are then used to address the specific provisions for each line of insurance.

Endorsements

Endorsements (sometimes called *riders* in health and life insurance policies) are used to change the insurance policy. An endorsement can expand coverage, reduce coverage, add a new provision to the policy, or modify an existing provision of the policy. An endorsement can be handwritten, typed, or a preprinted form. If legal, an endorsement takes precedence over the standard policy.

Exclusions

All church insurance policies contain exclusions. An exclusion is a claim that is not covered under an insurance policy. It is important for church leaders to be familiar with the exclusions set forth in their church's liability insurance policy, since these represent potentially uninsured claims that can expose the church to substantial damages. Further, the church would have to retain and compensate its own attorney if it issued on the basis of an excluded claim.

Common exclusions include intentional or criminal misconduct, injuries occurring outside of the United States, employment-related claims, and injuries caused by exposure to hazardous substances. Some policies exclude claims arising out of incidents of sexual misconduct. Church leaders may want to discuss with their church insurance agent the possibility of obtaining insurance to cover exclusions.

Deductibles

Deductibles are a common part of insurance policies. The deductible is an amount the insured must first pay before the insurance company becomes liable for financing the loss. For example, if the church has a $2,500 deductible and has an insured loss of $10,000, then the church pays the first $2,500 and the insurance company pays the balance of $7,500. As the deductible increases, the premium for the policy decreases. The deductible applies to each occurrence.

Duties in the event of a loss

The insurance will state what the reporting requirements of the insured are in the event a loss occurs. Generally, the insured must report the loss in a timely way and safeguard the property following a loss. Failure to properly notify the insurance company can void the coverage.

INSURANCE COVERAGE

For many church leaders, insurance coverage can be confusing and complex. When purchasing or reviewing coverage, it is helpful to break the coverage down into specific areas, and then to focus on one area at a time as noted below:

- *Property Insurance.* The main concern is the insurance of buildings and contents. Property insurance has levels of complexity because of what is included or excluded in the policy. As a result, leaders must be very careful to understand the "forms" that are used to write the policy. The options available are discussed in more detail in the following section on property insurance.
- *Liability Insurance.* Liability insurance provides coverage for civil claims. Liability coverage is generally divided into general liability, automobile liability, and workers compensation and employers liability. Each area is written as a separate policy. Some additional liability coverages are

important for churches, including directors and officers insurance, counseling or professional liability, sexual misconduct coverage, and corporal punishment and excess medical claims.

- *Workers Compensation and Employers Liability.* As a form of liability coverage, workers compensation and employers liability are handled as separate policies. This coverage is vital for churches, yet many churches do not obtain it.
- *Automobile Insurance.* Attention must be given to a broad range of concerns, including liability coverage, medical payments, uninsured or underinsured motorists, collision coverage, comprehensive coverage for physical damage or losses other than from collision, the use of non-owned vehicles, and the use of employee and volunteer drivers.
- *Excess or Umbrella Insurance.* It is advisable for churches to purchase additional insurance that goes beyond the limits of the basic policies. This is generally done by obtaining excess or umbrella insurance.

Each of these categories of insurance is discussed in more detail in the following sections.

PROPERTY INSURANCE

Property coverage is vital to most churches. Property coverage, however, is divided up into a variety of "forms," including special form, basic form, and broad form. Each form has a different purpose and defines what is included or excluded from insurance coverage. The *Special Form* covers everything that the policy does not specifically exclude. It provides the broadest coverage available, and as a result, is often selected. The *Basic Form* and the *Broad Form* are more limited and cover only those perils that are specifically named in the policy. Leaders should ask the insurance agent to explain the purpose of each form, what the form covers, and what is not covered. Take time to understand the coverage provided for each of the following areas:

- *Perils insured/causes of loss.* This is a good place to start. Have the agent explain basic form, broad form, special form, earthquake form, flood insurance, and other additional considerations. Know what is covered and what is excluded. If

something is excluded, ask if it is covered on a different form, and then review the specifics of that coverage to determine if it is something you need. Each of these concerns is addressed later in this section.

- *Buildings and contents.* Make sure you have a clear written definition of what is included in your building coverage. Built-in items, such as a pipe organ, pews, sound systems, and other permanently installed equipment are actually a part of the building in the valuation of your property. Review such items with your agent to determine what is valued as part of the *building* and what is valued as part of the *contents.* Also, property that is taken off the premises may not be covered. Consider having an independent replacement cost appraisal for both the building and its contents. You want to make sure you are adequately insured.
- *Personal business property.* Be aware that items of personal business property, such as musical instruments, pieces of art, computers, and so on, may require separate coverage. Review this concern with your agent. Discuss how personal property is defined, when and where it is covered, and for how much.
- *Personal property.* Know what coverage exists for property left on church premises by staff, church members, and others. For example, what would happen if an expensive coat was stolen during a church service? Would it be covered by the church's insurance?
- *Debris removal.* Debris often is left after a natural disaster, such as a hurricane, earthquake, tornado, or even a strong storm. Know what coverage is provided.
- *Coverage extensions.* Review with the agent all valuable furnishings, musical instruments, jewelry, silverware, antiques, artifacts, art, cameras, sound studios, TV studios, valuable papers, outdoor property, libraries, stained glass, bell towers, carillons, and other unique items that may require special coverage.
- *Business interruption.* This insures loss of income and pays expenses during a recovery period following a loss. For example, a church building may be destroyed by fire and the congregation is unable to meet for several weeks. The church's

income may dwindle during the recovery period. This insurance helps to cover those shortfalls.

Property coverage is provided on a *per occurrence* basis. That means that each individual claim is covered up to the limits of the policy.

The insurance coverage that you actually have is affected by a number of additional factors. Review with the agent the following policy provisions: deductibles, the valuation of property, inflation guard, coinsurance, and agreed value. In order to obtain the full level of coverage needed, also examine the following additional insurance considerations with the agent:

- Blanket insurance
- Builder's risk insurance
- Plate glass insurance
- Boiler and machinery insurance
- Personal property coverage
- Inland marine insurance
- Flood insurance
- Earthquake insurance
- Fidelity bonds
- Additional crime insurance
- Sewer, drain, and sump backup insurance

Each of these issues is discussed below.

Deductibles

Examine how changing the deductible affects the cost of the premium. Know how and when the deductible is to be paid. Ask how the deductible is affected by the coinsurance clause (discussed below).

The valuation of property

If a property loss occurs, the valuation is based on one of two options: *actual cash value* or *replacement cost*. The actual cash value is based on the depreciated value of the property. A church that has a policy with actual cash value would not be able to replace the lost property with new property without incurring additional expense. On the other hand, replacement cost provides funds to replace the property. Most policyholders prefer replacement cost over actual cash value. In some cases, a church may own a facility that is too large for the needs of the congregation. For example, many inner city churches have older, ornate buildings that

are costly to maintain and too large for existing space demands. In such cases a congregation may choose *functional replacement cost* that would enable them to build a smaller facility.

⦿ **KEY POINT.** If a church has expensive stained glass windows, they should be insured separately. In addition, attention should be given to other specialized property concerns such as carillons, chimes, pipe organs, steeples, bell towers, and fountains.

Inflation guard

Some policies contain an inflation guard provision where the amount of the insurance coverage is automatically increased to account for changes in value due to inflation.

Coinsurance and agreed value

Ask the agent to review whether your policy contains a *coinsurance clause* or uses an *agreed value*. If present, the coinsurance clause is an important part of the policy, and one that is not well understood by church leaders. Here is how it works. In exchange for a reduction in the premium, the insurance company requires that the church maintain coverage equal to a specified percentage of the property's value, generally between 80 percent and 100 percent. If the church fails to maintain the specified level of coverage and a loss should occur, then the benefit is lowered based on the following formula:

$$\frac{\text{amount of insurance carried}}{\text{amount of insurance required}} \times \text{amount of loss} = \text{amount paid}$$

EXAMPLE. First Church is required to insure its building for 80 percent of its actual value in exchange for a premium discount. The building has a fire and the loss is calculated at $900,000. The value of the building is determined to be $2 million. Based on the coinsurance clause, the church should have the building insured for at least 80 percent of its value or $1.6 million ($2,000,000 x .80). First Church has the building insured for $1,500,000. Based on the coinsurance clause, the insurance company would pay the following amount for the loss:

$$\frac{\$1,500,000}{\$1,600,000} \times \$900,000 = \$843,750$$

Church leaders need to monitor both the value of the building and the amount of their insurance coverage to make sure it is adequate. For coinsurance, the value of the building is calculated at the time of the loss and not at the time the insurance is purchased. When the insurance is first purchased, some effort generally is made to determine the market value of the building. As time passes, however, the value can change based on many different factors. The responsibility for maintaining adequate insurance rests with the insured, in this case the church, and not with the insurance company.

➤ TIP. When comparing the policies of two or more insurance companies, see if the deductible applies before or after the coinsurance penalty is calculated.

Another option is to remove the co-insurance penalty through an endorsement of *agreed value*. With agreed value, a penalty clause does not exist and the insurance company pays up to the limit of the policy. This reduces the potential for conflict if a claim does occur.

ADDITIONAL CONSIDERATIONS

Blanket insurance

Sometimes a church may own multiple buildings at a single location, or property at more than one location. Leaders may purchase *specific insurance* for each building or they may buy what is known as *blanket insurance*. Blanket insurance provides coverage for all of the buildings under one policy. The advantage of blanket insurance is that the total amount of the insurance may be applied to any single building. The disadvantage is that it might cost more and may have a stricter coinsurance clause. Churches with multiple buildings should compare blanket insurance and specific insurance.

Builder's risk insurance

If a church is constructing a new building it should carefully review the insurance coverage it has for the building during the process of construction, and what happens to that insurance once the building is completed. Building programs carry many risks and it is important to understand the insurance coverage and risks associated with the contractor, subcontractors, and anyone else who has an insurable interest in the building.

Plate glass insurance

While glass breakage is covered with the buildings, important exclusions and limits do apply and leaders should be familiar with those provisions. Many churches have expensive stained glass windows that require special coverage.

Boiler and machinery insurance

Churches that heat with boilers should consider this insurance, which may include the inspection of the boiler. Hazards associated with boilers are usually not included in the other property forms. Boiler accidents can create substantial damage. Also included is coverage for a range of equipment that churches commonly own, such as copiers, duplicating equipment, fax machines, phone systems, and computers. Several different forms exist for boiler and machinery coverage. Have each one explained.

Personal property

Often, staff members and church members leave personal items at the church, such as computers, pieces of art, personal libraries, or musical instruments. Carefully review the insurance coverage for each item with your agent. Unless additional coverage is purchased, items of personal property will have minimal coverage.

Inland marine coverage

The purpose of inland marine coverage (which has no apparent connection with its name) is to insure property that is taken off premises or is in transit. It also covers property that is very expensive, fragile, or unique in nature, such as historical artifacts or pieces of art.

The National Flood Insurance Program

Flood insurance is under the jurisdiction of the Federal Emergency Management Association (FEMA), but the insurance can be sold through private companies. Churches located in flood zones should review this program with their agent.

Earthquake insurance

Earthquake coverage is written as a separate form. Carefully review the deductible and the rating factor (brick/masonry, brick veneer, or frame) used to classify your building. Make sure your building is properly classified.

Fidelity Bonds

Fidelity Bonds are used to insure against embezzlement, theft, forgery, and fraud that may be committed by an employee. A church may purchase either *schedule bonds* or *blanket bonds*. Schedule bonds cover either specific employees or positions. A specific number of people are listed if the bond covers a position. Leaders must be careful to monitor the number of people who fill a covered position to ensure that the number employed corresponds to the number covered by the bond. On the other hand, a blanket bond provides blanket coverage for all employees, including new ones. One important exclusion on fidelity bonds is based on prior knowledge. If the church as employer becomes aware of prior dishonesty on the part of a covered employee, losses then caused by that employee become excluded from coverage. Make sure the coverage applies to the loss of monies that may occur while being taken for deposit.

Additional crime insurance

Many churches experience burglary of everything from computer equipment to lawn mowers. Churches are viewed as easy targets because they are often empty, and may even be unlocked. Churches can purchase additional crime insurance for the following:

- Theft, Disappearance, and Destruction (covers the disappearance or theft of money and securities).
- Robbery and Safe Burglary (covers property other than money or securities when the robbery includes an act of force or intimidation or when someone clearly witnesses the unlawful act. If a safe is burglarized it must be the result of forced entry).
- Premises Burglary (covers property, such as furnishings and equipment, when there is evidence of a forced entry or exit, but does not cover money or securities).
- Forgery and Alteration Coverage (covers the forged or altered use of stolen checks).

Sewer, drain, or sump pump backup

If damage occurs due to a sewer, drain, or sump pump backup, the insurance coverage is generally excluded or limited from most policies. Additional coverage can be purchased separately.

LIABILITY INSURANCE

The insurance industry has undergone a major shift with respect to liability coverage. Trends that began in the business community have spread into the nonprofit sector, including the church. In particular, three specific trends are evident. First, premiums have increased. Second, coverage has been reduced or more narrowly defined. Third, some companies have stopped providing coverage for some risks.

These trends have occurred with respect to medical malpractice in the health sector, product liability in the commercial sector, and sexual misconduct within the church. The problem with liability coverage is predicting the cost of potential litigation and claims. For example, a large denominational group located in the northeastern United States paid for a professional assessment of their potential liability risks over the next five years with respect to sexual misconduct claims. The report came back with an estimated amount somewhere between $5 million to $50 million. During the early 1990s, some church insurance companies began to limit or withdraw coverage for sexual misconduct claims. That trend is now starting to change. Limits are beginning to increase once again, but they are generally tied to loss control measures to reduce the exposure.

The classes of liability insurance

Liability insurance is divided into three classes that include general liability, workers compensation and employer's liability, and automobile liability.

General liability

The general liability of churches is connected to the following areas of exposure:

Premises Liability. A church or school may be responsible if a person is injured or if property is damaged as the result of some condition arising from the premises. The theory is so general that almost any cause can be argued as causing an injury. For example, failure to keep a playground in safe condition could lead to premises liability.

Conduct of Operations. Liability can arise out of the normal conduct of operations by employees or volunteers, either on the property or away from it.

For example, a volunteer driving a church van may cause an accident in which people are injured.

Completed Operations. Liability can arise out of some work that has been performed, but turns out to be defective. For example, a church could build a soccer goal that later falls because it is not properly balanced and injures a child.

Product Liability. The faulty design or a defect in a product can result in product liability. Generally, product liability does not affect churches.

Contract Liability. A church could, on the basis of a contract, become liable for the actions of another person. For example, a subcontractor doing work for the church may require the church to indemnify the subcontractor for any claims that arise out of the work that is performed.

Contingencies. A church could be held liable for the work of a third party. For example, if the church exercised sufficient control or supervision over the work, liability could arise. This form of liability often surfaces with respect to the work of independent contractors.

Additional liability coverage

Directors and officers insurance. Should churches obtain "directors and officers" insurance coverage for the members of their board? Does the enactment of the Volunteer Protection Act (and corresponding state laws) make such insurance unnecessary? Not at all. The legal protection provided by these laws is not absolute. They do not apply if a board member receives any form of compensation (in some states, travel expense reimbursements are excluded from the definition of "compensation"), and they do not apply if a board member is accused of gross negligence. Directors and officers insurance will provide coverage for such exceptions. Just as importantly, the insurance company is responsible for providing legal representation in the event a director or officer is sued directly.

Directors and officers insurance may also provide coverage for certain injuries or damages not covered under the church's general liability policy.

EXAMPLE. An Alabama court ruled that a church's "directors and officers" insurance policy covered a lawsuit brought against a pastor for improperly obtaining money from an elderly member.[2] The daughter of an elderly church member was appointed guardian of her mother's property. The daughter sued the minister of her mother's church, claiming that he improperly obtained funds from her mother by means of conversion, fraud, and undue influence. The minister notified the church's "directors and officers" insurer of the lawsuit and asked the insurer to provide him with a legal defense. The insurer asked a court to determine whether or not the minister's actions were covered under the insurance policy. The court concluded that the insurer had a legal duty to provide the minister with a defense of the lawsuit. It noted that the church's insurance policy provided coverage for officers and directors (including the minister in this case) in any lawsuit brought against them by reason of alleged dishonesty on their part unless a court determined that the officer or director acted with deliberate dishonesty. Since the minister had not yet been found guilty of "deliberate dishonesty," he was covered under the insurance policy. The court acknowledged that if the minister was found to have acted with deliberate dishonesty in the daughter's lawsuit, the insurer would have no duty to pay any portion of the judgment or verdict.

It is a good practice for churches to obtain directors and officers insurance for the members of their governing board, for the following reasons:

- Board members who receive any form of compensation are not protected by state and federal laws that extend "limited immunity" to officers and directors of churches and other nonprofit organizations. It is much easier for these board members to be sued personally. Directors and officers insurance will provide the board members with a legal defense to any lawsuit involving a covered claim, and pay any judgment or settlement up to the policy limits.
- Board members who engage in gross negligence or willful and wanton misconduct are not protected by state and federal laws that extend "limited immunity" to officers and directors of churches and other nonprofit organizations. It is much easier for these board members to be sued personally. In many cases, lawsuits naming board members as defendants will allege that they engaged in such behavior. To illustrate, assume that a child is molested by a volunteer youth worker who had not been screened by a church because

---

2   *Graham v. Preferred Abstainers Insurance Company, 689 So.2d 188 (Ala. App. 1997).*

the board flatly opposed any screening program or procedures. The lawsuit alleges that the board members acted with gross negligence in failing to implement a screening program. Had they done so, they would have discovered that the offender had been convicted of child molestation in the past. Directors and officers insurance will provide the board members with a legal defense to any lawsuit involving a covered claim, and pay any judgment or settlement up to the policy limits.

- Directors and officers insurance may cover certain claims that are excluded under the church's general liability policy.
- Directors and officers insurance is relatively inexpensive.

Counseling or professional liability. Today, many churches provide a wide range of counseling programs that involve both paid and volunteer counselors. In selecting coverage for counseling activities, it is best to choose a "blanket format" that covers all individuals, paid or unpaid, that provide counseling services. The other option, "position" coverage, is limited to listed positions such as a pastor or a staff counselor.

Sexual misconduct. Sexual misconduct coverage is vital to every church and provides coverage if a claim of sexual misconduct occurs. These claims can be very expensive and no church should be without this coverage. The amount of coverage available may depend upon whether the church has a screening program in place. It is in the interest of every organization to reduce this risk through proper screening and supervision, and to maximize the insurance coverage available.

Employment practices. Liability associated with employment practices is a growing concern for all organizations, including churches. This coverage provides protection against employment-related litigation involving wrongful termination, discrimination, and other such claims.

Corporal punishment and excess medical claims. Another special area of concern is insurance coverage for churches that operate schools or daycare facilities. Coverage for corporal punishment and excess medical payments should be discussed with the insurance agent.

Punitive Damages

Church insurance policies exclude punitive damages. This means that a jury award of punitive damages represents an uninsured risk. As a result, it is important for church leaders to understand the basis for punitive damages. Punitive damages are damages awarded by a jury "in addition to compensation for a loss sustained, in order to punish, and make an example of, the wrongdoer." They are awarded when a defendant's conduct is particularly reprehensible and outrageous. This does not necessarily mean intentional misconduct. Punitive damages often are associated with reckless conduct or conduct creating a high risk of harm. Unfortunately, it is not uncommon for church leaders to ignore significant risks. Church leaders must understand that reckless inattention to such risks can lead to punitive damages, and that such damages may not be covered by the church's liability insurance policy.

Liability coverage: occurrence versus claims-made

Liability coverage can be written under two different forms: *occurrence form* and *claims-made form*.

Occurrence form. This policy requires that the insurance company pay for any losses that arise during the policy period, regardless of when the claim is made. The occurrence form has been the traditional approach to liability coverage. For example, suppose a person slips and falls and files a claim against the church six months later. Under the occurrence form, the policy in effect at the time of the loss (six months ago) would cover the claim, regardless of who the current insurer is. Suppose a child is sexually molested at a church program when he is six years old and then files a claim against the church 12 years later. Under the occurrence form, the policy in effect at the time of the loss would cover the claim, even if that policy is now expired and the church has a different insurance company. In such a situation, though, many churches would have no idea of who their insurance carrier was 12 years ago, and would have no idea of where the policy is located. This illustrates the importance of saving insurance policies. A church or school that maintains an occurrence form on a continual basis will not have any gaps in its coverage, but it must maintain ongoing and permanent records of its insurance coverage.

10

Insurance and Risk Financing

Claims-made form. Under this form, the insurance company covers those claims made while the insurance is in force, generally retroactive to a specific date. Here is how it works. Historically, churches and all other organizations have used the occurrence form. If a church switches to a claims-made form, the insurance company agrees to cover any insured claim after a specific date as long as the policy remains active. Since the church already has coverage for past incidents based on previous insurance coverage using an occurrence form, no need exists to duplicate that coverage. An insurance company can, however, agree to write a policy without a retroactive date or to select one that overlaps with earlier coverage. Why would a church switch from an occurrence form to a claims-made form? One reason may be cost. The claims-made form is generally less expensive. The other reason, though, may be concern about past liability exposures. Suppose, for example, that a church feels it may be liable for injuries that occurred in the past and may face a claim for which it has inadequate coverage. Perhaps it is concerned that a claim may surface for the sexual molestation of a child. An insurance company may agree to write a new policy with a retroactive date that goes back a number of years. The church may feel more confident with new, higher levels of coverage than it had in the past.

Churches must be very careful when they switch from an occurrence form to a claims-made form or from one company to another. Suppose, for example, that a church has a claims-made form with a retroactive date of January 1, 1985. Prior to that time it had an occurrence form, so the coverage remains uninterrupted. Then, on January 1, 2001, it began a new policy with a different company and continues using a claims-made form. However, the new company establishes the retroactive date as January 1, 1999. Perhaps no one at the church pays attention to the date or understands its significance. Suddenly the church is left with no liability coverage for the period beginning January 1, 1985 up to January 1, 1999. The previous claims-made form is no longer in effect (although some extended reporting provisions stay in effect for a limited time), and the new claims-made form only covers claims beginning with January 1, 1999. In order for the church to maintain continuous coverage, each new policy must use the same retroactive date as the first claims-made form. Again, if a church switches from a claims-made form to an occurrence form,

it faces potential gaps in its liability coverage. Such a change should be fully discussed with the church's insurance agent and the church may need to obtain supplemental extended reporting period coverage.

Which form is best? The answer must be considered on a case-by-case basis. The advantage of a claims-made form is that it covers past losses which may be inadequately insured, and that could surface and pose serious liability for the church. In fact, that has happened with regard to some sexual misconduct claims. On the other hand, if a church has had adequate coverage in the past, and has retained all of its past insurance policies, it may conclude that maintaining occurrence coverage is in its best interests. A church that maintains ongoing occurrence coverage should have no gaps in its liability insurance. Churches that switch to claims-made coverage, or change from one company to another while maintaining a claims-made form, or switch from claims-made to occurrence coverage, must take special precautions—or a gap could surface in their liability coverage.

The chart on the next page summarizes the advantages and disadvantages of both forms of coverage.

WORKERS COMPENSATION AND EMPLOYERS LIABILITY

Workers compensation laws have been enacted in all 50 states. These laws provide compensation to employees as a result of job-related injuries and illnesses. The amount of compensation is determined by law and generally is based upon the nature and extent of the employee's disability. In exchange for such benefits, employees give up the right to sue an employer directly. Fault is irrelevant under workers compensation laws. The only questions are (1) did an employment relationship exist; (2) did the injury occur during the course of employment; and (3) what were the nature and extent of the injuries?

Workers compensation laws are founded on the premise that job-related injuries and illnesses are inevitable and should be allocated between the employer and the consumer as a cost of doing business. This is accomplished, in most cases, by the employer purchasing insurance to cover the costs of workers compensation benefits, with the cost of such insurance being passed on to consumers through price adjustments. As a result, the ultimate cost of an employee's work-related injury or illness is borne by the consumers of the product or service that the employee was hired to produce.

Churches are exempted from workers compensation laws in a few states. A few more states exempt activities not carried on for monetary gain, and some states exempt any employer having less than a prescribed number of employees. The crucial question is whether churches are exempt from those workers compensation laws that contain no specific exemption of churches, nonprofit organizations, or organizations employing less than a prescribed number of employees.

Most courts that have addressed the coverage of churches under workers compensation laws have concluded that churches are subject to workers compensation laws unless specifically exempted. One court stated the rule as follows:

> [T]he fact that [a religious organization] is a purely charitable enterprise does not of itself release [it] from the obligations of our workers compensation act, which, unlike the acts of some states, does not except charitable or religious institutions, as such, from its operation, nor exclude their employees from its benefits. Where the relationship of employer and employee actually exists between a charitable institution and an injured workman, the latter is entitled to the benefits of our act, otherwise not.[3]

EXAMPLE. A federal court in Ohio rejected the claim that subjecting churches to workers compensation laws violates their constitutional rights.[4] A church argued that the state of Ohio, through its workers compensation system, had "assumed lordship over the church in direct contravention to the biblical principle that Jesus is 'head over all things to the church' (Eph. 1:22) and that 'in all things [Christ] might have preeminence' (Col. 1:18)." In addition, the church argued that "it would be a sin to contribute to workers compensation out of church funds designated for biblical purposes and that tithe and offering money . . . belongs to God." The court concluded that these allegations were "sufficient to allege infringement of [the church's] religious beliefs." However, "the mere fact that a religious practice is burdened by a governmental

3 *Schneider v. Salvation Army*, 14 N.W.2d 467, 468 (Minn. App. 1944). See also *Hope v. Barnes Hospital*, 55 S.W.2d 319 (Mo. App. 1932).
4 *South Ridge Baptist Church v. Industrial Commission*, 676 F. Supp. 799 (S.D. Ohio 1987).

10

Insurance and Risk Financing

Claims Made and Occurrence Coverage

Coverage	Advantages	Disadvantages
claims made	• covers any lawsuit filed during the policy period, regardless of when the injury occurred • coverage limits are the current limits, not the limits in effect when the injury occurred • insurance premiums often are lower than for an occurrence policy	• must have carried "claims made" insurance continuously with the same insurer from the date of the injury to the date of the claim, or have purchased "prior acts coverage" • "prior acts" coverage can be costly • a brief lapse in insurance coverage for any reason can result in no "claims made" coverage • coverage for prior claims is lost if a church switches from a claims made to an occurrence policy • when a policy expires or is terminated, for any reason, coverage ceases (even for claims that are later made for injuries occurring during the policy period) • claims for injuries occurring in more than one year may be filed during the same year, meaning that the policy's "aggregate" coverage limit is more quickly reached (the aggregate limit is the total amount the insurer will pay out during that year for all covered claims) • claims must not only be made during the policy period to be covered--they also must be reported to the insurer (a technicality that is sometimes overlooked)
occurrence	• covers any injury that occurs during the policy period regardless of when a lawsuit is filed • no "prior acts" coverage needed if a church maintains a succession of "occurrence" policies	• does not cover lawsuits filed during the policy period for injuries occurring prior to the policy period • insurance premiums usually higher than for a "claims made" policy

program does not mean that an exemption accommodating the practice must be granted," since "the state may justify a limitation on religious liberty by showing that it is essential to accomplish an overriding governmental interest." The court concluded that a state's interest in assuring the efficient administration and financial soundness of the workers compensation fund, and in protecting the interests of injured workers, amounted to a compelling interest that overrode the church's religious beliefs. The court noted that the Ohio law did exempt clergy from coverage under the workers compensation, and this limited exemption sought "to obviate excessive interference with the religious ministry of churches." Also rejected was the church's claim that the workers compensation program would impermissibly "entangle" government and church, since other courts had upheld even greater reporting requirements as constitutionally permissible. The court observed that exempting churches from coverage under the workers compensation law would force injured workers to sue churches in the civil courts, "an even more undesirable result from a scriptural standpoint."

EXAMPLE. An Ohio court, in upholding the coverage of church employees under a state workers compensation law, observed: "The workers compensation law has been characterized by the broadest possible coverage with frequent amendments to insure that no class of employers or employees was unintentionally excluded. If the legislature had intended to exclude religious institutions, it had ample opportunity to do so. We believe that the legislature intended for employees of religious institutions to come under the protections of the [law]."[5] The court rejected the church's claim that subjecting it to the workers compensation law violated the constitutional guaranty of religious freedom. The court concluded: "[T]he state has an overriding governmental interest in compensating workers and their dependents for death, occupational disease, and injury arising out of and occurring during the course of employment. To accomplish this purpose, the state has enacted comprehensive legislation creating a system which requires support by mandatory contributions by covered employers. Widespread voluntary coverage would undermine the soundness of the program and be difficult, if not impossible, to administer with a myriad of exceptions flowing from a wide variety of religious beliefs. The assessments imposed on employers to support the system are uniformly applicable to all, except as the [legislature] provides explicitly otherwise. Thus, we find no constitutionally required exemption for [a church] from the operation of the Workers Compensation Act."

Some have maintained that workers compensation laws were intended to apply only to commercial businesses and thus should not be extended to nonbusiness activi-

ties, such as the operation of a church. Many courts have rejected this reasoning as a basis for exempting charitable organizations from workers compensation laws, largely on the ground that the term *business* is so broad that it encompasses charitable activities. One court has observed: "[I]t is well to remember that in His earthly career the Head of the Christian Church seriously declared, 'I must be about my Father's business.' Wherefore does not church activity qualify as business? This term has such recognition apart from pecuniary gain."[6] Another court, in holding that a church is engaged in a "business" subject to the state's workers compensation law when constructing a new sanctuary, observed: "The business of a church is not strictly confined to charitable purposes, spiritual uplift, and the saving of souls. Such, no doubt, is the ultimate object and purpose of all church associations; but it is a matter of common knowledge that, in order to attain such ends, it is also necessary to construct and maintain houses of worship in which the business of the church is carried on."[7] The court also noted that a church could be a *business* under a state workers compensation law since there was no requirement that a business be "profit seeking."

▲ **CAUTION.** *If a church is not exempt from workers compensation law, what is the effect of its failure to obtain workers compensation insurance? Most workers compensation laws are compulsory. The employer has no prerogative to remain outside the system. In a "compulsory" jurisdiction, a covered employer that fails to obtain workers compensation insurance will ordinarily be subject to a direct action by an injured employee, or may be treated as a "self-insurer" and accordingly be liable for the damages prescribed by the workers compensation law. A few states permit employers to elect coverage under workers compensation law. To coerce employers into electing coverage, these states impose various legal disabilities upon employers that do not elect coverage.*

Workers compensation laws only cover injuries and illnesses suffered by *employees* on the job. The term *employee* generally is defined very broadly to effectuate the objectives of the workers compensation law.[8] As a result, persons whom a church may deem self-employed for

---

5   *Victory Baptist Temple v. Industrial Commission, 442 N.E.2d 819 (Ohio 1982),* cert. denied *459 U.S. 1086 (1982).* But see *NLRB v. Catholic Bishop of Chicago, 440 U.S. 490 (1979).*

6   *Tepesch v. Johnson, 296 N.W. 740, 745 (Iowa App. 1941).* See also *Hope v. Barnes Hospital, 55 S.W.2d 319, 321 (Mo. App. 1932)* ("[T]here is nothing about the act as a whole which discloses a legislative pur-pose to have limited its application solely to industries and businesses within the ordinary sense of the word.").

7   *Greenway Baptist Church v. Industrial Commission, 636 P.2d 1264, 1267 (Ariz. App. 1981).*

8   *Mill Street Church of Christ v. Hogan, 785 S.W.2d 263 (Ky. App. 1990).*

income tax purposes may be deemed employees for purposes of the workers compensation law. In some cases, however, a court may conclude that a particular worker, in fact, is self-employed and accordingly not covered by the workers compensation law. To illustrate, a South Carolina state appeals court ruled that a construction company president who donated his labor in constructing a new church was not eligible for workers compensation benefits following an injury on the job.[9] The court noted that workers compensation benefits are available only to "employees," and that state law defined the term *employee* as one who works for wages under a written or oral contract of hire. The injured worker in this case "donated his labor in the construction of the church. There is no evidence he was paid wages or had a right to demand payment. There is also no evidence [that he] entered into a tithing agreement with [the church] so that his work could be considered as a credit toward his tithe obligation. We find no evidence of an employment relationship between [him and the church]. He was not hired by [the church] and he was not performing any paid service for [the church]." As a result, the court concluded that the worker "was a volunteer and not an employee" under the state workers compensation law. Accordingly, the church, through its workers compensation insurance carrier, was not obligated to pay benefits to the injured worker.

EXAMPLE. A California court ruled that a homeless person who was paid $5 per hour by a church for performing miscellaneous services as part of a "charitable work program" was an "employee" covered by a state workers compensation law.[10]

EXAMPLE. A Louisiana court ruled that a church music director who claimed to have suffered increased sensitivity to chemicals as a result of her exposure to pine scented Lysol at church was not eligible for workers compensation benefits.[11] The court observed, "It is well-settled that for an employee to recover benefits under the worker's compensation law, the employee must carry the burden of proving by a preponderance of the evidence that an accident occurred in the course and scope of his employment, that the accident caused his injury, and that the injury caused his disability. . . . Although the worker's compensation rules are construed liberally in favor of the claimant, the employee still must carry the burden of proving by a preponderance of the evidence that the injury caused his disability." The court conceded that the music director

was exposed to pine scented Lysol fumes on at least three occasions during her employment with the church. As a result, the only issue in this case was whether the music director was disabled as a result of these exposures. The court concluded that the evidence at trial failed to prove her disability by a preponderance of the evidence.

▲ **CAUTION.** *Churches are subject to workers compensation laws in most states. This means that they should obtain workers compensation insurance on all employees. Such insurance generally will relieve a church of any liability for injuries or illnesses suffered by employees in the course of their employment. However, many churches have not obtained workers compensation insurance, or they have obtained insurance for only some of their staff. This results in a dangerous gap in coverage, making the church potentially liable for some employment-related illnesses and injuries. Many church leaders wrongly assume that the church's general liability insurance policy will provide coverage. This is rarely the case, since one of the most common exclusions in such policies is any employment-related injury or illness. This exclusion is based on the assumption that such injuries and illnesses are covered under workers compensation. Church leaders should review their workers compensation insurance, at least annually, to ensure that all employees are covered.*

AUTOMOBILE INSURANCE

Automobile insurance is written using a standard form. Churches should seek comprehensive liability coverage that covers *any auto*. Different options exist within the policy that enable the insured to narrow the coverage, for example, to just specific autos, or autos the church owns. However, churches use many different vehicles—some they own, some they lease, and some are owned by others, such as volunteer workers, parents, or church members. In today's legal environment, churches need broad and comprehensive liability coverage with respect to the use of automobiles that includes all types of vehicles, whether the church owns them or not, as well as coverage for both paid staff and volunteer drivers.

In addition to liability coverage, churches may purchase coverage for physical damage for both owned and non-owned vehicles. Options are available that include comprehensive coverage, specified perils, and collision coverage. Attention must also be given to medical payments and uninsured or underinsured motorists. Each option should be reviewed with the insurance agent.

9 *McCreery v. Covenant Presbyterian Church, 383 S.E.2d 264 (S.C. App. 1989).*
10 *Hoppmann v. Workers Compensation Appeals Board, 277 Cal. Rptr. 116 (Cal. App. 1991).*
11 *Starkman v. Munholland United Methodist Church, 707 So.2d 1277 (La. App. 1998).*

HIGHER LEVELS OF COVERAGE

Excess insurance

Situations may arise where a church desires additional insurance above the limits of the basic policy. One approach to obtain such coverage is to purchase excess insurance. The excess insurance is a separate, additional layer of coverage. For example, a church may purchase a general liability policy that provides coverage up to $3 million. An excess policy might be purchased to pay losses between $3 million and $5 million. Normally, excess insurance will follow the same form, or provisions, of the underlying policy. The two policies should be coordinated so they have the same inception and termination date, and that the language is consistent between the two policies. Churches that purchase excess insurance should always make sure that the excess policy begins where the underlying policy stops, and that there is no overlap between the two policies. For example, if the underlying has a limit of $3 million, then the excess policy should begin at $3 million.

There are two main categories of excess insurance: *specific excess* and *aggregate excess*. Specific excess covers losses on a per loss, per occurrence, or per claim basis. For example, suppose a church has an underlying policy that covers losses up to $3 million (with an annual limit of $3 million), and excess insurance for losses between $3 million and $5 million. If the church suffered a loss of $4 million, the excess insurance would pay $1 million. Suppose, though, that the church suffered three separate losses of $2 million each. The excess insurance would not pay anything because no single claim exceeded $3 million. The underlying policy would cover the first $3 million and the church would be responsible for the second $3 million. Aggregate excess insurance functions differently. Rather than covering losses on a per loss, per occurrence, or per claim basis, aggregate excess covers losses that exceed a specific amount over a defined period of time, such as one year. If in our example the church had purchased aggregate excess for $3 million to $5 million, then the aggregate excess would have covered none of the first $2 million loss, $1 million of the second $2 million loss, and $1 million of the third $2 million loss.

Umbrella insurance

Umbrella insurance is a different form of excess insurance that provides both higher limits of liability coverage and more comprehensive coverage. Some losses that are not covered in the general liability insurance are covered under the umbrella policy. Every company has its own umbrella policy, and policies often differ from one company to the next. Umbrella policies do not cover workers compensation, unemployment compensation, or disability benefits law. Other exclusions will also apply and leaders should carefully review the umbrella policy so they have a clear understanding of what it covers.

SELECTING AN INSURANCE COMPANY

Selecting an insurance company can be a confusing decision. Based on our research, about 11 percent of churches use an insurance agent that is a member of the church. That increases to 25 percent for congregations with more than 1,000 attending Sunday worship. Undoubtedly, a major factor for that decision is trust. Churches want to have their insurance with someone they can trust, both in terms of protection as well as to receive a fair deal. Few leaders understand insurance, yet they know it plays an important role in protecting the church. Having someone they can rely upon to help make important decisions concerning coverage, provides a sense of assurance.

Church insurance has evolved into an area of specialization. Today, a number of companies dedicate themselves to the church market and work almost exclusively with churches and parachurch ministries. One advantage of working with these companies is that they have extensive knowledge and experience in writing church insurance coverage and in responding to church claims. They understand the broad and sometimes specialized needs that are common in churches, but which are often not present in the commercial or nonprofit markets. For example, insuring a pipe organ or a stained glass window, or responding to a liability claim regarding sexual misconduct, are tasks that these companies understand well. They deal with issues, such as the replacement cost of church pews, on a daily basis. Furthermore, they have experience in the courtroom when a church faces a lawsuit. These are important considerations that work to the benefit of these companies.

Price

Price plays an important role in the selection of an insurance company. While price is obviously an important factor to every church, it may be a poor indicator of the best value. Leaders must be careful when comparing the prices of one company to that of another. It is not simply a matter of price but of coverage, and of service. The premium a church pays covers more than insurance: it also pays for the insurer's administrative costs and the services of the agent. Thus it is important to know how well the company is run, its history and practice in paying claims, the support it provides to its policyholders, and the level of knowledge and experience that the agent brings to the church.

Rating

The A.M. Best Company provides ratings for liability and property insurers. Each company receives a "General Policyholder's Rating" and a "Financial Size Rating." The "General Policyholder's Rating" provides the key information that will be of interest to church leaders. Five separate factors are evaluated and then companies are assigned one of 15 ratings that range from Superior (A++) to in liquidation (F). One factor that should be taken into account in evaluating a company is the trend with respect to the "Best" rating over a period of several years. Other companies, such as Standard and Poor's Corporation and Moody's Investors Service, Inc. also provide rating services. Since each company uses its own individualized rating system, church leaders should be careful when they compare one rating service to another.

Knowledge of the church market

Some companies specialize in providing insurance to churches. As a result, they tend to have greater knowledge and expertise with respect to the special needs of churches, and in responding to some claims. On the property side, church buildings often possess unique qualities that require specialized valuations. Similarly, churches face unique liability concerns because of the relationship they have with church members and the general public. Companies that specialize in serving churches deal with these concerns on a daily basis. As a result, they have in place a comprehensive insurance program that addresses the specific and unique needs of churches. Other companies that insure few churches have less experience on these issues. In selecting a company, church leaders should seek references from other church clients of the company, and have a comfort level that the company is the right one for their needs as a church.

Claims administration

How a company handles claims is vital to the overall quality of service and satisfaction that a church will experience. Seek references from churches that have filed claims and find out what their experience has been. Ask how a claim is filed and managed. What is the typical time between filing and settlement?

Service

Value added services can be an important factor when buying insurance. While some companies emphasize providing the lowest possible price, other companies specialize in providing the highest quality of services. Each company appeals to a somewhat different clientele. The key is the nature of the services that are provided. Price may seem less important if a church must struggle with claims, cannot get through on the phone, and finds out in the midst of a crisis that they have inadequate insurance. On the other hand, leaders don't want to pay for services that they do not value. Ask the agent to review the full range of services that the company provides and evaluate them in light of the church's needs. Examples of value added services include support in risk management activities, construction services, mortgage and equipment financing, discount equipment purchasing, security protection, employee screening and background verification services, and legal and financial information that addresses the specific needs of churches.

Loss prevention

For the most part, insurance companies have placed more emphasis upon loss control (minimizing losses after they occur) than on loss prevention (reducing risks before they happen). In evaluating companies, seek information on their approach to loss prevention. What resources do they have that can assist churches to minimize risks? Do they embody a philosophy of loss prevention that is sensitive to the ministry needs of the church? Having an effective loss prevention program means more than handing out a few brochures on how to reduce risks. Rather, it should be visible in the overall philosophy, services, and commitments that are present in the life of the company and its agents.

Duty to Cooperate

Most insurance policies impose a "duty to cooperate" on the insured. This means that a church must cooperate with its insurance company in any investigation, or in responding to reasonable requests for information. Church leaders should be aware of this requirement and understand that a failure to cooperate may result in the denial of insurance benefits. There are limits to the authority of an insurance company to investigate. However, churches should never decline an insurance company's request for information without the advice and consent of a local attorney.

Duty to Notify

Most insurance policies impose on the insured a duty to promptly notify the insurance company of any potential claim. The duty to inform your insurance company of an accident or loss arises when the injury occurs, and not when a lawsuit is filed. The purpose of the notice requirement is to give your insurance company sufficient time to investigate the incident and provide a defense. Failure to comply with this condition can result in a loss of coverage. Here are some points to consider:

- Notifying your broker may not be enough. Many churches purchase their insurance through a local broker. Sometimes this person is a member of the congregation. Church leaders naturally assume that in the event of an accident or injury they can simply call this individual and everything will be "taken care of." This case illustrates that such a conclusion may not always be correct. A broker may not be deemed to be an "agent" of the insurance companies he or she represents, and accordingly when a church provides its insurance broker with notice of an accident or loss it is not necessarily notifying its insurance company.

➤ TIP. If you notify your insurance broker of a loss, insist on a written assurance that he or she will notify the insurance company in writing within the period of time specified in the insurance policy. If you do not hear back within a week or so, contact the broker again to follow up. Better yet, the church itself should notify both its broker and insurance company. The insurance company's address will be listed on your insurance policy. Ask the insurance company to

provide you with written confirmation of receipt of your notice.

- Written rather than oral notice. If your insurance policy requires written notice, then be sure you provide written rather than oral notice of a loss. If so, how soon after a loss? It is essential that these provisions be scrupulously followed in order to prevent a loss of coverage.
- A reasonable time. How soon does your church insurance policy require that notice be submitted to the insurance company following an accident or loss? Be sure you know, and that this requirement is followed whenever there is an accident, personal injury, or other kind of loss.

➤ TIP. If you change insurance companies, be sure to review the new insurance policy. Do not assume that it will contain the same "notice" provisions as your previous policy.

EXAMPLE. The church board at First Church is informed by a parent that her minor child was molested by a church volunteer. The volunteer is questioned, and admits having molested the child. This incident represents a potential "loss" under the church's insurance policy, triggering a duty to inform the church's insurance company of the loss within the period of time specified in the insurance policy. The church should inform its insurance company immediately. It is very important that it not wait until a lawsuit is filed to notify its insurance company. Such a delay not only hinders the insurance company's ability to investigate the incident and defend the case, but it also may result in loss of coverage under the policy. This could have disastrous consequences to the church.

CASE STUDY. A church member was injured when he fell on church property during a funeral.[12] At the time of the injury, the church had a general liability insurance policy that required the church to give the insurance company written notice of any accident "as soon as practicable." Immediately following the accident the pastor instructed the chairman of the board of trustees to notify the church's insurance broker about the accident. The chairman did so by calling the insurance broker's office. An employee of the broker assured the chairman that the insurance company would be duly notified. In fact, the insurance company was not notified. Nine months later the church received a letter from an attorney for the injured member threatening to sue the church unless it paid the

---

12 *Shaw Temple v. Mount Vernon Fire Insurance Company, 605 N.Y.S.2d 370 (A.D. 2 Dept. 1994).*

member a large amount of money. The church immediately turned this letter over to its insurance broker, who in turn forwarded it to the church's insurance company. The insurance company refused to provide the church with a defense of the lawsuit or pay any amount of money based on the accident since the church had failed to provide it with written notice of the accident "as soon as practicable" as required by the insurance policy. The church responded by suing its insurance company. It sought a court order requiring the insurance company to defend the church under the terms of the policy and to pay for any damages awarded by a jury. A state appeals court ruled that the insurance company had no legal duty to defend the church or pay for any jury verdict since the church had failed to notify it of the accident "as soon as practicable." The court concluded that when the church gave notice of the accident to its insurance broker it was not giving notice to its insurance company as required by the policy. In addition, the insurance policy required that the church provide the insurance company with written notice of any accident. Even if the broker were an agent of the insurance company, the church still failed to comply with the terms of the insurance policy since it provided the broker with oral rather than written notice of the accident.

OTHER MATTERS

Here are some additional points to note about church insurance:

- Retaining your policies. It is important for church leaders to keep church insurance policies permanently, since some claims (such as sexual misconduct) may arise years or even decades later, and a church may need to produce a copy of the insurance contract for the year in which the misconduct occurred in order to obtain coverage.
- Reservation of rights letters. It is common for churches to receive a "reservation of rights" letter when they report a claim to their insurance company. Under such a reservation, an insurance company agrees to defend an insured, but reserves the right to deny any obligation to pay an adverse judgment as a result of an exclusion in the policy.
- Periodic insurance review. Churches should appoint an insurance committee consisting of persons with some knowledge of insurance who periodically review the church's insurance coverage to ensure they are adequate.

SUMMARY

Most churches rely on insurance as the primary device to finance risks. Insurance, though, should be viewed as only one of the means available to finance risks. In considering the role of insurance, leaders should take into account the frequency and severity of risks, the financial consequences of specific losses, and the risk financing alternatives. In addition to insurance, the most common ways of financing risks include paying for losses out of cash flow, cash reserves, borrowed funds, or through noninsurance contracts. To make an informed decision, leaders need to examine and take into account the financial capabilities and goals of the church.

Since insurance is the primary and most important risk financing tool, attention should be given to understanding the insurance contract and the coverage being purchased. For the typical church, most claims will involve the property side of the insurance contract. Special attention should be given to the deductible level, the valuation of property, inflation guard, and co-insurance. Additional consideration should be given to blanket insurance if a church owns multiple buildings, or property at more than one location. Other important topics include builder's risk insurance if a building program should occur, plate glass insurance, boiler and machinery insurance, flood insurance, fidelity bonds, and additional crime insurance.

Liability insurance plays an important role in providing financial protection to churches. Liability claims can be unpredictable, and churches are more vulnerable today to litigation than in the past. Leaders should take care in understanding the general liability provisions of their policy, and the difference between the occurrence form and the claims-made form. Other special policies for directors and officers, sexual misconduct, counseling, and employment practices also play an important role in protecting against lawsuits.

Most churches employ several workers, including clergy. Workers compensation insurance provides important coverage if these individuals are injured on the job. Every church should have such coverage.

Automobile insurance is important to every church. A key concern is to maintain comprehensive liability cov-

10

Insurance and Risk Financing

erage for any auto. Insurance for physical damage can be purchased for both owned and non-owned vehicles, and for a variety of perils, including collision.

It is not uncommon for churches to purchase additional insurance above the limits of the basic policy. The two most common options are to buy excess insurance or umbrella insurance. Umbrella insurance generally expands the coverage in addition to providing higher limits of liability.

Finally, purchasing insurance also involves selecting an insurance company. Price is always an important factor in selecting a company, although it may not be a good indication of value or service. In making a decision to select a company, leaders should examine a company's insurance rating, its knowledge of the church market, how it handles claims, the services it provides, and its commitment to loss prevention.

Insurance Coverage Checklist for Churches

Coverage	Description
property	Covers many major risks to church property, including fire, smoke, lightning, hurricane, tornado. *Checklist:* • Check to see if unique items such as stained glass windows, pipe organs, handbells, artwork, and sound equipment require special "endorsements." • Obtain appraisals of unique items to be sure they are adequately insured. • Conduct periodic inventories of property to prove claims in the event of loss or destruction. • Check to see if coverage is limited to the market value of damaged or destroyed property. If so, consider obtaining replacement cost coverage. • Check on coverage for items of personal property owned by members or employees. Examples include expensive coats left in a coat room, or an employee's own laptop computer. • Check to see if boilers require a special endorsement. • Check the exclusions under the policy. Some risks, such as earthquakes, mold, and sewer or drain backup, may be excluded and require special endorsements. • If your church is located in one of 19,000 communities that participate in the National Flood Insurance Program, you can obtain flood insurance from insurers that participate in the National Flood Insurance Program (NFIP). Coverage amounts are often inadequate. • Check to see if your policy contains a "coinsurance clause." If so, you are required to insure your property for a specified percentage of its market value. If you don't, you become a "coinsurer," meaning that your policy will pay less than the stated limits in the event of a partial loss. These clauses make it essential for churches to be sure they have adequate coverage. This review should be done annually.
liability	Covers many forms of personal injury and damage to the property of others. Common examples includes slips and falls, sexual misconduct (coverage may be limited to the church, and exclude the offender). *Checklist:* • Check to see if sexual misconduct coverage is limited, and if higher amounts can be obtained by complying with specified procedures. • Check to see if liability insurance is provided on an "occurrence" or "claims made" basis. • Some policies provide minimal medical benefits to persons injured on church property. Additional coverage should be considered.
church-owned vehicles	Covers injuries and damages resulting from the use of church-owned vehicles. *Checklist:* • Check to see if your property or general liability policy contains coverage for church-owned vehicles. If not, be sure to obtain a separate endorsement for this coverage.
non-owned vehicles	Covers injuries and damages caused by members who use their own vehicle while performing services for their church. The driver's personal car insurance is also available, but if inadequate, the church will likely be sued. Often must be obtained as a separate endorsement. Essential for churches that allow members or employees to drive personal vehicles on church business. *Checklist:* • Check to see if non-owned vehicle coverage applies to rented vehicles.

Insurance Coverage Checklist for Churches (cont'd.)

Coverage	Description
counseling	Covers injuries caused during counseling activities. Often must be obtained as a separate endorsement. Essential for churches that provide counseling services. *Checklist:* • Check exclusions carefully. For example, some policies exclude sexual misconduct.
employment practices	Covers certain employment-related claims such as wrongful dismissal and some forms of discrimination. These are among the most common types of church litigation today. Many church leaders erroneously assume that their general liability policy covers these claims. In most cases it does not. *Checklist:* • If your church has employees, you should consider this coverage. The more employees you have, the more essential this becomes.
directors and officers	Covers several potential legal claims that can be brought against officers and directors directly. "D&O" policies also may cover claims not covered by general liability policies. While uncompensated directors of nonprofit organizations have "limited immunity" from personal liability under both state and federal law, this protection does not cover compensated directors and does not cover acts of "gross negligence." Must be obtained as a separate endorsement or policy. *Checklist:* • If your church does not screen youth workers, lets children ride in fully-loaded 15-passenger vans, or engages in other high-risk activities that may be deemed "grossly negligent," then this coverage is essential.
theft	Covers embezzlement and other misappropriations of church funds and securities by employees and others having access to money or property. Often must be obtained as a separate endorsement. This form of insurance is also referred to as bonding. *Checklist:* • Remember, the opportunity to steal, rather than a need for money, is often the primary reason for employee theft. Institute procedures to minimize unsupervised access to funds.
foreign travel	Provides medical benefits for injuries occurring during foreign travel. Costs of a medical evacuation may also be covered. Often must be obtained as a separate endorsement or policy. *Checklist:* • Most general liability policies exclude any injuries or damages occurring outside of the US. • Essential coverage for churches that send groups on missions trips to foreign countries.
umbrella	Covers legal judgments in excess of the limits on other insurance policies. *Checklist:* • Does your church have substantial assets to be protected, or inadequate liability insurance? If so, this coverage is essential to protect against catastrophic damages.
workers compensation	Workers compensation insurance provides benefits to employees who are injured or become ill in the course of (or because of) their employment. Many church leaders erroneously assume that churches are not covered by state workers compensation laws. In most cases this assumption is incorrect, and exposes a church to a substantial uninsured risk. *Checklist:* • Check to see if churches are subject to workers compensation law in your state. If so, obtain insurance to cover potential claims.

10

Insurance and Risk Financing

Compensation
| Planning Guide

For ministers and church employees

This guide was created by GuideStone to help ministries be good stewards of their employee benefits. Copyrighted by GuideStone Financial Resources and used by permission.

GuideStone®
Financial Resources

Do well. Do right.®

Three things you need to know before you begin

1. **The benefits of a compensation plan:**

   Your church can maximize its limited resources by implementing a sound compensation plan.

   ❖ It reduces confusion about expenses, benefits and staff income budgets.

   ❖ It ensures funds are spent appropriately.

   ❖ It lets ministers and staff know you value them with a detailed compensation plan.

2. **The dangers of a "lump-sum" or "package" approach:**

   Paying a lump-sum amount to your minister to break down as he desires can be unwise.

   ❖ It often causes ministers to pay higher taxes, increasing financial burdens for their families.

   ❖ It can lead to a financial hardship for the church if a minister does not set aside a portion of the lump sum for insurance coverage.

   ❖ It distorts the amount of actual income the minister has available to provide for his family.

3. **The eligibility requirements of a Minister for Tax Purposes:**

   Generally, a Minister for Tax Purposes is ordained, licensed or commissioned and fulfills a majority of the following: administers the ordinances, conducts religious worship, has management responsibilities and is considered to be a religious leader by the church.

   These ministers have a dual tax status. They are "employees" for income tax purposes and "self-employed" for the purpose of Social Security.

   ❖ They are exempt from federal income tax withholding. (Ministers must prepay their taxes by using the quarterly estimated tax procedure, unless they elect voluntary withholding.)

   ❖ They are eligible for a church-designated housing allowance.

   ❖ They must pay SECA taxes for Social Security coverage (employees pay half of the FICA tax and their employer pays the other half).

Create a compensation plan

As a church, you have a responsibility to take care of those who serve you, while seeking to be good stewards of your limited financial resources. This guide can help you achieve that goal. It is designed for use by the person(s) who determines pay arrangements for ministers and church employees.

In the next few pages, we'll help you build a solid compensation plan using six essential steps.

Step 1   **Determine the needs (pages 4-5)**

Step 2   **Establish written compensation plan policies (page 6)**

Step 3   **Provide for ministry-related expenses (pages 7-8)**

Step 4   **Provide employee benefits (pages 9-10)**

Step 5   **Determine personal income (page 11)**

Step 6   **Complete a *Compensation Planning Summary* (pages 12-13)**

As you take this step of good financial stewardship, remember that you're not doing this alone. We're always here for assistance or to answer any questions you may have. Contact us at **1-888-98-GUIDE** (1-888-984-8433) between 7 a.m. and 6 p.m. CST, Monday through Friday. You can also email us at *info@GuideStone.org*.

Turn the page to begin step one.

Step one: Determine the needs

Each minister and paid employee should complete a copy of this compensation plan review. By providing the required information below, the church can better estimate amounts that adequately meet the needs of ministers and staff. Please note the following:

- ❖ Unless otherwise noted, all figures are annual amounts.
- ❖ Estimates can be based on actual amounts from the previous year.
- ❖ Tinted boxes are to be completed by the church.

Name:	Job title:	Complete by: _____/_____/_____

COMPENSATION PLAN REVIEW

SECTION 1: Ministry-related expenses *(see pages 7-8 for more information)*

Personal vehicle expenses

Description	Minister/employee estimate	Amount budgeted to reimburse expense
Estimated business mileage	(miles)	N/A
Multiply mileage by the IRS standard rate to determine cost for vehicle's business use (visit *www.IRS.gov*)	$	$

Travel expenses

Description	Minister/employee estimate	Amount budgeted to reimburse expense
Estimated travel expenses for work-related events (food, lodging, etc.)	$	$

Ministry expenses

Description	Minister/employee estimate	Amount budgeted to reimburse expense
Estimated expense on materials for sermon preparation, studies or church functions	$	$

Hospitality expenses

Description	Minister/employee estimate	Amount budgeted to reimburse expense
Estimated expense for hosting church groups, speakers, etc. in a home or at a restaurant	$	$

Professional development expenses

Description	Minister/employee estimate	Amount budgeted to reimburse expense
Estimated amount for continuing education, workshops or learning conferences	$	$

SECTION 2: Employee benefits *(see pages 9-10 for more information)*

Medical insurance

Description	Minister/employee estimate	Amount budgeted to provide benefit
Estimated cost of medical coverage for you (and your family, if applicable)	$	$

Life insurance

Description	Minister/employee estimate	Amount budgeted to provide benefit
Estimated cost for your life coverage	$	$

Disability insurance

Description	Minister/employee estimate	Amount budgeted to provide benefit
Estimated cost for your disability coverage	$	$

Retirement plan contributions

Description	Actual contribution last year	Amount budgeted for contribution
403(b)(9) retirement plan contributions paid by church	$	$

SECTION 3: Personal income *(see page 11 for more information)*

Personal salary

Description	Amount budgeted by church
Salary paid to the minister/employee by the church	$

Housing allowance

Description	Amount budgeted by minister
Housing allowance, if applicable, that will be designated by the church next year*	$

Salary increase

Description	Yes	No
Did you receive a salary increase last year? Check either Yes or No.		

SECA taxes paid

Description	Minister	Amount budgeted to offset expense
Amount of self-employment (SECA) tax you paid on your church income last year*	$	$

*Applies only to Ministers for Tax Purposes.

Step two: Establish written compensation plan policies

Written policies reduce confusion by forming a standard for current and future actions. They also help your ministers and employees clearly understand the provisions and expectations of the church. The policies should provide clarity in four major areas.

1. **Ministry-related expenses:**
   Note: These should be funded by the church apart from the minister's/employee's salary.
   * Allowable business expenses (needs to be consistent with IRS rules)
   * Employee recordkeeping and expense account reporting expectations
   * Reimbursement rate for mileage expenses
   * Allowable conference and convention expenses
   * Reimbursement amount for books, periodicals, software, etc. (as well as who will own the reimbursed items)

2. **Employee benefits:**
   Note: These should be funded by the church apart from the minister's/employee's salary.
   * Medical, life and disability coverage
   * Retirement contributions provided by the church
   * Educational expenses eligible for reimbursement

3. **Personal income:**
   * Salary and any amounts designated as housing allowance for eligible ministers
   * Social Security withholdings for non-ministerial employees (see the section titled "Social Security" under step five for more information)
   * Social Security offset for Ministers for Tax Purposes (see the section titled "Social Security" under step five for more information)
   * Willingness to withhold taxes at the request of a Minister for Tax Purposes
   * How the church will designate the housing allowance (see the section titled "Housing Allowance" under step five for more information)
   * Procedure for personnel reviews and salary increases

4. **Personnel policies:**
   * Vacation
   * Sick and sabbatical leave
   * Outside speaking engagements
   * Hiring requirements
   * Employee classifications
   * Work hours and pay periods
   * Business use of cell phones and computers

Step three: Provide for ministry-related expenses

Ministers and employees naturally have expenses related to the work they need to accomplish. However, these expenses should never be a burden to them. As such, the expenses should be fully paid for by the church and should not impact any portion of a minister's or employee's personal income.

Examples of ministry-related expenses include:

- ❖ Vehicle use for business purposes
- ❖ Meetings, workshops and conferences
- ❖ Books, periodicals, software and audio or video resources
- ❖ Continuing education opportunities
- ❖ Provisions for ministry-related hospitality

Addressing ministry-related expenses with an accountable reimbursement plan (ARP)

An ARP is a plan you create to help explain terms, conditions and tax rules related to allowable ministry expenses. With this type of plan, the church creates a reimbursement budget, the minister or employee turns in an expense report and the church uses that report to reimburse the minister or employee. Also, it's important to know employees pay no taxes on reimbursements, and these are not included on an IRS *Form W-2.*

Requirements for an ARP

- ❖ All expenses must have a business purpose related to the minister's or employee's duties.
- ❖ Expenses must be verified with documentation of the amount, date, place and business purpose.
- ❖ Documentation should be provided within 60 days of incurring the expense, and any excess reimbursements should be returned to the church within 120 days.
- ❖ The church should consider using the IRS standard mileage rate for transportation and per-diem rates for meals. These rates can be accessed at *www.IRS.gov.*
- ❖ Unused accountable reimbursement plan money should not be given as a bonus or additional income.

How to create an ARP in *three easy steps*

1 Decide what expenses will be covered and outline a plan (see the *Sample: Accountable Reimbursement Plan* on page 14). Then determine how much money the church will budget to cover these expenses separate and apart from personal income. If applicable, you may want to use last year's figures in each category as a guideline.

2 Instruct ministers and employees to submit an expense report within 60 days of incurring expenses (see the *Sample: Expense Report* form on page 14). Receipts should be required for purchased items and, for automobile expenses, mileage should be reported.

3 Reimburse ministers and employees at least once a month for all approved expenses (this reimbursement should not affect their personal income). Additionally, advances can be given for anticipated expenses, but unused funds from those advances must be returned to the church within 120 days.

A word of caution about reimbursement arrangements through salary reduction

It is strongly recommended that a church chooses not to reduce a minister's or employee's personal income by the amount of an expense. According to Treasury Regulation 1.62(d), that type of salary reduction will qualify as a non-accountable arrangement, and the church will have to report the amounts on the minister's or employee's IRS *Form W-2* as income. In general, the minister or employee will have to pay more taxes if the church chooses this option.

Step four: Provide employee benefits

A strong benefit plan includes retirement plan contributions and medical, life and disability coverage for ministers and other employees. Having this type of plan shows tangible concern for your church's staff, which can reduce turnover and increase attractiveness for potential new employees. It also provides some of the following advantages.

Tax Advantages

Can save taxes

A church may pay for certain insurance benefits for employees without that money being reported as taxable income. Churches may pay for or reimburse employees for group health coverage, disability coverage and term life insurance up to $50,000 on a tax-free basis. Additionally, a church's contributions into its employees' 403(b) retirement accounts are tax-sheltered.

Health care reform impact: As of January 1, 2014, churches can no longer reimburse employees for individual medical policies on a tax-free basis. They may continue to reimburse employees for group health coverage through a variety of vehicles, including Health Reimbursement Arrangements (HRAs), Employer Payment Plans (EPPs) and certain Section 125 "cafeteria" plans. These vehicles – which include a range of tax advantages – can help employers and employees control costs.

Note: Because of the added complexity of these regulatory changes, it's important that ministries work with qualified experts when setting up one of these vehicles.

These tax-saving ideas are not "loopholes." They represent a wise use of tax laws to help your ministers and employees pay the least amount of tax legally owed.

Insurance coverage benefits

Provides protection for the church

Neglecting to provide insurance benefits for ministers and employees can be a dangerous liability, and it places an unnecessary burden on their families should an unfortunate event occur. As such, a church should provide ministers, employees and their families with the protection and peace of mind they need to focus on their ministries. Moreover, a comprehensive benefits package can help you attract and retain qualified, talented staff that will help your organization meet its ministry goals.

Provides employees with appropriate coverage

Churches and other ministry organizations should consider providing a range of insurance coverage for their employees, including medical, term life and accident, dental and disability plan options. Each one of these coverages works together to help protect the health and financial well-being of your employees and their families.

Retirement plan benefits

Prepares employees for the future

While they'll never retire from ministerial service, ministers and employees need income to live on once they leave paid service. This income can be used to provide for families, missions, church planting or other ministry endeavors. Historically, one of the best ways to build this income is through a retirement plan, such as a 403(b)(9) retirement plan. Churches should consider offering such a plan that includes an employer-provided contribution paid by the church. GuideStone recommends employer contributions equal to 10% of salary. Employees should also be encouraged to make additional contributions from their own salary.

Provides a plan exclusively designed for ministries

Ideally, churches should maintain a 403(b)(9) retirement plan designed exclusively for churches and ministry organizations. Ministers who receive taxable income from a church may participate. Additionally, all non-ministerial employees receiving W-2 income from the church (secretaries, custodians and church-school workers) can participate. Some of the features of such a plan include:

❖ Employees' tax-sheltered contributions provide immediate savings by lowering the taxable portion of their salary. Further, both contributions and earnings grow tax-deferred until they are withdrawn.

❖ Eligible ministers don't pay SECA taxes on their tax-sheltered contributions.

❖ Earnings on Roth contributions can be withdrawn tax-free if certain conditions are met.

A note about *403(b) plan regulations*

The IRS published additional regulations on January 1, 2009.

They impact all 403(b) plans, but, fortunately, they are not difficult to follow. The two primary requirements that affect all organizations with 403(b) plans are:

❖ Written plan document requirements. Employer sponsors must maintain written documents that describe all material plan provisions.

❖ More requirements to share information. There are additional steps participants, employers and plan providers must take to share information if your organization makes contributions to more than one investment provider or allows plan participants to transfer money from one 403(b) investment provider to another while in-service.

To find additional detailed information about these and other 403(b) requirements, visit *www.IRS.gov.*

Step five: Determine personal income

A number of factors should be considered when determining the personal income of ministers and employees. **Keep in mind that ministry-related expenses and the cost of benefits should not be considered part of personal income.**

Responsibilities and experience

Those called to the ministry usually do not follow that calling to become wealthy. However, they should not be expected to live on inadequate wages. Additionally, merit increases in recognition of exceptional service should not be considered inappropriate. To help determine an appropriate income, consider the income of other professionals in your community with similar experience and responsibilities.

Inflation

It is imperative for churches to consider inflation when reviewing pay each year. Historically, inflation has averaged around 3% annually. Every year your ministers' and employees' pay isn't adjusted to meet the rate of inflation, their income has less and less buying power as they seek to provide for their families.

Social Security

Churches with non-ministerial employees should keep in mind that the church is required to pay the employer portion of Social Security taxes. The employee portion of FICA taxes is then withheld by the church from the non-ministerial employees' salary. Ministers for Tax Purposes, on the other hand, pay SECA taxes, and they must pay all of this tax themselves. **Churches should strongly consider providing additional income to the minister for use in paying this tax.** This is sometimes called a Social Security offset and usually equals one-half of the SECA tax rate. When it is given to the minister by the church, it must be designated as taxable income on the minister's *Form W-2*.

Housing allowance (only available to Ministers for Tax Purposes)

Ministers who own or rent a home may save taxes if a church designates part of their income as a housing allowance. Ministers who live in a parsonage may also be entitled to a housing allowance designated by their church if they have eligible housing expenses. Churches cannot designate a housing allowance retroactively.

How to designate a housing allowance

The minister should present the church with an estimate of housing expenses (see the *Minister's Estimate of Housing Expenses Form* on page 15). The church must officially designate and document the amount of the minister's housing allowance in advance of paying the minister. This should be done every year. To ensure the church doesn't forget to designate a housing allowance one year, the church should make the designation for all future years until it is changed by official church action. This is called a "safety net" designation. The church should record this action in the church minutes and notify the minister. If circumstances change, the amount designated as a housing allowance may be revised during the year; however, no changes can be made retroactively. Remember, there are limits on how much a minister can exclude from income as a housing allowance. As taxpayers, ministers are responsible for reporting their income properly.

Since ministers who live in a church-owned parsonage are not able to build equity in a home, many are concerned about how they will pay for housing when they retire. Accordingly, churches can make added contributions (within legal limits) to a minister's 403(b)(9) retirement account that can be used to meet this need.

Step six: Complete a compensation planning summary

Use the worksheet on the next page to develop a comprehensive plan of financial support for your new budget year. Please note that the worksheet is designed so that the three categories of compensation (expenses, benefits and personal income) are not added together. Adding these together is similar to recreating the lump-sum approach, which is not suggested.

Also, tear out and make copies of the additional worksheets that follow so you may use them as needed.

As you use these forms, you'll want to be mindful of the federal reporting requirements for churches. This checklist will help you to comply with these requirements:

❖ Obtain an employer identification number (EIN) from the federal government (visit *www.IRS.gov* to obtain this number).

❖ Determine whether each church worker is an employee or self-employed.

❖ Obtain the Social Security number from each worker.

❖ Have each non-ministerial employee complete an IRS *Form W-4.*

❖ Compute each employee's taxable wages.

❖ Determine the amount of income tax to withhold from each non-minister.

❖ Withhold FICA taxes from non-ministers.

❖ Follow all payroll deposit rules.

❖ File IRS *Form 941* quarterly.

❖ Prepare an IRS *Form W-2* for every employee (including ministers).

❖ Prepare an IRS *Form 1099-MISC* for self-employed persons earning non-employee compensation of $600* or more during the year from the church.

❖ Complete any additional forms required by federal, state or local governments.

*This figure is subject to change. For the latest updates, visit *www.IRS.gov/form1099misc.*

Compensation planning summary

Now you know what makes up a compensation plan. Look over the compensation plan review (pages 4-5) you received from your ministers and church employees. Identify areas of inadequate support that should be addressed in this year's budget.

Use this worksheet to develop a comprehensive compensation plan for your new budget year.

Note: The worksheet is designed so that the three categories of compensation are not added together. This is intentional. Adding these together is an attempt to reconstitute the lump-sum or package approach to compensation and all its inefficiencies and distortions. Putting these three categories of compensation on separate pages of the budget may further reduce the tendency to lump these together.

Ministry-related expenses (not income)	
1. Automobile	$
2. Conventions/conferences	$
3. Books, periodicals, software	$
4. Continuing education	$
5. Hospitality	$

Employee benefits (not income)	
1. Life and health coverage	$
a. Medical	$
b. Disability	$
c. Term life	$
d. Personal accident	$
e. Dental	$
2. 403(b)(9) retirement plan contribution	$

Personal income	
1. Personal salary	$
2. Housing allowance	$
3. Social Security offset (taxable)	$

Sample forms and reports

Sample: *Accountable Reimbursement Plan*

1 The church hereby establishes an accountable reimbursement plan for all ministers and employees with the following terms and conditions intended to comply with all applicable tax rules.

The church will reimburse only reasonable ministry-related business expenses incurred by a minister or employee. Subject to budget limitations, these expenses will include:

❖ Business use of automobile, up to the current IRS standard mileage rate

❖ Business travel away from home: transportation, lodging and meals on overnight trips

❖ Convention, conference and workshop expenses

❖ Continuing education expenses

❖ Subscriptions, books and software, if related to ministry or employment

❖ Entertainment/hospitality expenses, if business connection requirement is met

2 The minister or employee will account for each allowable expense in writing within 60 days. Documentation will include the amount, date, place, business purpose and business relationship of any person entertained for each expense. A receipt will accompany the documentation.

3 The minister or employee will return advances that exceed actual business expenses within 120 days.

4 Under this accountable arrangement, the church will not report reimbursed amounts as taxable income on the minister's or employee's IRS *Form W-2*. The minister or employee should not report reimbursed amounts as income on his or her federal income tax return.

Sample: *Expense Report*

Employee name: *Rev. John Smith*

For the month of: *January*

Date	Description of expense	Business purpose	Amount
January 17-18	Mileage to conference	Mileage (457 x .56)	$ 255.92
January 17	Meals at conference	Meals	$ 53.25
January 17-18	Hotel	Lodging	$ 120.00
January 17	*Sunday School Teacher's Guide*	Ministry expense/books	$ 53.00
		Subtotal	$ 482.17
		Minus advance	$ 200.00
		Total reimbursement due	$ 282.17

Sample forms and reports

Sample: *Minister's Estimate of Housing Expenses Form*

To (church): _____

From (minister): _____

Housing allowance for (year): _____

Item	Amount
1. Down payment on a home	$
2. Mortgage payments on a loan to purchase or improve your home (include both principal and interest)	$
3. Real estate taxes	$
4. Property insurance	$
5. Utilities (electricity, gas, water, trash pickup, local telephone charges)	$
6. Furnishings and appliances (purchase and repair)	$
7. Structural repairs and remodeling	$
8. Yard maintenance and improvements	$
9. Maintenance items (pest control, etc.)	$
10. Homeowners association dues	$
11. Miscellaneous:	$
	$
	$
TOTAL EXPENSES	$

Minister's signature: _____

Sample: *Notification of Housing Allowance from the Church to the Minister*

To (minister's name): _____

This is to advise you that at the meeting of _____

held on ____/____/_____ (date) your housing allowance for the year ____ was officially designated and fixed in the amount of $_____ of the total payments to you during the year _____. Accordingly, $_____ of the total payments to you during the year_____ (and all future years until changed by official church action) will constitute your housing allowance.

If a parsonage is provided, add: *You will also have rent-free use of the home located at:*

_____

for the year _____. Utilities will be paid by: ❏ *the church*   ❏ *the minister*

This action is recorded in the church minutes.

You should keep an accurate record of your eligible housing expenses to provide proof of any amounts excluded from income for income tax purposes when filing your federal income tax return. You may not exclude a housing allowance as income for SECA tax purposes. It is your responsibility as a taxpayer to understand and follow the limits about how much you can exclude from income as a housing allowance for income tax purposes and accurately report your income.

Sincerely,

Clerk's signature: _____ Date ____/____/_____

About GuideStone

Founded in 1918 as a relief organization, GuideStone has grown into the premier provider of employee benefits for evangelical churches and ministry organizations. For nearly a century, GuideStone Financial Resources has been serving pastors and ministry staff by providing employer-sponsored retirement plans, personal financial services, institutional and individual investing, insurance and church risk management solutions. GuideStone Funds provides the nation's largest Christian-screened mutual fund family, giving values-driven individuals and institutions everywhere the opportunity to invest in performance + values. And the Mission:Dignity ministry comes alongside the "veterans of the Cross" to provide dignity for retired Southern Baptist pastors, workers or their widows who are with need. With a drive for excellence and heart for ministry, GuideStone is committed to serving those who serve the Lord.

Index

Index

Index

C

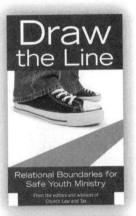

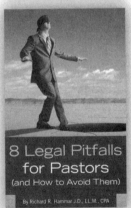

REDUCE YOUR CHURCH'S LEGAL LIABILITY

Does your church have what it needs to protect your ministry?

With *Pastor, Church & Law*, nationally known church attorney and CPA Richard Hammar, gives you comprehensive and practical legal advice—all in an easily-accessible and user-friendly format. In this four-volume set, you'll get the tools you need to:

- Avoid actions or practices that could result in a lawsuit
- Understand the complex definition of "church" in the eyes of our legal system
- Interpret the church's legal responsibility to employees
- Gain an awareness of the statutes and regulations churches need to abide by and from which ones they may be exempt

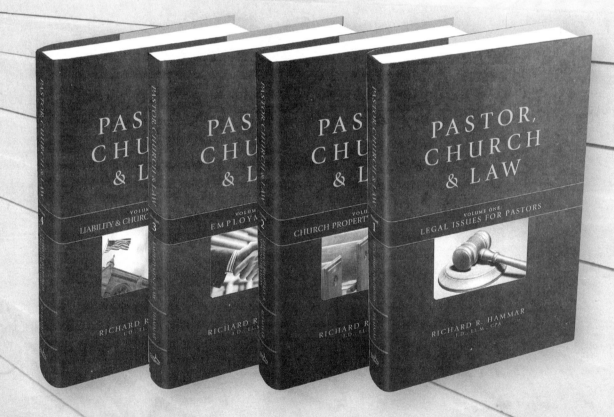

Start reducing your church's legal liability, ORDER TODAY!

ChurchLawAndTaxStore.com

a ministry of
CHRISTIANITY TODAY

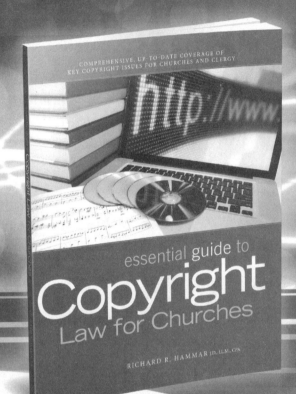